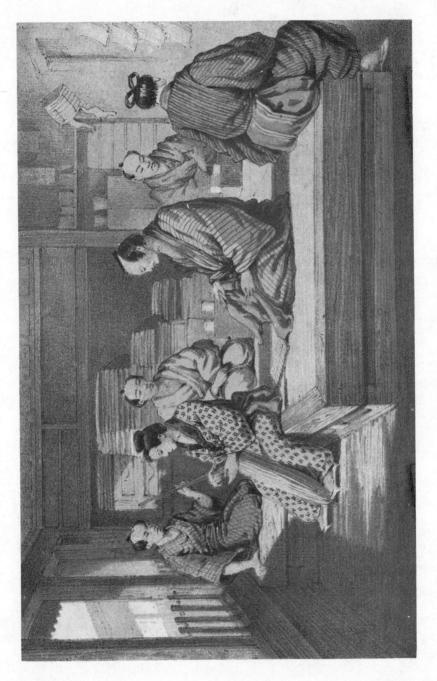

SCENE IN A SILK SHOP

THE

# CAPITAL OF THE TYCOON:

## A NARRATIVE OF A

## THREE YEARS' RESIDENCE IN JAPAN.

### BY SIR RUTHERFORD ALCOCK, K.C.B.

HER MAJESTY'S ENVOY EXTRAORDINARY AND
MINISTER PLENIPOTENTIARY IN JAPAN.

'Look ye! master Traveller: unless ye note something worth the seeing,
and come home wiser than ye went, I would n't give a stag's horn for all
your travels.'                                                    OLD PLAY.

WITH MAPS AND NUMEROUS ILLUSTRATIONS IN CHROMOLITHOGRAPHY AND ON WOOD.

IN TWO VOLUMES.

VOL II.

## GREENWOOD PRESS, PUBLISHERS
### NEW YORK

Originally published in 1863
by Longman, Green, Longman, Roberts & Green, London


First Greenwood Reprinting 1969

Library of Congress Catalogue Card Number 68-30995

SBN 8371-1866-2

PRINTED IN UNITED STATES OF AMERICA

# CONTENTS

OF

## THE SECOND VOLUME.

———◆———

## CHAPTER XVI.

## CHAPTER XVII.

# LIST OF ILLUSTRATIONS

TO

## THE SECOND VOLUME.

————o◦⟨◦⟩◦o————

### MAP.

(Engraved by E. Weller.)

### CHROMO-LITHOGRAPHS.

(By M. & N. Hanhart.)

### WOODCUTS.

(Engraved by G. Pearson.)

<hr>

*ERRATA.*

Page    Line                     Correction
 60     last     *for* Appendix A *read* Appendix B
177      34     *for* the British Minister, *read* If the British Minister

# A NARRATIVE

OF

# THREE YEARS' RESIDENCE IN JAPAN.

———◦◦❖◦◦———

## CHAPTER I.

NEARLY a month had elapsed after my return from
the spas of Atami, and little had occurred to break
the daily routine and monotony of life at Yeddo.
Nothing indeed was ever likely to occur, of a nature that
we should desire it,—an earthquake, a fire, or a murder,
being the only events travelling out of the beaten track!
The first incident, accordingly, which took place within
this vicious circle, was the sudden appearance, as we were
sitting down to dinner one evening, of the Abbé Girard,
pale and agitated, bringing with him, in a norimon,

Monsieur de Bellecourt's Italian servant, who had been attacked, while standing quietly at the gate of the French Legation, by two Samourai passing at the moment, and by one of whom he had been severely wounded. He was brought in, his clothes saturated with blood; and on examination it was found he had received a sword-cut across the upper part of his right arm, while in the act of warding the blow intended for his head. It was fortunately only a flesh wound, though several inches in length, and penetrating deeply; and being on the outside of the limb, where there are no large vessels to be divided, it was comparatively a safe wound. It was large and gaping, however, and quite sufficiently ugly-looking, to turn the good Abbé very sick, and compel him to retire to another room. The edges were soon brought together, and kept in place by a few stitches, while the bleeding from the smaller arteries was stopped, and the dressing completed with such materials as were at hand.

Where was this to end? Natal, an Italian by birth, unfortunately, like my linguist Dankirche, had had many affairs with the dangerous class, as had his master more than once; and although he went about habitually with an arsenal of weapons in his belt, revolvers, swords, and daggers, for self-defence, that did not seem to have protected him any more than it did my linguist from attack, though it probably enabled him, more fortunate in this than his predecessor, to save his life. It seems to have been a deliberate and premeditated attack, either out of pure bravado, or from long-nourished hostility. He was standing on the flight of steps at the gate of the Legation just before dusk, several of the yaconins on service at the Legation *being close to him*, when a couple of evil-looking and swaggering Samourai in full costume came past. One of them mounted the steps, and immediately began to pick a quarrel, by violently kicking a little dog at his side, into the street. On the first word of remonstrance, he drew his short sword, and aimed a furious blow at his intended victim's head. This was partially parried by

Natal, who raised his arm to protect his head as he sprang aside, and drawing his revolver, fired at his assailant, who then turned on his heel, and disappeared among the crowd,—the blood-stained sword still unsheathed in his hand, without a finger being stirred, either by the officers on service or the inhabitants in the street, to stop the ruffian! It is doubtful whether he was wounded by the pistol-shot, though reports to that effect afterwards reached the Legation. Nothing could be more disgraceful than the conduct of all the swarm of two-sworded yaconins and officials, cumbering the courtyard of the Legation with their presence. Several indeed were actual spectators *on the spot.* At first they denied that any of them were there, or saw what took place! And, when the asseveration of the wounded man was too persistent in pointing out the particular men, to be altogether discredited; the Ministers, through their Governors of Foreign Affairs, still had the air of treating it as a very doubtful matter what took place; and pretended to believe that the assailant only drew his sword when menaced with the pistol. But the means and the end were all in keeping, and the offender was never punished to our knowledge. The men on duty who so shamefully stood by while a foreigner under their special guard was being cut down, equally escaped, though nominally disgraced. There was a rule of immunity in all such cases. Everyone but the Government officers knew the assailant was an officer of a certain Prince* whose retainers enjoy a sort of notoriety as bold and turbulent swashbucklers, making their boast of it, and the power of their master to protect them. This would seem to be a state of things of no modern date, however. In the 'Memoires et Anecdotes' of the reigning dynasty collected from native sources by Titsingh, already referred to, there are some very curious illustrations of a state of lawless law in the code of honour of

---

* The same Prince of Satsuma whose officers and retainers on the high road recently fell upon a party of peaceable foreigners, among whom was a lady — killing one on the spot, and dangerously wounding his companions.

these gentry, and the extreme measures taken by their
chiefs occasionally, either to restrain the violence of their
people, or at least avoid being dragged into feuds by their
acts.    Although cases were not rare it seems when they,
like the chiefs of the ancient Scottish clans, adopted the
quarrel of their retainers and avenged them.

Titsingh says, 'When the subjects or vassals of one
Prince affront those of another, *the latter would be dishonoured if he did not avenge it.*' It is related of this same
Prince of Satsuma, (to whom the Loochoo Islands belong
as part of his hereditary dominions, and whose subjects
traffic from Japan there and through the principal cities
of the Empire,) that in order to avoid all quarrel with
other princes, he made a law ;—that if one of his people
should at any time be insulted by the subjects of another
Daimio, he was permitted to avenge himself by taking the
life of his adversary—provided that he performed the
Hara-kiru on himself immediately after! The life of two
persons, who by their bellicose and turbulent spirit were
the cause of their own troubles, appeared to him of too
little importance to drag their masters into quarrels which
might lead to great bloodshed.    And in order to give
greater effect to this principle, and at the same time
maintain a high spirit and sense of honour among his
people, it was also decreed that if any of his people were
insulted, and did not dare from cowardice to avenge
themselves, and the captain or any of his men belonging
to one of his ships should come to know it,—the coward
was to be conducted on board, and without delay or any
form of trial, to have his head struck off, and both head
and trunk to be thrown into the sea.    Titsingh remarks
' that in this manner peace is maintained and the people
generally treat each other with the greatest politeness—
endeavouring by every possible means to avoid all that
might create a dispute where the consequences must
necessarily be so fatal.'    And as a measure of policy,
there is no doubt the certainty of death, as the necessary
effect to both parties in a quarrel, must go far to check

brawls and violence even among the most turbulent. In other countries, if a man kills his enemy he may elude justice, and live to fight another day — but where there is no possible escape out of the country, and the offender is bound forthwith to be his own executioner, and follow his victim, it must greatly tend to simplify the administration of justice! Whether the Samourai in this case had an offence or an insult according to his code to avenge, and whether he scrupulously immolated himself afterwards, will never be known. But I have grave doubts as to the latter.

The following narrative, also given by Titsingh, may serve to illustrate this aspect of national manners and customs, in which we are more directly interested than may at first appear. About the middle of last century the retainers of the Prince of Owari (one of the *Gosankay* or 'Royal Brothers' of the reigning dynasty) had made themselves general objects of fear, by the deeds of violence they committed in open day on whoever had the misfortune to displease them. In the eleventh month of the fourth year Foreki (1754) a man in trowsers and cloak* met eight of the retainers of Owari in Sinagawa (a suburb at the entrance of Yeddo near to the British Legation, and of evil fame for its tea-houses and habitual brawlers) in the street *Sibagoutze-zogitscho*. He had the misfortune, in passing, to touch one of them, who immediately turned round and loaded him with abuse ; — which the unhappy man endeavoured to moderate by his excuses. But not content with words, they speedily fell upon him, and left him for dead. The victim of their brutality with difficulty dragged himself to the nearest guard-house, and there made himself known as being in the service of

* None but officers of a certain rank are allowed to wear trowsers or two swords. The 'cloak' referred to may be meant to describe the upper dress *Kami-shimo* — having projecting wings at the shoulders — as in the illustration, Vol. I. p. 256. This is not peculiar to any rank, but may be worn by all when paying a visit of ceremony. A cloak, properly speaking, is no part of Japanese costume — a sort of overcoat or wrapper is thrown over the shoulders, or worn as a coat, only in wet weather.

*Misou-no Yamassiro-no-kami.*   Being unable to walk, he was put in a cango and carried to his master's house, where he died shortly after arriving, saying that he had been set upon by a band of ruffians in the streets of Sinagawa, to whom belonging he did not know.

Misou-no Yamassiro-no-kami, indignant at the treatment his servitor had met with, immediately set himself to discover the offenders, and having been assured that they were people of the Prince of Owari he proceeded to the palace of the Prince—told him what had passed, and demanded the heads of the eight offenders. The Prince admitted the justness of the indignation expressed, and promised him satisfaction, but declared that he could never consent to take the lives of eight men to avenge the death of one. Yamassiro-no-kami, more irritated by this answer, insisted on his demand, declaring that if he did not obtain full justice on the spot, he would eviscerate himself in the Prince's presence, and that his death would not remain unavenged! Owari seeing him so determined promised him the satisfaction demanded, but Yamassiro apparently having no great faith in the sanctity of the promise, protested that he would not leave the house until execution had been done. Upon this the eight men were brought, and their heads cut off in his presence. ' *Cet exemple*,' observes the historian, ' *rendit leur camarades plus réservé.*' And well it might! *

---

\* May not this example from their own history be read with advantage by Foreign Powers — whose subjects are now exposed to the same treatment from precisely the same classes—remembering, indeed, the principle established among themselves, and accepted by the nobles of the land as a law, the penalty of disregarding which among themselves would be dishonour. *Can* Foreign Powers wisely or safely allow reiterated and murderous assaults on their subjects, without exacting adequate retribution? This law of honour, more imperative probably than any mere statutory enactment, which declares a Prince *dishonoured if he permits any subject or vassal of his own to be affronted, and does not obtain satisfaction,* cannot be without influence on all who live under it. If they apply the same rule to Foreign Powers—(and who can doubt that they do?)—there is no Treaty Power that can at the present time be regarded otherwise than as dishonoured and craven by the Japanese. We and all other nations of the West may, in our turn, regard with contempt any appreciation of our acts and policy by the Japanese; but the question to be considered is, whether foreigners can live at all in the country under such conditions? My own impression is they cannot,—and

Perhaps something in connection with these customs of vengeance and protection, may account for the seeming cowardice or indifference to whatever may happen, so invariably observed among the officers and guards placed at the Legations professedly for the protection of their European inmates ; and for that end made to accompany them on foot or on horseback whenever they leave the gates.    They have never been known to raise a hand to save a foreigner from insult or violence.    They would have allowed this last victim to have been brained at their side.    I have watched my own escort repeatedly, when these ruffling retainers have approached with an air of menace, and possibly meaning mischief as well as insult,—and seen them either look another way, or resolutely refuse to see anything that might be wrong! It was quite obvious, that for the life of no foreigner that ever stepped in Japan, would they incur the chance and peril of a rencontre—and a blood feud with one of these dangerous classes.    Hence, all these officers, guards and spies, inside the Legation gates ;—and escorts on horseback when we went out, were manifestly *no protection whatever*, though a great encumbrance.    Protection was the plea, and may to some extent have entered into the motives of the Government in placing them about us ;— but beyond and above this, I cannot help thinking, was another object, namely, that of cutting off the foreigners quartered in the capital by the force of treaties, from all free intercourse or communication with the population ;— more especially with the educated and higher classes, who might give information tending to expose the double game the Government was playing with Foreign Powers,— enlighten us as to the real state of parties, and themselves imbibe ideas prejudicial to the existing system of government.

As to the absence of any real or effective protection, a

*will not be permitted,* by those who commit the murders and violences,— if they have no respect for the nation, and no fear of the vengeance of the Governments, they outrage.

more flagrant case could not have been furnished; and it was not surprising, therefore, that a more than usual amount of mendacity and tergiversation marked all the proceedings of the authorities. It was impossible to avoid reflections far from reassuring, where such perfect impunity was known to exist, proved by more than a dozen examples now, and to the very persons from whom violence was to be anticipated. How long would the lives of foreigners be respected? It was evident the members of the several Foreign Legations, placed in the very focus of all hostility, lived on from day to day, by the sufferance only of a horde of ill-disposed men armed with deadly weapons, and perfectly secure from punishment for any outrage they might commit! Either the Government at Yeddo could not command the services of men courageous enough to defend Foreign Ministers and their suite from insult and murder, or foreseeing that this would entail a chance of conflict with their great Feudatories, and dangers affecting their own stability, preferred these half measures of protection for appearance sake, in case anything very disastrous should happen, — and deliberately took the chance of every foreigner being massacred. Despite the many successive cases of violence and assassination which had marked the two years past, there were some among the Foreign Legations who turned away from the contemplation of the only logical inferences to be drawn from the facts. And in despair perhaps of finding any remedy, buoyed themselves with a hope, that after all things might mend, or at least not produce the worst of those eventualities, which it could not be denied were among the legitimate consequences of inaction on the part of the Government on the one hand, and those menaced with destruction on the other.

The whole of my published correspondence with the Japanese government, proved that I had never deceived myself as to the real conditions under which foreigners were placed. As willing as any to hope for the best, I could not 'make my judgement blind,' or shut my

eyes to the probable effects of causes so clearly in operation, and so full of menace and danger.   It required
such an event as the deliberate and resolute attempt of an
armed band to massacre a whole Legation in the dead of
night, though surrounded by these soi-disant guards and
protectors, and an almost miraculous escape of the inmates
from destruction, to fully justify this prevision of the
future ;—and that also, as will be seen, was destined in due
time to be added to the chain of evidence.

I find on turning to the brief record which I kept
as a sort of almanac for future reference, the following
entry under this date—after the wounded man had been
sent away to his chief, who was at Yokohama.  'If
these guards are inefficient or disloyal enough to let us
be murdered at their feet, it is worthy of serious
consideration whether Yeddo is a place for Diplomatic
Agents?   If the Government of the country either *have*
not the services at their command of men capable of
doing their duty—or *having them* they prefer hazarding
our lives, to incurring the trouble and risk of defending
them (whether by efficient protection, or by repressing
with a strong hand the enemies from whom such dangers
come, might be immaterial) it certainly is a question of
grave importance, what steps can be taken, before these
individual murders and assassinations shall culminate in a
more general catastrophe, where all the Legations may be
sacrificed to a set of fanatics and cut-throats — and every
individual foreigner in the country murdered in cold blood
without means of defence or possibility of escape.'

--------

The emotions and the reflections excited by this last in
the long succession of similar deeds, became things of the
past.   There was no remedy within reach.   Practically,
there was no help for the evils that beset the working of
a treaty forced upon an unwilling nation, and a class of
feudal nobles ready to proceed to any extremity, with

apt and willing instruments always under their hand.
As Sydney Smith said of railroad casualties, until a
minister or a bishop was killed nothing would, or, as it
seemed, could be done; because there must be such a
demonstrative proof of the lawlessness and sweeping de-
structiveness of the plans contemplated, that not even
the most inveterate carpers and cavillers on the other side
of the globe could, in the consciousness of their own
security, find a plea for crying with the Romans of Gal-
gacus, 'Peace, peace!' where there was no peace, and
the sword had made a desert.

We were already far into the next month of November
without farther calamity, when one came upon us, which
not to have experienced in Yeddo would have partaken
of the character of a miracle. A few minutes before the
dinner hour, there was a rushing and scuffling of many
feet along the passages, the noise of which reached me in
my dressing-room at the extremity of the building, and
presently, high above all, came the ominous cry of
'CADJEE!' (Fire.) One must have lived in Yeddo, I
think, daily and almost hourly, accustomed to see and
hear of the wild havoc committed by the all-devouring
element, to thoroughly realise the sudden revulsion of
feeling such a cry creates, with the instant vision of the
beams and rafters blazing, and destruction swift and sure.

There was a rush to the spot, and I then saw that my
servants, with the lack of discretion and prudence usual
in Japanese,—whose constant familiarity with all the
horrors of fire, seems to make them only more perfectly
reckless and void of ordinary care—had lit a monstrous
fire in the dining-room stove, for there are no fireplaces
or chimneys existing or possible in this earthquaky soil.
The rafters had caught fire, and when I got outside, the
glower of a smouldering fire began to show by the side
of the pipe where it pierced the roof. Our own servants
and the large class of yaconins and police always on
service, fortunately supplied hands immediately; and, to
do them justice, if their discretion and judgement had only

been equal to their zeal, all cause of alarm would soon
have been at an end.    The mayor of the district also
came to our rescue at the first clang of the great Temple
bell, calling for the fire brigades.    At first, it seemed
almost inevitable that the whole place must be consumed.    There was little order or method — ladders
were deficient, and, when obtained, those who mounted
began by pitching off the tiles, in spite of my efforts to
stop them, thus letting air into the roof.    Fortunately, a
large pond was close at hand, well filled with water, and
by aid of a couple of little native engines, the fire was at
last finally declared to be extinct, with only a sad destruction of tiles, roof, and ceilings, and a few contusions and
bruises among the assistants.    It is in such circumstances
as these, that the large staff of Japanese officials having
authority, are really valuable.    All the gates were instantly closed, to keep out the mob, amongst whom are
always plunderers and some of the worst classes.    Two
or three yaconins were posted inside the house, with
arms in their hands, and guarded the passages leading to
my own suite of rooms, where the dinner-table was
spread, with the silver, &c., upon it.    For once I felt
they were a protection and a safeguard; and in effect,
nothing was touched or lost, though two or three hundred men must have been through and about the house.
A fat and burly carpenter, who had often been employed
in the Legation, rushed down with his men the moment
he heard the fire was at Tozengee; and a Vice-Governor
who had formerly been on service with me, though nearly
two miles off, jumped on a horse and came to the spot at
speed.    One had need of some such evidences of good feeling and loyalty to bear up against the strong and adverse
current of hostility and treachery.    I felt these instances
of devotion and interest went far to compensate for
all the flurry and anxiety of such an event as a fire in
the house—the inconveniences of which were felt long
after, for many weeks elapsed before the damages were
all made good.

About this time I met with an amusing instance of the kind of information given to the British public in respect to Japan. It was extracted from the columns of the 'Times,'—derived apparently from America, but still enjoying all the benefit of such a circulation as only the 'Times' could give it :—' The commercial and trading public, *officials and the higher classes*, encourage foreign intercourse ; while the masses are more prejudiced than ever, the latter complaining that the foreign trade enhances the price of food.'

The amusing part of this announcement consists in its not only being essentially inaccurate, but the exact converse of the truth. Although we hear a good deal from the Ministers of increased prices, and that these are attributed to us, there is no good evidence that the people hold this opinion ; and certain it is that the masses show no ill-will, but, on the contrary, great desire to trade, so far as we can come in contact with them. All that appears of hostility or restriction comes from the official and higher classes, held up for approval as sole encouragers of foreign intercourse ! The correspondents of our London papers are generally well-informed and trustworthy ; but when we are driven to some transatlantic sources, or even to our own local papers in such distant regions, for information, there seems no limit to the absurdity or inaccuracy of the announcements which our leading journals may be the means of circulating. On one occasion a description of my landing at Yeddo was copied from some American print, and went the round of all the English press, by which I was not only gratuitously gifted with a wife and two children, but the lady was made to comport herself with such vigour, in tapping the heads of the prying crowd with her parasol, that some of my friends in England thought it beyond a joke ; and at last, when it got transferred to the more permanent pages of a book on ' Japan — Social, Moral, &c.,' one of my relatives lost patience, and required a formal contradiction to be inserted in a newspaper which had quoted this veracious portion of the 'History of our Relations with Japan,' stating that I did not happen to possess either wife or children.

The year 1860 was now drawing towards its end. Early in the month of December I had an unwonted pleasure in the visit of two of my fair countrywomen, with their husbands—one an old China friend—the first that had ever set their feet in Yeddo; for the only lady previously in the capital was French by birth, though an English Consul's wife. They were well pleased with their short sojourn, not much heeding that they were treading on the ashes of a smouldering volcano, both literally and metaphorically. Yet the husband of one of them had unpleasant evidence of the fact in returning from a quiet ride through the city. A two-sworded retainer of a Daimio, something the worse for liquor probably, planted himself in the middle of the road in front of the horse, and by word and gesture refused to let him pass. One of my attachés was of the party, and, better versed in these sort of incidents, and what they might at any moment lead to, he turned round to those of my escort of yaconins who rode behind, to tell them to remove the man, who looked mischievously inclined, and was endeavouring rudely to obstruct the way; but they sat pale on their horses, awaiting the issue! So is it ever. We might be cut down and slaughtered any day in the public thoroughfares without hope of aid or rescue from any number of them; and it was difficult to avoid asking oneself sometimes—was not this likely to be the end? Certainly it was impossible not to feel that the more boldly and resolutely any Foreign Minister resisted bad faith and treachery in carrying out the treaties, and opposed the obstructive and reactionary policy of the ruling classes, the more likely was he to be marked out as an obstacle to be removed. Mr. Macdonald, who was there, seemed to have been seriously alarmed at the attitude of the bravo—drunk or sober. It seemed a moot point, not altogether decided in his own mind,

whether he would or would not draw his sword and run
' a muck' on the foreigner.  The defence of the yaconins,
when, on the return of the party, they were taken to task
for their supineness and inaction, was a pretence that
they saw he was too drunk to do any mischief,—an
unmitigated falsehood, for Mr. Macdonald could not
detect that he was drunk at all, and he certainly was
steady on his legs.   But what if drunk, with two deadly
weapons at his belt—was he to be allowed to try his
drunken strength on the limbs and bodies of foreigners?
And the Ministers thought the excuse a valid plea for
immunity both to the ruffian and the officers !

But the anxieties and causes of trouble existing at this
period were not limited to the acts of Japanese subjects.
Foreigners themselves, from time to time, threw in their
contribution to the combustible materials ready for a
general explosion, and wanting but a spark to fire the
train.  Towards the end of November, one of those untoward events took place at Kanagawa, which might well
have proved a source of great danger to the whole community, and did for a time threaten them with indiscriminate acts of reprisal and vengeance.  A British subject was
returning through Kanagawa from a shooting excursion,
with his gun over his shoulder, and his servant following,
with the result of his sport in the shape of a wild goose,
when a body of police pounced upon the servant.  His
master turned back to the rescue ; when they proceeded to
arrest him also, upon which he brought his piece down,
cocked it, and threatened to shoot them if they advanced ;
and in the scuffle the gun was fired, and an officer des-
perately wounded — one arm being shattered above the
elbow, and the charge passing across — or into his chest.
The foreigner was instantly pulled down, bound hand and
foot, and carried off by the police ; nor was it until the
middle of the night that the Consul could ascertain where
the prisoner was secured, and claim him out of their hands.

Nothing could have been more unfortunate or ill-timed
for the interests and safety of the community to which

the prisoner belonged, than this collision with the police. They had simply been performing their duty. The foreigner was violating a law of Japan which prohibits anyone using fire-arms within ten Re of the Tycoon's residence, and for which a Japanese is punishable with death. All foreigners had been warned that such was the law, and notice given to them to abstain from going out shooting, but, as the result showed, with little effect.

Great excitement prevailed among the Japanese *Yaconinerie* on the spot. Threats were rife, and a report circulated, that the brothers of the wounded man were determined to revenge him by taking the Englishman's life, at least, if not that of other foreigners. Blood for blood, and a life for a life — the rule under the Mosaic dispensation, and the *lex talionis* of Feudal days — is a law in full force in Japan. There could be no doubt he would be compelled to leave Japan for his own security, and it was not expected the wounded man could possibly recover. Although he did not die of his wounds ultimately, and was only crippled for life — it might very truly be said that this was more by good luck than good management. Hundreds have died under the best surgeons' hands, and with injuries far less severe. Part of the charge had severely lacerated the chest, and he had not the best, but the worst surgical aid, according to any European ideas of art. It was instantly proposed by two American medical men attached to the missionary establishment, to amputate, as affording the only chance of saving life. This could not be done, however, without the consent of the Government, and that was never given. Apparently it is not permitted in Japan to save lives at the expense of limbs. Fortunately, it would seem that the blood of the Japanese is not inflammatory, whatever their passions may be. A demand for justice was made, and the party accused was put upon his trial in a Consular court, before the Consul and two assessors from the community, called in by the Consul to assist. Every facility was given to the Japanese to satisfy themselves

that it was the desire of the British authorities to do that
justice when Japanese were concerned, which the former
were always insisting upon for their own people.   The
court declared the prisoner guilty on several counts, one
of which was maliciously wounding, &c., and a sentence of
deportation with a fine of $1,000 was recorded.   The
assessors dissented, and the judgement was accordingly
referred to the Minister, to whom the Queen's order in
council gives power to ' confirm or vary or remit altogether
the punishment' awarded by the Consular court.   In this
case the punishment appeared to me inadequate, whether
as regarded the evidence of animus and the injury
inflicted on the Japanese, or the mischief and danger to
the whole community which resulted, and I added three
months' imprisonment in addition, directing the $1,000 to
be paid as an indemnity to the wounded man ; who, if he
survived, would be rendered incapable of earning his
living by following his vocation.   Neither the fine nor the
deportation, it was very generally known, carried any
punishment ; because the first (as was ostentatiously
boasted) would be subscribed for by the prisoner's friends
and supporters in the community — and the deportation
would have taken place in any case by a voluntary act
of the accused, to escape the threatened vengeance of the
wounded man's relations.   The sentence was subsequently
made the subject of an action, brought against me by the
party convicted, who escaped his term of imprisonment
in Hongkong by a series of blunders and informalities
on the part of every one concerned, from the Consul at
Kanagawa to the Magistrate at Hongkong, and was
properly liberated by the judge on a writ of habeas
corpus, after one hundred and twenty hours' durance.   It
appeared on the subsequent hearing of the action, that
although the Minister had power to *vary* or remit, he was
still limited to fine and deportation — OR imprisonment.
Had I remitted the fine, or left out the deportation,—
neither of which really touched the prisoner in pocket or
convenience — I might have legally awarded twelve

months' imprisonment instead of three ; but this oversight on my part was fatal to the legality of the award, and the case for damages went to a jury of the Supreme Court at Hongkong, which gave, as substantial damages for wrong and injury suffered by the prisoner in one hundred and twenty hours' detention in the gaol, $2,000. To which they added, at the judge's suggestion, an intimation that *if* they had had full jurisdiction, they would have given from $15,000 to $20,000 in addition !

Considering that the said jury had no evidence before them whereon to found a judgement, except what the judge had himself ruled to be irrelevant, and expressly excluded on that ground as inadmissible ; both the question and the answer can only be considered as belonging to the curiosities of colonial law — quite as unique in their kind, as anything ever seen in a Consular court. The case is alluded to here, not to question or discuss the justice of the Hongkong jury's award ; but because the circumstances attending it from beginning to end, were calculated to exercise considerable influence on our interests and position in Japan : it furnishes, moreover, no bad illustration of the evils and anomalies attending the administration of justice throughout these regions, where something very like conflicting and antagonistic systems exist—in the jurisdictions of the Consuls in China and Japan, and the Supreme Court at Hongkong,— the one, administered necessarily by public servants unfamiliar with legal forms and technicalities, but bound to do justice on the merits of such cases as may be brought before them ; the other, provided with all legal machinery — law, lawyers, fees, and juries — and a summary jurisdiction, in the hands of a single judge, against which there is no appeal.

It is beyond doubt that had the prisoner been triumphantly acquitted on the spot of all blame, as many of the community desired, and contended he should have been, such a verdict would have been a source of imminent danger, not to the accused alone, who would probably

have paid the penalty of his life,— unless he speedily
disappeared, and made his escape from those who had
vowed to take it,—but to many of the best known and least
discreet of his supporters. Indeed, so general was the
conviction of this, that several took their passage by the
first ship, and it was a common report that the chief de-
linquent himself had arrived at the conviction, that he
ought to lose no time in getting away. The judgement
and nature of the punishment awarded was in effect a shield
of protection to him and to the whole community, whatever else it might be considered. This was no reason, of
course, why the accused should be either unjustly convicted or illegally sentenced, but the mere fact that the
life and security of many others besides the prisoner's were
jeopardied by his acts, formed a very good reason for
careful scrutiny of all the evidence brought forward on
the trial. It furnished the strongest motive at the same
time for rightly determining — whether in effect he could
justly be held *irresponsible* for all the injury and mischief
resulting? I thoroughly satisfied myself that he could
neither morally nor legally be so considered; and that he
had rendered himself subject to a much heavier penalty
than was ultimately imposed. The numerous Japanese
witnesses present on the spot deposed that they heard
him threaten the officer to shoot them,—that he deliberately cocked and pointed his gun at them ; and that immediately subsequent to this he did actually fire and
wound the Japanese officer close to him, who, so far as he
was concerned, as I have said, was only acting in the performance of his duty, and under the immediate orders of
his superior. Nothing but the clearest justification for
taking a life, could in the spirit of our laws exempt any
one in such circumstances as this evidence set forth,
from penalties of some kind. And as to the extent
and nature of those imposed in this case, it is only
necessary to look through the calendar of any assize
court, or even the police courts of the metropolis with a
summary jurisdiction for minor offences, to see abundant

proof that sentences of much greater severity are continually recorded by the judges and magistrates who occupy the bench at home, for offences and misdemeanours which neither in reality, nor in popular estimate, could rank with shooting at any person with intent to wound or do some bodily injury, and such was among the offences charged against the prisoner. ' To attempt in any manner to discharge loaded arms or to wound any person with intent to maim or disable or do some grievous bodily harm, or with intent to prevent the apprehension of another party,' subjects the person so offending against the law to 'transportation for life,' or ' not less than fifteen years,' or not ' *more* than *three years' imprisonment.*' And for how many comparatively trivial offences are more severe penalties than those imposed on the prisoner in this case, provided by the statute law of Great Britain, and without question — inflicted ?

That where there is illegality in the mode of assessing the punishment or delivering judgement—or informalities in carrying the same into execution, the defendant should have his remedy, is only right and necessary for the protection of the liberty of the subject. And that by regular process of law he should be declared free of the penalties, — though he may thereby escape altogether or in part the legitimate consequences of his misdeed, and such a result may defeat the ends of justice,— cannot be contested. For the vindication of the law under the assumed sanction of which judgement was given, it is right and proper that it should be so ; because it is a less evil that many guilty should escape, than that the law should be erroneously interpreted or misapplied, whether by design or error. This, and the liability to an action for damages in any judge who is convicted of error or misinterpretation, is the protection provided against such abuse. And that a jury should mark their sense of the importance of surrounding the subject in the East with every protection against negligence or illegality, even when altogether unintentional, which a liability to heavy damages could supply, is also to be anticipated and desired. If it may fall oppressively in some cases on an upright officer,—it has also the advantage of enforcing anxious attention to the actual state of the law, and his powers under it, without which a far worse evil might befall many under his jurisdiction, than mere pecuniary damages. It is well that Ministers, Consuls, and all other public servants in the East should know and feel, whenever they are called upon to exercise authority, or administer the laws, that no integrity of heart or desire to do right, no peculiarity of position however anxious or perplexing, will ever weigh in the minds of those, to whom a flaw in an indictment or a technical illegality may give the power to assess damages. At home a magistrate is equally liable to an action for acts done in his judicial capacity; but he is under the special protection of an Act of Parliament, commonly known as Jervis's Act, and if there be reason to suspect any local feelings or prejudices calculated to bias the judgement, he may move the venue to another court and locality, and thus insure impartiality. No such protection exists for the official in the East. He must be content to see the case tried in a locality where, it may be notorious, hostility exists to the whole system that gives judicial powers to his class; — and where no opportunity is ever lost of marking the feeling, by those who constitute the juries, out of court, before and after sitting in the jury-box, having no hesitation in loudly proclaiming it.* Public opinion in small colonies or communities — discussing and prejudging all civil cases — so far from aiding justice has a tendency to thwart or pervert it.

This is a very undesirable state of things for both parties. It tends to keep up a spirit of antagonism, which

---

* The great institution of trial by jury is somewhat shorn of its fair proportions, when the necessities of a tropical colony reduce the number of jurors to five, and a simple majority is required; that is, three out of five— nor does it tend to increase veneration or a sense of security, when the leading counsel for the plaintiff, after judgement, feels at liberty to censure and reproach one of the jurors for not having given his client larger damages.

is in the true interest of neither.   It weakens the hand of
the magistrate, on whose firmness and courage to do what
is right, must often depend the security and protection of
whole communities.  It encourages those who are disposed
to be lawless in such far Eastern ports, and from whom the
greatest danger  arises to the orderly and well-conducted.
I believe a good deal of the feeling of irritation and hostility, so frequently manifested in these regions by the more
respectable classes,— who have really everything to gain,
and nothing to fear, from the rigorous maintenance of law
and order,— arises from  causes which might  easily  be
removed, to the great advantage of our interests in the
East ; no less than to the benefit of Ministers and Consuls.
With this public object in  view, a few remarks of a sug-
gestive character may not be considered altogether irrelevant or impertinent.   There is perhaps something irritating
in the circumstance that the person with whom they have
daily social intercourse, and it may be some degree of intimacy, should the next day or after the last friendly meeting
be suddenly transformed into a judge,—with power to dispose under the law of their property, and sometimes their
liberty.  The proverbial impossibility of pleasing a worsted
suitor, can hardly fail to receive a new application of peculiar force in such circumstances.  Whoever thinks his judge
is right if the  judgement is a condemnation ?   And yet
in many cases this result must be inevitable.   Of course, if
the officer holding the scales of justice be young in years,
not a lawyer by profession, not infallible either in his law
or his judgement — and who is ? — the irritation and bitterness will be  intensified, by every  condition that can
possibly be held to tell against him.   Not all magistrates
and judges are either infallible or immaculate, even in the
home of law and liberty from whence we come,— or half
the lawsuits of each year would never arise.  Can we
hope they will be so in the far East, where the officers
selected must often be suddenly appointed to fill up an unforeseen gap made by death, or to occupy a newly-created
post, that cannot be left unfilled, even for a short interval,

without the gravest prejudice to the material interests of all
who are seeking fortunes in the country.    Consuls in the
East have administrative and political functions, as well as
judicial, imposed upon them, among which the latter are
only occasional and, so to speak, incidental,—while the
first two are constant and inseparable from the office.    To
remedy the major part of these evils thus briefly sketched,
it has been proposed, that to the bench of the Supreme
Court at Hongkong should be added one puisne judge, or
if necessary two, to constitute a full Appellate Court, and
that each of these in rotation should visit the Chinese
and Japanese open ports periodically, and as visiting
judges try the graver cases, thus relieving the Minister
and Consul alike of all responsibility in regard to them.
By this plan the several communities would be relieved
of one of the greatest of their alleged grievances; for
it is not likely such a judge would ever sin on the side
of great youth.    A lawyer by profession, it is to be
taken for granted all suitors and misdemeanants would
have *law*, and due observance of legal forms and technicalities, whatever else might be lacking.    Whether
they would thus make sure of justice in a more prompt
or more satisfactory form, they might learn by experience.
And at all events, if the value of a thing bear any proportion to its cost, there is very little doubt they would
have to pay for it at a sufficiently high rate compared
with consular justice (which to all its other sins has, I
think, added that of being nearly costless), to make them
disposed to value it highly, and to consider it a great
improvement on the 'cheap justice' they have been compelled heretofore to accept, *faute de mieux*.    It is not
often possible to propose any scheme, where passions run
high and interests are large, that can have a prospect of
being equally pleasing and satisfactory to all parties;—but
this, I think, may boast of that rare merit.    The British
communities would be liberated from the bondage to
'boy-consuls' and 'lay justice,' with its contingent or
possible illegalities and technical errors, of which much

has been heard. They might have law, profound and technical—to their hearts' content, with all the privilege of paying highly for it,—on something like the Hongkong tariff. The puisne judges, who would be made for such a service, could not be otherwise than gratified by their promotion—and if anyone doubts that Her Majesty's Ministers and Consuls would be the most rejoiced of the three parties in question, at their release from irksome functions and onerous responsibilities,—I wish them the benefit of a year's experience of the real cares and anxieties of office in those Eastern lands. This, or a somewhat similar system, has been adopted with success in the Levant; and a legal Vice-Consul (Chancelier) has been attached to the Consul-General in addition at Alexandria. Although it may be attended with greater practical difficulties,—from the distance of the ports and their comparative inaccessibility in winter,—there are none which need be insuperable. And sooner or later the *necessity* for some provision of this nature will, I have no doubt, make itself felt; and whenever this happens we shall hear no more of the expense or other obstacles which, for the moment, may be insurmountable.

Practically, British residents, I believe, have had little to complain of in the administration of justice at the Consular ports. They may, it is true, object to a *liability* to maladministration by inexperienced or unprofessional public servants, called upon to act as administrators of the law,—as a danger to which they ought not to be exposed. And it is, perhaps, natural that they should show extreme jealousy and distrust, if they see power confided to what they deem incompetent hands. I, for one, would very gladly see them relieved, even of the speculative and contingent, rather than actual injury; and placed in a happier frame of mind as to the guarantees for a perfect and unimpeachable legality in all the processes by which the liberty or the property of the subject may be affected. But, at the same time, I must declare my honest conviction, that they have had little reason to complain of any real injury; and that during the twenty years which the Consular jurisdiction has existed east of the Ganges, such as it now is, they have suffered no substantial wrong or injustice at the hands of those authorities. If any just ground of complaint existed, it would not, in my opinion, be for excess of authoritative interference, but rather that it had been short-handed in reaching delinquencies, which in the general interest ought not to have escaped punishment. The administration of justice has been prompt and satisfactory on the whole, as well as nearly costless. Technical errors and minor illegalities, or irregularities in the proceedings, may have been more or less common, and are perhaps inevitable under the circumstances. Where there has been neither legal training nor professional practice in the courts, it could not well be otherwise. But a decision on the merits of a case, where the points at issue are generally free from intricacies turning on points of law,—and such are the great majority of Consular cases,—may meet all the requirements of justice, if intelligence and honesty of purpose are not wanting in the presiding officer. If it be contended that a legal education and proficiency in legal forms and technicalities are both essential and necessary, for the protection of the subject in his rights and liberties, I have nothing to object; or, at all events, I have no wish to contest the point. But I would observe, in that case, the objection lies against the *system*, not the *individuals* who simply perform to the best of their ability duties forced upon them by it ; and it is scarcely fair, and certainly not generous, to make them bear the odium and the penalties of what is, or may be considered, objectionable in the first. Those who made the system and appoint the officers under it, know perfectly well that these have no legal education or professional qualifications. It is also frequently alleged, that to give judicial powers to unprofessional and more or less inexperienced officers, is to expose the subject to great danger of their arbitrary and oppressive exercise. But I would say, in opposition to this theoretic objection, that, judging from a large field of observation and some personal experience,— the tendency is *exactly the reverse*. There is far greater danger of the young and the inex-periençed, or the unprofessional judge, shrinking from the local clamour, and the liability of being ruined by vindic-tive damages from a prejudiced jury in a supreme court of appeal,— failing to discharge his duty firmly and fear-lessly, than of either exceeding his powers or using them oppressively.  I believe the real danger to be guarded against under the existing state of things, and in the in-terest of every community in the East, is that of Consuls being intimidated and *deterred from doing their duty*. And so far from those under his jurisdiction requiring pro-tection from wrong and injury at his hands and by the law, it is the public servant who stands most in need, exposed as he is to penalties for mere error of judgement, far more grievous and irremediable than any he has the power, if ever he had the desire, to inflict.  Local papers find a popu-lar theme for declamation in what they are pleased to style the abuses of authority, and the oppressive and arbitrary dealings of Eastern officials.  So far as my observation extends, and it has certainly not been very limited in scope — there is no part of the world where foreigners are freer from any vexatious restraints of law, and more constantly able to evade the legal consequences of misdeeds and an *abuse of liberty*, than in China and Japan.  There is no country (where law is held to be enforced and respected) in which manifest infractions are more leniently dealt with, even when they are brought under its cognisance.  In nearly twenty years, during some fourteen of which I exercised Consular jurisdiction, far removed from any superior, with all the judicial powers attaching to the office in the East, —I do not remember on more than two occasions re-cording a sentence of imprisonment against any of the resi-dent community : the one was for contumacy in refusing to pay a small fine, and lasted twenty-four hours ; and the other for an act of high-handed violence and confessed illegality, the term not exceeding a week.  Nor did I ever levy a higher fine than $200, and that only on one occasion. But it requires to have lived in the East, and among the foreign communities there, to have any power of realising the spirit in which all exercise of judicial power is regarded and canvassed. In London, or elsewhere in England, a man in a respectable station, young or otherwise, if he gets engaged in a broil, knocks another down, or commits an assault of more or less aggravated character, is without special warrant other than a constable's staff, made a prisoner, as a matter of course, and if he offer any resistance, is apt to be handled exceedingly roughly. He is then, equally as a matter of course, locked up in a nauseous cell, totally regardless of his respectability; and the next day he is put in the dock before a magistrate — fined, or, as will occasionally happen, sentenced to one or more weeks' — or months' imprisonment if he has endangered life or otherwise committed aggravated injury. But whoever hears of a hue and cry against the arbitrary tyranny and oppression of the magistrate? Let the same thing take place in one of the Chinese or Japanese ports, when the safety and material interests of a whole community are at stake; and let a Consul presume to inflict a penalty of fine or imprisonment upon a resident; — and he may esteem himself very fortunate if the press does not teem for weeks and months with declamation and abuse, on the standard theme of consular tyranny — or he be not subjected to all the harass, cost, and anxiety of an action in the Supreme Court of Hongkong, when, if any technical flaw can be detected, the risk of vindictive and ruinous damages hangs over his head. Let anyone take a file of a local paper at random, and it will be odd if he turns over many copies without an example which will fully bear out the truth of this picture. This is an evil, not of yesterday, but of twenty years' duration, and one that cries very loudly for remedy. I believe it may be found in the course suggested, and already partially acted upon in the Levant with happy effect, — by the appointment of a visiting judge. It may entail some additional machinery and expense, although, as regards the latter point, the fees, if on anything like the scale of the Supreme Court at Hongkong, might meet, if not the whole, a considerable part — and thus make litigation and violation of law pay their own expenses. The communities will be relieved of their standing grievance, but by far the greatest gainers will be the consular servants of the State. For let it be specially borne in mind, that if there were a legislation of a more stringent and summary character than, so far as I know, has ever been contemplated as applicable to British subjects in the Eastern half of Asia, it would only be in accordance with the exigencies of the case. Nowhere is there a greater influx, unless it be at some gold diggings, of the lawless and dissolute from all countries — and nowhere is the danger and the mischief they are calculated to inflict on whole Communities and on National interests greater than in these regions. In Japan more especially, an offence or act of violence that could have no other consequence in their own country, probably,—than some temporary injury or inconvenience to one or more individuals, — may here, among a sensitive and vindictive race, involve in massacre and ruin all the foreign residents—or set the spark to a train that will light up a war between two nations. Can these things, then, be lightly looked upon, even if the misdemeanants be, upon the whole, respectable and well-conducted? Are they not rightly, for the sake of so many others, if not in their own interest, made amenable to the laws, and held bound to be more careful not to infringe them, than in their own land? And if they take a contrary course, what more imperative duty can be laid on those who are charged with the maintenance of the peace, and held responsible for taking all due care to insure, not only the safety and weal of a community, but good relations between two countries,—than to repress vigorously and firmly all excess and license? It is their bounden duty to repress every act which they believe calculated to bring the nations they represent into disrepute or collision with one another, and their countrymen on the spot into peril; and to fail in this would be to endanger all under their control.   Whatever weakens a Consul's hand in the performance of such functions is an injury to all under his jurisdiction, who *must* look to him in all emergencies for aid and protection.   And I am satisfied that many of those whose course has this tendency would be the first to regret it, and admit the folly and mischief of persistence in it, — if they would take the trouble, or could ever be induced to look at the whole question, — stripped of local colouring and personal feelings.   These are only too natural, perhaps, to small and isolated communities, far removed from the wholesome influence of a public opinion formed under conditions of greater freedom from class interests and petty rivalries or animosities; and representing the common sense of a nation, instead of the passions of a small clique.   But it is not the less important that there should be a remedy against the possibility of such passions controlling and interfering with the free action of those in authority, to whom the larger and more permanent interests of a nation are entrusted, as well as the security and temporary interests of the few actually resident on the spot. Whoever occupies such places of trust and responsibility in China or Japan has the strongest claims to consideration and support on the part of those whose interests he must under all circumstances defend.   That he often receives so little of either on occasions such as this, is to be attributed to many causes, some local and others general.   Perhaps, if the truth were known, there are none of the Anglo-Saxon race who *like* the restraints which law imposes, when they themselves individually are concerned.   And it is only in far distant points, like the settlements in the East, the temporary home of so many mixed nationalities, that the chance ever occurs to them of resisting or offering objection in any tangible shape, without discredit, and consequences too serious to be lightly risked. Here the Foreign Representatives are isolated from all counsel or support,

and they have each, alone and unaided, to make head
against all difficulties.   They are surrounded by hostile
elements, native and foreign, and ever-recurring perplexi-
ties, entailing heavy responsibilities and much anxiety.
With an Oriental Government, and a treacherous and vin-
dictive race, to deal with on the one side, and some lawless
elements among those who claim their protection on the
other,—and often no means of compulsion save such as a
respect for the laws among their own people, and international obligations on the part of the Japanese, can supply,
neither of them much to be trusted—it may well be conceived, even by those who have never been so tried, that
the position is at once anxious and harassing.   A post
such as this brings with it too much wear and tear
not to leave, as time glides on, broad lines of care to
mark each year as it passes.   And these sink all the
deeper where there is no other hope to lighten the task,
than that which may spring from the prospect of a speedy
release.

The old year was at its last hour, and as I sat musing
on all the incidents marking the struggle that had filled
up its days and months, I could not help feeling how
uncertain was the future.   What the coming year might
bring of weal or woe to Japan, and the little band of
foreigners scattered amidst its millions, it was hard to
divine.   Christmas had been made more home-like than
any preceding by the visit of Sir Hope and Lady Grant,
and an influx of staff-officers fresh from their Chinese
campaign.   All the Legations, including the Prussian, had
their representatives at table, either in the person of the
chief or some of their staff.   We sat down twenty-three ;
and within that number of days, one of the guests, perhaps
the most light-hearted of the whole, lay wrapped in a
bloody shroud.

## CHAPTER II.

TOWARDS the close of 1860, the long-announced visit of a British squadron in the Japanese waters took place, the first since the establishment of the Legation ; and Rear-Admiral Jones in H.M.S. 'Impérieuse' with a couple of steam corvettes, the 'Scout' and the 'Encounter,' arrived in the Bay of Yeddo. The Admiral came on shore the morning after Christmas day, and took up his residence with me for a few days. Unpleasant rumours of danger to the several Legations were afloat ; but these were unfortunately too common to attract much attention. I paid a visit to present the Admiral to the Ministers of Foreign Affairs, before the last day of the year. Little took place worthy of note, unless it were the great desire expressed by the Ministers to purchase some of our largest frigates ! It is difficult to know with what object. They evidently desired to found a military navy, and thought the first step would be to obtain the ships and armaments ; without reflecting that if the object were to contend with Western Maritime Powers, they would merely be providing prizes on the first outbreak of hostilities, unless they were prepared with engineers and sailors to work the ships, and efficient men to fight them. Doubtless, with a large maritime population, they might in time hope to get up a navy to defend their own coasts even against Europeans; but it would require something very like a revolution in both their habits and institutions, as well as a long apprenticeship, before any moderate success could reasonably be looked for.  Some few men have been trained under the Dutch to work the three or four steam ships they already possess, *tant bien que mal*; but as for getting men aloft in a gale of wind, or really navigating a ship in the proper sense of the term, they have all to learn yet.  With what view were they so anxious to make costly augmentations of ready armed and equipped ships ?  Did they expect to be attacked by the aggressive action of some Foreign Power ?  Or were they conscious that their policy would before long bring one or more of the Treaty Powers upon them, in vindication of outraged rights ?  It was difficult to say, and as we returned from the interview I remarked to the Admiral, that whatever might be the real motive, or mixture of motives, I thought such plans of evil augury for the permanence of peaceful relations.

On January 1, the Rear-Admiral had already taken his departure from Yeddo to Yokohama, proposing immediately after to sail for Shanghae.  The visit was somewhat of the shortest, for any moral effect ; but I raised no obstacle.  I could not say there was any definite or immediate danger ; nor did I believe that the presence of his small force could materially avail to avert it, if any were impending.  Any show of force as a means of intimidation to be effective must be imposing, and anything short of this, was just as likely to irritate and produce an explosion as to defer it.

It was in this posture of affairs that the first of January 1861, brought me greeting, from my colleague the American Minister, who was on a visit to Kanagawa, to the effect that one of the Governors of Foreign Affairs had been sent down from Yeddo to warn him that the Gorogio (Council of State) were advised of a band of lonins to the number of several hundred, and supposed to be disbanded retainers of the old Prince of Mito, having combined with the intention of setting fire to the Foreign settlement at Yokohama ; and at the same time of attacking each of the Foreign Legations in the capital, and murdering their inmates. Mr. Harris had immediately despatched Mr. Heuskin, his secretary, to give me this information, together with that of a proposition made to him on the part of the Japanese Government, that all the Foreign Consuls should at once move over to Yokohama, where, it was stated, they could be more easily protected ; while he and the other Foreign Representatives should also consent to abandon their several Legations for a time, and take refuge under one roof within the circle of the castle moats, until these disturbers of the peace could be seized and the country reported in a quieter state.

This was not an auspicious opening of the new year. What I felt under such a notice, confirmed by a Governor of Foreign Affairs the same night, sent to me direct from the Great Council of State, and how painfully the utter uncertainty of all knowledge as to the real state of the country, and the authenticity of the facts reported by the Government itself, will be better shown in the following extracts from a despatch laid before both Houses by Her Majesty's command, than by anything I could write now, after so many events have intervened to modify both feelings and opinions : —*

'These alarms of a general massacre are, so to speak, periodical. Rumours of this kind have reached me, either through the Government or from other sources, many times already, even before the murder of the Regent in March last by a party of these said lonins (a name for disbanded soldiers and brigands), or the late Prince of Mito's armed followers, as is more generally asserted and believed. The Government then made very similar proposals to the Foreign Representatives ; and, failing in convincing us either of the necessity or the

* See Correspondence respecting Affairs in Japan, in March and April, 1861, laid before both Houses of Parliament.

expediency of the steps recommended, they sought to
induce us for a time not to stir outside our walls.   Failing
in this also, they took the opportunity of grafting upon
the establishment of spies, watchmen, and police officers
at the several Legations, a mounted escort of yaconins
(officials, soldiers, &c., of indeterminate rank and function,
in the Tycoon's pay) to accompany the members of the
several Legations whenever they stirred out.   This
arrangement has continued ever since, although it has
been repeatedly demonstrated, at our risk and peril, that
they are in reality no protection whatever, and look with
terror themselves upon any chance of collision with these
two-sworded bravos of the Daimios resident in the
capital, who keep many thousands of this dangerous class
as armed retainers in their service and afford them
sanctuary.   The Government can hardly believe, after all
they have heard from us, that any protection is in effect
afforded ; but they cling not the less tenaciously to the
appearance, by sending two or three of these useless and
poltroon officials with any member of the Legations who
may go out.   If they really saw cause of alarm, would
they not take some more effective means of securing our
safety ?

'So at the time of the Regent's death there was great
manifestation of alarm and anxiety on the part of the
Government, new palisades were erected round the
Legations, drawing within narrower limits the ground to
be watched and guarded, and the numbers of the guards
were doubled at night.   Precisely the same series of
demonstrations appear now.   A large addition has been
made to-night to the officers and police on duty, and
probably to-morrow an urgent request will come from
the Minister that I will not venture outside the Legation
until the danger be past, which I must disregard under
penalty of finding myself virtually a prisoner for the
whole remainder of my term of residence in the capital,
be it long or short.

' Under these circumstances your Lordship will readily

understand how difficult it is to form a decided opinion upon the actual amount of danger that may exist beneath these manifestations of alarm and anxiety on the part of the Government. How much of this is real, or what may be feigned in furtherance of a policy it is calculated to advance, must remain very doubtful in a country like Japan, where it is difficult to obtain even a modicum of truth, and no efforts are spared by the same Government to keep from us all sources of exact or reliable information ; and to mislead and deceive us as to the real state of things, even going so far as to throw obstacles in the way of learning their language.

'They have at present a great object to attain, and one which it cannot be doubted those who hold the executive power in their hands have much at heart, namely, the deferring of the opening of more ports, and the inauguration of a still more restrictive system, both as to intercourse and trade, than they have hitherto been able, or, perhaps, ventured upon attempting, to establish. I believe there are men among those ruling powers capable, in furtherance of this policy, if all less violent means should fail, of bringing about a simulated popular movement, in which foreign lives would be sacrificed, either those of the Legations or of the merchants at the neighbouring ports, or both.

'I say simulated, for, although I know to my cost that the general dearness of every article of consumption, the alleged cause of popular discontent, exists, so far as we are concerned, I have strong doubts whether it exists for the Japanese ; and if it does, I should be farther inclined to believe that it was artificial in its source, and brought about by the direct action of the ruling classes with a view to make out their case. And still I can see no sign of popular ill-feeling or hostility towards foreigners. If ever insult or menace is offered it comes from the bearers of two swords, and this class alone.

'I believe this the more strongly, because satisfied from my own observation that there are among the body of

Daimios and chief officers of State, some at least who look upon all foreign trade and intercourse as containing the seeds of revolution; and rather than these should be allowed to take root and germinate, they are ready to risk the chances of a rupture with all the Western Powers put together. And the whole course of the policy followed shows that these must be influential in the Great Council of State. In the first place they may argue that a revolutionary movement would be the worst evil that could happen to *them*, if not to the country, as it would be the knell of their existing régime, where the Daimios and officials are everything, and the people only their serfs, or voiceless. And in the second place, that, after all, great and powerful as those Western nations may be by fleets and armaments, there is a limit to their ability to inflict mischief in such a country as Japan. They might destroy Yeddo and one or two other large cities, but the Daimios, the persons chiefly concerned and the real authors of the counter-movement, could all retire to their territories and inland fastnesses, where they could hardly be followed; and there remain in comparative security until the Foreign Powers would be wearied out, their resources for war so far from home and their patience alike exhausted.* And, finally, they had better risk this, than see all the established institutions of the country overturned, themselves cast down from their hitherto exalted position, and the whole land impoverished and ruined by a foreign trade which brings an un-limited demand for articles wanted for their own con-sumption, and gives in exchange only silver, or things

* When the Japanese Mission was in this country, the Envoys were taken to a review at Aldershot. The soldierlike appearance of the troops of all arms, and the precision and rapidity of the movements, evidently made some impression;—and in the endeavour to ascertain with what feelings they witnessed the display, they were asked, incidentally, how they thought Japanese soldiers and arms would come out of a battle with such troops. Their first thought, as expressed in their reply, was a natural one, perhaps: namely, that their own men were formidable adversaries as sword and spear-men; but the next was more significant of the predominant feeling — viz., that it was no easy matter to transport any large force of artillery, cavalry, and infantry to the other side of the globe. In other words, they did not believe in the possibility.

which are superfluities and better dispensed with, to the enrichment at best of the few, and the serious injury of the many. Nor are these arguments invented for them by Europeans as a mode of accounting for effects by a preconceived theory. They have, at different times and piecemeal, been all brought forward by the Ministers — or by Governors of Foreign Affairs, who are often their mouth-pieces, — when discussing various measures with me, for retarding or avoiding execution of the Treaty.

'In so far as these views prevail, therefore, they who direct the government of the country have everything to gain, and nothing to lose, by throwing down the gauntlet. If ever this should be resolved on, there is little doubt that all foreigners in and about the capital will be swept away, as the first step. I do not wish Her Majesty's Government to understand that I see with any certainty such an issue to the efforts now making to establish friendly and permanent commercial relations in the country. But still we are now actually threatened with a catastrophe of this kind; and I think your Lordship should know that we carry on our relations under a menace, which may at any moment be carried into execution. Nor do I see what prudence or courage can do to avert such a calamity, if it were really determined upon. In all probability we should either have no warning, or none distinguishable from those we are now receiving at this moment, in time for us to escape; or there would be no British ship of war (still less likely that of any other nation) into which we could make our escape.

'Surrounded, therefore, by menace, doubt, and suspicion — by dangers, the extent of which we are utterly without means of verifying, it is hard to determine on what course to steer, or how disastrous results may most securely be averted. But taking all the circumstances into consideration, I have not felt justified in allowing Admiral Jones to leave without taking some steps to prevent my being left without a single ship of war within reach at this time.'

I wrote officially therefore to the Rear-Admiral — ' The Japanese Government inform me they have certain information that within a few miles or leagues from Yokohama, a band of some 600 lonins are collected, with intent to burn the Foreign settlement at Yokohama, and destroy at one blow both the trade and the merchants, and simultaneously or successively to attack the Legations, and murder their inmates. It is impossible to ascertain what amount of truth there may be in this, or the foundation that actually exists for the superstructure raised ; but I learn the rumour is general at Kanagawa of something of the kind impending. Under these circumstances it would hardly be prudent, I think, to remove the whole squadron ; I conceive that there should be one ship at least left as a security for British subjects and property at Yokohama and Kanagawa, and another opposite to Yeddo, in communication with the Legation.'

And I received for answer an intimation that having ' duly weighed and considered the substance of the documents,' he had determined,—instead of taking every ship away except the little sloop ' Pioneer ' (required to take a Consul to Hakodadi),—to leave the ' Encounter ' at the anchorage of Yokohama for the present.

Seeing that my first representation had so little effect, I wrote again ; and remarked, in a despatch to the Foreign Office, enclosing a copy of my letter to the Admiral, that for the urgent terms in which I had written to the Senior officer, I trusted sufficient justification might be found in the urgency of the circumstances ; adding, ' The signs of danger and alarm in the minds of the Government are too palpable to be mistaken, and of too serious a character to leave me any longer in doubt as to the reality of both. When the Regent of the kingdom was slain in the streets of Yeddo, in the midst of his own armed retainers, the manifestations of panic and distrust of their own powers of protection were far less apparent. As regards my own personal safety, and that of those attached to me, your Lordship knows that there is no protection to be looked for, from ships of war lying many miles off in the roadstead.    Nothing but the landing of a force to occupy the Legation could avail, and that I have not asked.'

To the Admiral I wrote, 'Since my letter of the 1st, various representations have reached me from official and other sources, which leave no doubt in my mind that some serious danger does exist of a very unusual character, threatening the lives of every foreigner in the capital and the neighbouring port, and that the Japanese Government distrust their own power effectually to protect them.    Not only is this the tenour of their communications to me personally, and through the Governor of Kanagawa to Her Majesty's Acting Consul, as I learn at this moment by an express from that officer, but my own observation of the measures taken by the Government here undoubt-edly proves a state of the greatest alarm.    The whole road from Yokohama to the Legation is kept by large patrols of armed men.    A Daimio has been given charge of this Legation, and some two hundred of his followers are here with two field-pieces.    Some crisis is plainly anticipated, and whether the blow is to be aimed at the foreigners alone, or the Government through the foreigners, there must be danger to both, of no light or ordinary character.

'Under these circumstances, I should utterly fail in my duty as Her Majesty's Minister and Representative, if I allowed you to depart, leaving only a single ship of your squadron as you propose, without again calling your attention in the most urgent terms to the present aspect of affairs.'

This had the effect of detaining the impatient squadron for a few days.    But understanding the reluctance with which a necessity for delay had been admitted, and that small-pox had broken out on board the flag-ship to such an extent as to require her either to put to sea or land her men, I came to the conclusion, that they had better go, as this would make a new complication, and the last danger might be worse than the first.    I could

learn nothing more definite as to the exact nature of the
danger announced by the Government, or their grounds
for alarm.    This state of things might go on for weeks
without any attack or overt act.    I therefore determined
to leave it to the Admiral's discretion when his departure
should take place, merely suggesting the expediency of
leaving a second ship.    Within forty-eight hours afterwards the Vice-Admiral's ship was out of sight, and the
second vessel also,—leaving me the 'Encounter,' as a
reinforcement to the sloop he found on the station when
he arrived.

---

Nothing changed in the position of foreigners for the
week following.    The alarm spread by the Government of
an impending attack continued, though with the usual
vagueness and uncertainty as to the true source and degree
of danger; and in this unpleasant state of suspense the
days passed on until the night of the 14th, when, about
ten o'clock, I received a brief note from Mr. Harris asking
me to send surgical aid to Mr. Heuskin, who had been
brought in wounded.    At midnight Dr. Myburgh, a
medical officer attached to the British Legation in the
capacity of Dutch Interpreter, went off immediately, but
soon returned with information that his patient was dead.
He had been waylaid on his return from the Prussian
Legation by a band of assassins, and mortally wounded.
    On the fourth day after, all the Corps Diplomatique
and the Consular body from Kanagawa assembled by
invitation at the American Legation to render the last
honours to the murdered man, when the American
Minister received a warning from the Government, that
if they persevered in their intention of following the
body to the grave, they were likely to lose their own
lives.    No one hesitated; but the fact of such a warning
seemed to indicate either an odious policy of intimidation on the part of the Government, or such deplorable
timidity and weakness as took from the Foreign Repre-

sentatives all security, or hope of vigorous measures for
their protection.   Not only were none taken on this
occasion — not a soldier called out — but there was a
total absence of any precautions to prevent a surprise
or sudden attack along the line of road, which lay for
more than a mile by the banks of a river ; and offered
great facilities of attack from cross-roads leading to it, and
bridges which traversed it at short intervals.

The whole of the Foreign Ministers, strongly impressed
with the significance of these events, and the sinister
rumours which continually circulated of plots for a general
massacre, met, by common consent, the next day at the
British Legation to consider their position,. and what
course it behoved them to take, not merely for their
own safety; but for the honour and dignity of their
respective Sovereigns, and the interests and lives of every
foreigner in the country.

I thus briefly described the facts to H.M.'s Secretary
of State:—

'The conference was attended by all, but an unfortunate
divergence of opinion on the part of the American
Minister, went far to neutralise the good effect that might
have resulted could perfect unanimity have been attained.
The French, Dutch, and Prussian Representatives and
myself were entirely in accord.   Mr. Harris alone of the
five present was willing to let things take their course,
and to confide in the good faith of the Japanese Government.   Neither the assassination of his Secretary nor the
warning at the funeral, and all that followed, seemed able
to shake his faith in their honesty of purpose and ability
to afford protection.   It was in vain under these circumstances that the rest of his colleagues, one after the other
pointing to a long series of assassinations, the constant
denial of justice, and a continued system of menace and
intimidation, showed the impossibility of reconciling the
views he entertained with the facts.

' A second conference two days later having been
determined upon, no decision was taken—and when the

day came, Mr. Harris not being present, a *compte rendu* was drawn up of both conferences, giving a full and detailed statement of the views expressed by the several Representatives who had taken part in either, with the grounds for a perfect unanimity on the part of the four signing, as to the most fitting course to be followed " to avert a great danger to Japan, no less than to the foreigners then in the country."'

The position of the Foreign Representatives was sufficiently embarrassing without this untoward complication of diversity of opinion on the part of one of the diplomatic body, as to the most fitting course to be followed at such a critical juncture, when the life of every foreigner was at stake, and peace or war might be the issue, according as a right judgement or the reverse prevailed.

Certainly it would be difficult to conceive any position more trying for a Diplomatic Agent, isolated from all material means of protection, equally cut off from all reference to his Government by five thousand leagues of sea requiring some six months for an interchange of letters, and pressed by the necessity of taking a decision upon more or less doubtful data. For in statesmanship and diplomacy alike, it has been truly said, 'Not only opportunities must be seized as they occur, the secret of success mainly depending upon this, but miscarriage must be risked, miscarriages through the faults of others as well as our own. Man has been left to shape his course in this world not so much by sight as by faith ; not with *demonstration* for his guide, but with *probability* only, in things temporal as well as spiritual.

Each to other like, more than on earth is thought.

For what can he do more, even in the most critical step that he is ever called upon to take, than plant his foot where there seems *most* cause to think he can plant it safely?' So it is even when life itself is involved, or the interests of nations ; he is compelled to decide upon the

balance of probabilities, where the wisest must often be
sore perplexed.  I remember meeting with the above
remarks about this time, and they seemed so peculiarly
apposite, that they were strongly impressed on my
memory.  Perhaps I found encouragement in the reflection they suggested, that however trying my position, it
only presented the same conditions of perplexity and
anxious doubt that must be the usual attendant of all
action in critical circumstances, where there is great
responsibility upon a single head.  In this instance, I had
at least the satisfaction of knowing that all my colleagues,
with a single exception, were perfectly of one mind with
myself.  We had determined at the second.conference,
with entire unanimity, to withdraw from Yeddo; sending
in at the same time a vigorous protest against the whole
system of intimidation and murder, of which we were made
the victims, *with the cognisance and seemingly tacit acquiescence* of the Government to which we were accredited.
Count Eulenberg, the Prussian Minister, was on the point
of concluding a treaty on which he had been engaged for
six months, such had been the obstinate resistance he had
encountered; notwithstanding which, he did not hesitate
to join in this decisive step, merely deferring his departure
until after the day fixed, then close at hand, for its signature.  Nothing could have been more generous or loyal
than this course, which required no small amount of
moral courage.  I even endeavoured to dissuade him,
pointing out that as he was in Yeddo only on an extraordinary mission, and not *en permanence*, he was not
really called upon to identify himself with those who were.

This decision taken, I immediately began my preparations for carrying it into effect, by sending to hire any
houses that could be found for the Legation, packing and
sending off a few articles of furniture, &c., and on the day
of my departure a week later, I addressed a strong representation to the Ministers of Foreign Affairs, to be laid
before the great Council of State, setting forth the grounds
for our common accord, and the motives of the step

resolved upon.    Among other things, I pointed out that
' The assassination of Mr. Heuskin, following close upon
menaces of a general massacre, communicated to the
Foreign Ministers by orders of your Excellencies, followed
up again by an intimation from the same quarter on
the morning of the funeral, when the Representatives of
the Five Powers were all assembled to render the last
honours to the murdered, that they themselves were in
danger of being attacked on the way to the cemetery, if
they ventured to proceed, were more than sufficient to
remove the last trace of doubt or hesitation in my mind,
and I think in the minds of most of my colleagues, as to
the necessity of instant and decided action on their part.

' But lest they should not have been enough, it would
seem as if it had been determined to furnish one more
conclusive evidence how little the Government could be
relied upon for our defence and protection, by leaving the
whole line of road, more than a mile in length, to the
cemetery open to attack.    There were no guards on the
ground, or extraordinary measures of precaution and protection — I do not say to resist the attack it had sent
warning was to be feared, but to prevent the possibility
of the most desperate men daring to attempt it.    Here
were the lives of all the Foreign Ministers in Yeddo,
together with the whole of their respective Legations, and
the Consuls from Kanagawa, declared by the Government
to be in immediate danger.    They were all at one spot
assembled, and yet it was not deemed worth while, apparently, to adopt a single measure for their defence and
protection !    This, indeed, was conclusive : that the
Government should allow a member of one of the Legations to be murdered, while the whole Corps Diplomatique
was under menace of a similar fate, and yet consider it
unnecessary, even in courtesy, to make any communication to Her Majesty's Minister at this Court, whose own
safety and that of the members of his Legation were in
question, could no longer be subject of surprise.    The
two courses were perfectly consistent with each other.

'Moved by these considerations, and perfectly convinced by all the experience of the past, of the hopelessness of any farther effort by mere remonstrance on the spot, to effect the changes which it was too plain could not be deferred without risk of the gravest complications, and, it might be, national calamity, if, unfortunately, farther lives should be lost, I took immediate steps, after the funeral, to communicate with my colleagues, and announce my resolution to avert, if possible, the dangers I foresaw in the continued supineness of the Government.

'I determined, with this view, to withdraw temporarily from the Legation at Yeddo, and I now write to acquaint you that I have carried this resolution into effect.   I shall take up my residence, for the present, at Kanagawa or Yokohama, where I can not only command means of protection, if required, from Her Majesty's ships, but also take such steps as may be needful for the security of my countrymen.   There I shall wait with calmness the result of farther communication with the Government of the Tycoon, free, for the first time for eighteen months, if not from the menace of assassination, at least from any anxiety as to such threats being immediately carried into execution to the peril and disgrace of Japan.'

That it was a momentous step we all felt, and I can say for myself that it was taken with the greatest reluctance; and only on the strongest conviction that it was the one most likely to produce a salutary influence on the councils of the Japanese Government; while indecision, or waiting upon Providence with folded hands, trusting to a Government that had shown nothing but ineptitude or apathy when efficient protection was required, could only lead to a repetition of similar acts of bloodshed, and in all probability the massacre so often menaced.   The main question was by what means this could be best and most surely prevented?   I and my colleagues believed this could only be done by holding the Government responsible for the security of life, not only as regarded the Legations, but foreigners generally, living in the country under the safeguard of solemn treaties,—a responsibility the Government had shown every disposition to ignore on a plea of inability. In the meantime, that those in Japan among the Daimios and their adherents, with or without the connivance of the Government,—who had from the beginning been inimical to the commercial and political relations initiated by Mr. Harris's treaty of 1858,—should by one means or other be deterred from the adoption of violent schemes of murder and intimidation directed against foreigners, was an obvious necessity, whatever else might be done or left undone. And that this could best be effected by sitting still and doing nothing, not even the American Minister, I fancy, could have deliberately believed, although he had nothing to propose, but remonstrances; the futility of which, unsupported by other steps, the painful experience of eighteen months had sufficiently demonstrated.

As the funereal cortége wound its way from the American Legation to the burial-place, many harassing and anxious thoughts must have filled the breasts of the chief actors. It was the middle of January, but the sun shined brightly; and not a fleck or a cloud was in the sky to dim its lustre. The place of interment was the same I had selected just one year before, when my linguist was slain at the gate of the Legation. Fine trees, consisting entirely of evergreens, and covered with foliage rich in colour, cast a pleasant shade over the well-kept grounds of the Buddhist temple to which the cemetery is attached. Here, lying back on some rising ground, not far from the banks of a little river which winds its tortuous way to the city—only too symbolic of the rulers of the land—a picturesque site as could well be chosen had been marked off for the dead. There was something very sad and impressive in the gathering which now brought so many nationalities together at the spot. A large circle of Europeans formed the principal group, while in the background the shaven crowns of some of the fraternity whose temple grounds were thus invaded might be distinguished.

In the centre of the group is a Roman Catholic priest in
his white robes, and on a terrace above the heads of all,
stand five Japanese dignitaries, Governors of Foreign
Affairs, whose attendance is anything but voluntary on
their part.  These, dressed in their Haka-ma of ceremony,
look coldly down upon the scene at their feet.  The
flags of four Treaty Powers are there, to which those
of Prussia, not yet in the number, is joined, and to the
right the Representatives of those Powers are all present,
surrounded by a strong guard of Prussian marines,—no ship
of war of any other nation being at the anchorage.  In the
centre is the newly dug grave, into which the sun pours
a flood of light, as if to rob it of half its terrors.  The
bier is covered by the American flag, for though Dutch
by birth, the murdered official was a servant of the United
States ; and as the service proceeded, notes of sadness filled
the air from the band of the Prussian frigate — a wail of
sorrow and complaint.  Farewell to the dead—ashes to
ashes, dust to dust !  The flags are lowered, while with
uncovered heads the Ministers each cast in a handful of
earth.  In mute sorrow it is done — in sorrow and humiliation too, for a murdered brother lies in that grave
over which the flags of five European Powers are drooped
in honour, yet were they all powerless to protect from the
hand of the assassin him now laid so low, and equally
powerless are they to secure future safety to those now
standing by the grave.

Redress for the past and Safety for the future—these
were the two things it most behoved every Foreign Representative there to obtain ; and they were precisely those
which the most sanguine could hardly hope to succeed in
securing.  The beauty of the site and clearness of the
sky, only contrasted the more painfully with the moral
features of the scene.  A foreigner in his prime, the only
son of a widowed mother,—cut down in his strength, and
murdered by a band of political assassins in the streets
of a great Eastern capital, where all but the few members of the Legations are still jealously excluded,—lay

in the grave,—round which the Representatives of the
greatest Powers in the West stood, mourning a wrong they
were indeed helpless to redress.   Surrounded by a hostile
class of Feudal chiefs and their armed retainers, living
under a Government either incapable or treacherous, they
were themselves under menace of being slain in the same
ruthless fashion, even while rendering the last duties to
the dead. And under this oft-renewed menace of massacre
or assassination, the Representatives of all the great Maritime Powers had lived for eighteen months past, isolated
and unprotected.   Singly pitted, as it were, against
the millions which surged around their dwellings,—cut
off from all friendly intercourse by the jealousy of
Eastern rulers,—watched, hemmed in, and yet unde-
fended,—it must be confessed the position of a Diplomatic Agent in this farthest Eastern station was anything
but enviable. It can hardly be realised in these modern
days in any European land, what it is—not for days or
weeks, but month after month, and not occasionally, but
constantly, year after year — to live under a perpetual
menace of assassination, with apt instruments for its execution ever at hand. Never to put foot in stirrup without
a consciousness of impending danger; never to sleep
without feeling, as your eyes close, that your next waking
hour may be your last, with the vengeful steel at your throat,
and the wild slogan of murderers in your ear ;— is not a
pleasant state of existence, and neither conduces to happiness nor health.   To anyone who cannot realise this, I
should seek in vain to convey the character at once
solemn and exciting, with which the whole scene of the
burial in that pagan cemetery was invested, in all its
accessories and associations.  By the side of the newly
closed grave was a plain tablet distinguished from all the
rest by its Roman characters — ' Dankirche, Japanese
linguist to the British Legation, murdered by Japanese
assassins on January 21, 1860 ; ' and this was January 18,
1861, when another Legation had furnished its annual
victim—a sacrifice apparently, to the rage of unknown

enemies, who might be thousands, or perhaps could be counted by tens and hundreds, if the Government were willing and true. As it was, all remained shrouded in dark and impenetrable mystery. Whence came the blows of the assassin, in such a long and seemingly endless series of murders and butcheries? The only answer to be got from the Government was 'Lonins, men of the Prince of Mito.'

It is somewhere related by Bruce, that a custom once existed in Abyssinia, when factions were violent and ready to tear each other in pieces for mutual wrongs, to compromise the quarrel by means of a camel. It was agreed that nobody in Abyssinia had been to blame on either side, only the camel, and the whole mischief, be it what it might, was the work of the camel. The luckless animal it was that had threatened to attack the Aga's castles, to burn his mother, destroy the cattle, or fire the town; he it was who had cursed the sheriff of Mecca, and destroyed the wheat!

The Prince of Mito in Japan seems to have played the part of the Abyssinian camel for the last two years; and now that even he, in strict accordance with Abyssinian precept, has been slain, his ghost still haunts the country in the shape of the prince's men; and lonins of Mito are made responsible for all the mischief threatened or done.

If only we could trust the Government of the country, trust their energy and their good faith, we might find patience to meet the evils which may be inseparable from the effervescence of a sudden contact between two compounds so differently constituted as European and Japanese civilisation. But it is impossible to have much intercourse with the ruling classes and their subordinates, without being perpetually reminded of the treachery and cruelty of the Venetian rulers, themselves Asiatic in origin and temperament.

To this day may be seen in one of the cells of the inquisition at Venice, traced in an unsteady hand, as in the dark, lines which speak of deepest perfidy: —

Da chi mi fido guardami Dio ;
Da chi non mi fido, mi guardaro io.

And the same profound conviction of betrayal and faithlessness to all engagements, in the end becomes too thoroughly established to be shaken by any lip-professions, or outward demonstrations of good-will and anxiety for the safety of those, whom they allow to be cut to pieces in the streets without raising a hand in their defence, or stirring a finger to bring punishment down upon the assassins. From whencesoever these successive blows proceed, there comes also, and always, a voice through the organs of the Government (not ashamed to be the medium of communication), which cries aloud: 'So are you all doomed; begone, or perish.' And so one after the other, by twos or by threes, and sometimes singly, the decimation goes on, without let or hindrance. How long? Whose turn shall it be next; and when will the measure of this iniquity be full? Where is it to stop; or must it be allowed to run its fatal course until all the lives are exhausted? These questions must have been present to many, who, on this bright day of January, under a sky which might have been that of Italy, stood round the grave of the *last*, and remained unanswered. From the grave came only the warning voice, ' Beware !'

All appeals to the Government of the country had hitherto been vain. It is said that the wolf, when learning to read, could make nothing out of the letters of the alphabet, however they were put before it, but ' *lamb* ; ' and so it was with the rulers of Japan. To all remonstrances they had but one answer, more guards, spies, and yaconins; more restrictions on individual liberty; more devices to reduce the Ministers of the greatest Powers in Europe to a state of degrading thraldom, in no way different save in the name to that of state prisoners. Any assertion of diplomatic privileges and rights,— to freedom of action and real independence,— was met by the ever-recurring announcement of danger. It came then to this at last; either Foreign Representatives and the whole Corps Diplomatique must accept the humiliating and derogatory position so persistently forced upon them,— while the Government to which they were accredited made a cool disclaimer of responsibility for any evil that might befall,—or vigorously resist such efforts. So far as I was personally concerned, I never felt a moment's hesitation as to which of the courses ought and must be adopted, whatever the individual risk, or peril to life. I believe there were none among our number, unless it were the American Minister, who conceived safety could be purchased, consistently with the honour and dignity of the national flag, at such a price as the Japanese Government attached, namely, the negation of all freedom of locomotion, or action — making the Legations so many prisons in all but the name.

A crisis had come, and upon the manner in which it should be met by the Foreign Representatives would greatly depend our future relations with the country. A greeting had come to the assembled Ministers of the Five Powers, when met together at the American Legation, to follow the last victim of this Machiavelian policy, spoken by the Government through their own organs — ' A great danger menaces all your lives from which we cannot secure you, if you persevere in your intention of following the body to the grave.' And then, as if to prove to demonstration the utter absence of good faith, *or concern for what might happen*, the whole route was left unguarded and open to attack. Now either they had good reason to know there *was* danger, and in that case they were bound, by every motive of national good faith and honour, to strain the utmost powers of the Government to avert it, and afford protection ; or no such danger existed, and the announcement was an infamy and an outrage. The Japanese Government, by its own acts, placed itself between the two horns of this dilemma, from which there was no escape. Even our American colleague on the day of the funeral seemed to have this conviction; unfortunately it did not last, and the next day his confidence in the Government that had thus pilloried itself, appeared to have returned stronger than ever. I and my colleagues

saw in this last proceeding an unfounded alarm, invented
to intimidate all the Legations, and carry out a policy
designed more thoroughly to isolate and place them under
restrictions, than had hitherto been found possible.  There
might certainly have been some foundation, some real
danger to be guarded against, only designedly exaggerated
in its proportions.  But in that case, why were there no
precautions, no preparations whatever to meet it, and avert
a catastrophe which might plunge the country into all the
horrors of a foreign war, in which every Treaty Power
would be their enemy?   Was it a simple exaggeration,
springing from the timidity and mendacity combined of a
Government given to large words, but very small deeds;
conscious, perhaps, of some hidden, but internal source of
weakness and fountain of evil?   In either hypothesis, it
was in the interest of all, that this state of things should
cease.

An event occurred at this time calculated to give greater
significance to the numerous sinister rumours afloat.   Hori
Oribeno-no-Kami, the most intelligent, experienced, and
respected of the Governors of Foreign Affairs, the one the
best versed in European business, and the most reasonable
and conciliatory of his class in all his intercourse with the
Legations, disappeared from the scene.   He died suddenly,
and a certain mystery as to the mode and time of death
gave rise to a suspicion that it was not unconnected with
the murder which had just taken place, and had been the
result of a discussion with the Gorogio or his own chiefs
the Foreign Ministers, on the subject of their foreign policy.
In effect, it was shortly known that he had committed the
Hara-kiru.  After a few days' delay, an official communication was received by the Foreign Representatives in Yeddo,
stating that he had ceased to hold office, 'having died
without the effects of medicine.'  A strange announcement to us, but the popular voice had no difficulty in its
interpretation.  It was the expression for an act of self-
immolation.   But what could have made one of the
highest and  most valuable of their officers, subordi-

nate only to the Ministers themselves, and their right hand apparently, destroy himself? Into what disgrace had he fallen? He was engaged as one of the pleni-potentiaries in negotiating the Prussian treaty on the point of being concluded — was it this? Had he been ex-pected to succeed, under pretext of framing a treaty, in deferring its conclusion indefinitely, and failed? He was, as I have said, one of the most esteemed of the Governors, corresponding in rank and functions to an Under-Secre-tary of State, and was universally regretted by the Legations. This event immediately following Mr. Heus-kin's murder seemed to throw some light on the causes of Oribeno's death. Some of the circumstances im-mediately preceding this deed of violence I have not yet related. On January 15, there was a gathering of plenipotentiaries and officials, Japanese and Prussian, at the temporary residence of Count Eulenberg, the Prussian Envoy. The clauses of the treaty with Prussia had all been agreed upon, after five months of refusals and delay, and in a few days it was to be signed. The presents to the Tycoon and some of his high officers were to be delivered — works of art (sadly thrown away), costly and choice volumes from the royal printing press, on Egyptian antiquities and scenery; speci-mens of superb binding; a portable magnetic telegraph, by which the Tycoon might communicate his orders the circuit of his palace; a fine series of photographic views; equestrian statuettes mounted on richly moulded pedestals of bronze, &c. Among the busiest of the party was Mr. Heuskin, who was rendering the same important service to Count Eulenberg which he had afforded to Lord Elgin, by acting as his interpreter. After dinner he mounted his horse to return, as was his daily habit, to the American Legation, where he resided; preceded by a mounted yaconin with a paper lantern suspended to his waist by a flexible bamboo, as is their habit. The Tycoon's arms are emblazoned on the transparency, and he was followed by two others, the ordinary escort of members of the several Legations, and especially insisted upon by the Japanese Government as a necessary protection. How little protection such an escort was really calculated to afford, had often been observed before when insult or minor outrages were in question. But still, where life was concerned, the Ministers insisted on the efficacy of the guard, and some were willing to believe it might not prove to be a mere sham, so far as defence was in question; and a reality only as part of a machinery designed to hamper the movements and insure the isolation of every member of the Legations, by a locomotory and ubiquitous surveillance. This was soon to be brought to the proof. When Mr. Heuskin had proceeded a few hundred yards along the banks of the river where we had just buried him, his road lay through some narrow streets in a densely populated quarter, in which the American Legation was situated. Shortly after entering these, where two or three intersected, a wild yell rose in the stillness of the night, and a band of some six or seven men lying in ambush for their victim, rushed from their covert with drawn swords. Dividing their numbers, while the main body fell upon the European, the others dismissed the leading yaconin with a blow of the flat of the sabre on his horse, accompanied by an injunction little needed, to take himself off. The two behind disappeared in another direction with equal celerity, while their charge, thus deserted, clapped spurs to his horse and endeavoured to dash through his assailants, who were striking furiously at him from both sides. He was only armed with a hunting-whip, but had he been better prepared for such a deadly onslaught it is doubtful from its suddenness, and the darkness of the night, whether he could have used a revolver. He succeeded to all appearance in breaking through the band, unconscious at the moment of being severely wounded, and was able to ride on a hundred paces when he felt that he was grievously injured, and calling to his horse-boy, still in sight, though some distance ahead, he endeavoured

to dismount, and fell to the ground in the attempt. He
had received a frightful gash across the abdomen, from
which the bowels protruded, besides several other thrusts
and cuts of less moment. There he lay, wholly deserted and
weltering in his blood, it is not known exactly how long.
It appears his assassins felt satisfied they had effectually
done their work, for they did not follow him up. And as
for his brave defenders bearing the Tycoon's arms, they
only returned with assistance after a long interval. He
survived but an hour or two after his arrival at the Legation — long enough, however, to tell the dismal tale, and
state distinctly all that had occurred. Fortunately, for the
yaconins had a version of the attack which rivalled Fal-
staff's. They had been set upon by at least thirty men, and
notwithstanding such terrible odds, kept by their charge to
the last — one only, when Mr. Heuskin fell from his horse,
being sent on to get assistance to carry him home. But
the dying man's testimony was too strong and clear.
Even the Government this time, wonderful to say,
hesitated to accept the yaconins' report. Of course two
Governors of Foreign Affairs were despatched immediately
with condolences, expressions of sympathy, and assurances
of justice,— precisely as had been done when my linguist
was assassinated in broad daylight under the flagstaff of
the British Legation a twelvemonth before — since which
nothing had been heard of the assassins except that they
could not be discovered. So had it been with eight successive victims — so it followed with this last! Such
assured immunity is perhaps the worst feature of the
whole, as obviously fatal to all security. And where was
the remedy to be sought? This was a question which
could not any longer remain without an answer—and the
four Representatives of Great Britain, France, Prussia,
and Holland, resolved a solution should be sought in
a determined protest, backed by the striking of their
flags, and their temporary retirement to Yokohama.
Many days were consumed in the necessary preparations
for the lodging of the Legations in the dearth of house-

room at the settlement of Yokohama; and it was not until the end of the month that either the French Minister or myself could embark, the 'Encounter' and 'Pioneer' fortunately giving us both the means. The Dutch Diplomatic Agent had preceded us — and Count Eulenberg, having obtained the signature of his treaty, prepared to follow in a day or two—Mr. Harris, the American Minister, alone remained, disapproving entirely of the course thus unanimously followed by all his colleagues. He indeed predicted that those who withdrew from the capital would never be able to return; but I had, as the event proved, a tolerably well-founded conviction to the contrary; while I felt certain that to remain was to *invite* the very dangers it was the desire of all to avert. It was a question of means to the end, and with opinions so diametrically opposed, it only remained for each to follow his own course.

# CHAPTER III.

WE had now entered upon a second phase of the crisis. The flags of four of the Treaty Powers had been struck, and their respective Representatives had each forwarded a strong protest to the Japanese Government, against a total denial of justice, and the absence of all efficient protection or security to life,—with what result remained to be seen. It had been made clear to the Japanese Government, that in withdrawing from the capital and striking their flags, we had no intention of breaking off relations with it ; and without implying any menace of hostilities if our reasonable demands were not complied with, they must have seen that there was a determination, on the part of my colleagues and myself, to effect some change for the better in our relations. In a circular to the British Consuls, I fully explained our actual position, and the objects we contemplated. They were told to explain to the Governors of their respective ports, that our object was not to create a rupture, but, if possible, to avert any such calamity, (while relieving the Government of Japan from a great danger) ; and to induce them, without farther delay, to take what steps might be necessary to place their relations with Foreign Powers on a better and safer footing; and 'above all, to give that security to life and property which had been greatly in default from the beginning, and latterly wholly wanting.'

To the Ministers of Foreign Affairs I wrote in the following unequivocal, but conciliatory terms, saying I had to urge upon the Government the importance 'of putting a speedy end to the present exceptional state of affairs. I am anxious for a peaceable and satisfactory termination ; and am ready to return to the Legation, and resume my duties in Yeddo, whenever I can see such material guarantee for redress in respect to past grievances, and security for the future, as may warrant this step. I have, in the meantime, left all my property undisturbed, under the charge of the officers in my house, and for the safety of which the Government will, of course, be responsible. Whether my return be prompt or tardy, therefore, depends entirely upon the Japanese Government. It is certain, sooner or later, that the Representative of Great Britain will return to Yeddo, the place of residence assigned by treaty ; but, if speedily, there will be the less time for new complications to arise, and affairs may be more easily arranged with mutual benefit (and on a better footing than hitherto, to my regret, has been found possible), if no time be lost.'

Having adopted this decisive step, and taken up a temporary residence at Yokohama, I had leisure to review the position, and meditate on what farther might be necessary to bring this species of interregnum to a speedy conclusion. While it would probably be the policy of the Japanese Government to leave the protesting Ministers self-exiled from the capital, by refusing their terms, and thus giving them a kind of stale-mate quite equivalent in the circumstances to a defeat—the tactics evidently contemplated by our American colleague, when he predicted that we should never return—it was my business and that of the only colleague remaining after the fourth week, Monsieur de Bellecourt, the French Minister, to force them to come to terms, and offer us those guarantees for greater security in the future which we were so fully entitled to demand. It was a struggle, however, in which they had all the advantage of a *chance* of winning by simply doing nothing, whereas it behoved us to make such moves on the political chess-board as should compel them to act. I speak only of the future, for as regarded the past, to insist upon any redress for things already done, would have been to enter upon a large field of complaints, and debates that might be endless. It was the future position of Foreign nations and their Representatives in Japan which it was most important to regulate and improve. I resolved, therefore, from the beginning, that I would welcome any fair guarantee for this, and trust, after my return to Yeddo, to convert what might be merely promises of improvement, into material results. Mr. Harris himself, as I wrote to the Foreign Office at the time, could not be more impressed than I was, with the consciousness that if satisfactory relations were ever to be established with the Government and people, we must needs be content with improvement by slow degrees, and put up in the mean-time with many shortcomings, and not a few wrongs. Nothing, indeed, could be more opposed to the whole tenour and spirit of my instructions, or less in harmony with my own sentiments and convictions, than a policy founded on coercion, and carried out by menaces. I knew, moreover, that any rupture of the relations established by treaty would be regarded by Her Majesty's Government, and by the whole nation, with equal anxiety and regret, as a calamity which no effort should have been spared to prevent, and no future advantage could well compen- sate. And no one will envy the position of anxious responsibility in which my French colleague and myself were placed, during the month following our withdrawal from Yeddo, in which time the question at issue was brought to a final solution in the only sense we desired.

The Japanese Government, exactly as I had anticipated, although manifesting considerable uneasiness and anxiety as to what might be the full import of our withdrawal and its consequences, very soon seemed to accept the *status quo* without making any effort to change our relations, once assured — as they soon were, and it is needless now to inquire how — that it did *not* mean war, or the commission of any act of coercion or hostility present or prospective.

Against such tactics as these I had two resources, which had not entered into their calculation; the one was the possible arrival of Admiral Hope with a squadron on hearing of the critical state of affairs, — rather a doubtful one I confess ; — and the other a measure strictly within the conditions contemplated by treaties, but which I could not doubt would be supremely distasteful to the Government at Yeddo, so much so indeed, that I could confidently look forward to their making great efforts, and almost any sacrifice, rather than see it carried out. Strong in this double reserve, one of which was entirely in my own hands fortunately, should the first fail me, as was but too probable, I sat down in patient expectation, merely suggesting to the Governor at Kanagawa indirectly, that if the Government at Yeddo *wished* to treat, they must send properly authorised agents, mentioning one of whom I had reason to think favourably, *Sakai Wookionoske*, a member of the Second Council of State, who had frequently taken part in my conferences with the Ministers.

I was not at all surprised to learn that this was considered impossible ; and a vain attempt was made to get into communication with us by means of two Governors of Foreign Affairs, sent down for that purpose. They were informed, both by my colleague and myself, that we could enter into no communication until a written answer had been received from the Ministers. It was farther intimated through the Japanese Secretary of the British Legation, speaking in our joint names, that the present exceptional state of affairs was not without its dangers, and that the first step towards putting an end to it would be the Ministers placing before us distinct propositions as to the measures they were prepared to adopt for the better security of life, and at the same time to put an end to the system of alternate assassination and intimidation which could no longer be tolerated. An official letter from the Ministers only arrived after a week had elapsed, couched in vague and unsatisfactory terms.

In the meantime, during my constrained residence in this infant settlement, I tried to turn it to some good account in the interest of the foreign residents and their location. And in order to ascertain in the most satisfactory manner in what direction my efforts could most avail, I requested the Consul to call a public meeting of his countrymen, and ask them to furnish a statement of their principal grievances and subjects of complaint in precise terms, more especially as regarded the principal of them, such as the currency, the free exchange of produce, and the occupation of land, with reference to the arbitrary restrictions, and official interference on the part of the Japanese authorities, of which many complaints had reached me. These, together with better security of life and property, a better custom-house administration, and certain local improvements in respect to roads, bridges, &c., seemed to exhaust the list of practical grievances in reference to treaty rights or privileges, and the interests of commerce.

And I may state here, that although many practical results were not possible within the month of my residence on the spot — the bases of an agreement with the Japanese authorities were established, from which in the course of the year many material changes for the better were finally derived — though not without reiterated efforts, after my return to the capital. What our actual position at the trading port was at this period, may be seen by reference to the proceedings of the public meeting to be found in the Appendix.*

The letter of the Ministers bore date February 9, in which they assured me that the neglectful conduct of

* See Appendix A.

the yaconins in Mr. Heuskin's case excited in them impatient sorrow ; that it was indispensable measures should be adopted, but this could only be done properly after repeated deliberation, which would require time.

It was now for us to move, since it was obviously the intention of the Japanese Government to leave us fixed in the swamps of Yokohama, until we were tired of our position. Accordingly, in concert with my colleague, Monsieur de Bellecourt, I answered immediately that I was glad to learn they fully acknowledged the existence of grievous causes of complaint, and the necessity of adopting effective measures for their removal. I added, that I could not feel surprised that the Government should deem the subject of such grave importance as to require repeated deliberations, or complain that these might necessarily occasion some delay in arriving at a satisfactory conclusion—but, as their Excellencies could fix no term for their deliberations, which might therefore be prolonged indefinitely, it was my purpose to employ this interval by travelling through the country, visiting all the ports, and more especially those on the east and west coasts, the opening of which, according to treaty, the Japanese Government desired to defer. After personal observation, I should then be better enabled to decide what advice should be tendered to Her Majesty's Government on this question, and when their Excellencies had concluded their deliberations, and were prepared to bring all pending questions to a satisfactory termination, they could let me know by courier should I not already have returned.

A very few days sufficed to prove that I had made no miscalculation as to the effectiveness of the new weapon brought to bear. In less than a week Sakai Wookionoske was in Yokohama, with plenipotentiary powers to treat with Monsieur de Bellecourt and myself, and to enter into such arrangements as might be necessary to insure our return to the capital. Three conferences followed on February 21, 22, and 27, at which it was finally arranged that a formal invitation, in the name of the Tycoon, should be sent to us requesting our return to the capital, under the conditions set forth in the minute of the first conference.

The formal acceptance of these conditions, and the invitation in the name of the Tycoon, were received within two days; and on March 2 — exactly four weeks from our departure — we embarked on board H.M.S. 'Encounter' and 'Pioneer' and returned to Yeddo. But we returned not as we went—for one of the conditions was that we should be received at the landing-place by two of the Governors of Foreign Affairs, and conducted to our respective Legations—and when our flags were hoisted, that the batteries should salute each with twenty-one guns.

Thus ended the grave crisis—ostensibly to the satisfaction of all parties; and there can be no doubt several important results had been attained. The conditions of our return were briefly, a formal pledge from the Tycoon, by and with his Council of State, to provide effectually hereafter for the safety of the Legations, and their exemption from violence and menace, thus recognising without reservation their responsibility;—the official invitation to resume their posts,—and finally the public reception of the Foreign Representatives who had left under menace of violence,—with marks of respect to the national flags, by a hitherto unused distinction of a royal salute at the moment they were hoisted. The last public homage and mark of respect I had rightly anticipated was that which cost the most to obtain—but finding it impossible to secure our return without this concession, it also was agreed to in the end. Under these circumstances it appeared to me as to my colleague, that the objects for which we had accepted so many sacrifices and such grave responsibility would be fairly attained by our return. The false position in which Foreign Representatives had been placed by the Japanese Government perpetually warning them, and through them all their countrymen, of danger and threats of massacre, under a practical disclaimer of responsibility, or, at all events, of their

power to prevent either the one or the other, would cease.
Their position would not, on the face of it, be one utterly
derogatory to the nations they represented.    Life, either
their own or that of their countrymen at the ports, might
not in effect be perfectly secured : this, in the present
state of the country and its government, might be unattainable, but there could be little doubt that a great step
towards that end would have been made.    Lastly, various
manœuvres and devices, designed apparently to lower the
Foreign Representatives in the eyes of the people, and to
restrict them from all free communication, were formally
repudiated ; and the maintenance of those existing, or the
creation of new expedients to the same end, if not rendered impossible, were certainly made more difficult.

# CHAPTER IV.

HAVING already given a detailed account of a journey through the interior of Japan, while describing the pilgrimage to Fusiyama, in which the casual incidents and subjects of observation occurring by the wayside, the mode of travelling, accommodation, &c., were all noticed as they occurred, I do not propose giving anything like an itinerary or daily journal of this second and longer expedition. A recurrence to subjects already touched upon, however interesting in themselves, or worthy of farther study on the spot, could only weary readers at a distance. My attention was moreover directed mainly on this second journey to such facts and incidents, as might help me to form a judgement of the relations actually existing between the ruling classes and the masses; of the developement of intelligence in the middle and lower ranks, and the influence which feudalism in its oriental phase exercised upon the population, rural and urban. For this purpose it was needful to carry my observations not only among the tillers of the soil, but into the cities and those great centres of life and activity where commerce and large intercourse might be expected to give a fuller, if not a more distinctive expression and form to national life. Of the political and social status of the Japanese, it must for many years to come be very difficult to form a decided opinion. But such opportunities for observation and study, as a long journey through the country affords, are peculiarly valuable for their rarity ; and the jealousy· with which, at Yeddo, all the avenues to any knowledge of the people and their true state are watched, and more or less effectually closed by the authorities.

But once in the country, far away from the Capital, and moving through different scenes every day, with only one set of officials to hamper your progress, or surround you with a network of designed impediments, their control may be to a great degree escaped. The work is too much for the number employed. They are weary every night, not only with the fatigue of continuous travelling, but the vain attempt to keep pace with the foreigners' restless and ever active pursuit after objects they but imperfectly apprehend. And at last, finding any meshes of a net which they can weave perpetually broken through by the strong will of those committed to their charge, they have frequent periods of utter discouragement, and for a time fairly give up the attempt. Their despair at the hopeless nature of the task assigned them, was sometimes legibly written in the puzzled and vexed expression of their countenances ; and in a way so serio-comic, that it was difficult to avoid smiling. There are so many more things in heaven and earth than enter into their philosophy, especially in the erratic habits and unceasing activity of Europeans. These are all so utterly opposed to their notions of what is natural, pleasant, and fitting in this sublunary scene, that I am satisfied they would just as soon have been given charge over so many lunatics, and felt quite as likely to fathom their motives, or divine what would be the next thing they would ask, seek, or do in any given circumstances. I think they must often sigh after the good old time, when Mynheer (never a very mercurial personage) was kept safe locked up in the farthest corner of the kingdom, and even when sent to Yeddo, was duly caged, and much too well trained in the way he should go, to want or to do anything which was not *selon les regles*, as set down in Japanese laws and customs for the use of foreigners.

It so happened that the head of the Dutch Mission, Mr. de Wit, whose society could not fail to be a plea- sure, as his companionship was a great advantage in all other respects, had arranged to travel the road on this occasion with me. And certainly no one could be less dis- posed than was my colleague to be put through the old series of Japanese ways and devices, either as regarded personal freedom or antiquated tariffs of expenses established 200 years ago, for the special benefit of the Japanese officials,— by which some 3,000*l.* of Dutch money must have re- mained in their hands, after payment of the actual expenses of the journey. About 4,000*l.* was always charged, and the whole cost in this instance, though we were by no means exempt from extortion, did not amount to 500*l.* for Mr. de Wit and myself, with three gentlemen attached to the British Legation. But this result was not achieved without effort and many battles — the two Ministers cor- dially joining in a determined resistance to all unblushing exactions, on the one side—and the whole array of Yaconinerie as steadfastly bent on maintaining time- honoured customs, and strong in their resolution *stare super antiquas vias.* But progress and innovation carried the day.

I think they only made one serious attempt to put us in the old harness, and as that was at the beginning — and signally failed, they probably gave it up as hopeless in the end. It came in the form of a proposal that we would pledge ourselves ' never to go before the escort, and always to stop at the places they should designate for meals or sleeping.' When it was objected that this would be to make them our keepers or masters, rather than attendants, it was observed, with a Japanese genuflexion, that it was only a *form*; if we would sign the engage- ment, when once out of the town, we could then do as we pleased. When informed that we preferred doing as we might judge best, without the previous formality of signing a bond to do only as others might please, they evidently concluded it was a bad case, and resigned themselves to their fate ; only wishing us very probably in the lowest depths of the bay, instead of preparing for a thirty days' journey in their company.

It may be thought this was not a propitious beginning, but it did not rest with us to make it other than it was. It followed inevitably from our relative positions and antecedents.  We could no more change it, than the season of the year, which was still less promising.  Towards the end of May the rains generally set in, and if *they* do not come, the sun does.  On consulting the meteorological records kept at Decima during the last ten years, I had the satisfaction of learning that the average of wet days in the month of June was twenty.  Twenty wet and ten hot days, did not offer a pleasant prospect for a month's journey on horseback, at the rate of three or four miles an hour; involving, therefore, six or seven hours every day in the saddle, either under a hot sun or a drenching rain. But here again force was put upon us, by a sort of necessity.  It was already the end of May when I returned from China, where public business had carried me as far as Hongkong — nearly a thousand miles homeward, if I could only have held my course onward !  Both I and my colleague must either undertake the journey *then*, under the aforesaid conditions, or renounce it altogether, and proceed to the capital by sea ; with the probability of no second opportunity again presenting itself — certainly not as regarded myself.  I had not the slightest intention of foregoing so interesting an expedition as the journey by land, or the important objects I had in view, even though I could not command all the most pleasant and desirable conditions. My colleague felt just as little disposed to take ship in preference, so, immediately after my arrival, preparations for our departure began.  These, as before in the first expedition, involved no small forethought and care for the commissariat.  Our party, originally intended to be three, was swelled to five by the addition of the British Consul, very anxious to join the expedition, and requiring change of air and scene for his health ; and an artist, for whom it was an opportunity never likely to return. As he was connected with the 'Illustrated News,' I thought it the best possible means of making Japan better known to the British public, a very desirable object in itself, and did not hesitate to add him to my suite. I would very gladly have attached a botanist also, but, unfortunately, although three arrived in the country within a week or two, none were within reach at the time.

Our departure was fixed for the 1st of June. The two or three preceding days were wet and stormy, apparently ushering in the south-west monsoon. The die was cast, however, and although the morning was anything but smiling, about ten o'clock the caravan got under way— some on horseback, some in norimons, filling the whole street of the usually silent Decima, where the hospitable house of the Dutch Consul General stands. Our Japanese escort — yaconins, ometskis, and interpreters, ' officers' officers,' and the 'servants of servants,' — in number untold. These with our own followers, and the baggage of the whole party as we left the town, stretched in a line which seemed interminable.

For an hour before starting a large space in front of the house had been filled with kicking horses and screaming owners, with a very mob of officials and their attendants, norimons, kangos, and their bearers. There were yaconins of all kinds and degrees — looking very much like my friend here, his sword-hilt covered up with his long mitten to preserve the weapon from the rain, which was pelting pitilessly on his umbrella of a hat — for it answers both purposes admirably — but accepting his destiny with a stoical philosophy and resignation which strips the worst lot of half its bitterness. The sketch on the following page is one for which the materials were seldom wanting during the journey ; although we were much better treated by the weather, after all, than we had any right to expect.

I have omitted to mention, that soon after the Governor of Nagasaki had been officially informed of my arrival and proposed departure by the overland route, he took an opportunity of urging upon me the danger of the journey, and general insecurity of the roads from the unsettled state of the country.   I confess I gave little heed to his warnings, taking them very much as matters of course, and a repetition of the play acted by the Ministers them-

DUTY UNDER DIFFICULTIES

selves, when my journey to Fusiyama was announced. Nor should I have thought it worth mentioning now, but that after-events seemed to prove he had some good and tangible reasons for his proceeding, and that he knew a special danger menaced us on the way, which was only too likely to cost us our lives.   But this is one of the evils inseparable from their system of pretexts and mendacity, and a reticence which will never let them speak out and tell the whole truth.   It is impossible to know when they are merely giving warning of danger, as a pretext for objecting to a diplomatic agent's giving effect to the treaties, or exercising any privilege which might enlighten him as to the true state of affairs; — and when it is given in good faith, because they know danger of a specific kind does actually exist, which it behoves him and them to guard against.

The Governor having in vain sought to turn us seaward by the general warnings of danger, sent his good wishes; and although we set off under a lowering sky, the clouds lifted for a short space and let us mount our horses, with a faint promise of fair weather. But we were hardly well out of the town, before the sluice-gates above us were opened, spoiling to the eye what would otherwise have been beautiful scenery. Our way led through several villages picturesquely grouped on the hill sides, and along the edge of the road. One of the first, just out of Nagasaki, Mr. Wirgman sketched, with a tea-house for the foreground, and such habitués as may most frequently be seen in such localities.

The corn harvest was in progress, and, by-the-bye, it has always been a mystery to me how the good people in Japan get in their corn, for it seems destined to be in the wet season that it must be gathered, as they cut their wheat in June. The rice harvest does not come until November, but last year, the autumn being also exceptionably wet, much of the crop was left to rot in the fields—a serious calamity to a rice-eating population like the Japanese. At this time of the year, green plots of the brightest hue indicate where the seed rice is thickly sown, for the purpose of being transplanted out during the month, after the ground has been well watered, ploughed, and harrowed, and finally made into a sea of mud!

Of all agricultural employments, rice-planting seems to be the least enviable I have yet seen, and we had ample opportunities throughout the journey of learning all its details. Men and women, with their backs bent

WAYSIDE INN NEAR NAGASAKI

and nearly up to their knees in a malodorous mud field, take each their basket of young plants, and separating them into small bundles, fix them at a space of about six inches apart, into the less fluid soil below, with no other implement than their hands.    The aram, a sort of lotus, the root of which is eaten, the sweet potato, and the bearded wheat appeared everywhere.    The latter was often planted in terraces raised with incredible labour along the face of the hills, supported by walls from six to nine feet high.    Trees, chiefly pines, are planted higher up, and these with other evergreens scattered over the country, keep the country from looking bare, despite the oceans of mud and fallow fields in the lower levels.    In the hedges, the honeysuckle and the thistle reminded us of home, while the azalias—pink, blue, and white, in all their delicacy of hue and texture,—mingling with the camellia and cape jasmine, which grew wild by the hedgeside, spoke of other climes than our own.    The rich tints of the evergreens, of which nearly all the hedges in Japan are chiefly formed, gave quite a peculiar feature also.    Vegetable wax-trees were in great abundance, as were the bamboo and cryptomeria. A few palms here and there gave farther variety, and a whole family of coniferæ clothed the hill-sides with a dark mantle.    In some places the nakedness and poverty of the sandy soil could not be entirely concealed, and pure sandstone cropped up so divested of soil that it seemed a marvel how trees of any kind could find sustenance in their vicinity.    Often, however, along the roadside what little earth had ever sustained them, had been completely washed away, and the root striking downwards, and stretching enormous distances horizontally, made a perfect network of gnarled and twisted timber, bare of all earth, sometimes embracing a huge boulder or rock, until they seemed to grow out of it, as though in the hungry search for something to cling to, even the sapless stone had been clutched with a loving embrace.*    One has seen something not unlike this in the world, where men and women both—

* See illustration, next page.

with natures as hard as the nether millstone, and with as
little feeling as any granite boulder,—have had loving arms
thrown round them, seeking stay and support from the
least congenial elements, when more kindly soil was
denied them by a hard fate.

HOW PINES GROW

And thus we journeyed through the island of *Kiusiu,*
one of the three largest of the group of islands which constitute Japan.   The road lay chiefly along the coast, now
and then stretching across a hilly promontory, wild and
beautiful.   The valleys were fertile and covered with
various crops ripening to the harvest ; the lower grounds
alone fallow, preparing for the rice under the most favourable circumstances,—the close vicinity of mountain and
hill giving abundance of water for irrigation ; and the
lower level of the sea affording ready means for drainage.

HALT BY THE WAYSIDE NEAR PALHIWA

SULPHUR BATHS URITZINO

Sometimes when the sun was high, and the baggage far in the rear, we would call a halt and sit down beneath the shade of some fine tree, never far to seek in Japan, and there rest long enough for an artist's sketch, as in a scene depicted in the lithocrome opposite.

During this nine days' journey there was a combination of every kind of scenery. Well-cultivated valleys winding among the hills, were graced with terraces stretching far up towards their summits, whenever a scanty soil could be found or *carried*, with a favourable aspect for the crops. We traversed some wild-looking passes, too, where hill and rock seemed tumbled in chaotic confusion from their volcanic beds. Frequent glimpses were caught of the sea-coast and bays, from which the road seldom strays very far inland. Pretty hamlets and clumps of fine trees were rarely wanting; and if the villages looked poor, and the peasant's home (bare of furniture at all times) more than usually void of comfort, yet all the people looked as if they had not only a roof to cover them, but rice to eat, which is more than can always be said of our populations in Europe. As groups of women and children crowded round the doors of the cottages, the whole interior of which the eye could easily take in at a glance, it would sometimes appear a problem how so many living beings could find sleeping room; or what provision there could be for the commonest requirements of decency, much less comfort. They must of necessity herd together very much like cattle;— but neither is that peculiar to Japan, unfortunately.

At Urisino in the morning, and Takeiwa in the evening of the third day, we found some hot sulphur baths. The first we visited was open to the street, with merely a shed roof to shelter the bathers from the sun. As we approached, an elderly matron stepped out on to the margin, leaving half a dozen of the other sex behind her, to continue their soaking process. The freedom of the lady from all self-consciousness or embarrass-ment was so perfect of its kind, that one could not help recalling the charitable exclamation of John Huss when he saw a pious old woman bringing a faggot to his stake, ' *O sancta simplicitas* !' O holy simplicity, which has no fears of a censorious world, is vexed by no arbitrary code of conventional proprieties, and feels no shame in the absence of covering. She had washed, and was clean; and with the consciousness alone that she had accomplished a duty, evidently saw no reason why all the world should not know, and see it too, if they chanced to come that way. There were great crowds of men and women luxuriating in them ; and I suppose it is the force of habit, but they certainly bear par-boiling, both men and women, better than any people I ever met with.

A photographic view and a sketch were obtained of the busy scene, although a midday sun made the first very trying work. The springs are close to the banks of a river, shaded by some noble trees ; and the scene is both lively and picturesque, with groups of votaries, nude and draped, crowding round the various reservoirs, and enjoying alternately the medicinal virtues of the waters, and the cool shade of the trees.

During this first part of the journey, the extreme richness and fertility of the soil were in striking contrast with the apparent poverty of those who lived on it. Even in the large towns, though there were of course better houses to be seen than in the villages and hamlets, there was no sign of activity or prosperity. A sketch of the road leading through the first village as we left Nagasaki, where the houses still partake of the character and something of the prosperity of a seaport and a place of trade, has already been given.* Some of the towns were both large and populous, with a much superior style of architecture. The view on the opposite page was taken in the principal street of Omura, a provincial capital of one of the Daimios, where we passed a night. A crowd collected to catch a glimpse of such novel visitors, and a few matchlock-men were passing at the moment the artist was sketching. But these are both

* See p. 70.

FROM OUR INN AT OMURA

specimens which show the best, not the worst aspect of town and country. Whether the poverty among the people is more apparent than real (their wants are so few), or the share allowed to the mere cultivation is really too small, I could not very satisfactorily ascertain. Nothing is so difficult, indeed, as to get any kind of information, either political, statistical, or scientific, in Japan; partly, I believe, in consequence of the dense ignorance of everyone on any subject not immediately concerning his own life and business; partly also due to our imperfect knowledge of the language,—but chiefly to their inveterate propensity to deceive and mislead the foreigner. It is enough that he should desire information on any subject, no matter how trivial or apparently unimportant, to make it their business or their pleasure, either to deny all knowledge, or tell him a falsehood, no matter how palpable. When Mr. Veitch was at Yeddo, on a visit to the Legation in quest of botanical specimens, he saw a pine-tree from which he desired a few seeds. ' Oh,' said the inevitable yaconins, ' those trees have no seed!' ' But there they are,' replied the unreasonable botanist, pointing to some. ' Ah ‚yes, true; but they will not *grow.*' On another occasion, I wanted some seeds of the *Thujopsis dolabrata*, the fine pine discovered by Thunberg, and a Governor of Foreign Affairs, promised they should be got, but after three weeks' time — and when it was too late to take other steps — he sent me a withered branch, saying that was the seed!

I heard that by the tenure of land in the Tycoon's territory, six-tenths of the produce goes to the cultivator, and in the territories of the Daimios only four-tenths. But I have no certainty of the truth or accuracy of the statement; for I have also been told that only *one-fifth* is retained, the other four-fifths going to the owner — rather a wide discrepancy this. It is said also that 100 Tsuboo (or 600 square feet) of land will produce on an average two piculs of rice each crop — a picul being 133 lbs. The whole subject of the tenure of land in Japan is involved in obscurity. Nor do I believe any foreigner at present can obtain trustworthy information. Another peculiarity in the physical character of the country has already been noticed, in the great prevalence of sand. The mountains were sandstone, and the rivers were sand, more than water. It could be traced everywhere in the soil, so much so that nothing but centuries of manuring of the most fertilising kind, and an unlimited supply of water, with all the patient toil of a Japanese population, could ever have brought it into the crop-bearing state. But they seem to grow everything, corn and rice in large quantities, buckwheat, millet, beans, especially a kind called *Daiko*, with a white flower, from which they make soy. This plant covered large tracts. A few patches of poppy here and there appeared, grown no doubt for the opium, but I fancy, to be used only as a medicine, for, except as regards a few in immediate contact with the Chinese colony at Nagasaki, I have not heard the Japanese are addicted to it as a narcotic stimulant. They prefer their *Saki*, made by distillation from rice, which is of every degree of strength, from weak wine to ardent spirits.

As another consequence of this geological feature, all the rivers are sand-choked. And this condition is not limited to *Kiusiu* alone; for all the rivers on the road, and we must have passed more than a hundred on our way to Yeddo, are obstructed by sand-banks, and the water is scarcely four feet deep anywhere. Often a wide margin of sand and pebble alone marks where a river has once flowed, and in the centre is a shallow rippling stream, in the midst of which sand-banks innumerable appear above the surface, and obstruct its course. During the wet season, no doubt from the close proximity of the hills and mountain ranges, the country below is subject to great freshes; and a large volume of water is poured down the ravines, flooding the plains and carrying the detritus of the soft sandstone and gravel and boulders in vast quantities on to the banks, and down even to the mouths, which are all obstructed with bars.

On the third day, when near *Takeiwa*, we came upon a coal mine of the Prince of Fizen. It lay within a hundred yards of the main road, and a cross-road led directly to it, but I found the way stopped by a newly erected and temporary barrier of bamboo of a very fragile kind, behind which squatted a couple of armed retainers. The treaty very explicitly states that 'The Diplomatic Agent shall have the right to travel freely to any part of the Empire of Japan;' and the better to prevent all doubts as to the meaning of the words 'travel freely,' it is stipulated that the diplomatic Representative of Japan shall have the same 'right to travel freely to any part of Great Britain.' It was not a bad opportunity, therefore, of ascertaining how far this right to 'travel freely' extended, in the conception of the Daimios. I turned round the temporary barrier accordingly, and had already advanced several steps along the road, before the guards had sufficiently recovered their surprise at the unexpected audacity of the proceeding, to vociferate orders to stop and come back. This was not at all my intention; and followed at some distance by M. de Wit and the rest of my party, I held on my way, while the two guardians, joined by some more of the retainers, tried to pass before us, and block up the passage. Under the guise of an escort, some armed retainers always accompanied us through each Daimio's territories, but in reality, as became abundantly evident on this and other occasions, to see *we kept the high road*, and neither deviated to the right nor the left. Amidst much vociferation and excitement, finding they could not stop me without proceeding to actual violence,—and despite their indignation, hesitating and fearing to resort to such extreme measures, —I gained the coal heaps and the mouth of the pit, which seemed to be only the opening of a horizontal adit or gallery into the side of the hill. I saw no sunken shaft, but a large quantity of coal was heaped up in the open air, exposed to rapid deterioration. Some of the coal itself appeared of tolerable quality, but small.

It is from this Prince of Fizen's territories chiefly that Nagasaki is supplied with coal for our ships, and great complaints are made of its quality. It is generally considered mere surface coal and badly worked. I learn, however, from those practically acquainted with coalmines at home, that this is really the most economical way of working. Either this Daimio, or another in the same island, ordered, through the Dutch, a steamengine to aid in the better working of his mines—but after it arrived, and was conveyed to the spot, he appeared to have changed his mind, declaring that it would take the bread out of his workmen's mouths—the old argument against all machinery and improvements. So the engine lies useless and spoiling, a sacrifice to the political economy of the rulers. Whether this was his own suggestion, or came from Yeddo, however, may be a question. Notwithstanding the sort of semi-independence in which these Daimio princes live in their own territories, evidence every now and then appears, that something of real subjection exists. For instance, in this very article of coal, in which we are so much interested, there is great danger of the supply failing the port of Nagasaki altogether, not from any unwillingness on the part of the Prince of Fizen as the proprietor to work his mines, and make money by the sale of the produce, but from the dishonest and oppressive interposition of the Tycoon's officials. Nagasaki was made a portion of the Imperial territories when the port was first assigned as a place of trade for foreigners, and since then not even the prince can sell his own produce, except to the Government. And the Government officials, taking advantage of this condition, not only fix the lowest price consistent with a bare remuneration of labour, in order that they may make the larger profit by re-selling to the foreigner; but they leave such long arrears of payment, that the prince, wearied out, had declared he would employ his people no more in getting coal, for which not even the amount of wages could be obtained.   It was understood, at the same time, that he demanded permission to send his own agents to Nagasaki to sell the coal, without any interposition of the Government officials—a permission not very likely to be conceded, seeing the profit made by these gentry.   But the difficulty will probably be temporarily got over, as in similar cases in Japan, by a kind of compromise.   Some, if not all, of the arrears will be paid up, and liberal promises given of better payment in future.   Another instance of the sort of real subjection in some things, in strange contradiction to the pretensions of independence in others, seemingly of greater importance, was related to me by Mr. de Wit at Nagasaki.   The Prince of Itzen, whose territories are also in Kiusiu, had young men instructed in the medical science of Europe by Dr. Pompas, a Dutch medical man, who is stationed at Nagasaki by the Dutch Government, and is farther salaried by the Japanese Government to give instruction in medicine, and constitute a sort of college. In order to get over some of the difficulty occasioned by the repugnance to dissection, manifested in the beginning but gradually disappearing, anatomical figures in *papier maché* had been sent for to Europe.   One was commanded by the prince to keep up the knowledge of those who had returned to his territory after they had finished their course.   When this arrived by the good offices of the Dutch commissioner, he was unable to receive it, because one ordered for the Tycoon's Government had not arrived, and it was unfitting that he should be supplied before the Tycoon.   Was this a mere act of overstrained courtesy on the part of the prince, or compulsory?   The Government officials said he *could* not receive it; and the prince, although he had desired very much to have the figure, did not in effect receive it, and I believe it was made over to the Government.

Thus, although the Prince of Fizen was unable to assert a right to dispose of the produce of his own mines, except to the Imperial Government under onerous conditions, he yet felt sufficiently strong and independent to close every avenue, except the main road, to the British Minister travelling through his territories under escort furnished by the Tycoon, and in virtue of an express stipulation of the treaties with Foreign Powers. And not only to coal mines did his prohibition extend, for a few miles farther on, seeing a high embankment apparently to a great reservoir or lake, at the foot of some hills *close* to the road, I turned off to see the nature and extent of the work, and all the way up the steps leading to the higher level, and while there, the prince's retainers attached to us as an escort, thought it their duty to vociferate and protest against this most innocent deviation from the high road. On my arrival at our first halting-place, as soon as I could find the chief officer of the Tycoon sent with me by the Governor of Nagasaki for my proper escort, I remonstrated against the unwarranted interference and incivility of the prince's officers. He and his colleagues professed to be extremely sorry, alleging it was because they were not there. True to their principles, and never failing to take advantage of any danger or disagreement to shorten the life that binds the foreigner to the side of his gaoler. They admitted a treaty right secured my freedom from such obstructions, &c. But the admission had no practical influence, and did not prevent every pathway and side street for the rest of the journey through his territories, being carefully guarded by detachments of armed men, from all renewal of attempts which were evidently regarded as unauthorised intrusion. Of course it might be said they were placed there to honour the passage of the two Foreign Agents, but the real object was much too apparent.

So that it was clear the right of the Chiefs of Diplomatic Missions '*to travel freely throughout the Empire,*' was limited by the Daimios in their own territories, to a right to travel *along the high road*, which is held to be under Imperial control; and they disputed my right, derived either from the Tycoon, or the treaties made by

ODAH

him with Foreign Powers, to turn a single step to one side
or the other.   In every town where we halted or slept,
barriers covered with curtains bearing the Daimio's arms
were raised, not only preventing any passage, but shutting
out the view of the streets branching off.  When our
officers were spoken to on the subject, they maintained 'it
was for our better protection.'   It might be so, certainly,
but in that case, the country must be in a more alarming
state of insecurity than even the Ministers have ever
represented.   It is much more likely that the Government and the Daimios, perfectly agreeing in their jealousy
of foreign intrusion, are accomplices in making all travel
as irksome and unattractive as possible.   Other and more
important matters occupied my whole attention immediately after my return ; but, later, I did not fail to bring
the matter before the Ministers, with a protest against a
mode of interpreting treaties which completely perverted
their sense, and neutralised all that was really valuable
in their stipulations.

During the first five days, the roads, without being
as bad as cross-roads in many European countries are to
this day, were nevertheless in striking contrast to the
fine broad avenues which constitute the Tocado of
Nipon.   They were all practicable for artillery, but never
was there a country less adapted to cavalry.   Paddy
fields, nearly always in a state of swamp, ever liable to be
flooded and cut up in all directions with drains and watercourses, alternate with inaccessible hills.   It was not
until the sixth day, on the way between *Kansaki* and
*Tatsiro*, that we came upon an improved line.   On each
side were beautiful valleys waving with ripe corn, skirted
by hills covered with scrub, while farther in the distance,
blue mountains formed the background.   The vegetable
wax-tree abounded always, and I heard when at Nagasaki
that 20,000 of these had been planted in the district soon
after the European demand for this article arose, although
the Dutch residents had never been able to find out the
place ; plainly proving that the Japanese were by no

means slow to feel the stimulus of a new demand and
increase the supply, while desiring to keep their proceedings a secret from the merchants.   There did not seem
to be much cotton grown in these districts — here and
there we saw a field, and occasionally in the villages saw
the women at work rolling the cotton for the spinning-
wheel or distaff, as in the following illustration : and a

PREPARING THE COTTON FOR SPINNING

thrifty housewife might also at intervals be seen reeling off
her thread on a large wheel.   We passed through several
small towns with houses presenting a better appearance,
while hamlets half-concealed in clumps of trees with
luxuriant foliage everywhere met the eye.   The dogrose,
honeysuckle, and buttercup, with the homely thistle,
continued as we went, to fill up the hedgerows.   While
riding on alone, it would be easy to fancy the scene was in
some picturesque English county.   We came upon a very
beautiful moss-rose growing by the side of a cottage. a
variety of the English species apparently, and with some
of the fragrance.   It was bought and packed with great
care, but in a few days it withered and died ; as little
disposed as its owners, it appears, to be thus suddenly
appropriated by the foreigners.   We also found a pecu-

VILLAGE LIFE IN JAPAN

liar kind of thistle, with bright red and yellow petals, which appears to be cultivated for the sake of the dye it yields, a coarser kind of red used to stain the lips of the women.   Hollyhocks were also growing in patches for a similar use, and the flowers spread on a mat were in many of the cottages.

VILLAGE HOUSEWIFE REELING COTTON

On our way to *Uzino* on the seventh day, we passed through many scenes worthy of the artist's pencil; indeed, the number of tempting pictures was truly tantalising, since it was clearly impossible to take even the slightest sketch of all.  A little wayside shrine, embosomed in trees, was approached over a ravine, across which nature or art had flung a great boulder of granite.  The scene, with a group of Japanese seated in the foreground, proved altogether irresistible.  Again as we descended through a rocky pass into the valley below, and caught the first glimpse of the cultivated fields and terraced hills with another range of mountains towering beyond, picturesque Japanese figures filling up the foreground, it was difficult to pass and take no note.  A very slight sketch was all *I* could attempt, and as for 'the artist' I despaired of

seeing him along such a road, before dark.    Once fairly
descended into the valley, the scenery changed in character, but was still equally rich in artistic effects.    I
endeavoured to fix the outlines with a few strokes of the
pencil, but the afternoon was far advanced, and there
were men and horses both in the party, with little feeling

ROADSIDE SHRINE.

for the beautiful, but a great desire for rest and the
evening meal!  So I closed my book with a pang of regret,
only consoled by the reflection that it was far beyond my
powers to have done any justice to such scenes, or carry
away more than the merest indications of all I admired.

On the eighth day, our way to *Koyonoski* lay chiefly
along the banks of a river, on a high causeway raised
some twenty feet above the level of the water.    We
passed several depôts of coal, evidently placed there for
embarkation, in some large flat-bottomed boats, a novel
sight on the sand-choked rivers of Japan,—certainly in
Kiusiu, where boats are to be seen only as exceptions, or
at some ferry where the water is a little deeper than
usual.    We had heavy rain all day, and the miserable

horse-flesh provided by the country under the yaconins'
superintendence, induced both M. de Wit and myself to
get into our norimons, only one degree less intolerable
than a broken-down baggage-horse which will only go
when its owner leads, at his pace, and when it is not
either kicking or biting, is sure to be stumbling.　I had
been persuaded against my better judgement to trust to
the resources of the country for post-horses, and only
repented it once — but that was the whole way.

*Kokura*, the fortified capital of BOUZEN and one of
the keys to the Straits between Kiusiu and Nipon, we
reached early in the morning fortunately, for the sun
beat hot upon our heads and shoulders long before ten
o'clock.　The roads were sheets of mud, and in places all
but impassable with the heavy rains that had recently
fallen; and though the scenery was beautiful as ever, it
was difficult, under such conditions, to enjoy it.　Our
spirits rose, however, as we approached the end of this first
and most trying stage of our long journey, and enabled us
better to appreciate the beauty of the approach.　Pleasant country houses, each surrounded by their garden
and clumps of trees or orchards, line the road which
leads to the provincial capital, for more than a mile.
It was holiday time; and all the inhabitants were at
their windows dressed in their best, or grouped on the
door steps to watch the cortége pass.　Among the
younger and fairer portion of the spectators were many
pretty faces, pretty in spite of red paint and rice powder,
where a modest shyness might be read, struggling with
intense curiosity to see the stranger — a conflict in which
the latter, I am bound to say, was not always the victor.
The entrance of *Kokura* is by a gateway, guarded by a
considerable force of armed retainers.　The walls were
high, and seemed well capable of defence against anything
but artillery.　After a short halt, we embarked on board
a junk, in the state cabin of which we had only the choice
of squatting, or lying down between the ceiling and the
floor.　At the opposite side of the Straits, after a two
hours' pull, we found H. M. S. ' Ringdove ' waiting our

arrival ; and we left the shores of Kiusiu, not sorry to
have ended this much of our journey ; for, despite all the
attractions novelty and great beauty of scenery could lend,
it was both fatiguing and tedious.   Some seven or eight
leagues a day on miserable ponies, led at a snail's pace over
indifferent roads when at their best, and at this season
often little better than a series of pitfalls, was rather trying
to the patience ;  even had this slow mode of progression
not been under one of two inevitable conditions, a hot sun
or heavy rain.  We had traversed the territories of several
Daimios; of the Princes of Omura, Fizen, Secousin, and
Izen ; and from all I had seen, I drew the conclusion,
that although the fertility of the soil is great,  and turned
to the best account by a plentiful supply of the cheapest
labour, yet little superfluity is left to those who have to
live by the cultivation of the land.  Whatever surplus there
may be in the produce, must be absorbed by the Daimios
and their thousands of hungry and idle retainers, who form
the unproductive classes in Japan ; and whose lords are,
I believe, owners of nine-tenths of the land.  Rent is usually
paid in kind, and whatever the exact proportion, the
general poverty of the people, in the midst of surpassing
fertility, goes far to prove it must be high.  The probability is, as I have heard, that the rates vary in different
districts, and according to the productiveness of the soil.
They are, as a race, so frugal and penurious, however,
that, judging by the general aspect of poverty, nothing
but a bare sustenance of rice and vegetables can be
left to the cultivators, with just enough over to buy the
very homely and scanty vestments they habitually wear,
—which in summer, the reader knows, are reduced to
the narrowest limits compatible with the use of any
clothing at all.  The prices of everything in ordinary
consumption are evidently very low, and a metal currency
must be very scarce, for we found bank notes, of a
tolerably indestructible paper well thumbed, for every
fractional sum — from thirty cash, or a fraction over a
farthing, to 500 cash and more.
    Political economists have laid it down as a rule, that

the cheapness or dearness of living in a country may be very well estimated by the minuteness of divisions in the coinage; as a liard in France, far below a farthing in England, indicated a corresponding difference once, in the cost of articles of daily and common use. If so, then living in Kiusiu must be very cheap, since a cash can scarcely be estimated at more than $\frac{1}{25}$ of a farthing; and is not, like the liard of France, or the maravedis of Spain, a nominal but a *real* coinage of copper, about the size of a farthing, only much thinner.

We did not arrive at *Simonoséki*, the town on the opposite side of the inland sea at its entrance where it separates Nipon from Kiusiu, until the ninth day after our departure from Nagasaki. From this port we had to take ship for Hiogo, at the farther end of the sea, and the beginning of the second land route. We could have gone on by land, skirting along the sea-coast, but it would have added greatly to the fatigue, and prolonged the journey nearly three weeks, without any corresponding advantage.

OUR JUNK IN THE INLAND SEA

# CHAPTER V.

SIMONOSEKI—THE 'INLAND SEA,' AND VOYAGE TO HIOGO.

THE *Suonada* Sea, on which we embarked to cross over to the opposite shore, separates the two islands of Kiusiu and Sikopf from the larger island of Nipon, which latter is to the Japanese the *mainland*—the largest of all the group of islands,—forming the England and Wales of Däi Nipon, or Great Nipon as they occasionally write it, for *Japan* is a name of our own invention.*

This inland sea, as it is commonly, though not very correctly termed, is about 250 miles in length, extending to the bay of Osaka, and is studded with a few rocks, and innumerable islands.   It is probably some fifty miles wide at its broadest part.   This was not my first voyage through it, having proceeded to Nagasaki by the same route ; and although everyone must have been struck with the change which scenery undergoes, by merely reversing the order of progression, in going to a place instead of coming from it, or ascending instead of descending ; still the charm of absolute novelty, and a first impression, cannot be thus obtained.   The few Europeans who had hitherto taken this inner passage had generally given very glowing descrip-

---

* The word Nipon in a Japanese mouth means the whole empire.  It is composed of two words written in Chinese character, JIH PUN, meaning the place or rising of the sun.  The Japanese, in conformity with the character of their own language, softened it into *Ni-pun* — the Dutch spelling it *Jeh-pun* — their *j* corresponding to our *y*, we took their spelling, and gave our harsher English pronunciation, and thus called it JAPAN.  So YEDDO for some time after the treaty was spelled after the Dutch JEDDO, but pronounced after our own way, making a word perfectly unrecognisable by a Japanese, as the name of their city.  One disadvantage of this was, that I more than once received letters intended for our Consul at *Jeddah* in the Red Sea.  Whether our letters ever went to him — *en revanche* — I cannot say ; but I think it is very likely.

tions of the surpassing beauty of the scenery.  I cannot say I felt disposed to fall into ecstasies of admiration on either occasion.  But ecstasies are comparatively rare, after the 'forties and fifties,' as the Germans would say, have been fairly entered in a man's life.  And even those who are not on the shady side of the great turning-post in the race, often feel on such occasions the force of Napoleon's somewhat cynical remark, that ' *L'enthousiasme des autres nous refroidit.*'  It is still more generally true that our impressions of scenery at all times are greatly modified by the frame of mind we may be in.  The state of bodily health, companionship, and associations, pleasurable or otherwise, all tend to make an atmosphere of the moment, through which everything is viewed.  Somebody has said, apropos to the *mer de glace* — 'What is the picturesque when one is struggling for dear life?'  What indeed?  Or what is beauty of scenery when there is nothing dear in life?  In either of these circumstances, one is much more inclined to agree with the Frenchman Lever describes somewhere, who, having been dragged over all the highest mountains of Europe in search of the picturesque, at last found courage to relieve his mind by an emphatic protest against any more sight-seeing.  ' *Aimez-vous les belles vues?*' he exclaimed, on meeting an Englishman enveloped in mist, during some laborious ascent, and looking no doubt as bored as the interrogator—' *Aimez-vous les belles vues?  Moi, je les abhorre !*'  We all know the weariness of listening to other people's raptures in the description of scenery ; but we are not all so ready to admit our insensibility to any such emotions when the scenes themselves are before us.  There is a conventionality even in our feelings, which often seems to compel us to adopt phrases and expressions as we adopt our costume, not because it is appropriate or to our taste, but because it is the fashion or ready made to our hands ; and it is less trouble to use it, than devise another which, though it might be better adapted to our individual wants, would bring us in antagonism with the rest of the world.  Some

years ago I was wandering a solitary traveller, though
not absolutely alone in a literal sense (in steam-boats and
railroads no one ever is) on the shores of the Lago Maggiore,
and I could not help *seeing* how radiant in beauty this
queen of the Italian lakes lay basking in sunlight and
shade, and how like an enchanted island *Isolabella* stood
out from the liquid mirror in which its hanging gardens
were reflected.  But I remember turning away, with only
an aching sense of weariness, — a consciousness of the
absence of pleasure, which is very near akin to pain in
many circumstances.  Young was not far wrong when he
wrote,

> Nature in zeal for human amity
> Denies or damps an undivided joy.

And they who travel in pursuit of pleasure or health,
would do well to take with them some of the first elements of both.  If not a mind at ease—not always attainable
—at least some companionship that is itself a source of
pleasure, independent of all external conditions.  But it
seems wisely ordained that pleasure is never so hard to
win, as when it is made a primary object of pursuit, or its
own end.  When we are employed in the performance of
active duties, it is rare, however adverse the circumstances,
that we do not find some pleasure or interest in our path, to
compensate what there may be of actual toil.  And having
this advantage in the present instance, the voyage through
the Suonada Sea formed an agreeable change, and I was
consequently in the best frame of mind to do full justice to
the scenery and its picturesque character.  It was, indeed,
anything but a solitary voyage, for our party filled to
overflowing the little ' Ringdove,' and she had to fold her
wings, and tug away with all her steam power at three
huge junks, into which the remainder had been transferred
with the baggage and commissariat.

Before we took our departure a day was devoted to
Simonoséki itself, and to the exploration of its shops and
temples.  It was evidently well situated for trade and

enjoyed some traffic, but of what nature was the question ?
Mr. Boyle, an English merchant, had received a passage in
the 'Ringdove,' and to him I consigned the task of taking
especial note of any foreign goods, and of such produce
as might be adapted to foreign markets.   The result was
not upon the whole very encouraging, as the following
brief report will show.

'*Simonoséki.*   A town at the entrance of the Suonada
Sea, situated at the south-west point of the Island of
Nipon in lat. 33° 56′ N., and long. 131° E.   The town
straggles along the shore about a mile and a half in length,
consisting of one main street, containing about 10,000 inhabitants.   The dwellings are mostly built of wood, but
the principal buildings are godowns or warehouses, constructed of mud and wood, coated with white cement or
stucco, and said to be " fire-proof," in which is deposited
the produce arriving there from other ports in the sea,
chiefly from Osaca.   The town is surrounded by high
hills, giving little indication of yielding those articles
which are exported in junks, such as sugar, rice, iron, and
oil.   It is evidently a depot receiving the European imports from Nagasaki for transmission into the interior, as
well as the produce from Osaca, pending its reshipment
to Nagasaki or elsewhere, where required,— the business
being conducted by agents of merchants residing at
Osaca.   In the shops were to be seen several articles of
Dutch import, such as medicines, glass, bottles, and
taffacelas, all of a retail nature ; but in much greater
quantity were exhibited for sale some of the principal
staples of British manufactures, such as grey shirtings,
camlets, prints, and long ells.   The prices quoted for
these varied from 50 to 100 per cent. above Nagasaki
prices, but as little reliance could be placed on these
quotations when given through a yaconin interpreter, it
is sufficient to know that British manufactures are
gradually working their way into the interior for consumption.'   I must add, that as regards the prices and Mr.
Boyle's conclusion, in which I entirely agree, he was not

content with trying to extort a true confession of selling prices, but he wanted to know what had been paid for the chief articles of import,—which was rather more, in most countries, than merchants like to tell.

There were other things to be seen at Simonoséki, according to the immemorial custom of the Dutch factory, whose chiefs always took boat here on their way to the capital, in their triennial visits as bearers of presents to the Tycoon. My colleague, Mr. de Wit, had the journal of the last Commissioner who had passed through, and with that sense of obligation so well known to all travellers, by which they are driven to see everything written down for them, often in utter ignorance whether the objects will repay the trouble, we proceeded as a matter of duty to exhaust the catalogue and test our sight-seeing capabilities. There was a certain ancient temple, where a cartoon, some three centuries old, of a great sea-fight illustrious in Japanese history was to be seen ; and also two swords, and other relics of the great soldier *Täiko-Sama*, who about the year 1582 founded a short-lived dynasty of Tycoons. Thither we proceeded at once, and without difficulty saw the cartoon, that is, as much as time and dirt had spared of it. A very wonderful fight it appeared to have been, in which the most remarkable feature was the utter inadequacy of the vessels to carry a tithe of the warriors represented as most valiantly fighting on their decks.

But the swords and other relics were not so easily to be seen, and as an instance of *yaconinerie*, and to all human comprehension unmeaning and motiveless lying, with an exercise of obstructive powers for the sole object of obstructing, I have seldom seen a happier example. Having exhausted the attractions of the cartoon, the temple, and the view of the bay — the last by far the best thing to be seen — my Dutch colleague recollected that his predecessor, Mr. Donker Curtius, spoke in his journal of the swords. 'Where are the swords? We must of course see the illustrious hero's weapons.' To

which head yaconin replies : 'Oh, the swords! what
swords?' gravely adding, 'There are no swords; this is a
temple.'

'True,' observed Mr. de Wit, ' but here nevertheless
are kept the swords and other relics of Täiko-Sama.'
Yaconin must inquire; had never heard of such things.
After a few minutes he returns, and we are informed
there were no swords to be seen. 'What had become
of them then?' 'There never were any!' This was
refuted by a reference to the journal in question, with a
full and particular description. ' But there is no priest to
show them.' 'Where is the priest then? let him be sent
for, we intend to see the swords.' ' The priest? the priest
was dead!' 'His successor then.' 'Oh! he had gone
over to Kokura.' We seemed fast coming to a dead lock.
In such circumstances experience has shown that a determination not to be foiled is often the best policy; and
when our yaconins slowly gained the conviction, that in
no other way would their tour of duty for the day be
ended, the priest appeared; and without any farther
ceremony or hesitation, some dusty cases were produced,
and a couple of old rusty swords exhibited, with less
reverence than could have been conceived. We were
allowed to inspect and handle them, and I verily believe
might have carried them away with us—'for a consideration,' to be in part expended no doubt in purchasing substitutes. I felt some curiosity to discover, if possible, a
rational motive for all the difficulty made by our yaconins,
but in this, as in a thousand other similar cases, I wholly
failed. When pressed into a corner and some explanation
was insisted upon, the chief offender declared it was a
mistake, he *thought* there were no swords. ' Then why
affirm there were none without inquiry, when you knew
nothing about it?' ' I do not belong to the place ; I knew
nothing about it.' ' And the priest that first you killed, and
then sent to Kokura?' 'Somebody told me he was gone,'
and so on to the end of the chapter! To attempt to
convict a Japanese of prevarication in a way to touch his

conscience, is to endeavour to seize an eel by the tail
in his own slime; he is sure to wriggle himself out of your
hand, and swim at large again, in a very sea of falsehood
as his natural element; and your attempt to land him on
the dry shore of Truth, no doubt is to him, as to his pro-
totype, a most unnatural and monstrous proceeding.

But the strangest of all the sights, which it seems
formed part of the programme, to which our predecessors
the Dutch had been invited from time immemorial, was
reserved to the last. It appears Simonoséki, among other
titles to fame, enjoys the questionable distinction of
originating the 'Social Evil,' one of the institutions of
Japan, as it exists in the present day. The same hero
and founder of a dynasty whose swords we had seen,
being sore pressed by the difficulty of keeping his soldiers
together while engaged in the long struggle of an inter-
necine war, and finding them anxious to return home to
their wives, originated the institution in question for the
solace of his followers. In nearly all the books that have
been written on Japan by Europeans more or less space
has been devoted to this subject;—but so far as I can ascertain there is nothing very peculiar, or sufficiently distinctive in the form the evil takes, or even the action of the
Government in licensing establishments, to make it worthy
of such particular notice. The law recognises the establishments maintained (as it does in some Christian countries)
and protects both parties to the contract; while public
opinion so entirely recognises the absence of any free will
in the unfortunate victims, generally brought up from
infancy to their vocation, that when freedom comes, as it
does by law after a certain period of servitude, no indelible stain appears to attach to them, and they may consequently, and it would seem often do in effect, find
husbands who prefer them, as being better educated and
more accomplished than those of their sex who are otherwise brought up. They thus merge the exceptional state
in which they pass the first years of their life, into the
ordinary marital relations. What influence this absence

of any impassable line between vice and virtue, prostitution and matrimony, may have upon the purity of women and the morality of the men, or on the domestic relations, can only be a matter of speculation, until we know more of the people and their modes of life than any foreigner can learn at present. Their popular literature might doubtless throw some light on this subject; but of that we must remain profoundly ignorant also, until some foreigner succeeds in mastering both the written and the spoken language. No doubt there is something very much opposed to our idea of the true foundations of morality and national life, in this easy transition from the depth of pollution to the sanctity of married life and domesticity. To us it seems as if the great barrier between virtue and vice was thrown down, and we vainly speculate upon the influence such social habits may exercise in the inner life of the nation. After all, we should probably fail entirely in arriving at a right conclusion. Polygamy and slavery as both have existed in the East from the days of the patriarchs down to the present time, do not apparently carry with them all the consequences we should *à priori* expect. What is the actual result of institutions which allow parents to sell their children to prostitution, and the victims, after years of harlotry, to return to domestic life, is a problem only to be solved by the knowledge of Japanese life in its closest relations, and for this we must wait. Of all things strange and incongruous connected with such a national 'institution,' nothing can well be more extraordinary or bizarre than the gala costume of the whole class, which is closely regulated by sumptuary laws, as is everything else in Japan. With a forest of metallic hair-pins of large dimensions, the hair is trained back from the face, which is elaborately painted and powdered. Rich brocaded robes lightly swathed round the waist and secured by a girdle of many folds, forming a sort of bag or muff in front, complete the costume. The robe descends below the feet, and sweeping behind in a train, gives them very much the appearance of mermaids, as these are pictorially rendered in the most authentic

GALA DRESS BY LAW ESTABLISHED

representations of such syrens.  The artist thought the
costume worthy of a sketch, and I give it as probably

THE SEA OF SUONADA

more to be relied upon for fidelity to nature, than any hitherto produced of their mythical sisters.

The junks proved of enormous dimensions ; but as the sea is well protected by high lands from storms, and steam was at our command, no difficulties were experienced — or made, by one of the best and most willing of commanders.*

During the three following days we pursued our way very leisurely through the quiet waters of what seemed

HELM OF OUR JUNK.

rather a great lake than a sea. We always anchored before nightfall, for, even if we had not had such *impedimenta* as the junks, until accurate surveys are made it would be unsafe to proceed by night, although there are probably

* Capt. Craigie, R.N., whose death I grieve to see announced by last mail.

not many sunken rocks or shoals — and all that we observed near the surface of the water have been very carefully marked by a stone buttress or pyramid carried
several feet above high-water mark.

Those of our party in the junks seemed to enjoy their
quarters, and their society ; although it must be confessed
the first were of the roughest, and not water-tight, while
the second was more original than refined.   To the artist

STEERSMAN AND HIS MATE

it was, of course, a mine of riches ; and whoever wishes
to gain a correct notion of the quarter-deck or poop of a
Japanese junk, rising to an abrupt angle of fifty degrees
from the main deck to the stern, will find it here most
faithfully portrayed, with the steersman standing at the

helm, which very much resembles the proboscis of a colossal elephant. How even sailors keep their feet on such
an inclined plane when knocking about at sea and the deck
is slippery with rain, I do not pretend to understand. One
of my servants, rather notable for his stupidity, found it
altogether beyond his capacity, and made a descent off the
poop into the lower regions which broke his ribs, and deprived me of his valuable services for the rest of the
journey. *Cahie* took such a dislike to a ship in any
shape after this, that he would fain have been carried in
a cango twenty days overland (at my expense) rather
than embark again in the 'Ringdove,' for a two days'
voyage. The Japanese landsman, although of a sea-going

SAILORS EATING THEIR RICE

race, has the greatest possible horror of the water, and
never willingly trusts himself on the fickle element.
When the Ambassadors were chosen for England, their
first and most anxious inquiry was for a remedy against
sea sickness. For a type of the Japanese sailor nothing
can be more graphic or true to the life, than the preceding

sketch from nature of two of the crew on the deck after the morning meal, smoking the pipe of idleness. And the one opposite of Japanese sailors at their dinner is in no degree inferior.

Of the general character of the scenery I have already spoken. In many parts, no doubt, it is exceedingly picturesque, and if never grand, neither is it ever altogether tame, or devoid of beauty. The marvellous richness and fertility which characterise the Japanese territory generally, is wanting ; but even in this respect, there are other portions which leave nothing to be desired. The passage between Hirado and Kiusiu, by which a steamer may enter when coming from Nagasaki, or pass out from within, is very beautiful beyond question. Although not really dangerous to a well-handled steamer, it has quite sufficient of the appearance of danger to lend additional interest to the scene, as the waters rush foaming and whirling, in

PASS OUT OF THE SUONADA SEA

treacherous-looking eddies, past the naked rock lying in mid-channel, and but little above the surface, leaving a bare passage for a large ship. Some of the coast presents undoubted evidences of volcanic origin. Mountains rise high to an apex from their base, and sometimes form a perfect cone, as may be observed in a preceding sketch.

When approaching near Hiogo a very singular view
presents itself in a hill some twelve hundred feet high,
which forms a flat table abruptly ending on all sides.

We landed at one or two places in the evening when
we anchored, but nothing could well be poorer or more
miserable-looking than the few fishing hamlets we saw —
and not even fish was to be had, though fishing-tackle
and boats abound everywhere. The country near the
coast seems for the most part poor and barren, with
patches of cultivation only in the sheltered nooks and
valleys. There is a large traffic undoubtedly through this
Strait. When Admiral Hope came through, a little later
in the year, some 1,500 junks were met in the passage. It
was not until the noon of the fourth day that we arrived
before Hiogo, the termination of the voyage, so serious

NEAR HIOGO

had been the drag of three lumbering junks. There was
a sort of chuckle, and expression of undisguised satisfaction on the face of the boatswain when he loosened the
hawser and cast adrift the nearest junk, thus severing all
farther connection with such undesirable mates.

HIOGO

# CHAPTER VI.

### THE PORT AND THE CITY — HIOGO AND OSACA.

HIOGO is the shipping port of *Osaca*, the great centre
of trade in Japan, lying some thirty miles distant on
the banks of a river, the mouth of which is about five
miles higher up in the bay. Hiogo is itself a town of
some extent, containing perhaps 20,000 inhabitants, and
pleasantly situated along the edge of a sandy shore, with a
range of wooded hills and mountains rising with gentle
slope from 1,000 to 2,000 feet behind. Several fresh-water
streams open into the bay, and offer facilities the Japanese
have well known how to avail themselves of, for docks and
inner harbours. The Bay of Osaca stretches about twenty-
five miles across, and affords excellent anchorage, well
protected from all winds, except perhaps from between
north-east and south; and I imagine a very heavy sea
cannot set in from without. The bottom appears to be

stiff mud, and affords excellent holding-ground.  So good, indeed, that the 'Ringdove' could only weigh her anchor with great difficulty.   There is a general depth of about five fathoms, with four close to the beach, and no dangers are known to exist.   I am indebted to Mr. Watts, the master of H.M.S. 'Ringdove,' for these particulars showing the great eligibility of Hiogo as a port of trade, with easy access and secure anchorage.   According to existing treaties this was one of the ports yet to be opened to foreign trade, with free access to Osaca.   January 1863 was the period fixed, but the Japanese Government had long manifested the most urgent desire to have the period deferred ; and even intimated, not very obscurely, that our insisting upon a treaty right in this direction, could only lead to *disastrous consequences to them and to us.* I had a special object, therefore, in visiting both places, desiring to form a judgement from personal observation, of the value and eligibility of that which we were so earnestly required to give up under menace of some hostile outbreak ; and also of the state of popular feeling so constantly referred to as the great obstacle to all progress.

Two pieces of intelligence greeted me on landing, of rather contradictory tendencies ; the one that the *Bettos*, as the horse-boys and grooms are called, with my own horses, had arrived from Yeddo to facilitate my journey ; — the other that a Governor of Foreign Affairs, Takémoto Dzus-hono Kami, had been sent express by the Gorogio to meet us, and, as I immediately divined, to make another effort to turn us from our route, and especially from Miaco. Accordingly, we were scarcely landed before a message was received from Takémoto, with a request to know when we could see him ?   As it was nearly dark and too late to explore, it was arranged that he should come at once while dinner was preparing, and in a few minutes the principal envoy with his attendant satellites, ometskis, and scribes appeared.   ' The Great Council were full of anxiety and alarm for our safety.   The country was in a disturbed state ; information had been obtained of divers lonins being abroad ; two had actually been seized ;' and in a word, they begged us to defer our journey and return by ship. What I have told in a few lines occupied Také-moto more than an hour, especially as it was his business to press for our acquiescence, and neither I nor my colleague felt in the least disposed to yield, attaching little faith to the declarations of danger from attacks of 'lonins' and 'the disturbed state of the country.' This was such a stereotyped formula from the beginning, that had any attention been paid to it, no Diplomatic Agent could have taken up his residence in Yeddo, in the first instance, or being there, have ever left the courtyard of his residence. That there was some special ground for alarm on this occasion, and a real and specific danger to be encoun-tered, we had reason to know, only when it was too late. Beyond the usual vague tâlk of the lonins as a dangerous class, Takémoto had nothing to tell us apparently. Never-theless, he showed the greatest unwillingness to take a re-fusal ; and when at last, as it was getting late and dinner had long been ready, we induced him to take his leave, it was only with the promise that he should again pay us a visit in the morning. The next morning he came alone, and told us he did so, because he had something *important* to communicate of a confidential nature, which he had not been able to enter upon the preceding evening when so many were present. The information had reference to some negotiations going on for the marriage of the Tycoon with a daughter of the Mikado, and the healing of some differences which had disturbed the councils of the empire—for something of rivalry and antagonism still exists, it would appear, between the Sovereign *de jure* and the Tycoon who governs *de facto*. It was difficult to avoid some suspicion that the whole thing was merely got up — seeing the impossibility of turning us back by menace of personal risk ; in the hope that serious danger to the Government and political considerations would furnish an argument of greater cogency. Nor, if these

were their tactics, were they far wrong, as under all the
circumstances neither Mr. de Wit nor I felt justified in
taking it for granted that the whole history of the relations of the Tycoon or Mikado was a mere invention to
serve the end — or assuming the reality of such complications, to disregard wholly the representations of the
Government to which we were accredited. We consented,
therefore, to avoid MIACO in our route to Yeddo, the point
on which the Council had evidently felt most anxious.
And the readiness with which Takémoto accepted his
compromise as satisfactory, sufficiently proved that we
were right in our supposition, and led us to infer that all
the warnings of danger to ourselves by the way had no
other foundation. The main object of the mission had
been to prevent our going to the capital of the Mikado,
apparently; and the danger to which we were exposed
in the rest of the route, only the make-weight in the
argument. Yet in so far as anxiety for our safety was
concerned, it would appear the real and most imminent
danger lay there. What amount of truth there was in
the rest, or what the real cause of the anxiety to prevent
our entrance into Miaco, must remain doubtful. The
Dutch Commissioners had often passed through. It was
the regular route to Yeddo. True, when Mr. Donker
Curtius, the predecessor of Mr. de Wit, was last there,
after new treaties and relations wih Foreign Powers had
been entered into, and the Dutch Commissioner was no
longer the bearer of tributary presents to the Tycoon, but
the Representative of a Sovereign claiming equality, he
had observed an ill-disguised uneasiness and fear on the
part of his escort, composed of officers of the Tycoon.
They evidently had no authority there; and were not
without anxiety lest their own dignity or safety might be
rudely compromised. The officers of the Mikado, it appeared, were not slow in asserting the suzerainty of their
master; and the undoubted inferiority of any power or
authority emanating from the Tycoon, in whom they only
recognised the Mikado's lieutenant. The population, Mr.

Curtius thought, seemed imbued with the same sentiment ; and, at all events, quite disposed to be rude and turbulent towards the intruding strangers and their escort. Was it to prevent our having an opportunity of observing such things? Or merely a desire to prevent such tangible evidence of our existence in the country? Or, finally, fear of some collision where they would be helpless? It might be any of the three or all, in addition to the alleged political grounds as to the negotiations going on.

This diplomatic joust having ended, we proceeded to take a survey of the town. Near to our *hongen* or resting-place, there was a beach gradually rising from the water which would afford a fine site for any future foreign settlement. Whether the officer accompanying me divined what was passing through my mind, or really contemplated the opening of the port at the time fixed by treaty and wished to throw out a feeler, I know not ; but to my surprise he asked me what I thought of the site for a foreign location ; and I had no hesitation in telling him that I thought it excellent. As we pursued our route, I found all the shops shut, and the population either hid away in their houses, or confined to the streets which lay out of our road. It required a very vigorous remonstrance to put a stop to this singular mode of showing a town. First, it was for our protection; then it was a mistake which would not occur in future ; and at last, driven from all their positions, the orders were rescinded, the shops opened, and the people were allowed to attend to their business. Hiogo seems chiefly devoted to the making of *Saki*—large distilleries and warehouses line the sea-shore, all dedicated to this object. One of the former we visited, but found nothing save the machinery of empty barrels, &c. Nor did we succeed in getting any reliable information as to the process; but all the means and appliances were of the simplest kind for its wholesale manufacture. We passed through the town skirting the bay, on the shores of which were many slips for building large-class junks and boats, and a considerable number of

both were on the stocks.   Having traversed the town in
its length, we turned by the banks of what was once
a wide river, but chiefly remarkable now for the abundance of sand and gravel which filled its channel high
above the level of the town, and the absence of water.
We returned home through the main street, but without
seeing anything in the shops of much interest or novelty.
I observed on our way back a new kind of passion-flower ;
and a colossal nettle growing by the banks of the river,
which seemed to follow the usual merciful law giving
giants a harmless disposition.   Certainly its stinging
power was in no proportion to its size ;— for concen-
trated venom we must go to the smaller species, both
in the animal and the vegetable kingdoms.

The distance from Hiogo to Osaca by land occupied
eight hours, being called ten Re, but something over
thirty miles.   Nearly the whole way lay through the
slopes and valleys intervening between the sea and the
mountain range trending inland.   We had to cross a succession of rivers ; some over plank bridges almost too fragile
for horses.   One, my favourite hack, positively declined
(evidently remembering a former experience, when he
lost his footing and fell backwards with me into the stream
below), and after a couple of steps, deliberately leaped
off, preferring to take the bed of the stream, which ran
in shallows interspersed with sand-banks over a width of
some two hundred yards.   Others had to be crossed in
boats, and several were forded ; all were more or less filled
with sand.   One only, the main stream on which Osaca is
built, some miles higher up, had boats of any burden upon
it, and appeared fairly navigable.   We were now in the
middle of June ; the wheat was still standing ; the rice
was being planted out from the seed-beds.   The soil was
of the same sandy character as in Kiusiu.   We noticed
here for the first time a novel expedient for insuring
means of irrigation in a well, sunk at the corner of each
field, with the primitive beam and stone for a lever.   A
couple of hours before reaching Osaca, we entered on a

wide plain, the sea on one side, and the mountains on the other.  Here much of the corn had been carried, and some was still on the ground in sheaves curiously stacked on pegs standing horizontally out from a stout stake driven into the ground.  The cotton, planted on each side of the rows of corn as an alternating crop, was just appearing ; while on the raised borders along the road and round each field, little heaps of rice bran appeared at regular distances, and for some time greatly puzzled us. We learned at last that beneath each a bean was planted, thus turning to profit every inch of soil.  What part the bran played, I could not satisfactorily ascertain.  There were fields of broad beans, also, the crop nearly over ; and of *brinjalls* or egg-fruit, a vegetable in great request in Japan, and common also in China and elsewhere in the East, of a deep purple colour and pear shape.  Azalias in flower abounded on the sides of the banks and roads growing wild.  About an hour and a half's journey from *Misinomia*, near *Amaga Saki*, we passed a castle of great dimensions, with a crenellated wall, and surrounded by moats into which a river had been turned.  It stood in the midst of a large park enclosed within a wall.

## OSACA

we caught a first glimpse of, when about a league distant, with the Tycoon's castle on a wooded eminence commanding a view of the river.  This is said to be the best of the five which he possesses, and is celebrated in Japanese history as the place of refuge of the infant son of the renowned Täiko-Sama, who, although he successfully imposed himself as Tycoon on the reigning Mikado, and long held in subjection the Feudatories of the realm, was unable to transmit his dynasty even to his son.  So short-lived and transitory often are the triumphs and the dynasties of the greatest conquerors.  Alexander the Great, and Napoleon, were not more fortunate ; and in the

West as in the East, it seems easier to conquer than to
keep.    That which is won by violence or craft, is so often
lost by the same means.

We were nearly an hour in traversing the suburbs
of this vast city, before we seemed to gain the great
thoroughfare, filled to overflowing with an immense but
very orderly crowd.   There was pushing and squeezing,
and from time to time a desperate descent was made by the
police on some luckless wights in the front rank pushed out
of line.   Blows on the bare head were dealt furiously on
all; but the weapon was a fan, and although in their hands
a very effective one, it could hardly do much mischief.  We
came at last to the main river, spanned by a bridge of three
hundred yards, well and solidly built, immediately below
which there is an island covered with houses in the midst
of the stream, something like the island of St. Louis in the
Seine.   Not a trace of hostile feeling was to be seen anywhere, though the curiosity was great to see the Foreign
Ministers.   As they had never before known any but
natives of Holland pass through their city, I often had
the honour of being taken for a Dutchman, the word
passing from one to another, ' Hollanda Minister,' and
as there were two of us riding in front, they no doubt
thought we were *duplicates.*  Here, indeed, as might be
seen at a glance, was a vast population, with whom trade
was the chief occupation ; and at every step evidences of
the greatest activity were visible.   Piled up near the
bridge I noticed glazed tiles for drains, and large earthen
jars for coffins — the Japanese being buried as he lives
with his heels tucked under him in a sitting posture — an
arrangement which has at least the advantage of saving
space in the cemeteries, still farther economised by burning
the bodies of the poorer classes, and merely burying
their ashes in a jar of small dimensions.   The Japanese
have some strange superstitions about either sleeping or
being buried with the head to the north.   In every
sleeping-room at the resting-places, we found the points
of the compass marked on the ceiling ; and my Japanese

servant would on no account let my bed be made up in any but the right direction.

Osaca, its people, temples, and theatres, its trade and manufactures, were all objects of interest, but scarcely to be examined in detail during a flying visit. Nevertheless, as all veteran sight-seeing people know by experience, much may be crowded into a short space of time when there is urgent motive, and not altogether without profit. The city itself is admirably placed on the banks of a large river, which, as it takes its tortuous course through the valley, divides into many branches, farther multiplied by canals, and these and the town together, in loving companionship, spread themselves over an immense plain, filling up the whole space from the hills for many miles towards the sea. We were lodged in a large temple, at the opposite side to that at which we entered, and one with as much pretensions to architecture as can ever be seen in this land of earthquakes. The porch for the bell which Mr. Gower photographed is given as a fair specimen of the best.* The first day we gave up almost entirely to shopping and the theatre, reserving a second day to be spent in perambulating the city by water, much as in Venice, and for a visit to the largest and most celebrated of the temples, and the Tycoon's castle. The sun was unfortunately in full power both days, and the scorching heat of its rays as they caught us between the houses was very trying. But travellers seem generally proof against all opposing influences, so we toiled on, preferring in the morning the fatigue of walking to any means of conveyance, that we might with greater facility turn into the shops, where anything seemed worth purchasing or examining. We were taken to some silk shops which were on a large scale, larger it seemed than the largest in Yeddo, and the display of goods was in proportion. From fifty to one hundred people seemed employed, and there was no lack of promptness

* See woodcut, Vol. II. p. 280.

in producing whatever we required. The first prices
asked were high, and we gave an order in two shops, to
send a certain number of articles to our lodgings, from
which, afterwards, I made a selection of tapestry, em-
broidery, and silks, according to my feeble lights in such
matters feminine,--sorely perplexed, and deploring the
absence of those who could alone choose with taste
and judgement combined. I dare say I shall have the
satisfaction of finding that there is 'nothing to wear' in
all my purchases!* At all events, they could not utterly
fail as specimens of textile fabrics, so they were all
despatched to the Great Exhibition. Of bronzes I saw
little to compare with the choice there is in Yeddo and at
Yokohama, where foreigners create a large demand. A
very quaint and elegant hanging night-lamp, and an
elaborately carved *chaufferette* for charcoal, alone took my
fancy, and these, to my surprise, I obtained without
difficulty, at a moderate price ;—for, just before, we had
been in a lacquer-ware shop, where we found only a very
indifferent show, and the prices were something altogether
fabulous. Strangely enough, this was precisely what Mr.
Donker Curtius had recorded in his journal of most of
the articles for sale, but lacquer-ware especially. Either
the yaconins accompanying us had, as is their custom,
exercised a sinister influence, whether to keep up the
delusion the Government would fain make us accept as
reality, that Japan is a very dear country, and that our
dollar ought not to be taken for more than a third
of its weight in their silver coinage, or in a smaller
way to make their own per-centage out of the extortionate prices. Attempts were made to purchase some
little dogs also, for which everybody seemed to have
unlimited commissions ; but no one felt disposed to give
thirty or forty kobangs (from forty to fifty dollars) for
a little pug-nosed, goggle-eyed monster, which has no
merit, so far as I know, unless it be its extreme ugliness.

* This was written in Yeddo. I found on my return that most of the
silks had their admirers, who were ready to find a good use for them.

Ten guineas for such specimens seemed dear to the most
determined dog-fancier in the party.    We were more
fortunate in our search after porcelain and pottery, aided
a little by chance.   In passing through one of the streets,
a quaint grotesque-looking piece of earthenware attracted
my eye, and long before my yaconins could wheel from
the front, or come up from the rear embarrassed by the
crowd, I had both priced and appropriated it, and was
already deep in the farther recesses of the store, with a
perfect wealth of 'palissy' pottery, with raised fishes,
and fruit gathered about me, and for the most part
priced, when the obstructives arrived.   I think they felt
that for once they had been outflanked, and that any
attempt to retrieve lost time might expose them to a
worse defeat, and so abstained altogether, in disgust and
despair.    Certainly, this was the only harvest I was
enabled to secure.    Many of the objects were unique in
kind, and nothing like them could be found either in
Yeddo or Nagasaki.   Some very perfect eggshell china also
was picked up here ; and when we left there must have
been a great vacuum on the shelves.   They afterwards
took us to a porcelain shop of their own selection, where
we could find nothing worth bringing away, and the
prices were some fifty per cent. higher.

By this time we had perambulated half the city, and
having worked our way to the vicinity of the theatre, we
were not sorry to exchange our walk for a seat, and our
own performances as actors for the less fatiguing part of
spectators.   We had inquired at what hour we could go,
and the answer was, 'They commence at ten in the
morning, and finish at six in the evening.'   And thus, it
seems, they continue day after day for a week together.
Their repertory must be as inexhaustible as the patience
of the playgoers.   For it is not one piece the whole day,
but often a succession.   We arrived between ten and
eleven, and stayed about an hour and a half, during which
time a piece something like the ' Miller and his Men ' or
the ' Forty Thieves,' with a little coarse love-making, and

a great deal of murder and fighting were got through, apparently to the entire satisfaction of a numerous, if not a very nicely discriminating audience.

The play-house is a building of considerable area, and covered over by matting on a scaffold at a much greater height than they could venture, with the fear of earthquakes, to raise any roof of more solid materials or permanent character. The pit consists of a number of little square compartments, into which a party of six may find squatting or kneeling room. At the sides, a little raised, are what may be considered a series of boxes, separated from the pit by a raised platform extending the whole length of the building, from the entrance to the stage, along which the principal characters of the piece make their *entrées*, at the end opposite the stage. Some twenty feet above the heads of the lower tier of boxes is a 'shilling gallery,' and along each side a tier of boxes on the same level, which are reserved for those who pay a higher price. We could not learn exactly what was the usual price for the various places, but, doubtless, exceedingly low, although for our party twenty itziboos were charged, with the observation that 'such was the price paid by the Dutch.' Although we had broken the force of such arguments, yet in this particular instance, as it was due to the precedent that we were allowed to appear in such a place of entertainment, we were not disposed to question the cost. In Yeddo I had never been able to gratify my desire to see this illustration of national manners, because no person of rank can be seen in such places, and it would have been a breach of all rules of propriety for a Minister to visit a theatre. So, at least, we were assured by the officials about us; and as it was tolerably certain the usual audience at all places of amusement was anything but select, the attempt to judge for ourselves had never been made. But here it was the established custom for the Dutch Commissioner, on his way through, to go to the theatre; and, accordingly, profiting by the license, to the theatre we went.

The piece, as I have said, was of a melodramatic character, except that there was very little melody. The female parts, as in China, are all performed by boys or young men, but the *mise en scène* was very much less rude than I had expected to find it. There was a drop-curtain, a revolving platform generally representing the interiors, with side slides to complete the scenery, and at each act all these changed. To me the audience was the best part of the play, I confess. They consisted entirely of the middle and lower classes, and had evidently come together in families or groups to spend the day; bringing with them their luncheon in lacquer cases, with all the ingredients for a midday meal. Some of the more well-to-do parties either had it brought to them while the play was going on by their own servants, or probably sent from some eating-house, in the vicinity. One immediately beneath us had a whole fish of large dimensions served; and all seemed to enjoy themselves *sans gêne*, but also, it must be admitted, in a quiet and orderly way. There were all ages and both sexes mingled together, as well as many gradations of class evidently. I remarked a Bonze with his shaven head accompanied by his wife or concubine. These were soon joined by another party, and they formed one of the merriest groups. Many of the compartments were obviously filled by a family each. Father, mother, grown-up daughters, young brothers and sisters; and when the piece proceeded, and a scene of indescribable grossness was going on, it was marvellous to see with what entire unconcern man and woman, young and old, looked on, either with amusement or indifference, but perfectly unembarrassed, and with no sense of indecency or indecorum. Really these people in some of their aspects are altogether bewildering when we try to judge them by our canons of morality or taste. The plot of the piece was not difficult to follow. The first scene opens at an inn by the roadside where the master of the house is absent, and his wife and the rest of his feminine establishment appear discussing his expected arrival, which immediately takes

place, but he comes with a jaded and preoccupied air ; and
his spouse, like a true wife, naturally seeks to learn what
he has on his mind.  All her blandishments fail, however,
and he dismisses them, with orders to get the rooms
ready for some travellers that will speedily arrive.

The scene changes to a secluded spot close on to the
high road, where two men, one young and evidently the
master, and the other a confidential attendant, lead in
a baggage horse, with a valuable pack ; the horse being
composed of a skin thrown over two men's shoulders,
which, with the thermometer at 90°, must have been
anything but cool.  A certain want of harmony in the
movements of the fore and hind legs, was a source of great
amusement.  There is a tomb and a tablet some little way
back, and this was evidently the object of their journey.
He was paying homage to the manes of his mother, who
had been murdered on that very spot, and taking a vow
to avenge her death.  While thus engaged, they hear
persons approaching, and retire behind a clump of trees to
observe the new comers, who are two men of evil mien ;
and the chief of the two turning round, sees the perpendicular wooden tablet on which it is usual to inscribe the
name and virtues of the dead.  He no sooner looks at this
than, reading the characters, he tears the tablet from the
ground, and breaking it, scatters the pieces on the road,
revealing that he himself was the murderer.  While this
is proceeding a great deal of bye-play is going on between
the youth and his attendant,—the impulse of the former
being to rush upon the murderer, and perpetrator of this
second outrage ; but he is restrained by his faithful servant.
As the last comers pursue their journey, the youth and his
attendant come forward.  By this desecration of his mother's
grave he has discovered her murderer, before unknown,
and learns that he is the chief of a powerful band of
lonins.  He immediately renews his oath to exact retribution ; and the next scene shows the entrance of the
same inn, and the arrival of the travellers with their
baggage.  Two of the boxes appear to be treasure, which

attracts the attention of the host to a suspicious degree.
He is very officious in having it brought in, assuring the
guests there are many lonins about, and that the roads are
very insecure.  (Very much what *my* hosts the Ministers
had been telling me.)  And it appears he had the best
reason for knowing the fact!  Something about him arouses
the suspicions of the ever-watchful servant, and he warns
his young master to be on his guard, for as night is coming
on it is too late to think of moving, but he will himself
keep sentry at his door all night.  Left alone, the attendant is revolving in his mind how best to secure himself
against the treachery he anticipates, when one of the
waiting-maids peeps in, evidently seized with great
admiration for the comely stranger; and, after a time,
seeing him alone, she ventures softly in, and begins to
make advances.  At first, he is rather amused with the
naïveté of the whole proceeding, and the unhesitating
avowal of love that follows; but having far other thoughts
in his head, he gets at last importuned, and endeavours
with a present to get rid of her.  The parts of Tarquin
and Lucretia seem in a fair way to be reversed, and the
curtain drops a great deal too late, if a Japanese audience
were susceptible of being outraged by anything gross or
obscene.  Their standard, whatever that may be, is
evidently not ours, or husbands would not bring their
wives, or mothers their daughters, to such plays.  With
every disposition to be charitable, and making large allow-
ances for differences in national character and manners, and
the widest scope for the undefined margin of things conventional, making that innocent in one country which is held
indecent or immodest in another—things which vary in
different ages, even in the same country, and still more
widely in different nationalities—it is difficult to conceive
how anything of purity or sanctity can enter into the lives
of those classes, at least, where not only the sexes of all
ages frequent the same public baths promiscuously, but
young girls and respectable matrons find their recreation
in witnessing such plays.  It is true there are scenes in

French plays, as in M. de Pourceaugnac, pursued by the apothecary, which would not be tolerated on our stage, and would be thought to the last degree indecent ; yet, on the other hand, there are scenes in Wycherly's and Congreve's plays, and sometimes in more modern plays at the smaller theatres in England, which would quite as certainly not be tolerated in Paris, for the very same reason, that they would outrage the French sense of delicacy and decency.  Nothing is more variable, therefore, than the standard each nation and century establishes in this respect ; and it requires a large experience of mankind to avoid erroneous conclusions in applying the standard of one to gauge the morality of another.   But I confess my difficulty in Japan, is to discover what the Japanese standard may be, or whether they have such a thing ?  And yet some must exist, for a gentle womanly and modest expression and bearing generally marks the women ; and the well-conditioned among the men have a certain refinement and delicacy in their manners ; while there is much habitual courtesy, even among the lower classes, with a considera-tion for the feelings and susceptibilities of others, and an unwillingness to give offence, which cannot well be sus-tained amidst universal grossness, and a coarse unbridled license.

But the curtain rises again, and upon scenes which there is no doubt are the peculiar delight of Japanese, whatever the last may have been : deeds of valour and heroism, of bloodshed and self-immolation, the staple of nearly all their story-books, so far as I have been able to dip into them.   It is night, the lamps are lit, and the landlord with his wife are in front of their house, when two more travellers arrive, who seem especially unwelcome to mine host.   Under pretence that the watchman is not at his post, he despatches his wife with the lantern to go the rounds, and then approaching the new arrivals, begins to converse with them, when there is a sudden recogni-tion on their part, and they claim old acquaintanceship with their host.   They recognise in him a man who fled from their own district some years before to escape the hands of justice, and after in vain attempting to mystify them, he admits his identity, appears overjoyed to meet them, and goes to bring them some saké for their entertainment. Returning stealthily behind, he seizes each by the neck, and either strangles them, or dislocates their spines in the most expeditious and effective manner, flinging their bodies to one side, just as his wife returns to assure him that all is right.

The stage revolves and brings round the sleeping apartment of the young master, his faithful attendant evidently on the alert. He draws his long formidable-looking sword, poises it in his hands, feels its edge, and then lays it across his knee ready for action, while his master sleeps within. Another revolution of the stage and we have again the outside, and from the platform at the end of the pit a grand entrée is made by the chief of the brigands in a complete suit of brilliant armour, rolling his eyes in the most alarming manner, and making furious grimaces at the audience as he takes a stage step with a flourish of an enormous spear, all to the great delight of pit and galleries, who cheer him enthusiastically. Arrived on the stage he meets the inn-keeper (now seen to be one of the band), who begins by showing his night's work in the dead bodies of the two travellers, and then reports that he has a rich young lodger in the house, with his servant and two boxes of treasure. Of course it is immediately resolved that the band shall be mustered, the house apparently broken into, and the travellers robbed and murdered. Then follow the scenes of mustering—a great number of pompously-declaimed speeches from every one of some twenty lonins, swearing fealty to their chief, which stretch to such intolerable length that Mr. de Wit gets evidently uneasy, thinks it is breakfast time, and is bent on summarily finishing his part of the play. But our escort look so unhappy at the bare idea of going away at such a critical time, that we succeed, with some difficulty, in detaining him. The stage is darkened, and now a man appears over the edge of the wall surrounding the courtyard, who rapidly descends, and is followed by several others, when they rush to the house to force their way in.

As I write, I cannot help being struck with the strange fact, that I sat there in the theatre at Osaca, studying the manners and customs of the people I had to live among, and was actually seeing rehearsed a scene precisely similar to one in which I was destined very soon to be a chief actor myself, with some of its tragic results. But I interrupt the play.

As the lonins approached, the sliding screens of the room were suddenly thrown back, and the servant appeared, sword in hand, on the raised verandah which surrounds all Japanese houses, and fought valiantly, finally retreating in the direction of his master's room. There is a change of scene, and the master himself appears, not in his plain undress, in which it seems he had been travelling incognito, but brilliantly arrayed for battle with a surcoat of shirt mail, plumed helmet, and flashing sword, with which he did instant execution, cleaving down the assailants right and left; then leaping from his vantage-ground, he flung himself among them, and engaged the whole band by twos and threes in succession, with extraordinary grimaces and antics, evidently in the most approved popular style. He was already surrounded by heaps of slain, when the dreaded chief himself at last appears, and after giving vent to some expressions of strong disgust at the slaughter among his followers, he deliberately prepares himself for a desperate conflict, and certainly Astley's never saw anything half so grand, or so absurd. For a moment he retreats, after a long struggle, to draw breath, swearing, as he goes, that it is the devil and no man he is fighting with; and in the interval the landlord appears, and is laid on his back in a moment. Finally, in a renewed struggle the chief himself falls, and just as both are about to be finished, the wife rushes in, and falling at the feet of the victorious youth, implores for mercy.

Will it be believed that at this intensely interesting crisis, my colleague resolutely got up, and without any regard to our feelings, declared it was long past breakfast time, and he could not wait a moment longer! It was very hard, and I doubt whether Tarasaki, our chief officer, and still more Horu, the interpreter, ever quite forgave him. I confess I was myself anxious to know, as a matter of national morality, how the whole would wind up. Whether, notwithstanding the atrocity of the villains and the dire provocation offered the brilliant young hero, it would be more consistent with their code that he should exercise generosity, and, in pity to the wife, spare the husband, or with Rhadamanthine-sternness execute justice? And I am willing to think my readers also will thank me for some notice of the dénouement, and, if not, it will be very ungrateful; for it cost me an infinity of trouble to arrive at it, having them partly in view as an inducement to persevere. Well, then, it appears *justice* not *generosity* was the ideal of the illustrious author, and in a last speech the young prince declared to the weeping wife that, although he was very sorry for *her*, the crimes of both the delinquents were of too deep a dye to be pardoned; the first having murdered his mother, and then defiled her grave; and her husband having plotted the murder of his own guests; and so they were either killed on the spot or handed over to justice, for that part of the story I could never learn, and gave it up at last in despair. They are, like the Chinese, a theatre-loving people there is no doubt; and parties often remain and spend a whole day seeing either a succession of plays, or one interminable piece of ancient history, and wars and battles innumerable. Many of the fair sex too, notwithstanding the absence of all refined or elaborate scenic appliances, listen with breathless attention to heart-rending passages of love and murder, weeping bitterly. When at Nagasaki, one of the Dutch residents gave me an instance within his own personal knowledge of the simple and childlike faith with which they allow a conviction of the reality to take possession of them. A friend of his met one of the young females in his establishment coming in one day, in a state of the greatest trouble and grief, sobbing as though her heart would break. 'Why, what is the matter, *Hana*? (flower, a common female appellation) what has befallen you?' 'O! I am so miserable,' sobbed out the desolate one. 'They have killed him, they have killed him! that poor lover — the husband caught him and ran his sword through and through his body.' 'Who did? where was it, and what have you to do with it?' he asked, conceiving it was some domestic tragedy which had taken place in the neighbourhood, any lack of chastity of their wives being, according to Japanese law and custom, punishable by instant death. 'O — oh! at the play!' 'Why you little fool, it is all sham; he has not been killed at all, the fine gallant, and is most likely very busy eating his rice. 'Oh no! he *is* killed, indeed, indeed. I *saw* the sword go into his body as he fell.'

Refreshed by our breakfast at midday, we again returned in the afternoon to our exploratory shopping; but this time on horseback, and consequently much less successfully. The next day we devoted to the navigation of the thirteen rivers and canals which run through the city in all directions. Certainly this is the Venice of Japan. At least a hundred bridges span these various streams in every direction, many of them of enormous width and costly structure. The banks of the main river are lined for two or three miles with the residences of Daimios, with broad flights of granite steps descending to the water's edge. And although they will bear not the faintest comparison with the noble palaces of Venice, and are merely long lines of wall, pierced at intervals with rather imposing gateways, yet their number and extent alone give an impression of wealth and importance. Thousands of boats filled with merchandise or passengers cover the broad surface of the waters; and every bridge was crowded to an alarming extent by the population, eager to see the foreigners. In truth, the Japanese in general

seem to take life and its labours very easily, and are
never too busy to collect in vast crowds to see anything
novel.   I took a sketch of one of the guard-houses on the
banks of the river, while 'our special artist' was engaged on
a much more telling view of a bridge and the adjoining
houses looking up one of the branches of a river opposite.
In picturesque features it scarcely yielded to a river scene
in Italy.   The same glorious sun was over all, and the
quaint projecting roofs and irregularly grouped balconies
and verandahs, lent something of grace and originality
to supply the place of architectural beauty.

Later in the day we made an attempt to reach some
celebrated temple, and, in a moment of· misplaced
confidence in our treacherous escort, were induced to
abandon our boats at the hottest hour of the day, believing
the distance was short.   It proved a long hour's hot and
dusty journey; and when we got there, beyond a pile of
buildings round a large courtyard, and a rather ruinous-
looking square pagoda in the centre, there seemed to be
nothing to see, which we had not seen a hundred times
before in exactly the same forms.   I had indeed long
given up looking at temples in Japan ; for after seeing one
or two, it is like looking at successive negroes—nothing
but a familiarity of acquaintance, which you do not desire,
can enable you to distinguish any difference between
them.   It struck some one, however, after we had rested
a little, and vented our wrathful feelings on our guides
for having beguiled us into such an unconscionable and
bootless journey, that from the top of the pagoda we might
get a good view of Osaca and the surrounding country,
which in some degree would repay us our fatigue.   But
we reckoned without our host—that is, our officers—as
a very short colloquy satisfied us.

'What have you brought us all this way to see?' 'This
fine temple.' 'The temple, where is it? Do you mean the
outside of the walls?' 'There is nothing else.' 'What,
have they no insides?' 'Oh no! the priests live there.'
'Well, but that pagoda ; the Minister wants to see the

VIEW OF OSACA

view from the top.'   ' Oh, it is very unsafe, the stairs are broken.'   ' Unsafe is it?  well, I dare say you have never seen it; let us judge for ourselves.'   ' We have not got the key.'   ' But I suppose you can get it ?'   ' No, we cannot without an order.'   ' An order from whom ?'   ' The Governor of Osaca.'   ' Why don't you say the Governor of Yeddo ? it would be just as true, and more out of reach !'   *Cosas d' España !* a little piece of *yaconinerie.* Not that there could be any rational motive for making a difficulty, any more· than at Simonoséki in the case of Täiko-Sama's old rusty swords ; but there must be something in the nature of Japanese officials which makes them find a certain pleasure in creating obstacles, besides the opportunity it gives of exercising their inventive faculty in alleging reasons which have no existence ; and lastly carrying out the general policy of their Government, no doubt carefully inculcated, ' In all things be obstructive—the less the foreigners can do, or see, or know the better !'   A rule which has the great advantage of being at once comprehensive and simple.

By the time we returned, if we had not exhausted the objects of interest in Osaca, we had very nearly exhausted our own powers.   One gets wearied, too, with the never-ending struggle against the systematic obstruction and deception practised by those ostensibly placed under our orders for a totally different purpose.   We did indeed visit the smelting works for copper, the produce of the Government copper mines, where it is a contractor's business to extract all the gold and silver; but with lame interpretation, and no one either willing or able to give an intelligible explanation of the processes, or the usual per-centage of gold and silver, or indeed anything else, little of useful information could be gleaned.   As usual in Japan, all the implements and appliances seemed very rude, though they might be effective.

We had seen Osaca, and enough to be satisfied that, as regarded the population, there was no reason why access should be denied to foreigners; indeed, to us

Yeddites, the unwonted absence of two-sworded retainers lowering at us from every street and corner,
made it appear a most desirable place of residence.
And, on the other hand, as regarded the developement of a large and flourishing trade, this great centre,
with its port of Hiogo, must be worth more to foreign
commerce than all the other ports put together. Of
course these were all so many good and excellent reasons
for the Japanese Government, or any dominant party
of the retrograde Daimios, to oppose all access. And the
menace of civil war and revolution would be the most
natural argument for them to use as a means of deterring
foreign Governments, from insisting upon a measure which
would certainly go far to produce a social revolution, in a
sense adverse to all feudal privileges and government.

Capt. Craigie took leave of me at Osaca to return to
his ship, and I asked him to make such observations as he
could, in his passage down the river, as to the facility it
might afford for trade. He found it below the town clear
of bridges, and for the first mile and a half sea-going
junks were moored, two and three deep, on both banks as
close as they could lie, leaving a clear passage in the
centre stream, which he estimated at about 120 yards
wide. He had no means of sounding, but the junks
lying in the river, he thought, must have drawn, at least,
eleven feet of water. The river meets the sea at about
five miles' distance from the city, and has no difficult
turns. The current was running at the time he went down
about one and a half knots. He saw no indications of a
bar, although, judging by all analogy in Japan, one probably exists. This he imagined to be the entrance having
the deepest water, although, no doubt, from the flatness
of the surrounding country there are many other smaller
ones.

# CHAPTER VII.

OSACA TO YEDDO.

WE had purposed making an effort to see the palace of the Tycoon, it having the repute of being the finest of the five he possesses, though, so far as I can hear, it has never been inhabited by any of the present dynasty. But our Vice Governor and his yaconins probably saw some grave objection to so daring a project, and therefore devised such a walk to the temple—we were not per-

CASTLE OF OSACA

mitted to see either —as would effectually satisfy even *our* sight-seeing appetite for that day at least. If such

was their design, they succeeded perfectly.   It was probably by way of amends, that the next morning they led
us by a circuitous route out of the city, from which we
had an excellent view of the outer walls; this being very
generally what they consider showing a place.   The
sketch made on the spot perfectly conveys its general
aspect and situation from the road.

We were now fairly on our way to Yeddo—the last
division of the journey; and as we had consented to
abandon our visit to Miaco, we had to take a circuit to
avoid it, which led us through a part of the country
where probably no European had ever set his foot.   Certainly not since the days of the Portuguese and Spaniards.
It took us fifty minutes on horseback, at a walking
pace, to get clear of the city.   We emerged on to a wide
plain, covered with rice, wheat, and cotton; the cotton
and the wheat often sown on the same fields; the wheat
being ready to cut as the alternate row of cotton is coming
up.   The ground for both requiring to be drier than for
rice, is always raised, from a few inches to a foot, above
the level of the paddy fields.   The wheat was here nearly
all carried (it was June 19), and the rice for the most part
had been planted out from the seed-beds to the fields.
We passed innumerable hamlets and a large peasant
population — noisy enough in the villages — and having
gone on in advance of all our escort, we found them, for
the first time, disposed to be troublesome, vociferating
after us ' *Tojin, Baba* '— Chinese, trafficker, or merchant,
their only idea of a foreigner being that of a Chinese and a
merchant.   Tojin is their name for a Chinese, and Baba for
a huckster or trafficker, also for an old woman.   Boys and
even men followed us from village to village to keep up
the annoyance.   Some of the party wheeled round once
or twice, and a very sudden scamper to the rear relieved
us for a time, but only until they recovered breath and
courage again to pursue.   I confess I was not without
suspicion that they had been set on by our own people—
that is, the officers of our escort—who, for some reason of

their own, had desired to delay our departure another
day, and were very sulky at being compelled to resume
their journey at our time instead of theirs; for it was altogether unusual, to that extent at least, and never occurred
either before or after.

At the other side of the plain we came upon a mountain range finely wooded, and rising some four thousand
feet. The road, which was most picturesque as it wound
circuitously over the summit, made the ride in the early
morning (for we had started at five o'clock) very enjoy-
able. From the summit there was a fine view across the
whole breadth of the plain, and a valley on the other side
lay before us, bounded by another range of mountains.
As we toiled slowly up, leading our horses, we heard
some very sweet notes of the *unquissu*, not unlike the
notes of a nightingale, and I think nearly the only bird
in Japan that sings. It had one or two very sweet notes.
They say the Japanese teach them to sing beautifully,

JAPANESE WANDERING MINSTRELS

which is the more extraordinary, if true, as they certainly
do *not* teach themselves; and if I had not lived among the

Chinese, I should have said they had the least conception
of either harmony or melody of any race yet discovered.
The discord they both make, when they set themselves to produce what they call music, is something that
baffles all description. Marrowbones and cleavers are
melodious in comparison, and the notes they bring out of
a sort of lute or guitar, is something too excruciating for
endurance. And yet they make it a study, and there are
professional singers and teachers who as sedulously cultivate their art as any in Europe. The professors are often
blind; to judge by their performance I should have
guessed them to be deaf also — certainly the audience
should be. I have a native artist's drawing of one of
these blind professors teaching a female pupil to play a
stringed instrument, called the *samiseng*, in great favour,
apparently, with the Japanese.

At *Okasaki*, where we passed a night, some specimens
of porcelain were bought; this place having a special
celebrity for all such ware, so much so, indeed, that it has
given a generic name, and *mono-saki* means in Japan 'porcelain ware,' just as ' china' does with us. Some of the
white porcelain seemed very fine, and was surprisingly
cheap, compared with prices at Yeddo or Nagasaki. For
eleven itziboos, or about fifteen shillings, I had for my
share a large basketful; some of the contents both good
and pretty.

As we advanced to *Goicu* the next day, the country
began to be closed in with hills on each side the Tokaido,
a river winding through the valley. We met a cortége,
with some Daimio of unusual importance, apparently;
for a train of little sand heaps marked the road for
several miles, in testimony of respect, signifying that the
road was freshly swept and sanded for him especially.
So, even with ourselves, there generally ran before us a
couple of little ragged urchins, dragging their brooms
after them, and shouting as they went for an advertise-
ment to all whom they might meet, the magic word
which brings every Japanese to his knees, ' *Sh'tani-iro !* '

or, rather, this was the word which should have been articulated; but, in their mouths, it was transmuted into a sort of monotonous cry or howl, which we often took occasion to leave far behind us, by pushing our horses on. So, at the entrance of every *hongen*, or hostelry, when any one of rank is expected, a heap of sand on each side of the door is the accustomed mark of respect.

As we passed along the road, we often noticed at this part of our course, a boy or man with a stall for the sale of small articles of refreshment; and, occasionally, by his side, a sort of framework or gibbet, from which a row of tortoises were suspended by the middle in the air. The poor little animals, wanting the *fulcrum Archimedis* desiderated to move the earth, were vigorously ' beating the air with vain endeavour,' and plying their limbs in the most futile but persevering efforts to make some progress, and escape from such an unnatural position. The torment devised for Ixion by the implacable gods, of perpetual motion without progress, was never more effectually realised. I confess I looked on these unhappy prisoners, exiled from their native element, and condemned to a life of endless effort without result, with a strong fellow-feeling of sympathy, struck with the analogy of my own position as a Diplomatic Agent in Japan. Doomed, like them, to unceasing effort, without any very sensible progress; with the added consciousness of the inutility of all attempts to make way against the crafty policy of those who, affecting to observe the treaties, found means of always evading execution, and in their weakness, finding an element of strength. Do they not keep the Representatives of Foreign Powers suspended in an atmosphere of delusive promises and vain expectations, without the only fulcrum that could avail to insure execution and progress—Force, with Fear for a lever? This is the only true basis of all power perhaps, where love is not; but especially it is so in the East, where the obligations of good faith, irrespective of either fear or affection, has no existence when

conditions have been imposed upon them, which they
consider injurious, or find otherwise distasteful.  The
observance of treaties with Eastern nations, so long as
these are the results, in the first instance, not of their
own free-will and desire, but the fear of a superior
Power, can never be otherwise than a matter of compulsion, however the thing itself may be veiled by euphuisms
of moral pressure.  And, to compel where there is no
effective force exercised or compulsion used, is not more
a contradiction in terms, than the attempt to obtain the
end, without appropriate and effective means, is an
absurdity in action.  The Japanese, seeing only conciliation, and forbearance, and long-suffering on the part
of the Foreign Representatives accredited to them, acting
under the orders of their respective Governments, treat
very lightly all remonstrance.  Great Britain is habitually,—though not very consistently, perhaps, after forcing
political and commercial relations upon them,—most reluctant to resort to coercive means for the enforcement
of treaties; while other Powers are, naturally, not less
reluctant, in the absence of material interests.  And thus
the Japanese, it is to be feared, have begun to imagine
that nothing will induce any Foreign Power (unless it be
Russia, which they really fear,) to go to war, and involve
themselves in all the trouble and cost of hostile operations at such an immense distance.  Thus fortified,
they play out their game of cross questions and crooked
answers, with imperturbable *sang froid* and untiring
vigour.  Under such circumstances, are not Foreign
Ministers at Yeddo much in the case of the unhappy
tortoises, and suspended, like Mahomet's coffin, between
heaven and earth; do they not give themselves an infinity
of trouble, to exceedingly little purpose, beyond that of a
sense of unutterable weariness at the end of each day.
Poor tortoises! I would gladly have purchased the whole
stock in hand, and given them their liberty; but I reflected, that if even those individual units were released,
they would immediately be succeeded by others under

precisely similar conditions, and it would, therefore, merely be to shift the burden on other shoulders, without any diminution of the sum of misery ;—and so I passed on my way, moralising how little good one can certainly effect in this world, even with the best intentions!

After descending the mountain, and traversing a wide valley, with the same crops growing as in the one we had left, we reached *Narra*, our sleeping-place. The day following we started again, soon after daybreak, for *Kasangi*, the next stage, which was said to be only three Re (or about eight miles), but it proved a good fifteen ; by which we acquired the experience, that long as the Japanese have been striving after a perfect uniformity, they are as far from success as Charles V. in the regulation of his watches, and have not even succeeded in preventing a very considerable diversity in the length of their Re in different parts of the country.  As they have two kinds of mat—one for the temples, and the other for the laity—and fans and mats are the units of all their measurement, if these vary, there is an end of unity!  A fan in Japan is little more than a foot English, and a mat is *usually* calculated at six in length.  It is to be presumed there are two standards of measurement in these, at least.  If this was temple measurement, all I can say is, that it was a very liberal one.  Fortunately, I had now my own saddle-horses, making that a pleasure which previously was an intolerable fatigue.  Nothing could exceed the picturesque character of the country through which our way lay this morning.  We rode through defiles of mountains, amidst a very chaos of hills and ravines ; the former tumbled wildly together, looking like a troubled sea of billows suddenly petrified.  It must have been the theatre of some long extinct volcanic action ; and, for miles, half filled-up craters seemed the leading feature.  The same sandstone formation, so constantly observed in Kiusiu, reappeared, and as the sun poured a flood of light upon the whole amphitheatre, it only seemed to make the desolation more clear. This was the circuitous route adopted, in order to leave Miaco to the left, which compelled us to take a cross-road, only some five or six feet in width, winding round the base of the hills, to a river of the same name as the town we were approaching. Here, for the first time, in little sheltered nooks and valleys where cultivation could go on, tea bushes were observed forming a border or hedge to the wheat and cotton fields. We came upon a patch or two of tobacco also, before reaching the river which ran through the valley, broad, rapid, and shallow. We crossed, with our horses, in boats; and on the opposite banks, a little farther on, we found our halting-place for the noon meal. A château of the Prince of Itzi was nestled into the face of the hill opposite us, which Mr. Gower succeeded in photographing, but is scarcely worth reproducing, for the Daimios' houses are something like themselves; there is little to be learned from the exterior.

Here, too, for the first time, we observed, not a ' *rope of sand*,' but a rope of boulders or paving-stones, which was worthy of all admiration for the simplicity of the contrivance, its cheapness and efficiency. It consists of a cylinder of variable length, some two feet in diameter, made of split bamboo woven in wide meshes, only just too small to allow the escape of a good-sized pebble, such as the streams roll down from the hills. And with these filled to any length required, they build up dams, and bank up rivers to resist the force of the stream. The only cost is that of the split bamboo, the cheapest of all their products, and the labour, the next cheapest article, required to make it into this sort of net, and fill it with stones; the last cost nothing but the trouble of picking them up. Here is an illustration, which I begged the artist would give me, of a device so ingenious that I could not help thinking, had the scene of the great wizard's exploit been Japan instead of Scotland, he might not have had such an easy victory over the devil, when he fairly

baffled satanic ingenuity by setting him to weave a rope
of sand.

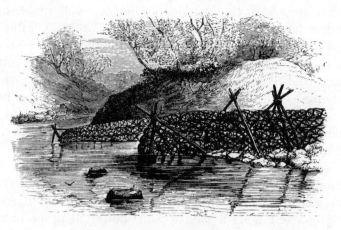

A ROPE OF STONES

Our baggage and commissariat were long in coming up,
and a four hours' ride made some refreshment desirable,
so we had a Japanese breakfast served.   It consisted of a
series of little dishes, some very nice, and others much
the reverse, to my taste.   But it was very daintily served.
Each of us had our own tray raised about a foot from the
ground, and three dishes, one of bamboo-root sliced, a
delicacy when stewed tender ; salt fish; a bowl of rice
with soy and divers lesser condiments, with a flask of
saki to aid digestion, all for the extravagant sum of three
tempos, or as nearly as may be, three pence.   As I looked
across the river at this country house of the Daimio, I
found myself speculating on the kind of life men of that
class led.   What were their occupations and amusements?
how did they bear the 'burden and mystery of this life'
without weariness, or being a prey to mortal ennui in the
absence of any absorbing interest or undergrowth of
small pleasures?   This speculation has often recurred to
my mind.   They are not permitted any social intercourse
with their own class.   None but blood relations may
visit each other.   So at least the Ministers have assured

me, when taxed with an offensive and hostile attitude in excluding the Foreign Representatives from all social intercourse with the Daimios. One can well understand such a law having been made by Täiko-Sama, after he had broken the spirit and reduced the power of all those banded in arms against him, as a safeguard against future plots and conspiracies;—and that the dynasty which superseded his own should from motives of policy have continued to uphold the same jealous system. But its effect on the social and intellectual life must be withering. It is cunningly strengthened by a purely conventional creed, which attributes inferiority to whichever of two Daimios or officers pay the other a visit. It is easy to conceive how powerfully this comes in aid to prevent all social intercourse among a class of punctilious and proud nobles, all claiming equality of birth and privileges. But this only makes it the more difficult to understand how their time is passed. Some plotting and attempts at combination do go on notwithstanding, as we have had tolerably clear evidence in the political troubles, which have taken place since the treaties with Foreign Powers were first entered into. A little treasonable plotting between factions, some in communication with the Mikado (not quite so entirely shut out from objects of sublunary interest as has been represented), to weaken, control, or depose the reigning Tycoon, must be a precious resource against a *tedium vitæ*, which otherwise would make mere existence a grievous burden! Then the compulsory residence six months every year, or each year alternately, at Yeddo, under more active surveillance; and the long journey there and back, must come in aid to kill time — for the existence of a grievance may even help to save them from utter stagnation. Some among the more able, restless, and powerful, may doubtless exercise direct influence over the councils of the Tycoon, and the policy or action of his Government; and now that the whole country has been moved to its centre, and the elements of change and disorder let loose by the new relations with

Foreign Powers, they may find a sufficiently exciting occupation in politics. But with all this, as they are several hundreds, there must be many wholly excluded from this redeeming excitement and field of exertion. The question, therefore, still recurs — What do they do with themselves and their time? They have a wife and are unlimited in the number of concubines, within doors. They have large or small territories and estates, which must be managed, and subjects which must also be taxed — and governed. No doubt that must afford some interesting occupation. But I cannot learn that they hunt or enter into outdoor or active occupation, or recreation of any kind. And to pass day after day, and month after month, inside their own houses and parks, we know in England and elsewhere, requires no ordinary amount of philosophy, and a very unusual frame of mind, to bear for a continuance — even with the sweetest wife and the liveliest children man can be blessed with. And I do not suppose multiplying the number of either, would materially improve the conditions. Altogether it has always been to me a very puzzling question, which nothing but a month's residence in the interior of one of these country houses could ever satisfactorily solve.

On the third day after we left Osaca, a deviation was made from the settled programme for our halting-places for the night, at the earnest desire of the Vice Governor and his brother officers. The grounds given for the change were as frivolous and unsatisfactory, as are usually any reasons given by Japanese officials. But as one never expects they will tell their true motives, one learns to regard those actually produced as mere forms, and to decide on other grounds. They said *Saki*, the place proposed, was more convenient—that it was nearer, which was undeniable — that all the houses fit for our reception at *Nieno*, the place originally marked for the night's halt, were under repair, &c. We took it for granted they had some good reason of their own, since they gave themselves so much trouble to alter the arrangements, and acceded to their proposal. But the next morning we reached *Nieno* in about an hour, and saw abundant reason for concluding that not only the motives put forward had no foundation, but that some other and urgent reasons existed which they had carefully concealed. In the first place, as to the houses being under repair, we found it was the Daimio's capital, and a very large place, while the town we stopped at was little better than a hamlet. As we advanced through the streets, we found every house and side street hermetically closed; not a whisper was to be heard, nor the face of a living being to be seen! The side streets were all barricaded and shut out of view by curtains spread on high poles. His own house, which we passed, was similarly masked by curtains. What did this extraordinary manifestation mean? Even in the adjoining villages, no women or children were to be seen. Information from our officers was hopeless. A series of evasions and fabrications, one more absurd than the other, was all that could be got from them. 'It was no doubt an order of the Daimio *Todo-idzu-mino-kami*, Prince of Itse and Isan — but perhaps it was only the act of his officers — it might be a sign of respect — or merely a mistake — it *might* also,' as they were fain to admit when pressed home, 'be a sign of anger and enmity.' Such was the construction put upon it by our servants, from whom the truth was much more likely to be got, so far as they knew it. The mystery remains unsolved to this day; no similar greeting awaited us anywhere else, only in all places where a Daimio's principal residence was, I observed we were jealously barricaded out of all but the main streets. Once or twice it was noticed, and of course we were assured it was for our protection and a proof of the anxiety to prevent all danger, or our being molested by the crowds. It *might* be so; it was very hard to prove the negative; and in our absolute ignorance of the country, and what actual danger or necessity for precautions might exist, it would obviously have been both injudicious and inexpedient to take any action in the matter. But it was impossible not to perceive that

the 'free right to travel through the empire,' especially
stipulated in all the treaties as the privilege of Diplomatic
Agents, was effectually limited by the several Daimios, with
the connivance of the Tycoon's officers, *to the high road.*
I think this gave me the first clear insight as to the actual
relations established by the treaties entered into on the
part of the Tycoon. He had made treaties, but the
Mikado had never ratified or sanctioned them, and the
*Daimios could not therefore be compelled to observe them.*
Without the Mikado's imprimatur they were binding and
obligatory upon no one out of the Tycoon's territories —
the ports opened to foreigners and the capital of Yeddo —
and not upon the Daimios and *their* subjects even at Yeddo!
For when these came within the limits of districts wholly
under the sway of the Tycoon, they made no scruple in
offering insult, or wounding and slaying the treaty-gua-
ranteed foreigner. The Western Powers had not made
treaties with the Empire or its Sovereign — but with the
Tycoon only reigning in five imperial ports with their
adjoining districts. Later, when I returned to Yeddo,
and startling events brought the whole question of
the Tycoon's powers under discussion, I found full
confirmation of the correctness of this view of the basis
of treacherous quicksands, on which our actual relations with Japan rest. Notwithstanding the affirma-
tion of the Ministers of Foreign Affairs, that the Mikado
had ratified the treaties, I think there can be little
doubt that, to this day, they want the sanction of the only
recognised Sovereign of the Empire. And this supplies a
key to much of the vacillation and weakness of the executive under the Tycoon's authority. They are paralysed by
the want of legality in the treaties, which they are nevertheless constrained to make a show at least, of executing
in good faith. Hence their confessions of compulsory
regard to ' public opinion,' of the impossibility of efficient
action contrary to it—and their last *petitio ad periculum* as
well as *ad misericordiam* — to be released from the clauses
which stipulated for the opening of Yeddo on January 1,

1862, and three more ports, Neagata, Hiogo, and Osaca. The riddle thus read leaves little farther to explain in regard to the jealous obstruction encountered through all the Daimios' territories. Of the sort of levee which, despite all these jealous precautions, attended us in all the larger towns where we halted, Mr. Wirgman, in the sketch facing, has given a very graphic picture. Not only the people, but the architecture of the streets, the costumes and characters of the population, are all equally faithfully rendered. This was taken at *Odah*, and shortly after leaving it he took an equally faithful view of village life and architecture on the roadside, with the women beating out their corn, wielding vigorously the most simple of flails. In passing through these primitive habitations, the traveller is often reminded of the scriptural warning of two women at the mill, precisely the same scene occurring which must have been present to the mind of the speaker when the prophecy and the warning were uttered. Two women standing at the same primitive stone mill— grinding the rice, by alternating action in each. These villages, as I have observed, are rather poverty-stricken, even in Nipon; and the interiors of the thatched cottages do not really promise much beyond mere shelter for man and beast, and not much better for the one than the other. Except a raised platform or matted room, where all the family, no matter how many in number, or of how many generations composed, must be huddled together at night, there is no provision for comfort, placing that at the lowest standard — and nearly as little for decency. The back yards are cumbered and dirty. The entrances, and even the mud floors by the side of the raised matted room, seem habitually resorted to, where there are young children, for purposes one would have thought the least refined or cleanly people might have objected to as unsightly and filthy. This is the more extraordinary, as it is in striking contrast to a great love of order and cleanliness in some other respects. In the larger establishments there is a separate kitchen

—by far the most picturesque part of the building. Here I used generally to seek the artist, when I failed to find him in the front, making one of his wonderful street sketches. It is vast and gloomy, with rafters blackened in the smoke, not cribbed and cabined in chimneys, but allowed free circulation. Here all that are not 'gentle' in blood or pretension generally congregate,— men and women; and every variety of occupation goes on harmoniously together, from cooking, eating, and chattering, to washing, bathing, and sleeping. A sketch of one of these interiors has already been given; but here is a very good type of the best-looking of the daughters

of the house—in such an establishment, generally sold to servitude for a term of years; a course, perhaps, less essentially differing from our apprenticeship than we might at first suppose.

Our way lay for many days through mountain scenery and fertile valleys, the hills generally clothed to the very summit with trees, chiefly of the pine family. The same sandy character of the soil, and the formation of the hills already noticed, continued until we approached within sight of Fusiyama, when it was exchanged for the dark rich mould which alone is to be seen within a hundred miles of Yeddo. Among the trees, the box of tolerable growth seems abundant; my attention was drawn to the fact by hearing that for artistic purposes the supply hitherto received chiefly from Turkey was beginning to fail. There might be a resource here against any dearth, but whether the Japanese Government would not look with alarm upon any attempt to export their woods, and take efficient means to prevent it, is more than I can undertake to say! I think it is very probable; for in proposing to the Government that they should furnish me with samples of all their woods to send to the Great Exhibition, I said that, *if they chose*, as they were rich in woods, they might find in their export a source of national wealth. They did send some twenty-six specimens, but I observed that any attempt to get at the prices was steadily evaded by the officers, who were careful to observe that they were generally *very scarce and dear.* In truth, there can be no free developement of trade in Japan, while the Government regards commerce with foreign countries as a detriment and a source of national impoverishment, instead of bringing prosperity and increased wealth. Their political economy and their policy must both change; and the one must precede the other, I fear, before foreign trade can be placed on any assured or permanent basis; — but nations and governments are difficult subjects for education, and usually uncommonly slow at learning a new lesson, especially the former, when the object is to build up, and not to pull down.

As we were approaching *Kamogawa* we passed a castle with moats and a crenellated wall, both apparently of great extent. I had ordered an express to be sent from Yeddo, to meet me at Miaco if a mail arrived, and although a courier had been sent to that city with orders to forward any despatches by the route I was now taking, I did not feel quite sure that there might not be some mistake. While meditating on the chances of their being detained at Miaco, or otherwise missing me, I saw two men stripped to their loin-cloths approaching at a quick trot, one of them carrying over his shoulder a carefully-secured packet, and everyone instantly getting out of their way. I immediately recognised by these signs an express with Government despatches, and for a moment hoped they might be mine; but without deigning to look at us, they sped swiftly on, and I had the greatest difficulty, by sending

JAPANESE POST — AN EXPRESS

a mounted officer after them, to get an answer that they were an 'Imperial express carrying despatches to the Government at Miaco.' Even this was not altogether satisfactory, for as the express courier who would have my own would be sent to Miaco by Government officials; and suppose he was carrying Government despatches, they might still be my unfortunate letters that I had seen speed past me. It was not until many days later, when a mail actually reached me from Yeddo, that I could assure myself on the subject. These couriers will travel in this way—being relieved at short stages and always going in couples, to provide against one meeting with any accident—at a very swift rate. From Yeddo to Nagasaki or Hakodadi, if not stopped by stormy weather in crossing rivers or bays, they will go in nine days a distance of some 350 Re or 850 miles; and may generally be depended upon both for punctuality and trustworthiness. I only know of one case where a courier of my own between Kanagawa and Yeddo mysteriously disappeared with an English mail; and I never was able to obtain either satisfaction or information from the Government. For such a journey as that to Nagasaki, the expense is usually twenty cobangs, or six pounds sterling, when express.

On the fourth day we had struck into the ordinary route, and had the advantage of the fine sanded roads and park-like avenues of the Tocaido. And now each day we met one or more cortéges of Daimios coming from the capital. As a general rule we had nothing to complain of; if some of the principal officers and armed retainers scowled at us, and seemed to think our presence on the high roads an offence, the greater number passed on their way, as we did ours, without any expression of feeling or opinion. In one case only, I was amused by a somewhat characteristic trait. Mr. De Wit and I were riding abreast and without any escort, having left them far behind, when, seeing rather a large cortége filling up the road as we turned an angle, we drew to one side of the road and went in single file. No sooner did the leading officer observe the movement, than he instantly began to swagger, and motioned all the train to spread themselves over the whole road; so that all we gained by our consideration and courtesy, was to run the risk of being pushed into the ditch by an insolent subordinate.* Thus it ever is in the

---

* The late savage and murderous attack on the high road by Prince Satsuma's people, is a sinister commentary on the chances we ran on the road, the circumstances were so closely parallel.

East.    To yield the wall is a sign of weakness ; to yield
in anything spontaneously is to provoke oppression ;   and
they who, from courtesy, step aside, are fortunate if they
do not get trampled down for cowards or fools.   This
is why the East is a bad school for teaching moderation.
There are but two classes clearly marked, the oppressors,
and the oppressed, and the only choice too often seems
to lie between them.

As we advanced through the country, men and women
both were all busily employed in planting out their rice.
This was the first time I had  seen any but isolated cases
of women being engaged in field labours in Japan ; for the
Japanese appear to me to be honourably distinguished
among nations of a higher civilisation, in that they leave
their women to the lighter work of the house, and perform
themselves the harder out-door labour.   Indeed at first I
was in some doubt here, for it was by no means easy to
distinguish the women from the men at a little distance,
with the heads of both covered, as the former were
travestied.  To guard the legs probably from leeches, as they
paddled in the mud, they all wore gaiters up to the knees,
and short cotton trousers.   When the neck was covered,
there was no very distinguishing difference between the
sexes, as the men never have any hair about the face.
Some of the ground was still under the plough ; a light
wooden frame with an iron-pointed ploughshare, drawn by
a small pony, turned over the soil with ease, though not very
deeply, nor is deep ploughing required, probably.  In some
fields they were ploughing in weeds and vegetables, apparently as manure.  Some of the ground had been put up in
ridges, and many were engaged, after it had been flooded,
in levelling them into the water.  The wheat in Japan
never appears to be sown broad-cast.  All that I have
seen has been drilled and planted in rows, much as the
rice is, a few stalks together.  Labour is cheap, and it is
to be presumed they find this the more profitable way.
The cape jasmine, one of the few flowers that has any
scent in this country, was everywhere in blossom in the

hedges and about the cottages, and so was the privet. As we moved through town after town, and village after village, in our daily journeys, I observed a good deal of ophthalmia ; blind people not unfrequently also. And among the children, scald-head is very common ; a disease generally held by the faculty to have some association with dirt. And the children do look dirty, despite the many washings they must undergo. But the truth is, people of the lower classes in Japan herd, and sleep, and bathe so promiscuously huddled together, that if there be any disease communicable by contact, they cannot fail to spread it. They seem to have a very inveterate form of itch, which Dr. Pompas in Nagasaki assured me was not to be cured by the ordinary treatment in Europe — yellow soap and sulphur it defies ; and it is disgustingly prevalent, so much so, that it is difficult to get domestic servants free from it.

As we approached *Mia* on the bay of Owari, we passed another great castle. And yet this phraseology is very likely, I fear, to mislead any reader. What constitutes a Daimio's château or castle, then, in Japan, is first a moat surrounded by a wall, generally built of mud intersected with layers of tiles, and plastered over ; sometimes with parapets and loopholed for musketry. A large gateway with massive overhanging roof ; a straggling group of ignoble-looking lath and plaster houses inside, rarely more than one story high ; and sometimes, if the owner is a Daimio of very great pretensions, his walls will be flanked with turrets ; and in his grounds, something like a two or three storied square pagoda will rise above the dead level of the other roofs, and look picturesque through the clumps of fine timber, with which the grounds of the owners are always graced, whatever else be wanting. *Kawana* is a place of some consequence, and might in the event of hostilities become an important position as a base of operations. It lies at the head of the gulf forming the Bay of Owari, which we had to cross over to reach *Mia* on the opposite side where the Tocaido recommences. We were six hours in performing the transit, but a violent thunder-storm, with rain, drove all our boatmen under cover, and, as is their habit under similar circumstances, they cast out their anchor, and took to their rice and pipes for a couple of hours.   The distance across is seven Re—say twenty miles.   The castle at Kawana is the property of Mat-zudaira Etchinno Kami, in the province of Sesein, and, to judge by the circuit of the walls, must be of unusual importance and magnitude.   They are washed for nearly two miles by the waters of the bay, and could easily be assailed from the water face.   They somewhat later objected to our surveying-vessels going near this bay on some plea that it was Mikado's territory, and *he* had objected.   I believe it was a mere pretext to prevent our gaining information, they did not think it desirable we should have.

And here, or at *Mia*, I should probably have ended my journey overland, by giving rendezvous to the 'Ringdove' to take me up in the bay; for notwithstanding many objects of interest on the road from day to day, the mode of travelling, especially in a party with a large attendance of servants and Japanese officials, is so wearisome, the rate of progression so slow; and the sort of camp fashion of living, with noise and clamour and confusion reaching from the courtyard and servants' offices to the sleeping rooms late into the night, and beginning long before daybreak each morning, becomes by constant repetition and iteration, irksome enough to make a fixed habitation and something like peace and tranquillity seem very desirable.   But my colleague was very unwilling to abridge his journey.   I think he deemed it a duty to do as all his predecessors had done before him, and as all the arrangements, even to the cooks and batterie de cuisine, had been made in view of the whole party continuing together to the end; I was compelled, somewhat reluctantly I confess, to continue as I had begun, and abandon all idea of cutting a long journey short.

The capital of *Nangoya* in the province of Owari lies

only three Re from *Mia*.  It is said to possess the highest
palace in Japan, but as it lay that distance off the Tocaido
and our direct route, any proposal to visit it without
previous negotiation with the Tycoon's Government,
and the consent of the Prince in whose dominions it was,
we had now had sufficient experience to know, was out of
the question ; and we wasted no time, therefore, in vain
efforts.

Between Mia and Ocasaki we passed through a clean,
flourishing, well-to-do little town called *Arimatz*, celebrated
in Japan for the manufacture of a peculiar stuff for ladies'
dresses.  It was certainly the most *comfortable* looking
town we had seen ; and we stopped to buy several
specimens, which, on the principle already intimated of
doubt as to my own capacity for choosing what might be
deemed wearable by my fair countrywomen, were duly
despatched after the silks and tapestry, to the Exhibition,
to take their place in the class of ' textile fabrics ' from
Japan.

The whole road to Ocasaki is a beautiful sanded
avenue, through an open country, though always with
hills or mountains in the horizon.  All level ground in
Japan would seem, indeed, but circumscribed plains or
valleys of variable dimensions, in great contrast to the
dead level and all but boundless plains of the great river-
courses of China.  Villages and towns follow in quick
succession ;  and rarely at a greater interval than one or
two leagues at farthest, along the whole route from
Nagasaki to Yeddo.  It is not always safe to judge of the
extent of population in a country from what we see along
the great trunk lines of communication and traffic,
whether by water or land ;  but, so far as a judgement
may be formed of the rest of the country which we did
not see, by what actually was seen, the population must
be quite as dense as it has been represented by Kœmpfer
and the Dutch writers.  At *Arai* we had to take boat
again, and the Prince of the place graciously gave us his
own lacquered boat for our passage across.  This is a

frontier station, like those in the passes of Hakoni, where a vigilant watch is kept on all who pass to and from Yeddo. And the better to enforce this, there is some rule that no one may pass the guard to the strand except on foot; from which, as Foreign Representatives attended by an escort of the Tycoon's, we were entitled to be exempt. And, although this was admitted, our head officer had very nearly succeeded in getting our horses embarked, while we rested to let the boats be got ready. Of course, it would have been 'the mistake' of some irresponsible menial, for which our really responsible officer would have been 'profoundly sorry,' with an inward chuckle that we had been outwitted, and compelled to pass through their caudine forks! We crossed the Bay of *Maisaca*, a distance of one Re, rather less than a league; but the whole way nearly in a sort of canal, most ingeniously engineered between two breakwaters, stretching right across the middle of the bay; advantage, apparently, having been taken of some sandbanks or islands, on which pine trees are growing. As we neared *Maisaca*, a great line of breakers out to seaward, marked a reef which would seem to close the bay.

The next day we breakfasted at *Hamamatz*. The road was still a well-sanded avenue, only interrupted at intervals by pretty, rural-looking villages, with fine clipped hedges, made of a species of pine-tree. The only thing which marred the Arcadian effect of the whole, strange to say, was the female population; and their faces, despite black teeth and red paint, were by no means the ugliest or most repulsive features about them. Really, considering what absolute and arbitrary power is exercised by Tycoon and Daimios, one is inclined to regret, if not to wonder, that there has never been an edict making it a high crime and misdemeanour for the fairer part of the population to appear without a vest, after sixteen years have passed over their heads. It is hard to say which would gain most, the men or the women; but, very

assuredly, there would be great gain and benefit to all
parties! I noted Hamamatz in my diary of the journey
especially, with red chalk, '*half-way.*' Happy day!
Decidedly, the journey was getting tedious ; and that my
narrative of it may not incur the same condemnation, I
shall very briefly touch upon what yet remained to be
seen.

Immediately after leaving *Hamamatz*, we had to make
our way across a plain traversed in all directions by
rivers and flooded watercourses, swelled by the rains,
and these had broken the bridges and dilapidated all the
roads. One of the villages we passed through was
entirely devoted to straw shoe-plaiting ; and, notwithstanding the enormous consumption there must be, it
evidently was not a trade on which people could grow
rich. It was, in truth, the most wretched and poverty-
stricken village I have ever seen in the country. They
all looked like beggars' hovels. The following day our
route lay over a range of mountains, with scenery finer
in character, and more massive and wild, than any we
had seen for many days. At *Cakengawa* they are
celebrated for weaving a kind of linen from the bark of
a creeper. I brought away some specimens, both of the
fabric and the raw material. Rain coats are made of the
same bark unwoven, and only slightly plaited, and these
are highly esteemed as both light and impervious. In
descending the hill, our attention was called to a great
boulder in the middle of the road, which is said to mark
the spot where the murder of a woman was committed in
revenge ; and every night, I was gravely assured, the
stone weeps!

Arrived at the banks of the river lying between
Kanaya and Okabe, it was found impassable by our
chief yaconin. The next morning, however, its passage
presented no difficulty, and we descended into a valley
almost entirely filled up with the pebbly bed of the
stream, nearly a league across. The stream, itself, rushing over this wilderness of stone, was not, in the largest

branch, above 200 yards wide ; but unusually deep, for our bearers were sometimes up to the shoulder, and as a false step would have precipitated norimon and passenger into the troubled stream, without a possibility of deliverance— since the norimon would have acted as a trap to drown one in — it was rather a nervous operation.  However, as our yaconins trusted themselves in such ready-made coffins, it was scarcely fitting that we should show less hardihood ; and so, trusting in Providence and the sturdy porters, we did as the rest, and were safely landed, while our horses breasted the current and swam across.  It was an admirable subject for a sketch, and even a photograph was taken.  This river, *Oigawa*, an abbreviation for *Oki gawa*, or great river, affords endless material for native artists and illustrations.  The women of the poorer classes are carried across on the men's shoulders, and as the men are themselves nearly immersed in the water, it follows that their burden below the waist cannot be very dry ; but, in Japan, such difficulties are easily met.  The lady tucks up her clothes as she gets astride her steed, and he, on arriving at the other side, sets her gently down ; and, before he is on his feet, or can turn round to receive her payment, the costume is all perfectly in order, and the lady escapes wet clothes for the rest of the journey, and probably a rheumatism for life.  Really, it is impossible to deny that a certain Spartan simplicity of costume and manners, has its advantages in such a primitive country as Japan, at least.

As we descended to the banks of the river, we obtained a first view of Fusiyama, and a glorious sight it was— he never looked grander.  The first rays of an Eastern sun just lit up the peak, while a fleecy mantle of clouds clung to the descending slopes.  It was like the old familiar face of a friend ; and I doffed my cap in greeting and salutation, to the great delight of the Japanese, who felt, no doubt, it was only a proper mark of respect to the majesty of their sacred mountain.

I felt now the journey was really drawing to a close.

Three days more would bring us into the old road traversed the year before in my first pilgrimage. The Hakoni range only lay between us and the sea shore, by which the high road to Yeddo took its course on to Foogisawa. From thence a sharp morning ride of five leagues would take us into Kanagawa.

So on the thirty-second day after we started from Nagasaki, I arrived at the British Consulate in Kanagawa, without accident or serious contretemps; right glad to have performed the journey; thankful, too, though less so, perhaps, than, as coming events soon proved, we ought all to have been, for our preservation from serious peril by the way.

OUR CHIEF YACONIN

# CHAPTER VIII.

RETURN TO YEDDO — ATTACK ON THE LEGATION IN THE NIGHT,
AND DESPERATE ATTEMPT AT A GENERAL MASSACRE.

ON my arrival at Kanagawa some public business detained me a couple of days, and it was not until July 4, that I rode up to Yeddo. The day was fine, and I mounted with a pleasurable feeling that at last the journey was over, and I was about to return to my home in the East. Is there any land or place of exile, where an Englishman does not turn towards the residence where he has been domiciled more or less permanently, however uninviting it may be in many respects, without something of a home-like feeling gathering round his heart as he approaches the familiar roof? God knows, our residence in Yeddo had few of the many blessings which in our native land is associated with a Home. No wife or children were there to greet us, no grace of womanhood cast its spell upon the hearth. There was, indeed, no hearth for either light or shadow to rest upon, in that Pagan temple of a heathen and hostile city. Yet, as I crossed the boundary river halfway, and saw on the opposite bank old familiar faces I had left behind, and some new ones arrived in my absence, all waiting eager to give me a cordial welcome back, I clasped their hands with a glad feeling to be among them, and at my post once more, despite its manifold anxieties and troubles. All the more cheerfully it may be, why should I deny it, that in one of those who had come to meet me, I saw Mr. Oliphant, the newly-appointed Secretary of Legation,—a relief which would enable me to turn my steps homeward in a few months.

We all mounted gaily. My escort, the same that had accompanied me all the way from Nagasaki, appeared to have felt it a point of duty to see me safely into Yeddo, and although it seemed to me a superfluous exhibition of zeal, I could not, without something of ungraciousness, decline their company. So that with the whole strength of the Legation in Europeans, and my escort of Japanese, had there been any danger to apprehend on the road, we made rather a formidable looking party to attack. I confess, nothing was farther from my thoughts than such a possibility. It was only by the kind of reflected light of after events, that I remembered having noticed the whole way, as we passed through the various hamlets on the roadside, an appearance of interest, a stir and excitement in the population, which at any other time would certainly have struck me as very extraordinary. We were so accustomed to pass to and fro on this road between Yeddo and the port of Kanagawa, that our appearance had long ceased to have any novelty. I simply thought that as I was returning after a long absence and with a larger escort than usual, the chief officer had sent on before, determined to keep up the usages of the journey on to the end, and had thus been the cause of a turn-out of the whole population. As I entered Sinagawa I did notice, however, with some surprise, that all the side streets were shut off by rope-barriers, and that the tea-shops and houses of entertainment where the soldiers and retainers of the Daimios go for dissipation, were all shut up; and I had intended to make some inquiry as to the reason for such unusual proceedings. But arrived at the Legation I thought no more about it. Despatches and letters, with newspapers of two mails, were all waiting my arrival, and I devoted myself to them without farther concern as to the incidents of the road.

The next day was a very fatiguing one. Numerous

packing-cases full of things from England and from China, had accumulated in my absence.   Trunks had to be un-packed, and many other matters required immediate atten-tion.   So that when the dinner-hour came round at seven o'clock, I was more tired than I had been in the longest day's journey.   I accordingly took leave of the other members of the Legation early after dinner, and before eleven o'clock I was in bed and asleep.   In the summer time, with a view to coolness and the better to insure a current of air, it was the custom at the Legation to sleep with the whole front of the house looking towards the gardens open : the sliding screens shutting in the lower part, merely closed to keep out the pariah dogs, which sometimes found their way into the grounds; but they had no fasten-ing, and merely consisted of a light framework of wood, covered with thin paper, so as not to exclude the light.

It is necessary to give some preliminary description of the building, and locality, to enable the reader to realise the events of this night.   The Legation was tem-porarily located in the reception rooms of one of the largest temples of Yeddo ; surrounded by extensive and beautifully wooded grounds.   The temple itself, with all its contiguous buildings, is a vast scrambling place, situated in the bottom of a valley, surrounded by a great screen of evergreen oaks, maples, and shrubs, forming for a quarter of a mile a sort of a shrubbery or jungle.   A cross-road leading into the Tocaido, ran over the hill at the back, where there was a private entrance opening directly upon a fine avenue ; from whence a flight of steps led directly to my own apartments, which were at this angle of the building.   The other side of the house was approached from the Tocaido or main street leading into the city, by an avenue three hundred paces in length, and through a suc-cession of courtyards, one of which, that leading directly to the entrance of the Legation, was stockaded all round and closed by a gate.   Along the whole of this avenue, and in the courts, were not only porters at the outer and inner gates, always closed at night, but a Japanese guard of Tycoons' and Daimios' soldiers to the number of one hundred and fifty, who had been placed there on service by the Japanese Government ever since the menaces of attack which had preceded the murder, in the streets, of the American Secretary of Legation in January of this year. Two watchmen of the Legation, and in our pay, were also on duty every night, whose business it was to go the rounds from sunset to sunrise.

The reader may now be enabled to form some sort of idea of the British Legation in Yeddo, and its situation ; and understand, what I had always felt, that if any attack should ever take place by determined men, such as made the onslaught on the Regent in open day, a more insecure or indefensible position could not well have fallen to our lot. From the road at the back, any number of men might have penetrated through the slight fence at night, without being detected by droning watchmen, and patrols who only went round every hour, and not with much certainty. And if they knew the locality they might have entered the house along the whole front at twenty different points, beginning with my own apartments, and walked right up to my bed. Perhaps it will be thought unaccountable imprudence or foolhardiness with such a possibility, and the often renewed menace of an onslaught, that greater precautions were not taken, at least so far as to close in this more exposed face of the house with shutters. But it was difficult to believe in the existence of the danger, or that whatever isolated attempts might be made on my life or that of others, a deliberately planned attack on the Legation surrounded by a hundred and fifty guards, would be ever resolved upon, unless something like a general rising should take place. Moreover, had it not been already insinuated in more than one quarter, that I in common with the Representatives of France, Prussia, and Holland, had a few months before withdrawn to Yokohama, without any sufficient cause, though directly menaced with precisely such an attack ? Had not Colonel Sykes in the House of Commons thought it necessary to ask what had induced me to leave Yeddo, since I had a Japanese guard of one hundred and fifty men, and 'there could be no danger to my safety?'

But the plain truth is, we hear of danger ever near and impending, until, as day after day passes and no danger assails us, we grow hardened and indifferent, the constant strain of suspense, and hourly expectation of an impending danger is so intolerable, that the majority of mankind get rid of it at any cost—the timorous by flight or suicide— the hardier by a sort of callousness, partly made up of incredulity as to the reality or extent of the evil threatened, and partly of a conviction that it had better be met when it comes, if come it must, with all the chances and contingencies attaching to it, than be made the burden and misery of a life, in anticipation.   Truly has Shakspeare said,

> Cowards die many times before their deaths,
> The valiant never taste of death but once.

And so it happened that on my return to Yeddo, as soon as the Japanese Government had been made to acknowledge their responsibility for the security of the Legations (which they had previously been disposed to question or evade), I made up my mind to accept whatever risk there might be, without allowing it to dwell in my thoughts.   I did not believe that any amount of prudence or precaution could really secure my life, if one of the more powerful Daimios resolved on setting their emissaries to take it; whereas the constant dwelling on such a contingency, would in the end unnerve me for my work, and make life not worth having.

But despite all threats and alarms, as I have already stated, I felt more than half incredulous of any Daimios, or band of men, attempting so desperate an expedient as an attack in force on the Legation,—desperate, not so much in view of the large body of guards, or the danger and difficulty of the deed,—as in the political consequences likely to follow their success.   It could hardly be imagined that Great Britain would allow her Representative and a whole Legation to be massacred in the capital, without exacting retribution. And something of the 'Divinity which hedges in a king,' I felt might also, perhaps, shield a sovereign's Representative.

I certainly lay down that night without a thought of danger. So much so indeed, that my two cases of revolvers placed on my dressing-table by the servants according to custom, remained unopened,— and one still locked, although it had long been my habit, in the possibility of a surprise, to sleep with revolvers under my pillow. I slept the sleep of the weary; when one of the young student interpreters, to whom the duty had been assigned of going through the premises the last thing, to see that the servants were in bed, and the lights out, chiefly as a protection against fire — stood by my bedside with his dark lantern, and awoke me with the report that the Legation was attacked and men were breaking in at the gate. I got up, incredulous, believing it was some gambling or drunken quarrel either among the guards or the 'bettos' in charge of the stables; but, taking a revolver out of its case, I was proceeding to the spot, and had scarcely advanced five steps towards the entrance, when Mr. Oliphant suddenly appeared covered with blood, which was streaming from a great gash in his arm and a wound in his neck — and the next instant Mr. Morrison, the Consul of Nagasaki, appeared also, exclaiming he was wounded, and with blood flowing from a sword-cut on his forehead. 1 of course looked for the rush of their assailants pursuing — and I stood for a second ready to fire, and check their advance, while the wounded passed on to my bedroom behind. I was the only one armed at this moment, for although Mr. Morrison had still three barrels, he was blinded and stunned with his wound.

To my astonishment no pursuers followed. One of the party now grouped around me broke open my other pistol-case and armed himself, but two others had no sort of weapon. Mr. Oliphant had encountered his assailants in the passage leading from his room with only a heavy

hunting-whip hastily snatched from his table on the first
alarm.   We had in fact been taken by surprise—the
guards first and ourselves later, and no sign of anyone
coming to our rescue appeared—of all the hundred and
fifty surrounding the house.

Mr. Oliphant was bleeding so profusely, that I had to
lay down my pistol, and bind up the wound in his arm
with my handkerchief; and while so engaged, there was a
sudden crash and the noise of a succession of blows in
the adjoining apartment.   Some of the band were evidently breaking through the glazed doors opening into the
court with a frightful fracas; still no yaconins or guards
seemed attracted by the noise!

A double-barrelled rifle had by this time been loaded;
but still there we were five Europeans only, including a
servant—imperfectly armed, and with two more disabled,
whom we were afraid to leave for an instant exposed to
the fury of a band of assassins of whose number we
could form no guess—neither could we tell from what
quarter they might come upon us.   Whether many or
few they were left in entire possession of the house for
full ten minutes.   It may well be conceived that suspense
and anxiety made the time seem still longer.   While they
were engaged breaking their way into the room, or out of
it—for this we could not tell, and uncertain at what
moment they might either come pouring through the
suite of rooms in which we stood by the open passage
adjoining the very room they were in—or through some
windows close to the ground within a yard of the point
they were breaking down; I had a moment's hesitation,
whether from the window immediately facing we
should not fire a volley into them at point blank range?
But we were so few, and they might be numerous enough
to rush in and overpower any resistance.   On the other
hand, *they* evidently had missed their way to my apartments—and every minute lost to them was a priceless
gain to us, since it could not be, that the guard to whom
our lives were entrusted would abandon us *altogether*,

unless there was treachery.  The unwillingness to leave
Mr. Oliphant lying helpless on the floor—even for a short
space, in the terrible uncertainty as to what point an
attack might come from, turned the balance and determined
me to stand, and wait the issue.  The noise subsided ; there
was reason to hope rescue had come, or at least a diversion
from without, and that the assailants had turned in some
other direction, or perhaps made their retreat.  Then only
I ventured with two of the party to leave the wounded,
and go to look for one of our number at a farther wing
of the building who had never appeared, and might have
been less fortunate.  While advancing I put one of the
students, Mr. Lowder, as a sentry at an angle commanding
a long passage leading from the entrance, and the
approach from two other directions—and had scarcely
advanced ten steps, when a shot from his pistol suddenly
recalled me.  A group of armed men had appeared at
the farther end, and not answering his challenge, he had
very properly fired into them, and as it was down a
passage, he could scarcely have missed his aim—at all
events they suddenly retreated.  And this was the last
we saw of our assailants !  A minute or two later the
civilian officers in charge of the place appeared with
congratulations on our safety ; how little due to them I
could not but remark !  Mr. Macdonald, the missing one
of my party, came in with them to my great relief ; his
apartment being partially detached on the other side of
the grounds.  It appears he had rushed out on hearing,
as he thought, some one break into his bath-room in the
rear, and after in vain attempting to induce a guard
immediately above him to come down, made his way
through a side-gate to the front, where he found a wild
scene of tumult and conflict.  In the courtyard of the
temple itself, and in front of that leading into the part
assigned to the Legation, there were groups fighting—men
with lanterns rushing to and fro, and gathering from all
sides.  He himself being descried by the yaconins attached
to the Legations (men of the pen and not of the sword),

was drawn aside ; and as he was a conspicuous object in his white sleeping-costume of jacket and pyjamas, they enveloped him in one of their own Japanese dresses.   It was easy to understand that many minutes elapsed before he could obtain any attention to his demand, that some of the guard should go into the house to our rescue.   Nor was it, in effect, until all the assailants outside had been beaten off, or made good their retreat, that there was any thought of the Minister and those with him inside,—or of the necessity of seeing that those for whom they were fight-ing outside, were not in the meanwhile being cut in pieces and deliberately assassinated within.   The whole guard had evidently been surprised ; everyone had been asleep, and turned into their guard-houses, and not a single one of the hundred and fifty could have been on the alert !

When it was possible to compare the evidence of con-fused actors in this midnight tragedy, and gather the facts from all sources, the whole plot and execution came out tolerably clearly.   On the body of one of the assailants killed on the spot, and also on the person of a second of their num-ber badly wounded and made prisoner, a paper was found, declaring the object of the attack, and signed by fourteen names.   One of these was taken from the wounded man all stained with his blood, in the presence of a member of the Legation.   So as far as regards its authenticity as having been *actually on his person*, there is no doubt whatever ; whether it be equally certain, that each of the band were not thus provided, by order of their employers, with a document to make the whole attack, in the event of failure, appear to be the act of a party of lawless lonins animated with a feeling of mingled patriotism and hatred of the foreigner, for whom nobody could be held responsible, is another question.

Here at all events was the document, written it appeared in a sort of mountain patois, by no means easy to decipher by educated Japanese.   After receiving the Government translation, I had others made by three different persons, all unconnected with each other, and although there were in one or two phrases considerable variation in the rendering, compared with the official translation, there was not sufficient between each of the three to leave any doubt that we had arrived at the true sense. The following translation seemed, on comparison of all three, the best:—

'I, though I am a person of low standing, have not patience to stand by and see the sacred empire defiled by the foreigner. This time, I have determined in my heart to undertake to follow out my master's will. Though being altogether humble myself, I cannot make the might of the country to shine in foreign nations, yet with a little faith and a little warrior's power, I wish in my heart separately (by myself), though I am a person of low degree, to bestow upon my country one out of a great many benefits. If this thing from time to time may cause the foreigner to retire, and partly tranquillise both the minds* of the Mikado and of the Government (Tycoon), I shall take to myself the highest praise. Regardless of my own life, I am determined to set out.'

Here follow the fourteen signatures.

It appeared the band of conspirators thus bound by an oath to attack the Legation, and massacre all its inmates, gathered together by previous concert in a house of resort to men of their class in the suburb of Sinagawa already referred to, not half a mile from the Legation. It is quite possible they may have been in their lair actually watching me pass the previous day. Had the Government any information or suspicion of this, and hence their extraordinary precautions? Or when they sent orders to the Governor of Nagasaki to seek to dissuade me ' *on account of the dangers of the route*' from proceeding overland ; and afterwards when they despatched a high officer in the person of Takémoto, one of the Governors of Foreign Affairs all the way from Yeddo to meet me at Hiogo, and again make strenuous efforts to turn me aside—if not from the continuance of the journey altogether, at least from Miaco, was this step motived by some knowledge of a

* Or ' the manes of departed Mikados and Tycoons.'

specific danger dogging my steps? Evidence later
obtained seems to confirm such a supposition. Long after
the event, I heard from Mr. Eusden, then officiating
as Her Majesty's Consul at Hakodadi, that for some days
before any intelligence of the event *could possibly have
arrived*, even by express, from Yeddo ; the Governor, on
more than one occasion, showed a restless sort of anxiety
to know if any tidings of my return had reached the
Consulate? When the intelligence actually arrived of my
return and the attack — received twelve days after the
event, by express — Mr. Eusden was immediately struck
by the interpretation the tidings gave to all these inquiries,
and the marked interest shown previously, for my safe return. It led to the conviction, in his mind, that it was
perfectly known at Hakodadi some great danger was
apprehended and impending at Yeddo. In effect, it
became, immediately after the event, a subject of common
conversation among the people at Yeddo, as I heard from
various sources, that the attack emanated not from a band
of lawless lonins, following their own evil courses, but
from a Prince of *Tsus-sima*, who, after a collision with the
Russians, and his humiliation by an interview forced upon
him by the commander of the Russian corvette, Captain
Biriliff,—hearing a 'great foreign chief' was at Nagasaki,
in his immediate vicinity, and about to proceed overland
to the capital, he had immediately despatched some of
his own people to follow and avenge the outrage he
had suffered at the hands of the Russians, by murdering me on the road, and bringing him the head. This
was carrying out the principle of *solidarité* among
European nations with a vengeance. The popular voice
attributed the non-execution of this mandate on the road
(where, considering how unguardedly we travelled, nothing could have been easier), to the circumstance that I
had already left before they reached Nagasaki, and
advanced so far, that they were unable to overtake our
party before we left Osaca, after which, we were traversing the territories of Daimios ; and to have committed

the deed within any of their dominions, might bring those chiefs into trouble with the Imperial Government, or produce a blood feud between them and their own master. Finally, it was generally asserted, that their design had been, as they followed my steps the whole way, to set upon my party on the road *from Kanagawa to Yeddo* ; but my unexpected detention at the former place a couple of days, and the uncertainty of their information as to the period of my departure, which was, in effect, left undecided until within a few hours of starting, had disarranged their plans. This would account for the unusual excitement of the population by the way-side, which made them turn out to watch my passage — assuming that some rumour of an intended attack had got abroad — and, also, for the vigorous steps taken by the authorities to close up all the approaches; and especially the whole of the houses of resort in Sinagawa.

Whatever might be the information possessed by the Government authorities, it seems but charitable to suppose that it amounted to little more than vague rumours that some design was on foot; for, assuredly, they gave me no special warning of a specific danger, either at Nagasaki or Hiogo; and, on my return, merely sent to congratulate me on my safety, without the slightest hint that they had reason to believe some farther danger was still impending.* And it is equally certain, as the event proved,

---

* The local press of China disseminated, as usual, some altogether erroneous statements as to the real facts. I met several months afterwards an extract from the 'Overland China Mail,' of July 12, copied into the 'Times,' and of course widely circulated, which formed an excellent illustration of the malice and recklessness with which facts are perverted in order to tell against those who may be invested with authority, and which not even such peril as I had escaped could soften or neutralise for a moment. 'It is believed that the Government sanctions these proceedings.' It is also reported that the Governor of *Kanagawa* had informed Mr. Alcock '*that such was the illwill of the people towards him,* that he could not give him assurance of being unmolested in his contemplated journey from Nagasaki to Yeddo.' The reader knows, that even assuming the Governor of Nagasaki, not Kanagawa, was meant, how entirely devoid of truth such a statement is, and will see how ingeniously the warnings Mr. De Wit and I both received in common and of a general danger, is made to turn upon personal illwill towards me alone.

that within the gates of the Legation they took no extra
precautions whatever to guard against a possible attack.
To assume, therefore, that they were in possession of any
positive and precise information at the time, would, under
the circumstances, be to charge them with direct complicity; and, to suppose that the surprise of the guard,
so ostentatiously kept up for our defence, was a premeditated act of treachery.    For a moment after an
escape which in every way seemed so providential,
with a laxness and tardiness of the guard, which ought
to have insured the success of such determined assailants,
I may have felt disposed to charge them with a piece
of Oriental Machiavelism worthy of an Eastern Feudalism
or a 'Moyen Age.'    Upon more careful consideration
of all the facts, I satisfied myself, however, that it was
nothing more than their habitual ineptitude in all matters
requiring prompt action, energy, and prevision.    The
Japanese can be lynx-eyed for a time; but the whole
power of the Government does not seem able to insure
in any of their employés a systematic, persistent, and
unsleeping vigilance.    The official classes are all, from
the highest to the lowest, too lazy and apathetic.    Theirs
is a lip and eye service always, in which they do as much
as may be needful to keep them out of scrapes that would
entail serious personal inconvenience, and prevent the loss
of their places, and nothing more.    The standard of duty is
placed as low, under such circumstances, as is compatible
with the performance of any.    Throughout the capital there
are guard-houses at short intervals, generally occupied by
boys or superannuated old men, who spend their whole
time (supposed to be devoted to the vigilant maintenance of order) squatted on their knees and heels, and
either dosing at their posts, or smoking the pipe of
apathetic idleness.    Thus it was quite consistent with
their whole system that Iko-mono-no-kami, the unfortunate
Regent, should be massacred by a band of Mito's men
immediately in front of the guard placed at the entrance of
the moat-bridge which leads to the Tycoon's palace.    There

would have been a want of fitness and congruity if he
had been murdered anywhere else! So, I do not know
that I could reasonably complain, if my own fate so
narrowly escaped being the same, and I had been slain in
the midst of a large force of the Tycoon's body-guard,
and the armed contingents of two Daimios charged
with my safety. The leopard will not change its spots,
nor the Japanese his nature, because it pleases the Tycoon
to enter into treaties with Foreign Powers, and throw
upon them a continued strain of vigilance and energy,
to which they are wholly unused and unequal.

The conspirators, or the Prince of Tsus-sima's emissaries, whichever be the most proper designation, having
missed their prey *on the road*, met, it appears, at their
rendezvous in Sinagawa, the second night after my
arrival, and there caroused and talked of the onslaught
they were about to make. The Government wished me
to believe the number actually engaged was only
fourteen — those whose names were attached to the
documents. Of course there would, in that case, be the
fewer to seize after their escape, and they were willing
rather to accept the awkward dilemma of admitting that
one hundred and fifty of their guards allowed less than a
tenth of their number of assailants to penetrate and take
possession of the Legation, and hold it, too, for ten
minutes; than the additional responsibility of having to
account for a larger number of assailants.

The number must, however, obviously have been greater,
or nothing but treachery and the certainty that they would
not be attacked on their way, could account for what without such aid would have been an act of stupidity or madness on their part, in attacking by the front instead of at
the back, where the road was perfectly clear and the
house entirely open. They came, on the contrary, before
midnight to the front gate, lying but a few steps back from
the great high road,— and finding it closed, they esca-
laded the fence at the side. The gate-keeper awakened
by the noise, seems to have come out and was instantly

cut down, and killed on the spot. They then proceeded up the long avenue to the first courtyard, a distance of three hundred yards, passing all the guard-houses, and on their way killing a dog, which no doubt was barking his alarm — the only sentinel awake ! A little farther on they met a horse-keeper of one of the yaconins, who seems unhappily for himself to have been outside the stables and to have crossed their path — him they killed also. A little farther on still, a cook in my service was met and severely wounded. Finally, a watchman, who happened to be close to the gate of my courtyard, was seized as a guide, and under threat of instant death, was told to show them 'where the accursed foreigners slept.' One would have thought four men successively and a dog could not at intervals, and separated from each other at different points along the line, have been cut to pieces without noise enough to waken *any* guard. Not so, however. They crossed the upper court beyond the great porch or open gateway leading alike to the front entrance of the Temple, and the Legation more to the right; and here it was they met one of our watchmen. Terror-struck at finding himself in the hands of such ruffians, he seems to have given only a feigned consent, and tried to make his escape. Being pursued, he was slashed frightfully across the body, before he found temporary refuge in a lotus pond. He survived, however, to tell his own tale, and indeed ultimately recovered. They then appear to have told off three parties — one proceeded round to the back of the stables through a passage leading directly into the house — another forced the gate of the court in which the main entrance was, and broke in the panels of the front door — a third made their way into the Temple adjoining the entrance hall of the Legation and the back of the premises. From thence, after wounding a priest in their path, some thrust aside the screens which alone formed the partition and entered there; while others proceeding on broke into a courtyard. A Chinese servant of Mr. Morrison happened to be sleeping in the hall ; and while listening in breathless alarm to the furious blows at the front-door, a man in chain armour, and masked, suddenly made his appearance from the Temple, forcing his way through a sliding panel.   On this — with the instinct of his race — he glided stealthily and silently away, and apparently unseen, to his master's room.   Fortunately it was one of the nearest in that part of the house, and awoke him in time to put a sword and revolver in his hands, which were lying by his side.   Mr. Oliphant, sleeping farther off, had by this time been awakened by the increasing tumult of the assault, and the barking of a dog.   Believing it was some fight among the servants, he seized a hunting-whip,— the first thing to his hand,— and ran down the passage, on which both Mr. Morrison's room and Mr. Russell's opened.   To rouse the latter and ask if he had any arms, was the work of a moment.   But finding none, he turned back, and at this moment encountered either two or three men advancing.   One immediately in front, he saw by the imperfect light of the stars, in the act of aiming a blow with a two-handed sword at his head ; and an unequal struggle began in the dark.   Mr. Oliphant parried as he best could the blows, seeking to disable his assailant with the heavy end of the hunting-whip, while retreating or borne back towards the room where he had just left Mr. Russell.   Fortunately, this gave Mr. Morrison time to throw back his screen opening on the scene, and to fire a couple of shots in the direction of the assassins. At the same moment Mr. Oliphant received two serious wounds, and Mr. Morrison himself a cut on the forehead. The pistol shots, whether they took effect or not, and it seemed probable that one at least of the attacking party was wounded, had the effect of checking the advance ; during which pause they both retreated and gained my room, meeting me, as I have stated, on my way out.

When the mêlée was at an end, some minutes later, and we went over the premises, we found an entrance had been effected from the Temple at another point, through some thin planking into a little court, on which the room of Mr. Lowder, one of the student interpreters, opened. The mark of a bloody hand was found on the sloping roof of the bath-room, over which apparently some wounded man had made his escape; and by the broken planking I picked up a sword and a leather purse, with a few cash and a seal in it, which had been dropped.

From the various marks, it was plain that an entrance had been effected at four points, and the assailants had come upon us in three separate directions. Whatever their number, and it is unlikely that they should not have been more than three or four at each point, a portion of the band must have remained on the outside long enough to give employment to the guard when fairly roused from their slumbers, and that for several minutes. It is inconceivable, therefore, that the original number did not exceed fourteen.

The danger did not seem wholly over when the first attack was repulsed. Frequent alarms from different parts of the grounds of the approach of an enemy continued during the next two hours, originating no doubt in the individual members of the scattered band making their way through the cover of the surrounding woods to escape. And all did escape, except two who were killed on the spot, nearly hacked to pieces, and a third who was badly wounded. The next day three more were tracked to their lair, in Sinagawa, but when the police arrived, two had committed the Hara-kiru and were dead, while the third had done his work ineffectually and was made prisoner. Later, the Governor gave me information that four more had been heard of in a village some miles from Kanagawa, where they had presented themselves travel-soiled and wounded, demanding of the priest food and money. If they did not boast of their feat of arms, at least they seemed to have made no mystery of it — but the priest, alarmed, under pretence of borrowing the money, went to give information, and they naturally suspecting treachery, made off before he returned with the police. Two since then have been reported as also having been pursued, and to avoid capture killing themselves. Of those first traced, and who had committed the Hara-kiru, there was a popular rumour that on their arrival at Sinagawa they had been bitterly reproached for cowardice by their chief—*they* especially, as the only part of the band that had been in actual conflict with the foreigners. To which they replied, that they had found us too well armed and ready to defend our lives; but not the less, being commanded to kill themselves, they did so on the spot. One of these, it was said, had a pistol-shot wound, and if so, he must either have been in the foremost party at which Mr. Morrison fired two shots, or the last fired at by Mr. Lowder.

The next morning when day broke, the Legation presented all the appearance of a place which had been carried by assault and sacked. The front panels of the entrance had been broken through, the screen partition between the Temple and the hall thrown down. The floors and walls of the passages were spattered with blood, the sliding panels crushed and broken, the furniture in many of the rooms was thrown down, and had been cut and hacked in their blind fury, or in baffled rage at finding all empty. The mosquito curtains were slashed, and the bed-post of Lowder's bed cut through, as well as a stout book on his table; as if they had sought to leave behind them tangible evidence of the strength of their arms and the keenness of their swords. They had careered through all the rooms in the house but those outlying châlets which Oliphant and Macdonald occupied—and the suite of rooms forming my own apartments at the opposite extremity. And that they should have missed these of all others, the main object of their search, although the marks of their sabres were on the panels at the entrance, and one at least of their number must have actually been on the threshold, is altogether inexplicable. Certainly a more providential escape from what, humanly speaking, seemed inevitable destruction, it is difficult to conceive. The fact of their having chosen the front avenue and entrance for their line of attack instead of the unguarded back, where all was open ;—and as they found at last, so thickly covered with wood that concealment and escape were alike easy, is difficult to explain. Had they come in that direction my death must indeed have been inevitable ; mine the first, if not all in succession, for the winding path down the hill led directly to my bed-room.

Early the next morning, after a brief rest of an hour or two, I proceeded to visit the wounded among my tardy defenders and followers. On the way I saw the wounded prisoner, a young man of two or three and twenty, ill-favoured enough and with a settled scowl on his face. Two of the juniors had seen him before, and though bound and wounded, he expressed his rage that they had escaped alive. I saw that same head again months after, and its lines must have been strongly imprinted on my memory, for the likeness suddenly flashed upon me. At intervals along the avenue, I found three corpses stretched on the ground, two of them the bodies of the assailants, who, as I have said, had been frightfully hewn about. I have seen many a battle field, but of sabre wounds I never saw any so horrible. One man had his skull shorn clean through from the back, and half the head sliced off to the spine ; while his limbs only hung together by shreds. The other was equally savagely maimed and hacked. If they had counted on the total inertness of the guards, they certainly must have discovered their mistake long before the last of them left the grounds. As I looked on these mangled and hideous remains, and thought such as they were then, it had been intended we should be, and such might still be the fate reserved for me from their confraternity, I confess to a shudder of mingled horror and disgust ;—quickly followed, however, by a deep feeling of gratitude to Him who saved us all from such a fate. I had need of trust in that same Providence to guard my steps in the way that lay before me, for vain seemed the help of man. Certainly the position was not exactly diplomatic, according to the ordinary acceptation of the term. A Minister under perpetual menace of assassination, and called upon to maintain his post, and defend the treaty-rights of a nation—not exactly by the sword, but by a bold front, in face of far more trying danger, than such as ordinarily besets the soldier in the field. The wounded had all been dressed, but I ascertained that many of the injuries were comparatively slight, and clean cuts with the sabre, gun-shot wounds and thrusts, even with the sword, not having yet entered into the lonins' tactics or means of attack. Some few were severe, and one of the Tycoon's guard died before evening. The following is an official return of killed, wounded, and prisoners, the Government sent me; to which should be added two of my own servants, a cook and a watchman, both severely wounded, and two of the inmates of the Legation, one so severely as to be partially maimed for life, the sinews of the left wrist having been severed to the bone. There is probably not in all the annals of our diplomacy an example of such a bloodthirsty and deliberate plot to massacre a whole Legation, and certainly none so boldly and recklessly carried into partial execution.

### Killed.

One of the Tycoon's body-guard and one groom . . 2
Two of the assailants . . . . . . 2

### Severely Wounded.

Two soldiers, one of the Tycoon's, one of the Daimio's.
    Two porters, one at the outer and the other at the
    inner gate (one died same day) . . . . 4
One of the assailants made prisoner . . . . 1
One member of the Legation . . . . . 1
Two servants of the Legation . . . . . 2

### Slightly Wounded.

Seven of the Tycoon's guard . . . . . 7
Two of the Daimio's guard . . . . . 2
One priest in the Temple . . . . . 1
One member of the Legation . . . . . 1
                                            ——

Total killed and wounded on the spot . . . 23
                                            ——

# CHAPTER IX.

THE LULL AFTER THE STORM—IMMEDIATE PROSPECTS AND POLICY.

THE position of the British minister at Yeddo, after this assault on the Legation by armed men, undeterred and unchecked by the presence of a large guard of the Tycoon's, was full of embarrassment. One thing alone was evident and certain, that he could no longer trust to the Japanese Government to secure his safety in the capital. Yet to abandon it a second time, and after such an attempt to carry out the long-suspended menace to drive all the Foreign Representatives out, would be to give a triumph to violence ; and to render a residence ever after impossible without a war, or some act of vigour on the part of one or more Foreign Powers that should strike terror into the hearts of those who plotted such atrocious deeds. It was above all essential that the position of Foreign Ministers as established by treaty should be maintained, if possible, without essential change, until their respective Governments could be informed of what had taken place, and their instructions received. How this was to be effected without great risk of renewed and more successful attacks of the same nature by those now baffled and defeated in their object, and consequently still graver complications, was the question ; or rather whether I had any means at my command by which the risk could be so far reduced, as to make it consistent with prudence and a sound policy, in reference to the ulterior object, to remain? The utter untrustworthiness of any Japanese guard as a means of security, had been abundantly demonstrated. And although the morning after the attack the Council of

State sent one of the Governors of Foreign Affairs to congratulate me on my safety, with an offering of some ducks and
a jar of sugar to express their joy, I felt in no way disposed
to accept either their assurances of increased vigilance,
or their presents; for I held both to be of about equal
value. I merely replied that I declined the last, and as to
the first, I also would adopt some means to secure myself
in future from being surprised in the midst of a Japanese
guard. 'Prave words!' as Fluellen says in the play. But
what means had I at my disposal? Notwithstanding repeated
commands and instructions sent out from home for efficient
protection and some show of force in the Japanese waters,
there was at this moment but one despatch-boat, the little
'Ringdove,' within call at Yokohama, for the protection of
the Legation at Yeddo and the Consulate and British
settlement at Yokohama, or any other interests in Japan.
Considering how little we had been favoured since the
first opening of Japan under treaty, I ought perhaps to
have considered myself fortunate that I had anything in
the shape of a man-of-war within reach. The same
emergency might have happened twenty times over, in the
first two years, without a British ship being on the spot
—or in Japanese waters. This no doubt was in part to
be attributed to the greater magnitude and absorbing interest of China, which, even after the war was over, gave
ample occupation to the reduced fleet. The reiterated assertions of writers in the local press of Hong Kong,
not themselves exposed to any danger, of the unmeaning-
ness of the constantly renewed threats of attack and extermination, may, unconsciously to the Admiral himself,
have had some influence. Something confirmatory of such
views might even be found in the action of the American
Minister; though he alone, among the Representatives
of all the Treaty Powers, professed to believe devoutly,
not only in the good faith of the Japanese' Government,
from whom these intimations of danger were perpetually
received, but in the absolute security of the Legations.
I could feel little surprise, therefore, if those at a distance

were often misled.  Visitors, moreover, came in shoals by every steamer from China.  All were naturally anxious to say they had seen the capital ; and the Legation offering the only accommodation or conditions indeed, under which British subjects could visit it, I was very rarely without guests, who came, stayed their few days, and went away delighted, to be able, on their return, to say they had been to Yeddo.  Of course, as visitors, the desire of everyone about me was to spare them references to danger tending to disturb their short period of enjoyment.  Much that they saw was novel and amusing, and pleased with their visit, they left Yeddo to speak of it as a charming place. As travellers will describe places they are not required to live in, and where they may have spent some pleasant days in the excitement of visiting new scenes, they naturally told the world what a beautiful country they had found, with a good-natured people ; freedom to ride about ; an outward show of guards and guarantees for security.  All very true in some respects, but utterly misleading as to the real amount of security, or the true nature of our position in the capital.  Probably the very same delighted visitors, if they had been compelled to take up their residence, would have very quickly qualified their praises in the sense ascribed to Moore in speaking of his beloved country Ireland, ' A beautiful country, sir, to live out of !'  We have lately had many accounts of Iceland, than which it is difficult to conceive a more barren or wretched place of residence, to those who are doomed by the accident of birth to live and die there — unless it be Aden, over the black scoriæ of which a burning sun from above sheds a scorching and withering blight.  Some of these books reached me at Yeddo, and I could not help being amused with the jaunty way in which all the accumulated horrors of ' geysers and volcanoes,' wide districts of 'extinct craters and fields of lava' (the homesteads of the poor Icelanders), are described as upon the whole very agreeable and charming features of the landscape ! It would be pleasant to set them down there for five years of their lives, and require them to write a book *after* a more mature acquaintance with these charming friends had qualified them to give a true picture. So it was with our unfailing stream of visitors to Japan — for even while the bloodstains were still on the sliding-panels and matting of the rooms, a new shoal arrived at Kanagawa, and I have no doubt thought it very absurd and very arbitrary in the Minister, that he declined the responsibility of any more of his countrymen at that moment, in such ' a charming place.' And ladies still reminded me, that they had an invitation to come with their husbands, and be put up at the Legation. Indeed, it is to the fact of ladies on one or two occasions having been guests at the Legation, I believe, that was mainly due Admiral Hope's indisposition to believe there was any broad foundation for the rumours of danger that reached him on the Chinese coast. It was not until he came to the spot himself, and that after an attempt at a wholesale massacre — calculated to carry conviction to the minds of the most sceptical — that he could see the necessity for any anxiety, or means of material protection. This was rather hard upon the members of the Legation, to whom the fair face of a countrywoman and the very rustle of a silk dress was, what the flowers and the one tree in the garden of the governor of Iceland must have been to the Icelanders! But if anyone argued from such premisses, that there could be no real danger in Yeddo, I should say it implied some ignorance of the fair sex. Without being altogether fire-eaters, in whom

*Danger and death a dread delight inspire,*

the seemingly most timid often find nerve for expeditions which many a masculine companion would willingly avoid, if it could be escaped with any decent excuse. I think they like coquetting with danger, as they sometimes do with lovers, when it does not come in such a questionable shape, as to threaten a too close intimacy with immediately disagreeable consequences. Just as dilettanti

explorers of the geysers are said to enjoy the idea of
' rousing Strokr,' and cannot resist a propensity ' to throw
him into a violent passion ' for their especial amusement—
always hoping after they have flung in their stones and
sods to such a degree that he collects all his strength and
shoots them back into the air ' in a hissing torrent,' that
they won't fall upon their own heads! One can understand that the ' temptation to tease the geyser,' and to
spend a week at Yeddo—with just a possibility of some
' horrid adventure,' or what is better, the narrow escape
from one, after running the chances, to visitors generally,
and to fair ones especially, about equal, and consequently
bad ground for any inference as to the absence of all danger.
I could not help being struck with the striking analogy
between the physical features in Iceland so graphically
described by recent travellers, and the moral characteristics and political state of Japan in the present day. For
although we had there, too, a good sprinkling of live and
extinct volcanoes, and no dearth of real earthquakes,
the analogy goes much farther. If, as Buckle and other
writers hold, the civilisation of a people depends very
much upon its climate, are we not at liberty to assume
there may also be some subtle affinity between the
physical condition of the earth and her children—
between the soil and those who live upon it? Certain it
is that the incidents of travel as described by these
explorers of nature and students of physical phenomena,
will admirably serve, *mutatis mutandis*, for a description
of the moral conditions of this favoured land.

For instance, one traveller tells us that the ground in
Iceland is pierced in all directions, and puffs of steam, jets
of water, and pools of seething fluid tell the visitor that
he is standing on a great cauldron, the crust of which
might be torn to fragments in a moment, were the riotous
vapours denied the means of escape. He feels that hundreds of safety-valves are at work around him, and
naturally wonders whether Iceland would not burst like a
boiler if these should happen to be clogged or destroyed.

This is precisely our position in respect to the moral elements around us; and nothing could more perfectly describe the situation of the Foreign Legations in Yeddo than the following account of the capriciously savage proceedings of the central boilers of the region :—

'The larger fountains generally give notice of their intention to play. This is only reasonable, for otherwise a curious traveller venturing too near the basin, might be drenched with scalding water by a sudden eruption; or, worse still, whilst peering down a tube, might receive the jet in his face, and recoil parboiled at a blow. The New Geyser, however, declines to give any intimation of his movements, and therefore, as Sir George Mackenzie remarks, it is necessary to deal cautiously with him, unless assured from a recent outbreak that his hour is not yet come. The notice served upon the public, in cases where due warning is given, consists of a series of detonations, which break on the ear like a report of distant artillery. The Head Geyser makes the ground quiver under your feet, as if an infant earthquake were gambolling below. Gun after gun is thus fired at varying intervals, as much as to say that a grand performance is just about to commence, and then the water begins to bubble in the pipe or to heave in the basin. Very frequently, however, the visitor, who rushes up, panting and agitated, on hearing the subterranean signals, is doomed to disappointment, for, after rising a few feet in a column, the liquid retires into the well, and leaves the spectator to ascertain (if the point is not already settled) whether patience is one of the virtues he really enjoys.'

'In the other respects, too, as well as in the hours of display, these thermal fountains are somewhat capricious in their proceedings. The quantity of water ejected, the height to which it is propelled, the mode of evacuation adopted, differ according to circumstances which cannot be accurately explained.'

Philosophers tell us that the same law prevails in mechanics and pneumatics which obtains in morals and

politics, and after reading such a perfect exposition of our
great moral Geysers in this volcanic region of the antipodes, I cannot doubt that the laws of action and
developement in both are identical! What the New
Geyser is to travellers in Iceland, Yeddo is to the foreign
residents in Japan—less fortunate than those, in being
obliged to stand permanently on the brink of this infernal
cauldron, long after its capricious phenomena have ceased
to afford either pleasure or amusement; and condemned
to wait for 'something to turn up,' without the support
Macawber derived from the hope that it 'might be to his
advantage.'

However, under existing circumstances, there was no
retreat possible. Even supposing this last demonstration
had carried conviction to the mind of my American colleague, the only other Foreign Minister then in Yeddo, and
led him to revise his opinion that we were 'as safe in our
Legations as in Windsor Castle,'—a favourite declaration
of his, I for one should have been as averse as ever he was
to abandon the position. There was no longer anything to
gain, and everything to lose, by retiring. The conditions
were all changed. The reasons which furnished the
strongest grounds for a temporary retirement from the
capital then, no longer existed. The Government of the
country, at that time, made an *ostentatious parade of their
inability* to secure the Representatives of the Treaty Powers
from outrage and murder; and fenced with their responsibilities in regard to such grave obligations. They had subsequently, as a consequence of that step, very fully and
formally acknowledged their responsibility, and recognised
the force of their international obligations. True, it was
now obvious the means they had adopted, as I believe in
good faith, had proved miserably inadequate, and all but
utterly failed in the end. The British Minister and the rest
of Her Majesty's Legation were alive : this was manifestly
due to a merciful dispensation of Providence, under which
a band of ruffians failed to reach my apartment, notwithstanding they had surprised the guards and poured through

the house sword in hand, holding possession undisturbed, save by such resistance as we ourselves were enabled to make, for a space of full ten minutes. They got lost in the labyrinths of passages, courts, and rooms, and missing their way in the darkness, never succeeded in finding my rooms, where, after the first mêlée, all the members of the Legation were collected for a last stand. But on the supposition that the Government had done their best, taking into account their habitual incapacity in such matters, were we to make it a *casus belli*? If not, then the only motive for such a step as striking the flag, and returning to Yokohama or on board ship, would be the personal safety of the members of the Legation. The risk of another and more successful attack of the same kind, despite an increased number of Japanese guards, was great, even in the opinion of the Japanese Government, who expressly declared they could not guarantee me against a renewed and more desperate attempt. Yet to retreat before danger and violence, where there is a chance of effective resistance, whatever may be the personal risk, is too repugnant to our habits and feelings to be accepted lightly as an alternative. I felt the responsibility of any decision, and during these hours of the night determined upon my course of action, till some more efficient means of defence could be secured. While the tocsin and alarm-bells were yet ringing through all the neighbourhood, I sat down to write a despatch to the Commander of the 'Ringdove,' requesting him to come up to the anchorage off Yeddo, and land me as strong a guard of marines and blue-jackets as he could spare out of his small crew. And at daybreak, when all farther danger for that night was over, I forwarded it by two mounted yaconins. Early the same day I cleared the house of my visitors—all, in fact, whose duty did not keep them in the Legation. About one o'clock Captain Craigie himself landed, with a guard of twenty of his best men, well armed; and to my surprise, accompanied by my French colleague, Monsieur de Belle-

court.  He had been staying at Yokohama, but the moment
he heard of the night's work, he generously put himself
on board the 'Ringdove,' with a party of his own countrymen, drawn from the ' Dordogne,' a French transport-ship,
and determined to share the anxieties and perils of the
position with me.   I acquainted the Government with the
steps I had taken to strengthen their hands, leaving the
outer circuit of the grounds to their own forces, suddenly
increased by them to 500 men, and reserving the defence
of the house and grounds immediately adjoining, to our
own people.   During the afternoon a survey was taken of
the scrambling buildings forming the whole of the premises to be defended ; and we all returned with the
conviction that a more indefensible position, against any
determined attack by a large body of men, or even
against the more stealthy approach of mere assassins at
night, could hardly have fallen to our lot.   Sentries were
placed when night drew near, so as at least to guard
against our being *surprised*, or murdered in our sleep.

Foiled and baffled in their first desperate attempt, would
they return with recruited forces and in larger numbers ?
This was an anxious question, which, as in the case of the
geysers, it was impossible to answer in any satisfactory
manner.   The movements and ebullitions of the hostile
elements in Japan seemed to the full as capricious and
beyond the reach of certain calculation, now ' breaking out
with unspeakable fury,' and again subsiding into mildness,
and tranquillity.   We could but hope an interval of
rest might succeed this unusually violent explosion.   If
we held our ground for even a week or two, while our
enemies were chewing the cud of their disappointment,
and ruminating on farther violence, the Admiral *might*
arrive.   He had himself fixed the 15th of the month as
the probable date of his arrival, and although I could not
count upon any certainty or rapidity of movement, where
Japan was in question, yet I knew he had received the
Queen's commands to come in person with a portion of his
squadron, and, therefore, sooner or later he must come.

For, although I had no faith in the power of a squadron or of ships of war generally, being able to prevent such an attack as this, and still less to extend any real protection if actually made, it had been decided at home that there should be such evidence of watchfulness and force at command as the presence of a squadron and the Admiral in person would afford.  It is, indeed, hard to say what would or could give protection, if any one of the hostile Daimios chose to give the word for a massacre.  Ships of war are only a protection in so far as they may deter the violent and factious from attempts,—and to do this they must be in such number, and assembled with such previous declaration of determined action in a given eventuality, as might overawe the hostile party in the country.  On the other hand, the menacing presence of ships might just as likely prove a cause of excitement and political fanaticism, prompting the more violent to acts of defiance.  The first of the long and dismal series of these political murders began with Russians for the victims, and when a much larger Russian fleet was on the spot than we are ever likely to have in Japanese waters, unless hostile measures should be resolved upon.  Nevertheless, it must also be said that the policy of Russia—which seems to consist in keeping no Diplomatic Agent at Yeddo, making no trouble about commercial rights, but always keeping a powerful naval force hovering about the Japanese seas, with commanders of a determined stamp, who, at the northern and other ports are apt to take the law into their own hands and vigorously enforce it, has apparently had the effect of making them more respected and feared than any other Western Power — respected because they made themselves feared, one cannot well doubt.

It was well worth an effort, and any reasonable risk, to hold our position until the Admiral should come.  When he arrived, I could determine in a more definite manner my future course of action, with a knowledge of what amount of support and cooperation I could count upon, in carrying out a given line of policy.  The 15th came and passed however, and even the 30th, and still no tidings of the Admiral. In the meanwhile, a surveying squadron, consisting of H.M.S. 'Actæon' with three gun-boats, came to our rescue. The news of the attack had reached Nagasaki, ten days after the event, by an express sent from Yokohama; and Mr. Annesley, the officer in charge of the Consulate at the time, very zealously sent a messenger overland to a bay where the ships were known to be. Captain Ward, the senior officer, instantly set sail for Yeddo with his little fleet — doubly welcome from the ready zeal with which he had come to our aid, in what he rightly judged to be a position of some anxiety, if not peril. The evidence it seemed to furnish, that when imminent dangers threatened, resources, even when least expected, were never far to seek, made his arrival still more opportune. It must have seemed to the Japanese something weird, as if ships could be evoked out of the sea when wanted. This relieved me of all anxiety for the security of the Consulate at Kanagawa, and also of the British community at Yokohama, which had been left to the guardianship of the Dutch brig, the ' Camelot,' in attendance on my colleague, Mr. de Wit, at that anchorage. Immediately on hearing of what had taken place, Mr. de Wit, who was on his way to Yeddo, wrote to the Japanese Government, saying he saw their promises of protection could not be safely trusted, and therefore declined to take up his residence in Yeddo until he had received farther instructions from his Government.

Thus a month passed wearily and anxiously enough, as will be readily conceived; chequered only by two reported gatherings for an attack on the American Minister's residence, who had no European guards. But the one came to nothing, beyond a reported reconnoitring of the defences by a body of armed men, to the number of fifty or more; and another night by the firing of two shots, a general turn-out of his guards, and alarm in all the quarter, with the fire-bells sounding the tocsin.

How, indeed, this month was passed may best be

realised by a glance at the divers reports that reached me from day to day of farther machinations, and the arrest of one or two of the assailants. Most of these came from my indefatigable French colleague, as we always interchanged our secret reports, gleaned with so much labour and difficulty. Surrounded as we were by Government officials, whose chief business was to *prevent* any information reaching us but such as they thought fit to give—and that was exceedingly little and bad of its kind—we were driven to means we should not otherwise have sought, perhaps, in order to supplement their spare allowance of truth. Here are a few extracts from the bulletins as they arrived :—

'Le 1ᵉʳ d'Août.— On dit que le premier Ministre des Affaires étrangères, un des Princes à forteresse, ne ferait plus partie de Gorogio—Koudze Yamata no Kami aurait été obligé de retourner dans son domaine, situé en *Simosa* (forteresse de Saki-jado). Selon les bruits qui courent, "Les malveillants de la province de Istals en Djousin (la province de Mito) auraient brisé les portes de son château," &c. Si ces données étaient exactes, elles sentiraient bien la guerre civile, ou un commencement de guerre civile.'

'2ᵐᵉ d'Août.—Je viens d'avoir avec . . . un entretien dont je vous parlerai à l'occasion, parceque j'ai été frappé du peu d'intérêt que ces messieurs semblent apporter sur questions les plus majeures, tout en protestant du bon vouloir du Gouvernement. Vraiment, je ne sais si je vois mal, mais il me semble que tous ces gens-là n'éprouvent guère de souci pour dire à demi-mot, Ah, mon Dieu ! laissez-nous donc tranquilles avec toutes vos grandes phrases ! C'est compris ! Il n'en sera ni plus ni moins ! Il semble qu'ils soient à bout de patience, et qu'ils supportent tout comme des gens ou *condamnés* ou décidés (je vois plutôt *décidés* que *condamnés*).'

'8ᵐᵉ d'Août.—Je ne vous confirme pas encore l'exactitude de mon *bruit* de ce matin sur l'attaque des Ministres. Mais je vais vous donner, sous toutes réserves bien entendu, les renseignements qui viennent de me parvenir, et qui sont d'une nature trop sérieuse pour ne pas nécessiter d'autres contrôles.

'Voici ce qui vient de m'être dit par un Japonais. Est-ce un *émissaire*? Est-ce homme franc? C'est ce que nous saurons bientôt. Je rapporte seulement.

'Il y a encore à Yedo des *Mito Lonines*;—avant hier les membrès du Gorogio, *Naito Kino Kami* et *Matsdaura Bonzen no Kami*, sortant du palais, où ils avaient été visiter le Taicoon, ont été attaqués par des lonines, qui se sont jetés, le sabre à la main, sur leurs norimons. Leur garde ont fait bonne contenance, et pendant qu'ils combattaient, leurs maîtres pouvaient sortir et rentrer chez eux sans blessures.' . . . 'Les deux attaques auraient été *successives*, c'est à dire, que les deux membres du Gorogio, sortant à peu près ensemble (mais cependant séparément) du palais, auraient été attaqués par la même bande.' . . . 'Les gardes de l'un des deux Ministres auraient réussi à faire deux prisonniers. Les assaillants de l'autre Ministre auraient prit la fuite.'

'Y a-t-il eu attaque? Ou toute cette histoire n'est-elle qu'une broderie? Il est important de le savoir, afin que j'éloigne de moi ces porteurs de fausses nouvelles. Et encore avec tout ce que nous savons, voyons et supposons, ne peut-on pas se demander (car vraiment l'esprit se déprave en contact de tant de mystères et de subterfuges), en cas où il y aurait eu réellement attaque, si cette attaque était *sérieuse* ou seulement *théâtrale*?'

'11^me d'Août.—Ce matin vous aurez reçu comme moi l'avis de l'inquiétude du Gouvernement au sujet d'un fameux *Lonine* de Mito, qui vient de s'échapper — on le tenait de surveillance et il a disparu.'

'14^me d'Août.—Je vous félicite bien de ce succès (a secret and confidential conference with the Ministers), au moins ils finiront peut-être par ouvrir les yeux!'

'17^me d'Août.—Les grandes affaires Japonaises seraient annoncées, c'est à dire, celles qui concernent les relations du Taicoon avec le Mikado au sujet *de mariage* — le mariage aurait lieu. La future Impératrice ou Taikonesse (*mia* en Japonais) arriverait de *Miako* dans le neuvième mois de cette année — c'est à dire, vers le mois d'Octobre.

'Le Taicoon irait lui-même l'année prochaine à Miako sur une escadre Japonaise, et non par terre.'

Then followed, on the 17th, a menacing placard on *Ando Tsoussima-no-kami's* door; followed, on the 18th, by an attack, real or simulated, on the American Lega-tion. M. de Bellecourt might well say 'l'esprit se déprave,' in such an atmosphere of assassinations, menaces, and rumours — each day bringing its contingent. I will complete this page of our history in Japan by a copy of a memorandum made at the time for the Foreign Office, of 'rumours and reports' in circulation from day to day in Yeddo and Kanagawa, which reached me from other sources.

'The Governor of Yeddo a few days after the attack on the Legation was said to have been murdered in his house by a band of lonins in league with those who attacked the Legation, and in revenge for the vigour with which these were being pursued. Next day he was said only to be sick, and suspended for the moment in his office. Finally it appeared that he had committed the Hara-kiru; having offended by intruding his opinion at a grand council of Daimios (he not being a Daimio). The council was said to have been convoked to determine whether the Tycoon should obey a mandate to go to Miako to pay homage to the Mikado as a preliminary to a marriage with the daughter of the latter, and the composition of certain differences for some time existing. The Governor sent in a very strong but ably drawn-up opinion against it. This opinion was adopted, but a rival and former Governor took advantage of the opportunity to ruin him by charging him with a violation of the laws in offering it. Upon this had been grafted a report of a duel between two Daimios. It was a "*duel à mort*" it seems, but not a hand-to-hand fight.

'Three lonins were reported to have been watching the new stockades and fences putting up at the Legation, and to have said with bitterness they were too strong to be broken through.'   (A great mistake on their part, if they ever arrived at the conclusion, for I demonstrated to the chief officials on service some time after this that the separate bamboos could all be slid upward, and any number of lonins might enter without the least noise or difficulty.)

'The Governor of Kanagawa urged the danger of an attack on the British Consulate, and wished Captain Vyse to go over to Yokohama, where he would be more easily protected, and in the meantime to admit a party of yaconins inside his house.   The Ministers urged the same thing when the interview took place.   Three nights before all the gates of the streets about Kanagawa were closed and the servants spread an alarm that the lonins were at hand, and already engaged with the Daimio's guard on the hill.   Four were actually seized in a tea-house, which was surrounded, and but one escaped.   There did not seem to have been any fight, but a body of them were about, giving countenance to rumours of an intended attack on the Consulate.   Captain Vyse had a guard of seven men from the " Ringdove," and a Dutch brig of war and a French armed transport were close in at Yokohama, in the absence of any British ship, for the protection of the Foreign settlement.'

Yesterday a report came in that two men had presented themselves at the Prince of Satsuma's *Kamiyaski* (or Palace) demanding refuge, and on being refused instantly killed themselves.

Afterwards modified into a report that 'fifty men demanded entrance and sanctuary, and on being refused killed the gate-keeper and dispersed.   Again, that one only presented himself, asking asylum for fifty, and on being refused killed himself, sure of being denounced !'

I may as well add here, though the account reached me somewhat later, the translation of a letter said to have been left in their house by four officers of the Prince of Mito, who have made themselves lonins.

'19th of 8th month.

'We become lonins now, since the foreigner gains more and more influence in the country, unable tranquilly to see the antient law (of Gongen Sama) violated; we become all four lonins with the intention of compelling the foreigner to depart.*

'AKIYAMA TETSONDJIRO
'TATÉMI TOMÉGORO
'ATSOUMI GORO
'MITSOUNGI SAUDA.'

Such were the conditions under which the Legations in Yeddo had to be maintained during the month succeeding the attack of the 5th July.

* It is very interesting to note the curious similarity that exists between the Feudal laws and institutions of Japan now, and those which marked our own national life in the Anglo-Saxon era. In England every freeman was bound to find a lord, a burgh, or a guild to become security for him, and if he could not do this he became '*a friendless man.*' Now a friendless man was synonymous with a *stranger* or an '*outlaw.*' Every man who met him had a right to kill him. This is precisely what exists now in Japan. As a noble or the head of a house is responsible for all who are of his family or claim his protection — when any of his people are resolved upon a desperate enterprise, they formally renounce the protection and declare themselves lonins — in other words 'outlaws' and 'friendless men'— after which no one is responsible for their acts, and this is considered highly honourable and a proper thing to do.

# CHAPTER X.

THE rumours and reports in general circulation, given
in the last chapter, will have sufficiently shown the
harassing and critical position of the Foreign Representatives in Yeddo. I had resolved on sending home Mr.
Oliphant, disabled for the time by his wounds, and
to make him the bearer of the Tycoon's letter to the
Queen, together with my own despatches, setting forth
as fully and accurately as I could the state of affairs.
It was natural to expect that the Government would
be mainly guided by such information as it might be in
my power to afford on the spot; and there was a great
deal that Mr. Oliphant could personally supplement from
his own observation, having both seen and suffered much
in the short period of his second sojourn in the capital.
The better to prepare him for this responsible duty, I
took him with me on several occasions in my conferences
with the Ministers of Foreign Affairs, and more especially
the two last, which were both confidential and secret,
none of the usual officers and attendants being allowed to
hear what passed. This was an opportunity I had long
desired for speaking out openly and freely to the Ministers as to their general policy, and the dangers incident
to it; but the difficulties in the way of so great an innovation on the established mode of intercourse, where all

interviews with the Foreign Representatives were public, and everything that passed took place in the presence of the Governors of Foreign Affairs and a large retinue of subordinate officials and attendants, were so serious that I had hitherto sought in vain for an occasion when I could, with fair prospect of success, make the proposition to send them all away.  The circumstances were peculiarly favourable now; and I therefore determined to make the effort. I calculated that I held in my hand means which, properly used, would not fail to convince them it was their interest to yield, and the result proved I was not mistaken.  I went to present Admiral Hope, who had landed the day before, together with Sir Hercules Robinson, the Governor of Hongkong.  I knew the Japanese Government was most anxious for the success of their own proposition, to defer the opening of the ports, and were satisfied this could not be attained, unless with my support.  They were not quite at their ease, either, about the view that might be taken by Her Majesty's Government of the late attempted massacre,—and Mr. Oliphant was just about to take his departure for England, with the Tycoon's letter and my despatches on both these subjects. Lastly, I had reason to know they were much disquieted and anxious about the proceedings of the Russians who had located themselves in the island of Tsus-Sima.  Profiting, then, by this rare combination of favourable circumstances, after a few minutes' conversation on general matters, I told them that the present aspect of affairs in Japan, and the state of its foreign relations, were very critical; that the proposition of the Government that we should abandon important treaty rights, at the same time that an attempt had been made, in the heart of the capital, to massacre everyone in the Legation, would naturally demand some resolution on the part of Her Majesty's Government of a decisive character; and that they might have the latest and best information, I was about to send Mr. Oliphant, crippled as he was by his wounds, to give in person more full details than I could possibly write.  In this view,

also, I had brought him with me, notwithstanding the
state of his health, that he might hear what the Ministers
should desire to say, after hearing some things I also
wished to say to them of very grave importance, but
which I could not communicate otherwise than confidentially, and to no one but themselves.  I added, I was of
course aware it was contrary to their custom ; but now
they had entered into new relations with Foreign Powers,
they must see the necessity, from time to time, of adapting
their modes of intercourse to the exigencies of a new
situation ; and that it was not in their interest that what I
had to communicate should, in the first instance, reach any
ears but theirs.  They were evidently strongly impressed
with the novelty and importance of my proposition, and
a conviction of the expediency of hearing what I had to
communicate ;  for, after a feeble resistance, and more
for appearances possibly than from any strong wish to
succeed, they consented ; — first to the withdrawal of
all the Governors of Foreign Affairs, except three ; then
these also, and, lastly, the Ometsky, or chief spy, with
all the subordinates and attendants of every description.  I, on my side, had previously arranged the withdrawal at the same time of Sir Hercules Robinson and
the naval officers, which prevented the appearance of
anything derogatory or invidious, as a concession on their
side only.  I then drew my chair nearer to the Ministers ;
made Mr. Myburgh, acting as my secretary and Dutch
interpreter, come between us, with only room for the
Japanese interpreter of the Ministers, Moriyama, on the
mats, and with the Admiral and Mr. Oliphant drawn
close on my left also.  The conversation was carried on in
a tone so low, that had anyone been behind the screens
in the vicinity, the Ministers must have felt it would have
been impossible to overhear what was passing.

After three hours thus spent it was getting late, but
so slow is the process of a double translation, that neither
the Ministers nor I had concluded what we each wished
to say.  It was accordingly agreed that the conference

should be renewed the next morning at eight o'clock, as the Admiral was to embark in the afternoon. It was most satisfactory in this beginning of better things, that the second Minister, when we were really done, declared that he had often desired such an opportunity of speaking without reserve ; and certain it is that he evinced the deepest interest in the communication I made, and the utmost anxiety that the conference should not be unduly curtailed,—while he on his side entered spontaneously upon very delicate revelations for a Japanese. I consider this 14th of August saw a new phase commenced ; and it will, I think, be seen hereafter that this striking innovation marks an epoch in the history of our relations.* The want of such opportunity for confidential exchange of opinions and information I had always felt to be an insuperable obstacle to any steady or sure progress with Japanese rulers. This was the first commencement of really confidential relations, and was not only a present benefit, but might prove the pivot on which all future intercourse between foreigners and Japanese would turn. To penetrate them with views which I could only hope to recommend to their acceptance if I could secure the means of speaking to them confidentially, and without a crowd of officials and witnesses of all classes, was an advantage of the utmost importance to the maintenance of that good understanding it had been my unceasing effort to establish—and one the more to be rejoiced in, that it was calculated to be equally beneficial to both countries.

I cannot, of course, make any statement here of what passed in these two important interviews—but the past, the present, and the future were all discussed in the most earnest and amicable spirit on both sides. And I

---

* Innovation of any kind in such a country, however expedient and necessary, is unfortunately always a source of danger to those who take the initiative. I was not surprised, therefore, to find later, that in a document said to have emanated from a body of malcontents, assembled round Miako, under covert protection of some of the leading Daimios, hostile to foreigners and to the Tycoon, this departure from established custom, among others, was enumerated as one of the crimes for which his Government was denounced.

cannot help hoping that much information was given and received, which placed the relative position and interests of the two countries, and, indeed, of Foreign Powers generally, with Japan in a much clearer light than they had ever appeared before to the Japanese Ministers; and by so much, at least, on a more satisfactory and intelligible basis than had previously been found possible.

My persistence in remaining at the Legation after the attack; merely gathering round it some better and additional means of defence in a guard from H.M.S. 'Ringdove,' and taking my usual rides with no better defence than a number of useless yaconins, had borne good fruit. It was not without some risk, certainly, but nothing is to be obtained in the present state of Japan without risk, and danger too, and the stake was sufficiently important to justify the step. Our position in the capital I am persuaded had been more firmly established in consequence, and at the very time it seemed most endangered and shaken. The attitude taken by M. de Bellecourt and myself tended I think to hold those in check, whoever they might be, who thought the Foreign Representatives were to be finally driven from the capital by menace and violence, and so far must have discouraged renewed attempts. These taken in conjunction with the new relations just established with the Government, were important results of what I may almost without metaphor term our six weeks' campaign in the capital — held against all enemies in what might in a military point of view certainly be deemed a most indefensible position — even against Ionins (if such were our enemies), with no better arms than swords—but of untold number and under powerful protection.

These two results went far even to modify my opinion of our position in Japan, in reference to the future. And if a two years' experience in the country would not allow me to write in a very sanguine spirit, yet I could not help taking a more hopeful view of *possible* improvement, than I should have felt justified in, but a few weeks earlier.

The position of the Foreign Representatives in Japan was indeed without precedent, certainly, in modern times. For any parallel we must go back to the middle ages in Europe, and to our early relations with the Sublime Porte, when Constantinople represented ' the East,' and ambassadors did not always escape personal indignities, and performed their duties in danger of the Seven Towers, if they gave offence to the Grand Turk. It is not surprising, therefore, if this conflict between actualities, and diplomatic canons of a later and more civilised era founded on existing international law and usages, should carry something of perplexity with it, and prove a source of harassing anxiety to those who were compelled by their position to try and reconcile the two. To maintain treaty rights without resort to the only arguments carrying weight; to preserve peaceful relations, and yet neither compromise the true interests nor the dignity of his country, constitute only a few of the more trying conditions attached to a Diplomatic Mission in Japan. Diversity of opinion as to how such seeming impossibilities may best be compassed is inevitable, where many minds and interests are concerned. This was well illustrated by the communications I received from my several colleagues at the time,— as to the conclusions to be drawn from passing events, and the course of action which might most fitly be adopted under the circumstances. But these diversities of opinion were rather the natural fruit of the atmosphere of doubt in which we were placed, by the absence of any positive information or thoroughly reliable data as to passing events — the real state of parties, or the action of the Government,—and never caused any real divergence of action or disaccord among the members of the Corps Diplomatique, with the one lamentable exception already referred to in the case of the American Legation. Indeed, in the midst of all the troubles and anxieties inseparable from the position of a Foreign Minister in Yeddo, the uninterrupted harmony and cordiality of my relations with all my colleagues was one of the few conditions of our exile on which I can look back with unmingled satisfaction.

As to the actual state of our relations, there was, indeed, much room for improvement. Life was insecure, trade was being daily restricted, and no remonstrance, protest, or argument within the scope of diplomatic means, had hitherto much availed to turn the authorities from a policy, the manifest tendency of which was to nullify the treaties, restrict all intercourse, and ultimately revert to the former state of isolation, by the expulsion of foreigners. To make trade unprofitable by restrictions, extortions, and prohibitions imposed on their own people, with whom their power is absolute; and render life not only so insecure, but intolerable in the conditions of residence, that no foreigner would long submit or find such an existence endurable,— seemed really to have been the chief object kept in view during nearly two years. This was the summary of their policy; and if these milder measures failed, the bravo's sword, for assassination, was always in reserve, and held *in terrorem* over the heads of the intruders on their soil, to be resorted to as occasion might serve, without ruth or scruple.

Who were the authors of this truly Oriental system, in which bad faith and assassination were the most prominent features? The Tycoon, by the mouth of his Ministers, speaking as a Government, denied all parentage and repudiated all responsibility. As to the systematic obstructions and restrictions of every kind, in which *Government agents* were the active instruments, they were either denied;—or defended as being no other than legitimate measures, to ensure regularity and prevent smuggling. So of obstructions to all intercourse with the people, or freedom of action on the part of foreigners, those which could not be proved against them were denied; and what could not be denied, even by Japanese, was defended as evidence of good faith, and necessary to our protection from the evil-disposed, 'who at the present moment abound, and are very dangerous even to the Government, though all outcasts, and *men of low degree* ! '

Such had been the continuous and unchanging course of events, since the first hour of the opening of the ports. The situation of all the Western Powers at this moment might be summed up in a few words. The treaties had in all their more important stipulations been systematically and persistently rendered inoperative ; and they now proposed, as a political necessity imposed upon *them* by the nature of the case and the exasperation of the public mind, the suspension of all farther execution, by deferring the opening of other ports for a term of years. Having thus provided against any developement of trade, and avowed the necessity of preventing its extension for the present, under plea of which they were doing much to destroy it, they also allowed the lives of the Foreign Representatives, and all other foreigners, to be so demonstrably insecure, that the authors of such a system might be pardoned if they counted with some certainty upon their not being long molested by the presence of such hated intruders into the country. Trade hampered and manacled, life menaced, national rights violated, with outrage to the flags, and without a hope of redress or amelioration—all with impunity. This in résumé depicts the situation.

Yet even among Europeans, and the Representatives of Foreign Powers, there were not wanting some who were disposed to give a much more favourable interpretation of the facts. Several possible, if not plausible explanations of the apparent inconsistency and half measures of the Japanese executive, consistent with the absence of any really hostile animus on their part, were suggested. First, the necessity of preventing the shock of a too abrupt transition from an old to a new state of things,— in trade, as in political relations. Secondly, the necessity of avoiding a revolution in the country, with which the Government said they were threatened, by parties opposed to them profiting by the excitement and confusion incident to such radical changes in the policy of the nation, powerfully assisted as these might be by a large class affected in their interests by a rise of prices entirely attributed to a new order of things, contrary to old laws and customs.

Thirdly, pressed by these and other causes of dissatisfaction and trouble incident to all sudden and great changes, it was farther suggested that the Government probably saw itself compelled by its critical position to keep up with any hostile party the appearance of making nothing but unwilling and compulsory concessions to prevent their rushing into open rebellion, in which foreigners and the native Government alike would become objects of attack. Equally might they have been compelled to be the proposers of an agreement to suspend execution of some clauses of the treaties, and from the same circumstances. Nor can it be denied that in this line of argument there is much appearance of reason and truth. Of decided bad faith as regards protection to foreigners for their lives, I did not think there was any sufficient evidence. No doubt there was a total failure of justice in the punishment of those who took life, and nearly equal fatuity was shown in the measures ostensibly taken for their protection. But much of this may be inherent in their system of administration and special circumstances, not perhaps very fully known to us. The first *may* have been due to a political necessity in regard to powerful and hostile Daimios who protected their instruments; and as to the insufficient and inappropriate means they successively took to prevent life being taken, all that could be said is, that they seemed a good deal in accordance with their habitual modes of proceeding, and a nation's habits cannot be exchanged in a year, even in matters of police. I acquitted them of deliberate bad faith in the latter particulars, and believed that they really desired to afford the protection they professed, because had they ever willed or consented to a general massacre, there was nothing whatever to have prevented a St. Bartholomew or a Sicilian Vespers on a small scale. We were but a handful of foreigners, all counted, not two hundred I think, scattered in four different ports, incapable of any effective resistance, and generally deprived of means of escape. In Yeddo always, for on those rare occasions when a ship of war happened to be at the anchorage, it lay of necessity some five miles from the shores. Bodies of irresponsible lonins, outlaws, and outcasts, could always be secured to attack a Legation or assassinate a foreigner; and if one attack failed, another and another might follow, and in the end make success certain. I think this is conclusive. That their protection was ineffective, and always would be so, unless close imprisonment within four walls in the midst of a guard of jailors were accepted, was in my opinion, however, equally certain. Even Mr. Harris's faith in his own safety had this important reservation, 'so long as he observed the precautions recommended by the Japanese Government, and used by the Japanese themselves.' What those precautions were had been sufficiently shown. Their inability, by any other and less objectionable or inadmissible means, to protect the Legations in Yeddo effectually, either from insult or murder ; while there was undoubted evidence of an actively hostile party seeking their destruction, was so clear, that I am convinced no British Minister, so long as this state of things should last, could be fitly resident in Yeddo without means of defence drawn from our own forces. This involved a guard permanently for the Legation, and a mounted escort of European or Indian troopers. The footing in a word would be somewhat like that of a Resident in India exposed to a similar danger, though it might and would of course be on a much less expensive scale. A guard of from twenty to thirty men at the Legation, and a mounted escort of a dozen troopers in addition; and finally a residence built with some reference to attack and in a defensible position, would, I conceived, meet the requirements of the case. Without some such provision loss of life, fresh complications and treatment so injurious, that it could not long be tolerated with any regard to our national credit, could not be otherwise than inevitable. We can only look for a cessation of danger and the necessity for such measures, from some political change in the country. Either increased strength of the executive, or diminished vigour and daring in the party or parties now apparently fighting their own battle with the Government of the Tycoon, over our bodies.

In these conclusions I was glad to find Admiral Hope when once on the spot, and able to judge as to what the actual conditions of a residence in Yeddo were, entirely concurred. I am indeed bound to say when he at last arrived, nothing could be more cordial than the desire he manifested to give Her Majesty's Representative the most effective support. And it was quite evident from the interest he evinced in all the measures calculated to ensure the Legation against any farther outrage, that had he ever realised when at a distance the actual danger menacing us, there would have been no room for complaint at apparent unconcern. It was mainly through Sir James Hope's effective and prompt assistance that I obtained for our troops on the coast of China, within three months from this time, a well-mounted escort, commanded by an efficient officer. And although their adoption was made a subject of remonstrance by the Japanese Government, and was not unattended with anxiety ; I feel now that only such means could have given the necessary safety, and that they have in more ways than one had a most salutary moral effect both on the population and the Government.

All that remained for me to do had now been effected, to maintain our ground and give time for the arrival of final instructions from Her Majesty's Government. The site for the five Legations was marked out on a commanding table-land, having a tolerably direct communication with the water. The Government undertook of their own accord to make it defensible by a deep moat and double palisade, and I consented in the interval while it was building, occasionally to vary my residence, and relieve them at intervals of the large expense attending the guarding of

Tozengee with a force of 500 men which they insisted upon as necessary in addition to our own small guard of marines — and also of the anxiety they felt, or professed to feel, for the safety of the Legation, even after such measures of precaution.  Nothing farther was left, but to wait patiently the lapse of months that must take place before Mr. Oliphant could arrive at home and any despatches or instructions reach me.

Part of this time was employed in putting together the materials that lay to my hand for the narrative which may now be very soon concluded.  I had leisure to consider very deliberately both the actual state of foreign relations, and the future prospects of these, as well as their bearing on the destiny of Japan.  And some of the reflections suggested at this period will be found in the following chapters.

# CHAPTER XI.

REVIEW OF FOREIGN RELATIONS WITH JAPAN — IN THE JAPAN-
ESE TERRITORIES THE PRESENT IS HEIR TO THE PAST IN A
PECULIAR SENSE — INFLUENCE ON EXISTING RELATIONS — HOW
THEY MAY BE DEALT WITH, AND WHAT THE ALTERNATIVES
OFFERED.

SUCH was the aspect of affairs soon after the end of the
second year following the opening of the Ports.   An
attempt to kill Her Majesty's Representative, and all the
other members of the Legation at one blow, placed though
they were under the protection of the Tycoon's body-
guards, and the armed retainers of two of his Daimios,
opened a fresh page in the history of our relations.   Prior
to this the outrages had been limited to *menaces* of
*massacre,* and isolated acts of butchery or assassination in
the streets.   But this last deed was a conclusive demonstration of the existence of a hostile party, which would
stop at *nothing* — not even the murder of the Foreign
Representatives within the gates of their Legations.
True, the Japanese Government had often warned them of
the existence of such dangers, and of plottings and designs
for the murder of all the Europeans, as a means of ridding
the country of their presence for ever, and effecting a
total rupture of relations with Foreign Powers.   But it
was hard to believe in designs as short-sighted as they
were atrocious, upon any evidence less conclusive than
the events of this July night.

We had, apparently, arrived at a period when parties in
the State hostile to foreign intercourse, had resolved on
keeping no measure henceforth with us, and were

determined to force on a rupture of relations. And whosoever the active agents might be, it seemed the ostensible Government (the Tycoon and his Council of State) exercised no controlling power to prevent any deed of atrocity. For the attempted massacre of the British Legation was but the culminating point of a long series of outrages and assassinations, attended with perfect impunity to the perpetrators.

Assuming, in this aspect of affairs, that Great Britain, from a love of peace, and a horror of new complications in the East, with contingencies of war in the distance,— would rather contemplate the abandonment of all her treaty rights in Japan than incur the risk of a contest to enforce or maintain them ; and, consequently, would be willing to adopt the views set forth by the Japanese Ministers in their letter to the Foreign Representatives — attribute any failure or obstructions to trade to natural causes beyond the control of Governments ; and the in-security of life to popular discontent and hatred, for which the Tycoon could just as little be held responsible — what would be the immediate result of such entire acquiescence ? If wholly unconditional and unlimited, it hardly could be doubted that trade would gradually cease. Its growth had been checked from the beginning by the action of the authorities with the native dealers. Although this was questioned by some few of our own merchants, there was really no doubt about it. We must, at all events, renounce the opening of more ports. And if we still maintained a Diplomatic Agent in the capital, and Consuls at the ports, we must also be resigned to see them reduced to a state closely analogous to the Dutch of old in Decima — free in name only, and prisoners in effect ; shut out from all intercourse with the people of Japan, whom it is our interest, by free communication, to conciliate and enlighten. To what useful end, then, would all this expense, trouble, and humiliation have been accepted ? If it should be expedient to maintain political relations independent of any commerce with this country, and for reasons connected with other and larger interests in the East, it would still be a question whether it might not be worth some serious effort to maintain our Diplomatic and Consular Agents in a position less humiliating and derogatory than that which the Japanese, of their own free accord, were ever likely to concede.

But, before entering into any question of this nature, or passing on to the future, and a description of the means available for the improvement of our position or affairs in this country, a few remarks of a retrospective character are required, if we would either understand the present, or be prepared to deal intelligently with the future. Nowhere is the present more completely interwoven with the past, or the impress of a nation's history and traditions more indelibly and plainly stamped in the lineaments of an existing generation than in Japan. The present is heir to the past always and everywhere, in the life of nations no less than of individuals; but the present is linked to the past in Japan, in a sense so peculiar, that it is worthy of special attention.

This study of the past can alone furnish a key to the character and policy of the nation, in the possession of which lies our best hope of the future, and of turning what it may have in store to good account. We *must*, indeed, read both the present and future of Japan by the light of the past, for by such reflected light alone can either be rightly understood.

The rapid growth and progress of modern nations in Europe has left Asia so far behind, that the elder race has become as a child in the grasp of the younger, and incapable of any effective resistance in actual conflict. There is a dull consciousness of the fact in the Asiatic mind, and of the giant power wielded by the younger and still despised branches of the great human family. And only thus is the collateral fact to be accounted for: that no people or nation of Asiatic blood ever yield to the superior strength of the European, without a dogged and determined resistance, and a struggle often continued long after all hope of final success must have died out of their hearts. Like the Greeks of the Byzantine empire, and later, the polished but effeminate Italians of the middle ages, the Chinese and Japanese are brought in contact with races surging in upon them from unknown lands beyond the outer limits of their civilisation—barbarians, in a word, far superior to themselves in bone, and thew, and sinew, in prowess and military tactics, but still barbarians, and thus *inferiors* in all that constitutes superiority in *their* estimation: in knowledge of their language, litera-ture, religion, and philosophy—the only religion or philosophy they recognise as having a real existence or value. As Goths and Vandals could trample down and sweep before them any array the effeminate Byzantine Court could marshal in the field, so can we the hosts of China or Japan, though the latter makes pretensions to be considered warlike. But the result is still the same. The triumph over their weaker frames and their ignor-ance of arms, does not command any respect, or *mental recognition of superiority*. They bend their necks to superior force, but harden their hearts and console themselves under defeat, by hoarding in secret a cumula-tive and rankling contempt for their conquerors.

And thus, when beaten in the field, they fall back on fraud and cunning, the traditional arms of the weak; and, it must be added, the only ones much relied upon by the Asiatic. Resistance does not cease, but only takes another form. The power of passive resistance possessed by a whole race, with habits and institutions antagonistic to the foreigner, and to all change, is a tower of strength to the rulers; and a barrier to the stranger's progress, which may prove long impassable. But, besides the obstacle created by the inert mass and bulk of the opposing body, rulers like the Daimios in Japan can always draw, from this great arsenal of ignorance, and passions easily aroused into activity, the weapons of treachery and violence, which leave the stranger, fixed on the soil, exposed to a vendetta, and compels him to stand in defence of his life.*

Such exactly is the position of the foreigner in Japan at the present moment. And against this kind of instinctive resistance, stirred up in the mass by designing rulers, no Western Power can hope to come out completely victor in a single generation; for it has arrayed against it the most baffling and exhausting of hostile elements. Russia has had some evidence of this in Poland. Prior to any real advance, such as shall be beyond the power of a privileged class to arrest, there is required a change of convictions among the people as to their true interests; which, for the most part, must be allowed to break in slowly, and advance by steady degrees. Like a New Zealander's *pah*, it is to be carried by the sap, and the superior skill of the engineer, and not by assault, which only leads to an idle sacrifice of life, and the danger of a defeat.

But it is clear that for such a gradual process to make way, there must be a beginning,— the trenches must be opened and the sap laid ;—and here precisely lies the difficulty. Our greatest grievance in Japan is not their present spirit of resistance — their antagonism and dislike to innovation ;— but the systematic and determined way in which the Rulers set themselves to work, with all the means at their command, to make a *beginning impossible*, by cutting off all communication with the people, and especially the educated, and with all persons exercising any influence in the country.

They seem to have intuitively seen where their real danger lay ;—and warned and enlightened by past experience, and some gleanings of history as to European progress in

---

* Here, again, the strange analogy of institutions and national habits with the Anglo-Saxon era cannot be overlooked. 'In the Saxon-Danish era, the hundred in which a criminal lived was bound either to make good his offences or to deliver him up.' 'It is probable,' the same writer remarks, 'that when both parties belonged to the same district, this duty was fairly performed; but when the murdered man was a detested Dane, or a still more hateful Norman, nobody ever chose to know how he came by his death.' Nothing could better or more accurately describe the existing state of things in Japan, and the position of the foreigner.

the East, they have resolved to meet us on the threshold. Determined that we shall not plant the first germs of anything that can bear fruit hereafter, they exhaust their ingenuity in effecting that end. They seem to see as clearly as we do, the importance of access to the minds and hearts of the people, and so have taken their measures accordingly to close up all the avenues. This they have chosen as their field of battle, and the stronghold of their power against the inroads of the foreigner, confident that, so long as they can maintain this ground intact, all the European nations together must recoil, baffled and defeated, as often as they come to the attack.

Hence all the jealous watchings, the restrictions and limitations encountered in every direction ;— the army of spies and two-sworded yaconins, true ' sbirri,' who know only their master's will. Hence, too, outrages, insults, and assassinations, with a remittent character of febrile violence ;— now striking a blow, and then dying off into mere mutterings of menace or insult, to recur again inevitably in the same order, and with persistent regularity. We have forced ourselves upon them ; but it is their business to see that neither present profit, nor hope of future advantage, shall come of it,—and this is the policy they have devised to that end, and perseveringly carry out with all the subtlety and utter disregard for life, which might be anticipated in Asiatic rulers, plotting against a formidable adversary.

If, on the contrary, the Japanese as a people could be brought in contact with us, even at a few points ; and within the sphere of new influences of thought and feeling, Europe might take patience. Ten or twenty years are so little in the life of a nation ! But the misfortune is, these Rulers will not allow the Treaty Powers to take patience for an ally,—listen exclusively to its counsels, and sow and plant in faith, that in due time the seed will bear fruit. The Daimios will not leave them any ground of such trust for the Future, and are ever stirring up violence in the hope of intimidating, and ultimately, by menace and assassination combined, of driving every foreigner out of the country.

To check this tendency to resort to violence and a system of terrorism; and to secure such points of contact and means of communication with the people as shall sooner or later enable us to leaven the mass with sentiments and feelings less favourable to the absolute power of the Daimios, and less indifferent to the prospective advantages of foreign trade and intercourse, appears, therefore, to furnish the very key we are seeking to a policy of the Future.

But we must still turn our regards backward to the Past for additional light, and abundant evidence will be found to prove, that although forced into renewed relations after an interim of two hundred years, they have never for an instant changed their policy, or entertained the design of making any effective or permanent change.

On the contrary, it would seem to be the Alpha and Omega of *their* policy to secure the means of returning to their isolation. They would have new guarantees, if possible, for its unquestioned enjoyment hereafter; in the conviction European Powers would acquire by experience, of the hopelessness of farther effort to keep up friendly relations, and the uselessness of entering into hostilities, for the costly and very profitless privilege. This good result they hope to draw from the evil days on which they have fallen; and then their patriotic efforts will be amply compensated.

There is a characteristic speciality in this tenacity of purpose which bates no jot of hope, even when all their outer defences seemed beaten down by a *force majeure* which they did not deem it prudent or possible to resist by arms. For in other respects, they only shared a common fate in yielding a reluctant consent to proposals for treaties, they would never voluntarily have entered into. All treaties that have ever been made with Eastern Governments, from Constantinople to Yeddo, have been extorted either by force or its equivalent. No Eastern potentate has willingly accepted the proffered friendship and alliance of Western States, unless the King of Siam may be considered an exception. The Japanese, however, unlike all other nations or tribes of the East, are not content with a sullen and passive resistance, but regard these compulsory treaties as a means of more completely insuring their emancipation from a foreign thrall, and an undisturbed isolation ever after!

Doubtless some portion of this intensified antagonism and hostility may partly be traced to their insular position, but greatly also to their antecedent history. Three centuries ago they voluntarily and trustfully made treaties with the principal Maritime Powers of Europe, and the relations thus established all ended disastrously in a forcible disruption, after years of civil and religious war convulsing the country. The Dutch alone were then excepted from a decree of extermination and expulsion directed against all of foreign race, and professing a Christian creed; and the natives of Holland were excepted only on condition that they would submit to be imprisoned in a sea-girt quarantine at Nagasaki, and under the most jealous guard.

Thus it happens that Europeans of this generation appear in Japan as the heirs and representatives of the past, in a way peculiarly fatal to any friendly settlement on its shores. On them indiscriminately, weighs heavily not only the antagonism of race common to all Asia, but an inheritance purely Japanese, which has been carefully hoarded by the ruling classes. One of mingled hatred and fear, of religious and political fanaticism, only too faithfully transmitted from father to son through many successive generations. Not merely without diminution, but with an accumulation of interest, which, now the opportunity presents itself, they seem eager should be paid off in addition to the original capital.

From the day that men of Western lineage first set foot on the coast, when Commodore Perry made his Treaty in 1853, there is abundant and conclusive evidence to show they were looked upon as the legitimate heirs, if not the lineal descendants, of the Mendez Pintos and Xaviers, adventurers and proselytisers, merchants and missionaries, who followed fast in the wake of Vasco da Gama, in search of new fields, where gold was to be gathered, and souls to be saved. The Americans flattered themselves (as they confess) that the plea, ostentatiously put forward, of being wholly disconnected with any nations whose antecedent relations had given ground of complaint or distrust, would be received as exceptional ground for favour. Never was hope more vain, as they now know by experience. The Japanese allow no distinction of nationalities to stand between them and their one object; which is the expulsion of *the foreigner* and a return to their isolation. Their distrust of Foreign Powers is indiscriminate, and their hatred perfectly impartial. They slay the secretary of the United States Legation, and attempt the massacre of the inmates of the British Legation with equal readiness and satisfaction. If the Russians attack them at Tsussima, the English at Yeddo may pay the penalty!

In a word, we are all descendants of Ishmael, and have no claim to the promised land. Descendants of those who, within the first century of their appearance in the country where they were received with a friendly welcome, drained it of its gold, convulsed it with civil and religious wars, and spread fierce dissensions where they had found only peace and union,—we return, after a lapse of two centuries, to claim the inheritance of men who were either crucified as the worst of criminals, or expelled, with execration, as disturbers of the peace and revilers of their gods,—at once the reproach and curse of the country,—of those against whom a law of the empire was made, declaring, that ' so long as the sun should shine,' no foreigner should touch the soil of Japan and live. From that date it became an act of loyalty and patriotism, worthy of all praise in a Japanese, to aid in rooting out and exterminating the hated race. This time-honoured law of Gongen Sama, the founder of the present dynasty of Tycoons, or as the Ministers affirm of older date, has never been abrogated.  It could only be rescinded by the Mikado, or, at least, with his sanction; and, practically, it certainly never has been repealed, for if the necessary sanction was obtained, the Tycoon's Government have never dared to make it public.  There is no doubt that the spirit of this hostile and intolerant legislation still survives in the hearts of a large and influential number of the governing class, and is quoted as justifying all Japanese in proceeding to any extremity against the stranger.  It would have been of just as little avail to introduce a clause of toleration for the Christian religion in the treaties, because the Japanese Government still maintain their right to make it death to a Japanese to listen to the missionary, or take his books.  It could only have made the other clauses for the establishment of trade and free intercourse objects of greater dislike, without in the slightest degree advancing the cause of religion.  They remembered the past, and still, apparently, hold a conviction, founded on some experience of the practical working of the Romanist system, that an ecclesiastical power which exercises complete dominion over the souls of men, leaves very little for the temporal sovereign.

The long and doubtful struggle and devastating wars which preceded the casting forth of the foreigner, and the extermination of all converts to his religion, in the 17th century, and which ended, as we know, with the fall of Simabara, beneath the ruins of which lay buried 37,000 of its defenders and Christian converts,—has left an indelible impression on the national mind, identifying us with trouble, dissension, and calamity.

Here we have both cause and effect plainly traced. We can understand the enmity we experience from the educated and privileged classes, and measure its depth and strength.  There are men among the ruling class ready to put into force as sanguinary decrees as those of Gongen Sama, and to enact over again all the tragic scenes of that time of blood and torture. The intervening period of two centuries has been little more to them than a long sleep,—from which they awake to find the foreigner once more seeking to effect a lodgement on their soil, and plant the seeds of more religious wars and civil feuds, with their consequences of revolution and national impoverishment.

If it be asked, 'what data exist for such sweeping conclusions?' it may be answered, too many for citation here in detail; but, first and principally, the authority of the Daimios and the Government of the Tycoon, both speaking by the mouths of the Ministers of Foreign Affairs. These, as members of the Great Council of State, represent a Cabinet, which, as the Tycoon is merely a youth, must be held to exercise the power in his name, under the influence and control of those strong enough to uphold a Government; whether these be the more influential of the Daimios or a large number of the lesser nobility. This declaration of irradicable and uncompromising hostility was the burden of nearly every official interview, and a vast number of written communications. The letter of the Ministers, accompanying the autograph letter of the Tycoon to the respective Treaty Powers, requesting no more ports might be opened, was only one among many; but the latest *written* expression of this political programme,— as the attack on the Legation, was the last *in action* — is to be found in a communication sent by the Ministers to M. de Bellecourt, which admirably sums up and confirms the narrative as it has here been given, and it has the advantage, also, of being authentic. Under date 27th July 1861, the two Ministers of Foreign Affairs forwarded an official note, containing the following passage referring to the declarations of two of the lonins who were wounded in the attack on the Legation, and made prisoners, adopting the French translation. It ran as follows :—

'Suivant leurs déclarations il paraîtrait que tous ceux

qui sont impliqués dans cette affaire sont des vagabonds de la province de Dziosiou, que des prêtres et des gens de basse classe se sont joints à eux, et qu'ils persévèrent avec obstination dans leur opinion qui a *pour but de rétablir l'ancien système gouvernemental, parcequ'ils considèrent la conclusion des Traités avec les Puissances étrangères comme contraires à l'ancien état de l'Empire*; enfin qu'ils avaient tramé cette conjuration par la raison que les officiers et les bourgeois sont dans l'indigence depuis l'ouverture des ports, à cause du renchérissement des marchandises, et parceque le sentiment national devient inquiet. Il est à présumer qu'indépendamment des quatorze conjurés connus, il y en a encore beaucoup du même genre.'

'Il y a quelque temps on a arrêté un individu s'efforçant d'exciter l'inimitié contre les étrangers. Il disait, que si par suite du meurtre des étrangers, les relations entre notre Empire et les Puissances étrangères étaient rompues, l'ancien système gouvernemental qui excluait les étrangers du pays serait rétabli, que l'Empire deviendrait alors considéré et puissant, et qu'il pensait prouver ainsi son patriotisme, bien qu'il pût y perdre la vie. La crainte de la mort ne semble pas modifier la persistance de son opinion erronée.'

There is, indeed, one notable difference between the statement endorsed by Ministers, and that which has been made in the preceding pages. According to the Ministers the hostility is all to be found in the lower and unprivileged classes and among the priests, without complicity or participation on the part of Daimios, or their relations and retainers; whereas there can be no doubt, as I have already pointed out in a preceding chapter, the exact reverse is the fact. Obstacles to trade, and danger to life, restrictions and vexations to which merchants and Ministers in different forms are subjected, may with more or less certainty be traced as coming from above, and not from below. The *Tycoonat*, to borrow a convenient name coined by the French, including the whole hierarchy and system

of government, Tycoon, Daimios, and Councils of State, are
the true sources, and furnish the only active power in
operation.   It is more convenient, and safer to the ruling
powers, to place the hostility which creates insuperable
obstacles to any extension of trade, free intercourse with
the people, or even security to life, in the mass of the population.   It is safer to refer to popular excitement and public
opinion as the source of the evil, than to the opinions or
machinations of any number of Daimios,* who could be
held responsible both for their acts and opinions, and 143
of whom have castles and capitals accessible to attack.†
They have wit enough, apparently, to realise the truth of
Sydney Smith's saying, without having heard it: that
responsibility is in an inverse ratio to the numbers involved.   And the policy attributed to the Bourbons and
petty sovereigns of Italy, of seeking to discourage
locomotion, internal and external trade, and almost every
branch of industry, except the ordinary operations of
agriculture, exactly represents the policy of the Japanese
rulers.   In trade, especially foreign trade, they see the
elements of wealth and the growth of a middle class, which
could not long be retained in a state of serfdom.   What
took place in Europe by the same developement of wealth
and intelligence, among the mercantile classes, enabling
these to break the chains of a feudal tenure, and create free
cities as centres of resistance, would follow here.   Foreign
trade and intercourse do carry with them inevitably the
germs of a social revolution to these Eastern states; and
whether by instinct, or by a higher exercise of reason
aided by some fragments of historical knowledge, they
know and feel the danger to existing institutions, and all
their class privileges by which the Daimios are sole lords
of the soil, and the whole of the population but labourers
to till it, with shopkeepers to distribute the produce;

* See Tables I. and II. of the official list of Daimios in Appendix.
† See map of the provinces, with the capitals of 143 Daimios marked, vide
Appendix.

neither having voice in the government, nor any pretensions to take part in the administration.

Why these same dominant powers, Tycoon, Councils of State and Daimios combined, entered into treaties with Foreign Powers in recent times, if such were their principles and ruling motives, may well be asked. And no question more frequently recurred in the beginning of our relations, or seemed less susceptible of satisfactory answer. But the difficulty has gradually disappeared, under the light thrown upon the affairs of Japan by recent events; and with fuller information on many points. This has already been touched upon in a previous chapter* when describing how the second American treaty was made.

When Commodore Perry first appeared in 1852 to try the effect of 'moral pressure,'—backed by a considerable squadron, much dissension ensued among the magnates. Not however, as the Americans represented, and were probably led to believe, by the Japanese themselves in order to mislead; not because *any* were friendly, and desired such relations. There may be some, like the late American Resident Minister, who still cling to this idea, as part and parcel of that which constituted his special pride—the ' opening of Japan to the civilised world,' by his tact and diplomacy, in dealing with a people who saw in his countrymen only *friends*, and against whom alone, of all the Western nations, the Japanese had no griefs of old standing. But their number must be very small at the present day, who believe that there either existed then, or can be found now, liberal and enlightened minds among the members of the Daimio class, who *saw the advantages of free trade and intercourse* with *foreign nations, and desired nothing better.* The plain truth appears to be, that all in various degrees were inimical to a departure from the old established policy of the country, the central idea of which was ISOLATION. When a new

* Vol. I. Chap. IX.

course was pressed upon them, by such cogent arguments as Commodore Perry advanced with his squadron, and Mr. Harris, four years later, ingeniously borrowed from the proximity of the victorious forces of England and France at the mouth of the Peiho, very violent dissensions ensued in each case as to the best policy. Whether it was better in their then defenceless state boldly to reject all overtures *coûte que coûte* ; or, as the other and prevailing party contended, to accept the treaties thus forced upon them, without giving them effect—or only just so far as might be found essential to avert a premature rupture, and solely with the view of gaining the time necessary to put their coasts in a state of defence, and make preparations for resistance, was the real subject of discussion. These defences, we know, have ever since been vigorously advanced. Large numbers of cannon have been cast ; new batteries erected ; steam ships have been bought, and enough powder expended in ball practice and drill to have supplied ammunition for a campaign. These preparations for contingent hostilities were far too obvious and significant to escape the notice of the Foreign Representatives ; and Her Majesty's Government had been more than once advised of the facts, and the unavoidable inferences, namely, that the Japanese either regarded a collision with some Foreign Power, and an attack, as probable at no distant period ; or they had themselves determined on a rupture, and were preparing to resist any attempt, on the part of one or all, to enforce the treaties. And if the progress of affairs and the succession of events since the opening of the ports be carefully studied, it is difficult to feel any doubt that the latter course was the one really contemplated from the beginning.

In the meantime there is reason to believe that in order to gain time, the least violent and reactionary of the party were put in office to maintain relations between the Government and the Foreign Representatives with outward professions of amity and good faith, but secretly under a pledge steadily to pursue a system which should render virtually inoperative all the more important clauses of treaties in respect to trade, locomotion, and freedom of intercourse : and more especially to instil a feeling of insecurity and danger into the mind of all foreigners, beginning with the Representatives themselves, as the effect of a strongly excited state of public feeling, increasing and fast becoming uncontrollable. In support of which various outrages and assassinations would not be wanting, until one of two things must result — either the Foreign Representatives would be reduced to the state of prisoners in the capital, or they would be driven to abandon the position as wholly untenable. It would not matter very much which ; the desired end would be clearly in view in either case.

If this were not really the policy and preconcerted line of action among all who exercise a controlling power in the Government of Japan, it would be something marvellous that the whole chain of effects should so perfectly and exactly correspond to the attributed causes. If those comprising the Council of State had no foreknowledge of the various murders and acts of violence perpetrated in one continued sequence against foreigners, and culminating in an attack on the British Legation, it was not a little remarkable that the Ministers should be so ready and anxious instantly to turn to profit such deeds, in manifest furtherance of the very policy here suggested. Is a linguist murdered under the British flag at the gates of the Legation ?—reason for exercising more jealous control over all access to the Minister. Is the Regent murdered ? —reason for surrounding the Legation with more police and guards, and never allowing the Minister to stir out without an escort :—reason for urging all the Representatives to go within the circle of the castle moats, and under one roof, to be under safeguard, and constitute themselves stateprisoners. Is the secretary of the United States Legation slain in the streets ?—reason for the same panacea, more guards and gates, more restrictions on the liberty of the Minister — reason for deferring the opening of the ports, for appeasing the public mind, in a state of such wrathful excitation at the prospect of more trade and more ports accessible, that the Government could not be responsible for the consequences, if refused. It is not easy to believe in the perfect good faith of a Government under such circumstances. And how can we trust to their professions of a sincere desire to observe the obligations imposed by treaties with the reservation ' So far as the state of *public opinion will permit,*' which, by their own showing, is not at all? At the same time that we see great contradiction between the professions and the acts of the Government, giving evidence of insincerity in the dealings of Ministers with Foreign Representatives, wholly inconsistent with their often expressed desire to carry out the treaties in good faith ; we are bound in justice not to forget that whatever be the state of parties in Japan, the reopening of foreign relations has proved a bone of contention, threatening once more to excite a civil war, and has actually led to a whole series of tragic events. Such a series of tragedies might well seem to justify the forebodings of those who denounced the initiation of this policy of concession, even though only provisional, as calamitous to the nation ; and are not calculated to soften their feelings of animosity towards the foreigner. Nor is there any assurance that we are near the end of this dismal chapter in their history. The lives of the members of the Great Council were menaced, the Ministers declared ;* and a Governor of Foreign Affairs was sent recently to inform the British Envoy of an attempt at assassination on one of the Gorogio, by a single man ; other accounts say by two.

So much of the past it is obviously necessary to have in mind, as inseparably connected with the present situation, and the success of any measures which may be devised with a view to improvement in the future. Great efforts have been made during the past two years, to

---

* Subsequent to this date the Foreign Minister, Ando Tsusimano Kami, *was* attacked and severely wounded by a band of eight, while on his way to the palace.

reconcile the Japanese to the establishment of trade, and the peaceable residence of political agents at the capital. But it must be confessed many of the foreigners in whose hands the trade lies at the ports, have ill-seconded those efforts by their conduct and proceedings; and it is the less surprising, therefore, if the efforts of diplomacy, however patiently and perseveringly continued, should have met with very indifferent success; too little, indeed, under such untoward conditions, on the European and the Japanese side alike, to authorise any very sanguine hope in relation to the future.

There is so much that is natural in the fears, the hostile spirit, and the general distrust of Foreign Powers manifested by the Japanese rulers, that however deplorable the result, no one can be surprised, or even condemn — without reference to extenuating circumstances, which are so many pleas of justification. It has even been contended by a friend of the Japanese among the Europeans, who has been longest resident in the country, under the old prescriptive rule of Decima and Dutch policy, that 'after all the Foreign Powers were wrong to have asked for more ports than Nagasaki.'

If we persisted in the undertaking, despite all these formidable obstacles to success, in seeking to establish trade and friendly relations with a semi-civilised Eastern race, who desire neither, and are in danger of being plunged into civil wars and dissensions, if they escape foreign war as the first consequence,—it was clear we must accept the task with these untoward conditions attaching to it.

Other wards there may be in the lock to be turned, before the secret of all our difficulties, and of Japanese policy, can be laid open; but there are valid reasons for stopping here, and not pursuing the subject further at present. Enough has been said to show how many and serious are the obstacles created by the traditions of the past. Foreigners are under the ban of a law which dates back more than two centuries, and justifies all who seek either to kill or expel them.   A law unfortunately associated in the mind of every Japanese with civil and religious war—with a long and bloody struggle, in which the Foreigner and his Religion were alike held up to execration, as the immediate cause of all the evils under which the whole nation groaned and suffered.   We cannot wonder, then, that our reappearance on the scene, after such antecedents, should be regarded by the ruling classes, if not the whole nation, with a mingled feeling of fear and hostility.

After this retrospect, and careful analysis of our present position in connection with the past, there were several questions pressing for solution.   The object of our treaty is no doubt trade, this first and chiefly.   But no trade, present or prospective in Japan, it might be thought, would justify our going to war for its advancement.   And yet it seemed doubtful,—unless we were prepared to enforce in some way the stipulations of treaties granting free exchange of produce and intercourse, with immunity from outrage and violence,—if any effort would be made by the Government to keep good faith with us?   Treaties extorted by force or pressure, can only, as a general rule, be maintained by the same means.   All our experience in the East points to this conclusion, and the history of treaties between European States even, is not very different.   If we scruple to enforce engagements, not spontaneously entered into by one party, and neither for the extension of trade nor religion, think such a course expedient or justifiable,—all that can be said is, it might have been better never to have made the treaty.   But neither nations nor individuals are always logical.   And although it is not unusual to appeal to the 'inexorable logic of facts,' even facts get sometimes grouped together in anything but a logical order of sequence.

Western Powers, and we more especially, have great interests in the East, of which Japan is an outpost.   We have

prestige and an empire to maintain, as well as a commerce
so vast, that nothing which Japan could ever contribute
to swell its amount, would perhaps be worthy of much
consideration.    Whether having once entered into treaty
with Japan, we can cease all farther relations and retire,—
retire, too, before violence and menace,—is a question,
unfortunately, which cannot be decided with exclusive
reference to that country.   Japanese trade we could very
well dispense with.   The tea and silk they supply can be
procured elsewhere.   Their coals are useful, but may be
paid too dearly for in national dignity.   They are rich in
metals, but these they hoard and will not freely give, and
*they* also may be had elsewhere, and nearer home.
Finally, any trade we might create with Japan, would
not be so much in *addition* to that possessed with other
countries, as in *lieu of* an equal portion somewhere else ;
while the profits on any of our manufactures they may
take, will probably never pay the cost of a small squadron
to protect it.

    But putting trade with Japan aside, our prestige in the
East is a power which supplies without cost the place of
fleets and armies.   We cannot *afford*, therefore, by any
ill-considered backward steps, to damage or jeopardise
this, seeing it is the great economiser of our national
resources.   So far from being a measure in the interest of
economy it might prove the very reverse.   And any act
or course of policy which may serve to indicate either
fear or weakness, is calculated to affect the power and
the integrity of the whole empire.   In this chain, not a
link can be broken or damaged, even in such an outlying
and distant region of the East as Japan, without some
danger and prejudice to the whole.

    In these latitudes we are confronted with Russia and
her fast increasing establishments on the Manchourian
coast.   From the extension and prosperity of her commerce
we have nothing to fear, but rather cause for rejoicing.
Seas covered with a commercial navy are pledges of peace

and not incitements to hostile aggression, on the part of the nation possessing it. But predominance of a military kind, by ships of war and fortified harbours, becomes a source of danger to any commerce less efficiently protected. Something of this latter predominance Russia appears to be seeking now in all the seas between the coast of China and Manchouria on the one side, with the Japanese Isles as a fringe and the eastern coasts of America on the other; between which lie all the treasures of a yet undeveloped but certainly increasing trade in the Pacific. The possession of Corea and Japan, or portions of them, would give to any aggressive Maritime Power almost inexhaustible resources, in coal, the precious metals, in iron, lead, and sulphur — in harbours of refuge and fortified depots — in timber and labour for ship-building — and even in hardy seamen. The means of attack these would supply to Russia, in the event of any designs against the commerce of Great Britain, both in the China seas and the Pacific, from the shores of Australia to those of America, gives us a pressing and momentous interest in any question of annexation or conquest in the Japanese seas, the only link wanted to complete *her* chain of empire round the world.

While we have treaty rights ostensibly in Japan, conquest or annexation without our concurrence would be difficult. Looking to the recent acquisitions of Russia in China, and other evidences of a fixed policy of advance in this eastern extremity of Asia towards unfrozen seas and ports denied her in the West; and a lion's share in the *spoliâ optime* of the trade, in the seas between the coast of America and China across the Pacific; there can be little doubt Japan would become a portion of the Russian empire at no distant date, if other European Powers retired.

But assuming on this view of the consequences of any complete abandonment, on our part, of Japan, a decision to maintain our relations in *some form*, as imperatively required by major interests having little reference to the value or extent of any commerce with Japan, or the farther difficulty arising from invested interests in trade, (which has already taken a larger developement than could have been anticipated, and with which those most directly interested declare themselves well satisfied), it has to be determined how the exigencies of such a position are best to be met, with the least danger of collision, and at the smallest cost, whether of life or national dignity?

If the actual trade of Japan be a secondary object in comparison with the interest involved in the larger political and commercial field, and these could best be advanced by relinquishing the former, as an object of immediate effort, it might be sound policy to do so. This may, at all events, deserve consideration, for there is some reason to believe that a mere political connection without trade (alleged to be so ruinous and productive of discontent and trouble) would be much more likely to be acquiesced in by the Japanese Government, than the present state of forced commercial activity. Possibly the vendetta against foreigners might cease under such altered relations. If even a residence at the capital of a Diplomatic Agent should still be insisted upon as the head of a Mission; a Legation might be little else for a time than a college for students, such as the Russians so long and patiently maintained at Pekin. The same result might probably be obtained, and with like good fruit. If this, with one or two Consular Agents at the ports now opened, but no importunate demands for execution of treaties, removal of limitations, or covert restrictions on trade, &c., were all we desired, the hostility now manifested might cease, or at least greatly diminish. This seems very much the policy of the Russians, who even avoid locating a Diplomatic Agent in the capital, and keep their Consul General at Hakodadi visiting Yeddo from time to time, only as occasion may require,—while they are especially careful to keep a powerful squadron always in the Japanese seas. This, be it observed, is the very reverse of our policy, or practice rather, which has been to keep an effective Legation in the capital, battling for all our treaty rights, and no force at all in the Japanese waters.  And the result has certainly not been encouraging.   Much would depend, probably, upon the degree of suspicion with which they might look at the Legation, and its quiescent attitude of study and retirement.   And much judgement and tact would be required not to rouse this in the first instance by any indiscreet display of eagerness, even in acquiring the language.  The Americans, on the other hand, took effective means, through their Minister, not to give umbrage by any too great display of restlessness or activity. The single attaché, poor Heuskin, it is true, did rather sin against the system, and the wish of his chief, by an active prosecution of the study of Japanese and much locomotion, —and he paid the penalty of his life for it.

Between these two courses, firstly of a total withdrawal, and secondly of acquiescence in the deferred opening of the ports, with the possible diminution of profitable trade at those now open,—a result partially aimed at by the efforts of the Japanese even while we are insisting on our rights,—it only remains to be determined whether any other alternative offers, save the one to which of all others Her Majesty's Government and the people of England are likely to be most opposed as neither justifiable nor expedient, namely, the adoption of coercive measures to compel the execution of the treaty in all its stipulations.  By whatever measures of a coercive nature we might seek to attain this object, it should be clearly seen that there is war in the background, more or less near, but tolerably certain sooner or later to come. During the last two years whatever a conciliatory spirit could suggest, with temper, patience, and forbearance in all things, had been tried.  Diplomacy had well-nigh exhausted its resources to induce the Japanese Government to take a different view of its interests, and to act in accordance with the spirit of the treaties entered into.  Little more remained to be tried in this direction, nor could much hope be entertained that better success would follow a longer persistence in the same course.   The hostile elements in the country had only to all appearance been gathering strength; and the policy followed by the Japanese had been growing day by day more unmistakeably obstructive and threatening. The conclusion would seem to be, that if there was to be any amelioration, Foreign Powers must change their tactics: and if these involved a struggle and the nation were passive, the feudal classes alone being actively engaged in such a contest (and this is what might be expected from all that is known of the country, always assuming that no revolutionary element came into play), the struggle could hardly be a long one. For some of the more hostile princes struck down, the rest would probably see the necessity of coming to terms, and sueing for peace, with a better estimate of our power to make our treaty rights respected, and compel observance, than has yet entered into the conception of Japanese Rulers. So possibly we might purchase peace, and trade with freedom from all obstructive limitations, as well as with security to life and property. But by no other means that suggest themselves, after long and patient study of the people and their rulers, does this end seem attainable—if once we break with the Daimios and the Government which masks them—to enter upon a course of coercion. As regards the masses and bulk of the population, we cannot look for anything better than indifference or neutrality. Of foreign trade, and the benefits which might flow to them from its extension, they know nothing, or perhaps worse than nothing, in the belief that to this Foreign trade they owe the increased dearness of provisions and other articles of consumption, which has more or less existed since the opening of the ports. The battle would be with their Princes and Feudal Chiefs only, unless these should succeed in rousing a latent fanaticism of patriotic feeling which no doubt exists in the Japanese character, nourished by all their traditions and historical associations, no less than by their insular position and long isolation from the rest of the world.

If once driven to enter into campaign, we should be liable to incur their hostility from lawless acts of spoliation or destruction on the part of troops, a danger which would be greatly increased if we entered into such a struggle with allies, instead of single-handed. In any movement in the country, the want of *interpreters* and means of communication or information would be one of our greatest difficulties, both as regards guides and supplies. A few Japanese know English or Dutch; but we could hardly count upon securing the services of any of these, or trust them if they offered to act against their own rulers. Among ourselves, or foreigners generally, no one yet has more than a limited knowledge or command of their oral language even. Assuming then that the cost of any efforts to extort by force or intimidation the full execution of the treaties would be great, and the issue too uncertain to permit an idea being willingly entertained of resorting to hostilities, either for the protection of any existing trade, or even its farther extension; we must turn to the terms of compromise actually offered by the Government under a pledge of greater security, and the abatement of hostile feelings. The future which the Japanese would fain present to us for our acceptance, and as the price of our renunciation of any new ports and right of residence for any but the Legations in the capital, is not without promise, though much shorn of advantages and privileges contemplated in the treaty. It may be shortly stated as comprising greater security for life, and the cessation of hostility; limited trade, but friendly relations and facilities within those limits, now virtually denied. How far even this moderate promise may be counted upon, when the concessions which are to be its price are made, is unfortunately open to doubt. If we would be on the safe side some material guarantee would not be superfluous, assuming that one could be framed which the Japanese might be induced to contemplate without too much irritation, and as only an *equivalent* for all they demand.

In any circumstances, the Treaty Powers will have to consider, not only the cost of any line of policy which may be determined upon, but the practicability of arriving at any satisfactory solution of the questions raised. Some effective guarantees for security to life, if not for any rapid developement of trade, might prove far more valuable than an extended field of commercial operations.

As a Mission was on its way to England for the express purpose of obtaining our consent to defer the opening of the ports, an opportunity would occur for declaring the stipulations under which we could accede to the wishes of the Japanese Government — defer all hopes of a rapid extension of trade, and accept a great apparent loss. We might observe, that however well disposed, this could not be done under an appearance of yielding to menace and violence; and having unfortunately been subjected to much of this, the Government not only owed us some reparation, but recent events rendered it necessary that we should stand free from the reproach or possible suspicion of yielding to fear, in surrendering rights—by the free concession on *both sides* of things equivalent. This it might be shown was a condition rendered imperative by the course of violence and intimidation which had ushered in, and apparently prepared the way for the Japanese proposals; and on no other terms could Great Britain stand justified either in its own eyes or that of the world.

In reference to the concessions demanded on their side, we might say we were not unwilling to take into consideration the state of the country as represented by the Government — the real difficulties they might have to contend with from the state of parties — and on our own side, were anxious not to precipitate them into a civil war, or even push the extension of our trade in any way to the injury of the Japanese people. But we might add, in all such negotiations between States, it was not usual for important treaty rights to be relinquished without some fair equivalent, and in this case such a condition could not be waived for the reasons already given, however well disposed Great Britain might be. What that equivalent should be would therefore become the first and principal thing to settle. And this might be no more than the greater *validity* of the existing treaty, with *new guarantees for its observance*, in the modified shape it would take, under a convention to defer the opening of the ports, in a sense altogether consistent with the wishes of the Tycoon and his Government.

If it were possible to carry this policy out, and in the way here indicated, it did not seem, on the most careful consideration of all the circumstances, that any better or more satisfactory solution could well be found, having in view the actual condition of the country, and the difficulties inseparable from it. Our progress in Japan will not be what in the beginning may have been over sanguinely anticipated — but more may be gained ultimately, by *foregoing something in the rate of progress*, than by impatience and too great eagerness to advance. The great object at this time was to avoid precipitating the country into a civil war; with which, to all appearance, it was seriously menaced ; and on the other hand it was no less desirable to avert the necessity for any hostile measures on our part. If both these ends could be accomplished without seriously compromising either our prestige or national dignity—and securing our position at Yeddo, and means of acquiring the language with no more loss of trade, or other material advantages, in the interval than would no less assuredly follow, were a more uncompromising or overbearing course to be pursued ; then we might rest satisfied with the conviction that nothing better was possible under the circumstances, and that great evils to both countries, without promise of corresponding advantage, could only thus be averted.

Whatever policy might ultimately be adopted, it was

perfectly clear that to compel without compulsion was an impossibility. A great change was needed, but this must in a considerable degree be a change of convictions—and no lesson is well learned all at once. Any change likely to be beneficial and permanent in the minds of the Japanese, must break in slowly upon their old traditions and habits of thought — and move forward by steady and gradual steps. But this slowness, if a subject of regret in some respects, makes the final victory more certain, and insures its completeness. New ideas, new principles and sentiments, must be allowed to permeate through and through the masses, and rather by a process of percolation from the upper to the lower strata, than by the force of an irresistible pressure from without or below.

What seemed most important, therefore, was to secure a fair commencement to a more gradual process of infiltration and leavening in the mass. Hitherto, and with more or less success, those who are the custodians of power in Japan have directed all their efforts to prevent this. *If we could neutralise this action*, we should probably effect more in the next ten years by peaceable means, and with mutual advantage to all parties, than in double that period by any measures of hostility and coercion. We can do little towards changing the current of Japanese ideas, until we can communicate our own through their language, and it will take some years yet to give us fair command of this first and most essential instrument of conversion and civilisation.

However inviting such a programme might be, it still behoved us to keep distinctly in view another class of facts and considerations, the tendency of which, it must be confessed, was rather adverse than favourable to this policy of deferred hope and conciliation. We have already had painful experience in China of the rule attending all concession to the supposed difficulties of the Government of the country, and their alleged inability to give execution to treaty stipulations. There can be very little doubt, as I explained in the first chapter of this book, that our consent to waive the opening of Canton from time to time, was the indirect, if not the immediate, cause of the second war.    Just as little doubt is there that the whole plea of inability from the hostility of the people, &c., was a pretext as futile as it was false, invented merely to *delude us into a course in accordance with the policy of the Government*, which was at heart hostile and designedly obstructive.    We know now that either *Seu* or *Yeh*, or even the first Viceroy *Keying*, had he chosen, could have opened the gates of Canton at once, without the slightest danger of popular commotion.    The only hostility exist-ing in the minds of the people was so purely factitious, and entirely due to the action of the Government, which, with signal bad faith, were doing all in their power to generate and increase such feeling,—at the very time that they were professing the utmost good-will, and the most earnest desire to give honest execution to this, as well as every other clause of the treaty.    They put forward a false plea for a dishonest purpose, and without the slightest intention of ever complying with the treaty stipulations.    When they induced plenipotentiary after plenipotentiary to defer from year to year the opening of Canton on the plea of giving time ' to soothe the people and prepare the way for a peaceable entrance,' they deliberately took advantage of the respite to raise new obstacles, create the very difficul-ties in the feelings of the people, which they alleged already to exist, and make it each year more and more impossible to admit the foreigner.    There was an ominous family likeness between the course followed by the Chinese Mandarins, and that now proposed by the Tycoon's Government.    They too pleaded for time ' to prepare the minds of the people;' they would close Yeddo to all but the Foreign Representatives, while *their* residence continued to be one of danger and harassing surveillance ;  and defer the opening of Hiogo, Osaca, and Neeagata for a long term of seven years.    But was it possible to believe that it was their honest purpose really to profit by this time to remove obstacles and put down

opposition ? Was it likely, that if even those immediately
about the Tycoon desired to do so, that they would be able
and willing to take any *effective* measures to that end, so
as to secure the desired result ? To neither of these vital
questions was it in the power of any Foreign Representative, I think, to give a confident or satisfactory answer in
the affirmative.

What should we be doing then by concession ? Gaining
time and only deferring an evil day that, if this hypothesis
were correct, *must* come sooner or later, and with increased calamities the longer it is deferred ? This was at
least a possible result, and formed by no means a pleasant prospect for future Governments and Plenipotentiaries. I wished nothing but peace and prosperity to the
Japanese ; and had spared no effort with their Government
to imbue them with juster notions than I fear they yet possess, of the power which other States possessed to compel
the observance of treaties, and their own want of means to
offer any effective resistance ; and above all, the danger
that must inevitably attend a persistence in any course of
deception and bad faith. But it was impossible to close our
eyes to the lessons and experience each day afforded. If
we find them timid, submissive, and anxious to avoid all
cause of quarrel with Russia, while they presume not a
little upon the policy of conciliation and forbearance of all
the other Powers ; it is difficult to avoid the conclusion
that the strong-handed and very summary measures
taken by the naval officers of the former Power at
Nagasaki, Hakodadi, and elsewhere, on more than
one occasion, and the ever-constant presence or pro-
pinquity of large squadrons, have had a beneficial influence. To the Japanese, as to all the semi-civilised
races of the East, Force represents Power, and inspires
Respect, and nothing else does. They will talk of the
necessity of conforming all their acts to reason and good
faith, and talk by the day or the month, but deliberately
disregard both, exactly in the proportion in which they
believe you are prepared to bear it without an appeal to

the idol of their worship, and the only God they fear or will propitiate — the God of war.

It may well suggest itself as a doubt, therefore, to Foreign Representatives on the spot, with their own experience of the inefficacy of reason and argument on the one hand, and that of the Russians on the other, who adopt a totally different system, whether we best consult even their interests, as a Government and a nation maintaining relations with the Western Powers, by allowing them to think they may persévere in the same system of deception and bad faith without check or danger?  It is very true, we have forced ourselves upon them, and many may see reason to regret such a step was ever taken by Foreign Powers.  They neither desired nor were ready for the relations imposed upon them, and are quite incapable of appreciating any advantage in our acquaintance.  The questionable policy of the proceeding is indeed fully shown in the danger of collision it unavoidably entails, seeing the impossibility by fair and peaceable means of inducing the virtual rulers of the country to keep faith, or observe the stipulations of treaties so utterly distasteful and obnoxious to them.

Unfortunately, to retrograde safely and with dignity, is often more difficult for nations and their Governments than to advance.  And the question now is, not whether it was wise or expedient to enter into treaty relations with Japan in the first instance; but having taken this step, what course it best befits us to follow, singly or in concert with other Treaty Powers, with reference to the evils which such relations inevitably bring with them? If the inclinations and prejudices of the Daimios, as a class exercising a decided influence on the policy of the ostensible Government, are to be taken into account for our guidance, we ought to withdraw from the country altogether.  Or, if we are to listen with confiding ear to the pleas of danger, and the inability of the Government either to avert it, or give execution to the treaties which the Tycoon alone has ratified, we must put in abeyance their principal provisions; all, indeed, that possess any substantial value. Assuming, or supposing, that we are not prepared to accept either of these alternatives, then there are certain conditions of good faith and honest execution which it would seem necessary to insist upon, because they are vital and essential to the realisation of any of the objects for which the treaties were framed. Some are even essential to the continued residence of foreigners in the country, with reasonable security to life and property, or immunity from continued outrage, submission to which would be impossible to any Sovereign State in the position of Great Britain; and could not permanently be endured, even from so distant and puny an adversary as the Japanese. True, we have borne all this and more, this thirty years past, from Mexico, with all its elements of disorder and misrule rampant and hydra-headed. But this has constituted the difficulty of dealing with those who perpetrated the wrongs, or holding any Government responsible. It has been a country without a Government, and given over to the wild license of armed factions. To exact redress, it was necessary to contemplate the occupation of the country, and possible necessity of providing for its administration, in the absence of any fit materials for an effective or permanent Government—the dilemma which France is now experiencing. Such is not the case in Japan. There are here elements of strength and order, which the existing Government represents and controls. It may be subject for consideration then, whether under such circumstances we should do well or wisely to trust entirely in the future, as we have done in the past, to conciliation and forbearance. There may be parties in more or less intimate connection with the Government, ready to suggest to them that such a policy on our part is due to the impossibility of the British Government adopting any other course, or resorting to means of reprisal and coercion under any circumstances. A rougher and sterner discipline may be needed with such men as the Daimios and

their supporters, to teach them the wisdom of maintaining
peaceful relations by observing the obligations of treaties;
instead of provoking to acts of hostility a Power that can
at any time crush their best efforts at resistance; and,
whatever may be the treacherous suggestions they may
receive from foreign sources, *will do so*, if all milder
means should fail.

# CHAPTER XII.

THE GOVERNMENT OF JAPAN AND ITS ADMINISTRATIVE MACHINERY
— RELATIONS OF LIFE : OF RULERS AND SUBJECTS — HUSBAND AND
WIFE — THE RELATION OF THE SEXES — THE POSITION OF WOMAN
IN THE SOCIAL SCALE — INFLUENCE OF ART AND CULTURE —
RELIGIOUS SYSTEMS.

OF the Government of Japan we have much yet to
learn, both as regards the actual machinery, and
the official hierarchy under which the administration of
the affairs of the Empire is carried on.   The relative
position, weight, and influence of the constituted powers—
Mikado, Tycoon, and their respective high officers — all
need farther elucidation.   The old and the new noblesse, in
their relations as feudatories of one or both Sovereigns, and
to each other, and to the people especially demand careful
consideration.   These may be held to constitute the moral,
as the mere administrative machinery supplies the more
tangible elements of a Government.

As regards the last, and the hierarchy established
among the officers of the Tycoon's Government, I have
various data, some of them derived from official, and
others from private sources of a more or less reliable
nature.   The lists of Daimios, with their revenues and
territories ; of the Tycoon's Court and administration,
given in the Appendix,* are taken from the official
Red Book of Yeddo.   This was very difficult to obtain
in the first instance, simply because the Government
of the Tycoon did not choose we should have any books,
maps, or other means of information, even of those open
to all the natives, and purchaseable by them for a few

* See Appendix D.

cash.   The book in question is as common among the Japanese, as our own Red Book, or the Gotha almanack. I doubt not, could it ever be traced how the copy I possess came into my hands, it would fare very ill with any parties concerned.   I have in addition met quite recently with a contribution to one of the local journals on the subject of ' titles in Japan,' which appears to be written by one well-informed on many particulars connected therewith, not generally known; and I think the writer's information, upon the whole, is correct.   The paper will be found in the Appendix.*

The following brief summary of the public officers, with their relative duties and ranks, in addition to the lists, &c., contained in the Appendix, will, I hope, serve to give the reader a tolerably clear idea of the whole.

The SEOGUN, or DAI-SEOGUN, rendered in the Treaties TYCOON, is the chief.   Kœmpfer styles him Crown-General, Vice-Regent, Generalissimo, and Emperor indifferently. The truth being, that the successor of the originally usurped authority of executive chief, which has become, for the last two centuries, hereditary in the families of the descendants of *Jejassama*, otherwise *Gongen Sama*, receives various titles from the reigning Mikado.   The first in order and most common is, SEOGUN, or DAI-SEOGUN. Though authorities differ even in Japan as to its exact meaning, it seems derived from, or to be the equivalent of, the Chinese term, *Ta-tsiang-kiun*, ' the great chief, or commander of the army;' and, as the Japanese are supposed to be a nation of soldiers, he who is at the head of the army, is virtually the head of the nation.   Hence nothing will induce a Japanese, at Yeddo, to admit that the Tycoon's title only means a generalissimo of the army.   What rendering the inhabitants of *Miaco* and the Mikado's territory might give, is not so clear.

After the Tycoon, irrespective of the Gotairo, or Regent, an office that only comes into existence when the Tycoon

---

* See Appendix F.

is a minor, the *Kokushi* follows next in importance. It is a Council, composed of either eighteen or twenty-four (for there is some doubt which is the number). Among these are some of the most powerful Daimios of the ancient aristocracy, who represent the Mikado at Yeddo. Although ostensibly they take no active part in the Government, there seems very little doubt that not only are they a serious check on the Tycoon and his own Council of Ministers, but something very like control and direction must be among their attributes and the functions they exercise. The theory appears to be that they are a consultative Council, with whom there is no initiative or active participation in the administration of affairs;—and the Tycoon need not recognise their existence, save only in cases where there is a question of departure from the fundamental laws or traditional customs, when their sanction and that of the Mikado are both essential to give validity or legality to any change; as, for instance, such a step as entering into Treaties with Western Powers, which for more than two centuries had been prohibited.

In such a grave and momentous question as a total change of national policy, there is reason to believe either law or custom renders essential an appeal to a Great Council of all the Daimios possessing a revenue over 50,000 kokous of rice,* said to number some 342. How they are convened, in what manner they deliberate and give their opinions or votes, is not known, I believe, by any foreigner. The necessity of convening such a Great Council of the nation was urged on Commodore Perry, by the Government of the then existing Tycoon, as the reason for a year's delay in giving him any answer. How far truly or not, of course, may be open to question.

Next in order follows the *Gorogio*, or administrative Council of the Tycoon — his cabinet in effect; consisting of five Daimios of the third class — I believe always

---

* See lists of Daimios, with their revenues, Appendix D.

selected from among the more modern aristocracy, and never from the elder stock.   How they are nominated, whether by the free and uncontrolled choice of the reigning Tycoon, — at the dictation of others,—or in compliance with some understood limitations, no foreigner, I am persuaded, is in a position to speak with any certainty.   There was much during the three years to lead those in direct communication with the members of the Gorogio who acted as Ministers of Foreign Affairs to conclude, that other and more influential or powerful Daimios, than they had any pretensions to be, held a controlling power ; whose nominees the Council probably were, and subject, in matters connected with the Foreign relations of the country more especially, to an overruling influence or more positive dictation.   Or numbers among the inferior noblesse may compensate for individual importance, and the check may be in this body — both on the Council of the Tycoon and on the chief Princes too.

Subordinate to this first Council of Ministers is a second Council, consisting of eight members—Daimios also, but of the third or fourth class, and with small revenues.   Their functions, so far as can be learned, are purely administrative.

Next in order should be enumerated the *Buñios*. These appear to be very numerous, and with very various functions.   A variable number of this class, from five to ten generally, act as Governors of Foreign Affairs — performing many of the duties of Under-Secretaries of State in Europe, and are called *Gaikoku Buñio*.   From this class are selected all the Governors of the towns, and the consular ports, as also the Judges.   The *Gisha Buñio*, the Governor of Yeddo, is an officer of such high importance that he is said to rank next to the Gorogio.   All the Samourai, and two-sworded men, and all the Bonzes or priests of the whole empire, are said to be under his jurisdiction.   The *Matchi Buñio* may be considered as a sort of civil Governor, under whose jurisdiction are placed all the rest of the inhabitants of the capital.

Many of the more subordinate offices are filled up from a large class of Government officers, not Daimios but belonging to the *Hattamotto*, or vassals directly dependent on the Tycoon, corresponding to the 'gentry and literati' of China, so often quoted in official correspondence, and receiving annual salaries, ranging from 3,000 kokous to 200 pios of rice, or say 2,000*l*. to 38*l*. A classification and enumeration of these will be found in the Appendix.* As regards the military administration and means of defence, a certain number of Daimios holding fiefs from the Tycoon probably, said to be twenty-six in number, are entrusted with the defence of the Tycoon, and obliged to furnish military contingents. It was some of these who were called upon to supply guards to the Legations, when the Tycoon's Government deemed such measures of protection necessary. And it was one or more of these military retainers who attempted in the night to cut his way to the room of the British Chargé d'Affaires after my departure.

Into the farther question of *honorary* offices, rank, and order of precedency as established between the Mikado's Court and the Tycoon's, I do not propose to enter in any detail—first, because I consider most of the information we possess too uncertain and imperfect to be much relied upon; and secondly, because although we have heard a good deal of the Tycoon's investiture by the Mikado, and of the fourth rank being assigned him,—by which he is placed not only lower than that of other Daimios, or courtiers and ministers about the person of the Mikado,—I think such distinctions have little influence on the real march of affairs. It may be true enough that according to the Red Book of Japan, the *Quambuku* or Prime Minister of the Mikado is classed as the second person in the realm, and takes rank before the Tycoon,— but practically what does this amount to? Does it give him any real power to direct, or meddle with the administration of affairs; or merely to approach three mats nearer

* See Appendix D.

the august person of a powerless Mikado, or receive more genuflexions in the day from other superannuated courtiers, condemned like himself to a life of utter insignificance, in all save a name or a title? He may come next after the Sovereign *de jure*, as an Archbishop of Canterbury, or a Speaker of the House of Commons, and take precedence of a Prime Minister—but with a like absence of any real significance or share of power. So there may be whole classes of *Daijo-daijins*, or *Sho-dijo-daijins*, *So-daijins*, &c., and all taking official rank before the Tycoon, who yet have no more voice in the administration of the Empire, than so many paste-board and bedizened dummies among the properties of a provincial theatre. These high-sounding titles I can only regard as so many fossilised relics of a past order—which have no vitality or real significance in the world, and no interest for the actual living men around them, who constitute the Japanese nation.

Japan appears to be actually governed, at the present day, by a sort of federal aristocracy, recalling in some respects that of the Lombard dukes ; — and France under the Merovingian kings ; or the early state of the Germans when their kings were elected out of particular families. A confederation of Princes and territorial Seigneurs possess the land, enjoying apparently very much the same kind of jurisdiction as our own barons in the days of the Saxon rule or the first Plantagenets. The Prince of Satsuma with his colonial dependencies of the Loochoo Islands ; the Prince of Xendai with large territories ; the Prince of Kaga, and many others, each with larger revenues and more men-at-arms, probably, than the virtual and *de facto* Sovereign the Tycoon himself could bring into the field — might any one of them play the part of an Earl of Warwick. If not in the present day, yet not three centuries ago, these were in the habit, separately or in combination, of setting not only the Tycoon, but his and their Sovereign, the Mikado, at defiance with arms in their hands. It was their feuds and rebellions which in the twelfth century gave to Yoritomo the means of usurping the quasi sovereignty of the Tycoonat, only then constituted by the victorious commander-in-chief of the imperial armies, which were originally set in motion for their subjugation. *Täico-Sama* towards the close of the sixteenth century did much to break the still dangerous power of these semi-feudatory but really independent princes. He only succeeded, however, by courting the alliance of some of the more puissant of them, and leaving their sovereign rights or pretensions untouched. There are many who thus succeed to their hereditary dominions and honours with all rights and immunities attaching from time immemorial, without any formal recognition or investiture by the Tycoon. Their allegiance is obviously more nominal than real, and is held by the slightest tenure. They are strong in their feudal rights and feudal power, while he is weak in his avowed subordination to the only acknowledged Suzerain of all, the Mikado, who is invested not only with all the prestige of hereditary descent in an unbroken line from the first Supreme rulers of the Empire, but tracing back through such ancestry, according to Japanese traditions, a divine origin. He adds the infallibility and pretensions of a Pope of the middle ages, to the temporal rights of sovereignty of a later era. And although he has been shorn of much, if not all, of his real power, as Popes have been ere now, and this ever since the Crown-General Yoritomo's successful usurpation ; — yet still the supreme dignity, rank, sanctity, and prerogatives have ever been the undisputed attributes of the Mikado, and his alone. Täico-Sama, the great soldier-hero of Japan, in the latter end of the sixteenth century, when invested with the command of the armies and administrative functions of the sovereign, did but continue the work of Yoritomo, his great predecessor, in still farther reducing the power of the Mikado, from whom he held the trust, to narrower limits ; at the same time that he broke down the strength of many of the great feudatories. And when his son perished, self-immolated in the castle of Osaca, where he was besieged by his guardian and father-in-law, Yedai (or otherwise

called Daifu-Sama—king or prince of Quanto), known in
Japanese history subsequently as *Gongen-Sama*,* the
founder of the present dynasty of Tycoons—these several
changes of the dynasty in nothing affected the Mikados
or their succession. They continued inheritors by right
divine of their phantom sceptre, preserving still some
remnants of their former unlimited and absolute power.
Their investiture is still theoretically essential to the Tycoon
to consecrate his election, as is their sanction to any changes
in the fundamental laws, and their ratification to any new
treaties. The want of this, in the case of the treaties with
European Powers, there is every reason to believe, as I have
shown, lies at the root of our difficulties in Japan. The
Tycoon, on the first appearance of an American squadron
in 1853, driven by a certain pressure and dangers which
seemed to him imminent, entered apparently into treaties
without this needful sanction of his Suzerain; against his
fiat, it is said, and is *therefore* powerless to give them execution throughout Japan. In the absence of this, and a formal
ratification, he can at most pretend to give them effect
throughout his own territories, in which the Consular Ports
are situated, and with *his own subjects*. The Daimios hostile to the innovation as a body, and never sorry, it would
seem, to use their allegiance to the Suzerain of both, as a
check to the encroaching power of the Tycoon, do not
recognise these treaties as binding upon *them*. This brief
summary of their history was necessary here to show how
this nation is governed on a feudal basis, with two hereditary Sovereigns, one by right divine and the other by
successful usurpation supported by material force, who is
himself held in check and controlled partly by the traditional respect for ancient customs and laws, and still
more by the hereditary Daimios professing a nominal
subordination but keeping up a real antagonism. The
whole country is thus parcelled out in large and small

---

* This frequent change of name and designation, taking place often in a
lifetime, is most bewildering to a foreigner. As much, no doubt, as are our
changes of name and mode of address when a commoner becomes a peer, or
succeeds to a new rank and title in the peerage.

territories over which feudatory chiefs rule absolutely,
although ostensibly the subjects of a Suzerain and an
executive chief of the state; and amenable to the laws of
the Empire, but opposing and limiting the authority both
of Mikado and Tycoon, as occasion serves or their interests
and passions dictate. We have in presence, therefore,
a dual system of Sovereigns, each with their separate
court, high officers, and nobles; next a class of nominal
feudatories, the bonâ fide rulers of the country in detail
under a feudal system. And over all, intertwined and
twisted round every individual member of this tripartite
hierarchy of two Sovereigns—their courts of great officers
—and a class of great territorial barons, each of whom
enjoys a petty and semi-avowed independent sovereignty,
there is cast like a spell an elaborate network of espionage,
which seeks to control by treachery and finesse those who
cannot be subjected by overt force, and to bring all under
one bondage or system of government. This part of the
Tycoon's administrative system involves a duty which
sends his officers into the several princes' territories, a
service, it would appear, of veritable danger. There was
presented to me one day a Japanese of considerable official rank, who for obvious reasons I will not more particularly describe, of whose history I had an outline.
One of the incidents, to the credit of his wit and astute-
ness, which most struck me, was the fact of his having
been the only one of seven ometskys or spies sent successively into the Prince of Satsuma's territories,—who
ever came out alive.

The Mikado and even his power, however shorn of what
it once was, may still exist. The Tycoon is after all, but an
executive head ruling under the shadow of his suzerain
prerogative—and he again is limited and checked at
every turn, as I have shown, by one of the most powerful
oligarchies ever seen, since the palmy days of the Venetian
Republic with its Council of Ten, under whose secret and
inquisitorial dominion the Doge himself felt insecure alike
of life and power. And if they brought one Doge to the

block for treason, the Tycoons are in certain understood cases, either by an order from the Mikado, or of difference with their Great Council, obliged either to perform the Hara-kiru, or abdicate.

When we speak of the Government of Japan then, all the separate threads of rule linking together by a slender hold, three hundred and odd principalities, and three hundred lesser Daimios with territories, must be gathered up, and traced into the hands of the second ruler of the Empire, and through him into the feeble grasp of the Suzerain of all. They each in several degrees exercise rule and government, and help to form what must seem to us an ill-fused amalgam of all governing and legislative powers. By these separately and collectively all the agencies of Government, civilising or otherwise, are set in motion and controlled for good or for evil, in the history of the nation and its civilisation. Of anything like real municipal or self-governing bodies, I can find no trace. There is a sort of subordinate system of wards and heads of tens and hundreds in the *Otonos* of towns and villages severally and collectively responsible for each other's good conduct, which has some faint resemblance to our own tythings and hundreds, which formed the foundation of our own municipal system of decentralisation and self-government. But these are here what ours were when still in the germ; and seem wanting in any vital elements of a representative character, on which all power of growth and developement depend.

Here, as in Great Britain in the days of the Saxon kings, the great bulk of the servile population are *adscripti glebæ*. Some are domestic slaves, both male and female. With the Japanese, as with ourselves in those early days, a source of servitude is found in a law which required every freeman beneath the rank of a thane, to be either the recognised follower of some lord, or the member of a family or guild or burgh who would be responsible for him. Even wealthy traders, to buy the privilege of wearing one or two swords, and also the protection of a powerful Daimio, will often pay a large sum for the privilege of being rated as one of his retainers, and wearing his cognisance.   Thus, if there are any free-men in the proper sense of the term — the oppression to which they are exposed by the armed classes, often in-duces them to surrender their liberty into the hands of some superior who is capable of affording them protection. Besides these several causes of slavery or serfdom, poverty, crime, and debt help to swell the ranks.   Parents, too, have undoubtedly in some cases, if not in all, the power to sell their children.   And as they are inveterate gamblers, I have little doubt in Japan, as in China, a man often stakes wife, children, and finally himself in the hazard of a die.   On the other hand, I had frequent occasions of observing, that precisely as with the Saxons in the tenth and eleventh centuries, the words ' freemen ' and ' slave,' * as understood at the present day, are hardly applicable, for a large proportion of freemen are in a position in which this would not with us be considered altogether free ; and the majority of the slaves live in a state of comparative freedom.

Let us now endeavour, if we may, to ascertain of what character are the effective agencies actually brought into play by the multitudinous and often antagonistic rulers of Japan, under this most complicated and imperfectly welded system of aristocratic and oligarchic government. Apart from the fact that the feudal system itself is repressive in its tendency, limiting and curtailing the exercise of all free energies, a Government which rests on espionage, secret and avowed, and delation, as among its chief instruments, sows mistrust broadcast through a whole nation, undermines all confidence between man and man, and makes truth and faith equally impossible among the mass subject to such influences.   'All lies,' it has been well observed, ' are discivilising ; ' the ' greatest savages have generally been found the most incorrigible liars and

* ' The Anglo-Saxon Home,' by John Thrupp.

the greatest thieves.'   It is not to be wondered at if mendacity among the Japanese has become something more than a bad habit, an institution and part of the necessary machinery of their system of government and administration.

'Different races of men,' Mr. Thrupp observes, in his 'Home of the Anglo-Saxon' already cited, 'and different nations, are usually found to possess particular vices and virtues to a greater degree than others, which thus not only become characteristic peculiarities, but have a material influence on their national character and manners, and require therefore to be duly considered in treating of their social history.'   And entirely agreeing with the writer, I am led to place at the head of the list of Japanese vices this one of mendacity, bringing as it does inevitably dishonesty of action.   The Japanese traders are accordingly what might be expected, and rank among the most dishonest and tricky of Easterns.   This seems a hard thing to say of a whole race, or a class even, yet the incessant examples of the most ingenious and deliberate fraud in the trade carried on at the ports, and Yokohama more especially, as being the emporium of the largest trade, leaves no doubt on the subject.*   Bales of silk are continually sold with outward hanks of one quality, and the inner ones of coarser material most craftily interwoven.   Jars of camphor with the top only the genuine article, and the rest powdered rice.   Tubs of oil the lower half water.   Money taken for contracts, and immediately appropriated to their own use, and unblushingly confiscated.   But it may be said *we* have fraudulent tradesmen too, at home and abroad, and unfortunately the fact is beyond all dispute, as Dr. Hassall and Parliamentary Committees have proved to demonstration.   In free, self-governed, virtuous England, is it not

---

* This is true, at least, of all whom foreigners are allowed to trade or have any intercourse with—those specially licensed by the Government, and probably not substantial and responsible men, but mere agents or servants, and not the most reputable.

hard to buy any article of food which has undergone mani-
pulation, or even medicine to preserve life, that is not
adulterated, and often by the most deleterious compounds?
Or, to buy a length of cotton which answers to the
measurement written upon it ; or a bottle of wine or beer
containing a statute pint or quart measure ? Yes, all this
is true, and sad as true. Commercial morality appears to
have a code of its own even in the most civilised countries ;
and perhaps it may be still more broadly stated, that the
moral standard of the most advanced nation, is very far
from perfect truth or honesty. We must admit then, I
am afraid, that it is only a question of degree, between
the Japanese who sells rice dust for camphor, and the
English tradesman who sells red lead for Cayenne pepper,
or alum and bone dust for bread. But still I maintain
the Japanese have the bad preeminence of far surpassing
us, in ingenuity and universality of cheating. In reference to mendacity, it requires some acquaintance with
yaconins and Japanese officials to know the full force of
the term ; or, to what perfection such a system may be
brought. Truth is not to be obtained at any price, for
love or for money — by a foreigner at all events. I do
not believe any real progress is possible so long as a
nation preserves this characteristic, and all true civilisation
is necessarily progressive.

There is as total a disregard of truth among
the Japanese of all classes, as can well be conceived —
compatible with the existence of any bonds of society,
which, after all, must presuppose *some* trust or faith either
in words or oaths. There are people in every nation
who lie — some from habit, some from vanity, and others
to advance their interests ; 'the gainful lie' is, unfortunately, common in all classes and races. And it was not of
the Japanese that Bacon spoke, when he said, 'A mixture
of a lie doth ever add pleasure,' but most likely of his
own countrymen. If, in ancient times, at the other
extremity of Asia, 'all Cretans were liars,' and their descendants, the Greek of modern days, amidst all his

pretensions, has less claim, perhaps, than any of Cauca-
sian race, to a character for veracity ; they have had, in all
ages and nations, a wide fraternity to keep them in countenance.  The chief distinction between the European and
Eastern civilisation, in this respect, seems mainly to be in
the one, the general repudiation of falsehood as a legitimate exercise of ingenuity, and its recognition in the other.
It is no disgrace or discredit to either Japanese or Chinese
to be detected and convicted of the most flagrant lie ;
there is not even the ·Spartan feeling of shame at being
found out.  But how the several relations of life in a social
state are maintained, where there is so little trust or
faith, and no acknowledged obligation to speak the truth,
is difficult to understand.   In matters of justice, the
problem is solved by a system of torture, which either
extorts the truth or kills the recusant.   But in other relations, some other and less brutal instruments of verifica-
tion must obviously be relied upon, for arriving at such
approximation to truth as may be essential for the conduct of affairs, in all the ordinary transactions between man
and man.   But if, as Bacon farther speculates, ' the
inquiry of truth be the love-making or wooing of it,'
there must be a great deal of such wooing in Japan, and
a surprisingly small portion of the ' belief of truth, which
is the enjoying of it.'  So far as this consummation is
really ' the sovereign good of human nature,' I am afraid
my friends, the Japanese, are wofully lacking.  The very
necessity of the case, I conclude, must supply a partial
remedy, by suggesting and enforcing truth, in an interested sense, as the best policy.  When Colonel Chartres
exclaimed that he would give ten thousand pounds for a
character, it was no doubt because he felt that it would
be worth ten times more than that sum to him in plying
his vocation.  So in my dealings with the various shopkeepers I was in the habit of seeing for the purchase of
their wares at the Legation, they certainly manifested a
keen appreciation of the value attaching to a character for
truthfulness : and, to their credit, I must add there were

many who would not palm off a plated for a silver article, or venture on any gross fraud of that kind. And to the honour of their discrimination, I must also say, they soon learned to take me at my word, instead of chaffering and haggling over a price they knew to be greatly in excess ' of what they were willing to accept. I have seen, when some one of their number, admitted for the first time, was asking an extortionate price, the older habitués check him, and have overheard the warning that it was ' of no use — that they knew my yea was yea, and my nay—nay in truth,' and that he would simply be left with his goods on his hands, if he did not deal more straight-forwardly. Of course, that they should often ask twice as much as they were willing to take, vow a modern work was either an antique, better than the oldest, and declare no second of the kind could be found, was in the fair way of their trade — do not picture and curiosity dealers in every mart in Europe the same?

But, after all, to return to the moral problem which universal lying such as exists in Japan suggests, there must be a real pleasure in the practice, for there is no denying it has its inconveniences. There must be many inducements and temptations to depart from truth, be-sides a mere regard to some present *interest* or *profit*; for, on a searching inquiry into the veracity or authenticity throughout history of all the wisest and wittiest sayings, and of many of the reputed doings of the noblest men in all ages and countries, some of which have become familiar as household words and undoubted as gospel truths, how many come out of the crucible with any shape or consis-tency? M. Fournier laid a sacrilegious and ruthless hand on all these heirlooms of the past, in a book which he entitled, ' L'esprit dans l'Histoire,' or ' Recherches et Curiosités sur les Mots Historiques,' and sad havoc he has made of the world's most cherished traditions on the subject. Alas! for witty and brilliant retorts — for heroic inspirations in the hour of action. Alas! for King Arthur, and Charlemagne, or even William Tell. Alas!

for 'Dying Words' and 'Speeches.' Good-bye, all! fruits only of the inventive faculties of biographers and historians, falsehoods stamped by Genius and handed down from age to age for admiration, to feed the strong propensity to hero-worship.   Let us say no more of Japanese mendacity, M. Fournier has dried up the ink with his scorching and withering scrutiny; and one is tempted to adopt the last phrase of the syllogism and exclaim, not only all Cretans, but 'All men are liars,' at some times, and in some things;—since it can be proved of nearly all the most celebrated 'Mots Historiques,' that either the people never lived, or never said the things attributed to them, or did not say them on the occasions, or in the terse and epigrammatic forms in which they have been written for all posterity.   Thus it follows that the Japanese are by no means the only people who delight in the inventive faculty—for the sake of inventing.

Let us leave the Japanese alone, then.  The human heart and mind retain the same essential features everywhere, unchanged by time, or space, or outward mould.   The only difference is to be sought in those external circumstances of government and institutions, education and public opinion, which all combine to supply more or less efficient checks on our evil propensities.   Men lie and cheat, gamble and steal, in all countries; only in some there is a strong curb in constant play, and in others a loose rein is given.   Nor, indeed, can we very well set up ourselves in any rank as immaculate censors of these nations, according to the dictum variously attributed to James I. and Sir Henry Wotton, that our diplomatic corps was composed of 'men of quality, sent abroad to lie for the benefit of their country.'  The Japanese stay at home and lie for theirs.

While meditating over these things, and the degree of importance to be fairly attached to this characteristic feature of Japanese life, a clever article in the 'Quarterly' fell into my hands, grouping in a startling juxtaposition these 'historical lies,' which made me pause.   The writer begins by showing that Themistocles *may* have said, ' Strike, but hear,' though Herodotus, the earliest reporter of the debate between the admirals, made no mention of it; but, at all events, it was not to the Lacedemonian admiral, for this debate was with the Corinthian Adeimantus. Robert Bruce may have been taught perseverance by a spider; but it is remarkable that the same teacher is assigned to Tamerlane. It appears Omar is no longer to be charged with burning the Alexandrian library, any more than the Legate at the sack of Beziers, in 1209, with the order, ' Kill them all— God will recognise His own,' so circumstantially related; and M. Fournier devotes a section to prove that Charles IX. did *not* fire on the Huguenots with an arquebuse from the window of the Louvre in the massacre of St. Bartholomew. So François premier, far from writing to his mother after the battle of Pavia, 'Tout est perdu fors l'honneur,' wrote something considerably different, and less epigrammatic. The patriotic devotion of Eustache de Saint Pierre and his five companions, of which Froissart gives such touching details, when they delivered up the keys of Calais to Edward III., by whom they were doomed, but for his queen's intercession, was never intended to be hanged, seeing that he was in connivance with the besiegers, and was destined to be rewarded by a pension. Whether Mazarin continued to his last gasp surrounded by a bevy of ladies and gallants is doubtful, to say the least, though historians and painters will have it so; and another popular picture of Leonardo da Vinci dying at Fontainebleau, in the arms of Francis I., is opposed by a double *alibi*. And so of Sir A. Callcott's picture of 'Milton and his daughters,' one of whom acts as his emanuensis, though it is authoritatively declared they were never taught to write. Whichever side we turn, deception and delusion meet us, and for no gainful purpose of profitably lying. Cambronne did not utter the grandiloquent ' La garde meurt, et ne se rende pas.' The Duke of Wellington did not say, ' Up, guards, and at them.'

The Abbé Edgeworth did not say, on the scaffold, 'Fils de St. Louis, montez au ciel;' at least, he himself told Lord Holland he had no recollection of having said it. Pitt did not make the often-quoted speech, when twitted with his youth, for it was written and invented by Johnson. Le Comte d'Artois did not make the eminently successful hit, in an address at the Restoration, 'Plus de divisions; la paix et la France! Je la revois, et rien n'y est changé, si ce n'est qu'il se trouve un Français de plus.' In vain His Royal Highness, who had extemporised a few confused sentences, on reading his 'neat little speech' next morning in the *Moniteur*, protested his innocence. He was told 'there was an imperative necessity for his having said it.' And it became history accordingly.

It is obviously only a question of degree: though the habitual disregard or the love of truth vary greatly in different nations. In some the second is hard to distinguish, and this is the case in Japan. There is a good deal of lying, gambling, and drinking; a certain amount of stealing and cheating, with a tolerable per-centage of cutting and stabbing, but I must declare my opinion that there is not altogether more of these vices than in many European populations placed under a Christian dispensation; and one would believe, under more favourable circumstances for the practice of Christian virtues.

Among the discouraging agencies at work to prevent the realisation of any sanguine hopes of progress and improvement, are, I conceive, first, their feudal institutions; and secondly, the highly artificial and unsound system of government — based upon espionage, necessarily sowing distrust, and encouraging mendacity. The Rulers have just sufficient knowledge and intelligence to see and understand that the enlightenment, intellectually and morally, of the mass of the population, must lead inevitably to fundamental changes, the first of which would be the destruction of their jealous, restrictive, and feudal tenure of power. Hence the persistent and implacable hostility with which all the more powerful Princes and Daimios regard the establishment of foreign relations and the extension of commerce, notwithstanding that the pecuniary interests of many as producers might be bene-fitted by foreign trade.*

But besides the Feudal form of Government, and an administration based on the most elaborate system of espionage ever attempted, which is essentially a discivilis-ing agent, and acts as an impediment to progress intel-lectual or moral; there are certain other vices grafted on the national character, possibly by such administrative system, but much too intimately blended with the parent tree, to be either easily or promptly got rid of. And these also constitute serious obstacles, for which I hold the Government in some degree responsible. I allude to the relation of the sexes, the intercourse sanctioned by law, and the position of women. I believe a great deal of undeserved laudation has been bestowed on the Japanese in this respect. I do not wish to enter here into the question whether they are as a nation more or less immoral than others; but in a country where a father may sell or hire out his daughter for a term of prostitution, not only without penal consequences from the law, but with its sanction and intervention, and without the reprobation of his neighbours, or not more than would be expressed in England if a family well to do let their daughter go out to service instead of keeping her at home, there can be no healthy moral feeling. And that such things are, I know to be a fact. I would also say, that even though a people may be free from the institution of slavery; though neither serfs nor domestic slaves could be bought and sold like chattels or cattle, and transferred from one master to another with the same facility (and the negative is only partially true as regards Japanese; for

* *Might* be, but as I have already shown, and shall have occasion again to prove, they never have been benefited, owing to the manœuvres of the Tycoon's Government and officials, by which all the profit realised by the opening of a new market for Japanese produce, part of which belongs to the Daimios, is intercepted and appropriated by a hungry swarm of custom-house and other officials, maintained for that very purpose, apparently, at the three Consular Ports.

girls are so bought and sold with all due legal formalities, though only for a limited term, and so I believe may both boys and men); yet where a legalised system of concubinage exists, I do not see how the sanctity of the domestic relations can be maintained. And yet without this the very foundation of national growth and dignity —of national progress and civilisation — must either be wanting or undermined.

What peculiar counterpoises may exist, to mitigate the otherwise ruinous effects of these radical vices in their national system of government and their institutions, we may at present be unable to discover. Some, I believe, there must be — as in China, in the unprecedented and in every way extraordinary authority given to mothers over their sons. Though they themselves may have been bargained for, and sold to husbands with no regard whatever to any will of their own, or any rights of womanhood; and during their husband's lifetime have been treated by them as household drudges or slaves — yet the power over the son restores the balance and redresses the wrong, by placing woman as the *mother* far above man, as the son, whatever his age or rank. Perhaps the right of women to succeed to the throne even of the Mikado, of which there are numerous examples both in ancient and modern times, may be one of these. Certainly their position seems from many indications to be more tolerable, if not independent and respected, than some of the premisses would lead us to expect. Nor is there any deficiency, as far as one can judge, of attachment between parents and children. We have a great deal yet to learn, however, on this subject also. There is no lack, it would seem, of parental and filial affection; the philoprogenitive organ seems indeed very fully developed — if there be such an organ, for phrenology has long been at a great discount.

There can be but one legal wife, and the son of the concubine cannot inherit with the son of the wife. This may in some respects rectify the disorder introduced by the bondwoman. But of one thing we may be certain,

that since male and female infants are brought into existence in equal numbers (with a slight fraction for greater
waste of male life), everywhere and in all circumstances,
the same law of nature has destined them for each other
in pairs; both for the satisfaction of the appetite on which
the propagation of the species depends; and the exercise
of the parental affections, based as these are on natural and
universal instincts; and precisely in the proportion in
which this great and fundamental law is violated by any
sanctioned monopoly or prevalence of promiscuous intercourse, will be the impossibility of a nation so offending,
attaining the highest civilisation. And where a government sanctions this, if even with a view of only correcting
the more palpable disorders attending it;— the question
will arise whether it is not doing evil that good may come,
and with the usual evil result. Whether, in a word, the
tendency of all such legislation is not still farther to
degrade the woman, and identify the government with
the evil. At the same time, as regards polygamy or
concubinage, we must in fairness remember this has been
the established law of Asia since the days of the patriarchs,
—and it may be hard measure to hold any government
of an Eastern race in the present day, responsible for not
having initiated a totally new principle of life and legislation. So in regard to the Social Evil, it must be also
admitted to be a question of policy how far a government should, by direct intervention, seek to moderate an
evil it is plainly out of its power to prevent or eradicate,
— a question on which many governments in Christian
countries have arrived at opposite conclusions, and adopted
different principles of legislation.

I cannot help looking upon what I would call radical
defects or vices in the national character and institutions,
as the chief obstacles to rapid improvement, or any sensible
progress in a right direction; these, more than any defects
of mere government either in form or administration, apart
at least from their active agency in producing or fostering
these very evils. I believe with Mr. Mill, that for the

general developement and perfecting of the human faculties and of mankind in societies, freedom of thought and of individual action are indispensable ; and it is difficult to conceive a system more determinedly repressive of all freedom of thought, speech, or action, than that which the Japanese Government has adopted.  And I also believe that in so far as it is incompatible with the free developement of man's best faculties—tends to repress the natural aspirations of the moral and intellectual nature, and denies the means of cultivation and exercise of all that are normal and ineradicable, it can only subsist so long as the radical vices just described enervate and incapacitate the subject for vigorous action in the assertion of the inalienable objects of his own life as a human being.  Could these be eradicated, the rest would follow certainly and of necessity.  The Government would change because it would no longer be an efficient instrument in the hands of its administrators, and it would break in their hands, if they persisted in retaining it, with a violence proportioned to the firmness and tenacity of their hold.  Doubtless it would be in the power of those now in possession to prepare the way, and greatly facilitate the desired improvement in the civilisation of the people ; how far it may also be in their power to retard, and eventually prevent such improvement and consequent progress — is the problem which time and events can alone solve.

As regards the Government and the effective agencies it employs, we see nothing elevating or ennobling, but, on the contrary, much which is undoubtedly demoralising and discivilising.  How far independent of the Government, —religion, philosophy, and the cultivation generally of the intellectual and moral faculties among the people may supply a counterpoise, and hold out any hope that ultimately they will both supply the deficiencies and correct the evils which it has tended to bring upon the nation, is a grave question, and all the more difficult that we do not know much either of their literature, their philosophy, or scientific culture and attainments.  Nor are we well versed in their religion, though on this head more information seems at our command. All their philosophy and moral ethics, and much of their religion—Buddhism and Confucianism certainly (by far the most widely spread systems in Japan) came from the neighbouring continent, and are Asiatic in origin — the first Indian, and the second Chinese. All their science, I believe, came from Europe through the Dutch. If they have originated anything themselves, we want the means of tracing it; but whence-soever derived, we know that scientific culture is not altogether wanting, any more than intellectual attainments of a respectable kind.

Cultivation, however, is not civilisation — just as little as it is religion, though each may be powerful civilising agencies. Both must indeed enter largely into the highest civilisation of which man is susceptible, and can hardly be entirely wanting in any. Intellectual culture the Japanese have to no inconsiderable extent. Culture in art, literature, and philosophy,— borrowed or original, does not very materially matter. And there is perhaps a more general diffusion of education than most nations of European stock can boast. But the question is, what kind of culture, and what are its tendencies and influence? If the industrial arts are civilising agencies, as they undoubtedly are, the fine arts may be so in still higher degree. They are, or *may be so*, for this is a necessary distinction. Art in all its forms, in poetry, painting, statuary, and music, appealing to the moral and emotional side of human nature, may tend to cultivate and develope all the higher moral faculties, or only address themselves to and develope the baser desires and passions. In the one case, they are civilising agencies of the highest kind; in the other, they are quite as obviously debasing and discivilising. Of the in-fluence which art can and does legitimately exercise in pro-moting man's moral and religious developement, making sense, under the guidance of the imagination, subservient to the spirit, much may be said, and in support of its general cultivation. Yet if we look to Greece, and later still to Rome when it wielded the empire of the world,

and art attained a higher excellence in many directions
among both pagan races than it has ever reached under
Christianity, we cannot but see that a people may have the
highest artistic and literary culture, and yet be thoroughly
pagan in spirit and brutalised in their lives.    For what kind
of existence did the Romans live, whose pastime was the
wholesale butcheries of the amphitheatre? The most civilised people of the earth, then, found their chief delight in
watching wild beasts rend human beings to pieces ; — or
men and prisoners pitted against each other for the not less
brutal and deadly combat.    With Cicero's eloquence and
finely rounded periods, with Virgil and Horace's sweet
numbers, with statuary and architecture in high perfection,
were they—considered in a rational and religious point of
view—any better than *barbarians*, making all intellectual
culture subservient to the basest uses, and pander only to the
grosser senses ? Was the Roman patrician with his greasy
woollen garments, his disregard of human life and suffering,
his ignorance of all feeling of domestic privacy, and of the
tastes, habits, and virtues inseparable from it,—his repudiation in war of all the rights of nations, and of the
claims of humanity,—with his slaves and his wild beast
shows, his scepticism, and disbelief in the immortality of
the soul,—really nearer to the ideal of man in his most perfect developement than the Hottentot or New Zealander of
to-day? Immeasurably in advance as to intellectual culture,
was he so by a hair's breadth as a religious, responsible,
and moral being ? This test applied to nations, and to
progress in arts, sciences, commerce, education, political
institutions — affords a ready and a certain gauge of the
true character and worth of such progress as they seem
to indicate.    Christianity has afforded a standard wanting
to the most cultivated and civilised of ancient nations ; —
and by that standard we are bound to weigh all civilisation and its various elements, law, politics, education, the
condition of women, the mutual relations of classes, the
security of property, the prevention of crime, its arts, its
science, and its commerce, its institutions, political, social,

and ecclesiastical,— and pronounce judgement honestly according to the issue.

Viewed in this light what has art, taken in its most comprehensive sense, done for the Japanese? Does it ennoble and civilise by cultivating the moral faculties, or degrade and barbarise by developing the animal passions and all the lower and grosser parts of their emotional nature? We do not know much, anything indeed, of their poetry, and little of their philosophy, except the general fact, that it together with their whole code of moral ethics and much of their jurisprudence are all derived from China and Confucius. Of art in other forms, we can perhaps better judge ; and except so far as it carries with it culture of the mind and intelligence, and gives developement to some of the more genial faculties,— to humour, wit, and mirth,—it is to be feared it has small pretensions in Japan to be considered a valuable civilising agency in its present developement and application; while it does act unquestionably over a wide area of the least cultivated, in pandering to the lower desires, and often to grossness and obscenity. All that creates amusement and innocent mirth, we may admit as good, so far as it goes. So in like manner, whatever tends to refinement ; but coarseness and indelicacy are essentially barbarising agencies, and are unmitigated evils. Art in Japan seems to me to contribute to both these results in a large degree, and thus whatever good it effects, may be more than counterbalanced by the unquestioned evil.

Their civilisation is not, however, as I have said, without moral and intellectual agencies in active operation. There is even a larger admixture of these than probably will be found, out of China, in any other part of Asia. For although there is no lack of sharp and effective law founded on physical force—the torturer's rack, and the executioner's sword being often in requisition — and voluntary immolation by suicide supplements largely the whole system in which life and human suffering count for very little,—yet viewing the administrative and legislative

systems together, so far as we are able to gather the leading principles from their details, both seem to rest more on
an appeal to the intellectual and moral faculties than actual
force as a means of control.   The frequency of deliberate
suicide in certain given cases, as a custom having all the
force of law, is itself an evidence that they hold honour
dearer than life, and are far from the low and base estimate, which would place the preservation of life itself as
the highest good.   There is always hope for a nation that
sees something above and beyond the possession of worldly
goods — or life itself, the most prized of all possessions.
Something of the feeling of duty as the true motive for
exertion, without reference to any possible or contingent
reward in wealth or distinction, mingles with their patriotism also.   All patriotism is so far an ennobling passion or element in national character, if for no other
reason than that of lifting man out of the circle of selfish
aims, and impelling him to sacrifices for that which is
outside of self, effecting that *sortir de soi* which George
Sand, with her usual eloquence and more than her usual
discrimination of right and wrong, has taken for her last
theme.   Just in proportion as duty, and not reward, is
the motive for action, all effort is ennobling, and all labour
civilising ; while even a desire for personal distinction, the
highest form which desire for recompense can take, where
reward of some kind is the real motive power, has often
a contrary tendency.   When this sense of duty mingles
in every act, and supplies the paramount motive for all
action, as it does when Christianity is really efficient, and
underlying the whole, all the elements of civilisation in its
best and most perfect aspect are in operation.   This we
cannot look for in pagan countries, nor even in Mahommedan lands, from errors in the foundations of their faith
and religious system—we cannot have it therefore in
Japan.   But inasmuch as the religious element is never
wholly wanting, and does mingle more or less in the daily
life and motives to action of every race and people, the
Japanese among the rest, and not always without ennobling

and beneficial influence ; it would seem a grave error to
consider any form of civilisation as entirely divested of its
saving and elevating power.  What the religion of the
Japanese is, or what it may amount to, in its collective
influences, cannot now be ascertained with all the fullness
or accuracy to be desired.  No European is yet, indeed,
in a position to speak from his own knowledge on this
subject.  All, or very nearly all the information we
possess, has hitherto been derived from the painstaking
labours of the early writers, especially Kœmpfer, who
did not himself know the language, and had exceedingly limited sources of intelligence in his intercourse
with the natives.  That there was an indigenous religion
as old as their history, one formed by and for themselves in long past ages, the Sintoo, which survives to
this day ; that some ten or fifteen centuries ago or more,
this was overlaid by the Confucian doctrines — a code of
moral ethics, not a religion in the proper sense of the term
— and about the seventh century both were in great
degree supplanted by the Buddhist faith derived from
China, we do know with tolerable certainty.  But this
is nearly the sum.  Of course we have ample information as to what both the Buddhist and Confucian systems
embody in India and in China respectively.  What we
do not know, are the modifications and transmutations
these may have undergone in passing through the alembic
of the Japanese mind,—and by slow accretions and changes
in the lapse of ages.  Of the doctrines and true character
of the Sintoo religion, either in its original or present
form, we can know still less.  So far as any personal
means of information has enabled me to form an opinion
on the one essential point here, I believe what Kœmpfer
has said in respect to the Sintoo religion is true as
regards any faith the Japanese generally may have.  'The
more immediate end which they propose to themselves
is a state of happiness in this world.'  They have indeed
some, but very obscure and imperfect notions of the
immortality of the soul and a future state of bliss or

misery.  But so far as I have seen, the educated classes scoff at all such doctrines, as fit only for the vulgar and the ignorant; and believe with all the ancient poets and philosophers that after death there is no future, or as Catullus expresses it in his Epistle to Lesbia:—

*Vivamus, mea Lesbia,* atque amemus.
Nobis cum semel occidit brevis lux,
*Nox est perpetua, una dormienda.'*

But apart from these enlightened rationalists and sceptics, there does seem among the masses a certain kind of belief in a supreme God, but one who scarcely looks down upon this world, and many inferior deities, who influence more or less directly man's destiny, and determine his happiness or misery.  They do, evidently, also believe in the future existence, in some form or state,—of a portion at least of those who live distinguished in this ; for they deify and offer worship to their great men and sovereigns, precisely as the Greeks and Romans did of old.  They believe also in a devil, or satanic agencies, and pay particular respect and worship to foxes, as being the incarnation of the evil one.  We can know little more of the religious doctrines or faith of the Japanese as a nation, until some among the educated Europeans have attained sufficient command of the language, written and spoken, to read all their works, sacred and lay, on the subject, and converse freely, even on abstruse subjects, with various classes of the natives in their own tongue.

As regards material civilisation, there can be no doubt they may take rank in the fore-front of all Eastern nations, and but for the fact that their mechanical appliances are inferior, as well as their knowledge of the applied sciences connected with mechanical industry and arts ; they may rightly claim a place with nations of European race.  As it is, if the policy of the rulers permitted freer intercourse and trade, so as to bring them in competition with Birmingham or Sheffield, and Manchester, notwithstanding all our advantages of funded knowledge and civilisation of a higher order;—our steam and river machinery, and the marvellous perfection to which all mechanical appliances have been brought; I believe the Japanese would hold their own, send out swords and cutlery to rival Sheffield, and silks and crapes to compete with Macclesfield or Lyons in the markets of the world;—cheapness of material and labour, with natural ingenuity and skill, compensating the difference in machinery. Of course they would copy and take hints; for they have little of the stupid conceit of the Chinese, which leads them to ignore or deny the superiority of foreign things. On the contrary, they are both eager and quick to discover in what it lies, and how they may make the excellence their own.

# CHAPTER XIII.

THE CIVILISATION OF JAPAN—SOCIAL AND POLITICAL CONDITION—
DURABILITY OF THEIR INSTITUTIONS — HOW SECURED HITHERTO,
AND ON WHAT DEPENDING — DREAD OF INNOVATION AMONGST THE
RULING CLASSES A PRIMARY CAUSE OF THEIR HOSTILITY TO
FOREIGNERS—THEIR PROGRESS IN ART—ILLUSTRATIONS OF POPULAR
SUBJECTS—MANNERS AND CUSTOMS—THEIR LOVE OF THE HUMOROUS
AND GROTESQUE.

SPEAKING of our own civilisation, it was said very
truly the other day, apropos to Social Science meetings, that although Christianity introduced new ideas,
new responsibilities, new duties, new sanctions, and new
aids; yet, at the present moment, judging from such
shrieks of despair, as the meetings of the Social Science
delegates imply, we are all in want of a new moral
system.

But if neither the art, science, and letters of the Greeks,
as I observed in the last chapter, nor the cultivation and
intellectual developement of Rome, nor lastly, in the fullness of time, the advent of Christianity and the religion
of the Gospel, have done anything effectual to change the
whole moral nature of man, and a fatal proclivity to evil
and crime, what does the progress of humanity, and the
boasted advance of civilisation, amount to?

This question presents itself very forcibly when we turn
to Japan, with a view to inquire into the civilisation developed amidst such isolation, though borrowed in the first
instance from the Chinese. From China, they borrowed
a religion, a written language in the ideographic character,
a philosophy, and a literature; everything in fact which
ministers to the intellect, and promotes social progress.
Religion, law, politics, education, the condition of women,

the mutual relation of classes, the security of property, the prevention of crime and its punishment, the statistics of disease, poverty, and sin, on which social philosophers are so constantly engaged, as means to the end of improving mankind; to what do all such efforts lead, so far as the actual progress and improvement of mankind, from one generation to another, are concerned ? To what have they led among the inheritors of the Greek and Roman triumphs of art and intellectual conquests? What is their fruit in this nineteenth century of the Christian era ? Is moral evil or crime on the decrease ? Is there not, as has recently been observed, rather a conviction, that if in some special departments particular vices are lessened, in other directions, new elements of evil have been developed? Whatever civilisation has done, it has not, to all appearances, materially diminished the sum of human misery and crime. Is all civilisation, then, but a vicious circle, and our efforts from century to century, but the oscillations of a pendulum, which so far as it sways to the one side, must of necessity swing to the other? As old evils are rooted out, and old diseases disappear, must it always follow, that there will be a similar outgrowth of new evils, moral and physical, modern remedies seeming to generate their own peculiar forms of disease and rottenness ? Is it only to be a change of *form* in Man and in States, not an essential change of nature or condition?

The lust of conquest, scorn of all moral obligations, frenzy, political corruption, and folly, which have been the characteristics of times the most remote, of the Pharaohs and Babylonian kings, of Alexander, Attila, or Tamerlane — are they unknown in our days? Are there not wars, and rumours of wars, keeping all the States of civilised Europe in constant care for their frontiers, against unscrupulous allies, and necessitating ruinous taxes to maintain armaments for defence? The fullest developement of constitutional freedom, and the widest bases of Republican Government in a new world, unfettered by old institutions and traditions, have plainly not sufficed to prevent an exhibition of frenzy and civil war, which neither the Greeks of old, nor mediæval Italy, ever developed with more suicidal madness.

In estimating the true worth of Japanese civilisation, it is well to remember, then, what are the actual products of our own boasted progress in all the different departments of human activity and social or political life, determining not only the moral worth, but the destinies of individuals and nations alike.    Much is said and written about the obligation of the Western States to spread the blessings of true religion, a knowledge of the Gospel, and all the advantages of an advanced civilisation to Oriental races, whom we regard as in a state of comparative barbarism.    But, if we would see the true bearing of all such clap-trap phrases and popular harangues, we must bring something of a philosophic and truth-loving mind to the task, and examine in what the civilisations of Europe and Asia agree, as well as in what they differ.    And, if we find that, as regards the fruit of both, in good and evil, there is a far nearer approach to identity than our pride would willingly admit, and that mere variations in *form* have been mistaken for essential differences in *substance* and *principle*, it may, perhaps, tend to moderate the rage for thrusting upon them, by a coarse machinery of propagandism, all kinds of panaceas drawn from European sources, for the evils that beset Eastern despotisms and Oriental institutions,— forgetful that the latter have the immense advantage over any we could give, of being indigenous to the race and the countries, and assimilated by long growth and mutual adaptation.    If, moreover, we find that they do actually attain all the principal ends of our own social and political institutions, to an extent which no modern graft from a foreign soil could possibly effect, were the most perfect success to attend the operation, we may well pause in our empiric efforts to force ourselves and our specifics upon them against their will.

In an article headed *L'Angleterre et la Vie anglaise*, which appeared recently, a French writer tells his countrymen and the world in general, that 'La civilisation Britannique s'appuie sur deux livres, la Bible et Shakspeare.' Like many other continental sayings about us, it is more epigrammatic than true. There are certainly very few Englishmen who could accept this very limited view as either affording a fair account of our civilisation, or a correct definition of its leading characters. I will take warning, therefore, and avoid the temptation to deal with so grave a subject in epigrams.

It has been very truly remarked, that 'It is one of the hardest things in the world to form a just estimate of a foreign country. We seldom see other nations fully, and still more rarely judge impartially of what we do see; such is the disposition to under-rate and to over-rate, according to our own special tendency.' The same writer goes on to remark, with equal justice, ' When we remember the contradictory representations we daily hear and read, of the countries in our own immediate neighbourhood, modesty may well restrain us from pronouncing any dogmatic opinion on those which are physically, intellectually, and morally more remote.' In the case of such a country as Japan, it may be added, the difficulty of judging well and impartially of what we so imperfectly know, amounts almost to an impossibility. We need not wonder, then, if one set of writers have described Japan as a paradise, while others following later, should feel disposed, upon larger experience, to depict it as a pandemonium. I will try, as much as in me lies, to avoid both extremes, and to state fairly all that I know or have observed, and no more, leaving it to the intelligent to draw their own conclusions. But, so strongly have I felt the difficulty of doing justice either to the Japanese or the subject, embracing as it does the whole range of questions affecting their civilisation and social condition, that this chapter remained for many months unfilled up, with a mere heading and in a skeleton form, though materials for its completion were abundant, and had been continually accumulating from my first arrival.

The political constitution, the social condition, and even the commercial relations of Japan, all enter into the question of their civilisation, besides being in themselves subjects of great interest and importance.  But, first, we want a definition of what Civilisation is — one that shall be both comprehensive and definite, and yet in accord, if possible, with some generally received notions on the subject—for the word is made to signify a great variety of conditions, real or imaginary ; and to convey to different minds many totally different views.

We must begin, as I have said, with some clear idea of what civilisation imports ; or, at least, what we ourselves mean by it, when we are seeking to decide upon the claims of any Eastern race to be considered *civilised*, and in what degree they approach that somewhat vague and Protean standard of developement and progress.  This is necessary, in order to determine the scope, no less than the method of inquiry.   If, ' to give and preserve what is vital in religion — religion as Christians know it — and with this to stimulate the highest aspirations of the heart, and the noblest conceptions of the intellect ; not only to abate superstition and inculcate tolerance, but to introduce in the place of the first a living faith and true motive to action, the highest of which humanity is susceptible,'—if this be civilisation, the Japanese have it not.  And, if this be the civilisation which we desire to communicate to Eastern races and naturalise in their soil, all honour to those who put their hand to the plough, and, whatever the difficulty of the task, the cost, or the sacrifice, will not look back.   All honour, indeed, I say ; but do we so understand civilisation in Europe, its gifts or its duties ?  What if there be no such civilisation yet existing in Europe ?  What, if passing in review all that can be said in favour of the civilisation of the most advanced countries in the Western world, we feel compelled, in candour, to pardon Kœmpfer closing his elaborate history of Japan by a chapter bearing the following significant title, 'An inquiry whether it be conducive for the good of the Japanese empire to keep it shut up, as it now is, and not to suffer its inhabitants to have any commerce with foreign nations, either at home or abroad?'

This is not an inquiry I intend to follow his example by making; not, perhaps, that I should see very serious cause to differ from him in many of his conclusions; but simply because I conceive the question already and irrevocably decided by the Treaty Powers, so far as any practical issue is concerned. Whether it might be argued *à priori* as conducive to the good of the Japanese empire to keep it shut up, would be merely a speculative question here; for shut up it can never be again. The gates have been forced off their hinges by commerce, by rival nationalities, and contending interests combined. There are many Western Powers too deeply committed, probably, to retire from the scene now: while any one of these is far too strong to be forcibly excluded, by any effort of the Japanese, when such exclusion would involve either loss of prestige, or national dignity, independent of any more material interests it might compromise. Unless, therefore, all the Treaty Powers could agree to retire together,—not a very probable contingency,— such an issue may be regarded as impossible in respect to any one of the number. The expediency or policy therefore of such a measure is hardly worth discussion. The only time when such an inquiry could have possibly been made with advantage to either party, would have been before Mr. Harris, the late Minister of the United States, entered into negotiations in 1858 for the second treaty with America. Whether the Minister, or his Government, took any thought on the subject, is another matter. But once the treaty made, the die was cast, for good or for evil; and nothing was left thenceforward, but to grapple with the difficulties which the throw entailed upon all the Treaty Powers, who chose to follow the American lead. What these are, and how they may best, or are most likely to be, overcome, are the only practical questions.

As regards civilisation, it has been observed that 'Nations and individuals attain the highest state which their fundamental convictions will allow.' And this is so far true (although natural capacity and original differences of organisation must not be overlooked), that some inquiry into the fundamental convictions of a people, as well as their general culture and capacity for anything better, appears to form the preliminary step in any advance towards right conclusions. And it will soon be obvious that no appreciation of the civilisation of a nation can be worth much which does not take all these elements into account ; while the practical difficulties in the way of any fusion or intercourse are greatly influenced by degrees of affinity and repulsion in those directions. Some progress in this inquiry has been made in the last chapter, but a good deal of ground has yet to be turned over before the harvest. I observed that in any such inquiry the religious convictions could not be omitted or overlooked. For although religion and civilisation were not exchangeable terms, and in no sense identical ; yet true religion was not only a necessary adjunct, but an essential element in all the higher forms of civilisation. However important and necessary it may be in practical life, and in legislation, to keep the two distinct, and under no plea to allow them to be confounded, lest we should debase the one and retard the other ;—there is no theory of civilisation which can be either comprehensive or complete, that excludes religion from consideration. We need not be reminded that nearly all religions have comprised a system of morality and of doctrines regarding man's rightful dealings with man, while all bring into play religious faculties and sanctions to enforce that morality, whatever it may be. Though religion and civilisation are two different things, therefore, each having their distinct domain, they are so far identified with each other (as is the soul to the body), that none but the lower and material forms of civilisation can exist without religion as an element of elevation and progress.

It is true that a large and more or less influential section of philosophers and writers on Social Science have adopted as the exposition of their theory of civilisation and its sole end, the greatest happiness of the greatest number ; yet if happiness in the ordinary and merely worldly sense be meant, the definition is essentially bad and false.  Happiness, however generally prized, is not after all the greatest good, much less the sole end of life, or its true aim in this short and manifestly probationary stage; where the appointed means for perfecting human nature under a Divine government seems to be much more frequently pain and suffering, and sacrifice of worldly goods and present pleasure or *happiness*, than worldly enjoyment, however refined and harmless.  Even equality of condition appears to be no more than happiness the means, nor the appointed end. Yet these together generally constitute in popular estimation the main ingredients of what is called happiness, or any popular estimate of what is needful to constitute it ; worldly goods, present pleasure, and equality, as implying the greatest liberty of enjoyment.  If this be so, and it is scarcely open to dispute, it may well admit of doubt, whether this modern and somewhat utilitarian shibboleth of philanthropy, can furnish the right solution of so intricate a problem.

So also there may be, as De Tocqueville observed in his work on democracy in America, a tendency in the civilisation of the West to advance towards ' equality of conditions ; ' but whether that will be a general levelling of the higher, or the raising of the lower to a better level, remains to be seen.  Yet upon the issue it depends, whether this said civilisation shall combine a greater share of happiness and enlightenment on the totality of mankind, or on  a small number only, raising, it may be, the few nearer to  perfection, but widening  the distance between them and the mass.

We hear  much  of  the  inequality  of  conditions  in

European societies of the old race ; and the evils flowing
therefrom ; the disparity of rank and wide distance between the rich and poor ; and in more modern and democratic societies, equal praise is heard of the equality that
reigns, and the absence of all lines of demarcation between
the highest and the lowest in the social scale.   If we were
to take this for our stand-point of view, or gauge of the
civilisation of Japan, I should have nothing favourable
to report.   But the evils attributed to these distinctions
and disparities, however broadly or indelibly marked in
the older and monarchical states, are not so clearly the
offspring of such forms of government, as of a common
humanity under all circumstances ; — for a law of inequality runs through all nature, and evidently is of
Divine origin and dispensation.   And on the other hand,
this democratic panacea fails miserably in its promise to
remove all the maladies of the body social and politic,
and even secure the dead level of equality which forms
the ideal of such a system.   This is never attained,
despite the abolition of patents of nobility, hereditary
honours, stars and ribands.   And it arises in great measure, no doubt, from fundamental errors in the original
conception of democracy, as a means of improving the
human race, reforming its political institutions, and removing all social evils.   It contemplates an enforced, unnatural, and impossible equality, and sets out with a false
estimate of what constitutes a *true* equality.   I have nowhere seen this so well and forcibly stated, as in a work
entitled ' Letters from the Slave States,' by James Stirling ;
and some of his observations bearing on this part of the
subject are altogether so apposite and conclusive, that I
need make no apology for quoting them at length.   I
could not better place before the reader my own convictions, and the conclusions upon which my estimate of
Japanese civilisation is based, or the guage by which I
am disposed to test their claims and fix their place among
the nations, where different phases of civilisation have
been developed.   For the instruction of the whole family

of man, these seem to have been infinitely varied under Jewish, Pagan, Mahommedan and Christian influences; which forms of civilisation, as we now can see, have been the determining causes of national progress or decay. These phases of civilisation, no doubt, have been modified in their turn, in a thousand different ways, by special causes more or less peculiar to each separate country or race, and wholly independent of religious influences or creeds. Among which, as regards Japan, its utter isolation must be steadily kept in view, as entering into any problem connected with the growth of its institutions, and the form or degree of civilisation developed.

Mr. Stirling observes, that 'The popular notion of equality is no less superficial than that of liberty. The democrat prizes an outward, material equality, not the essential inward equality that is rooted in man's humanity, and that exists in spite of all outward differences. Hence he is not satisfied with essential equality: he must have an outward monotony of condition. The people must all ride in the same car, and sit at the same table, and vote at the same polling place. It is considered a degradation for one to serve another, and the very name of servitude is abominated. In all this there is a want of true wisdom and true dignity. It is right to assert the dignity and worth of manhood; but it is a weakness and a folly to rebel against those civil and domestic distinctions which originate in the nature of things, and which therefore carry no real dishonour with them. So with service. There is nothing essentially degrading in one man performing certain menial offices for another. The degradation arises only when the office is performed in a menial spirit. In itself, all labour, even the most menial, is honourable, when performed in the true spirit of duty. The Americans will cease to disparage domestic service, when they learn to take a higher view of human equality; when they better understand true equality, they will tolerate the necessary distinctions of society.'

And again, giving the principle a larger application, he

remarks—'Democrats on both sides of the Atlantic have a confused notion of the fundamental principles of liberty and equality, which, properly understood, may be resolved into one.   They see in liberty only the freedom to exercise the unrestrained will of the individual—in equality, a gross similitude of material circumstances.   Whereas true liberty is that subordination of all wills to an universal law of justice, which secures to each its own unrestricted sphere of action ;  and *equality in the highest sense, is the equality of men as free intelligences which such a subordination effects.*   Well understood, therefore, liberty is not opposed to law : rather law is the essential condition of liberty.   But the vulgar in all times have confounded the spiritual unseen law of justice, and the material government which is its necessary embodiment.   Justice must be administered by some organised power, and forasmuch as the holders of that power have often turned it to their own uses, shallow and impartial men have jumped to the conclusion that all law, all government, all authority, is despotism.   Hence monarchy means with them tyranny, because many kings have played the tyrant; and democracy means liberty, because every man gets his own way.   But all this is sheer confusion of thought.   Where the universal law of justice prevails, no matter in what form or under what name, there we have liberty ; but where that law is disregarded or dishonoured, we have despotism or anarchy, according as the law is abused by its appointed representative on the one hand, or disregarded from any want of efficient embodiment on the other.   If, as is usual in democratic communities, we confound the " people " with the numerical majority of the nation, and set up their will, be it holy or unholy, as the supreme arbiter of affairs, we confound the brute force of numbers with the divine authority of right and justice, and thereby lay the foundation of a whole system of political blundering.   The end in view is *the predominance of justice.*   If that end be attained, it matters little by what machinery it is worked out.   If it be not attained, then the most specious constitution is a blunder and a failure.'

It has elsewhere been observed that Christianity failed eighteen centuries ago, in producing the democrat's ideal equality, as it has also failed in all that period in curing the ills to which our flesh is heir,—ills many of them far too deeply rooted in our common nature, we may certainly infer therefore, to find a remedy in forms of government or social institutions. Yet Christianity was the best and most democratic of all constitutions, with a Divine sanction for its authority,—and if it failed in realising the republican's dream, there is the less room for surprise if such democracy as man can invent should fail more utterly and miserably. But there is this broad distinction between the two, that failure cannot be very correctly attributed to Christianity, which never gave any promise of making all men equal in each other's eyes, or in reality, so far as natural gifts and outward conditions are concerned. It made no promise of ameliorating all the evils of humanity, but rather prophesied its own failure. But Christianity introduced new ideas, responsibilities, ends, and sanctions ; it supplied a new and higher principle of action, utterly repudiating all baser motives, and taking no account of worldly distinctions ; but it never gave any promise of removing such distinctions and inequalities, whether of rank, wealth, or political power ; or of eradicating crime and folly, by the creation of a political Utopia. Whatever civilisation exists in Europe, indeed, has taken its form, and all the best types of its developement from Christianity ; and to trace the growth of modern civilisation irrespective of its influence, is of course impossible. But it is different with reference to civilisation in the East ; no law of Christianity prevails there, to raise it above the lower standards of the heathen and Mahommedan world.

That *all* should fail in bringing the world forward in the march of improvement, every religion, and every form of government, or even in securing advance by any certain and clearly-marked stages, presents a problem for Social Science, which is to all appearance as far as ever from its solution. Civilisation, before and after the advent

of Christianity, has had a large field, and still halts far
from the avowed end.  Of all forms of government, which
is there that has not been tried under every possible combination of circumstances ?  Despotism, feudalism, limited
monarchies, republicanism and democracy in their most
unlimited expression, all have had their trial, and what
have they done?  How does the account stand if we take
stock of the social state under each, and note the degree
of civilisation attained?  The impotence of charts and
constitutions, republics among the rest, to lift a whole
nation above the common infirmities of our nature, or
save a body politic from the errors, follies, and wicked-
nesses of the worst government, is often, in those which
are the 'last-born of Time' sadly illustrated.   One is
disposed to ask with Philarète Chasles in his 'Etudes
sur les Hommes et les Mœurs au XIXᵉ. Siècle,' '*Sans le
sentiment réligieux, sans le dévouement, sans la souffrance
acceptée et bénie, y a-t-il une force sociale possible?*'
And no less earnestly to join in the farther conclusion,
'La souffrance est sainte, dit l'évangile, admettons donc
ce que le simple bon sens nous crie, c'est à dire, que le
devoir impose la souffrance à des degrès divers.   Rien
de plus puérile que cette morale de l'utilité.   Il n'est pas
utile personnellement à l'homme de mourir pour sa mère,
de se battre pour son pays, de s'exposer à la contagion
pour sauver des pestiférés qui meurent.'

As to our present European civilisation, of which we
are apt to boast as something far surpassing all that has
gone before, whether in ancient or modern times, before
or after Christ ; it has been very naturally asked what is
the meaning of all these Social Congresses ?  They have
a meaning, no doubt, and spring from some want which
they are intended to supply.  Social Science means, we are
told, 'the art of improving society, and both as to principles
and details we have almost everything to learn!'  This in
Europe,— in England in the nineteenth century, with all its
vaunted freedom, art, science, wealth, and religion.  Is this
the civilisation we would so fain bestow on other races ?

What are its fruits? Is moral evil or crime on the decrease in our own land, despite the 50,000*l.* a day spent in religion and education,—and the Chancellor of the Exchequer alone knows how much more on justice, and means for punishing the criminals who live and grow under a system, political, moral, and social, which a thousand years has been spent in perfecting since Alfred was king. Progress is a taking word, and civilisation, like the cardinal's red mantle, covers a multitude of sins and crimes. It is like a tinkling cymbal which drowns the noise of all other discordant things ; but there is enough yet in the old world and its modern institutions to teach humility and modesty, in our appreciation of the benefits either our institutions or our civilisation are capable of conferring upon another race or people, were they nearer akin to us in social habits and religion than the Japanese. There is vice and crime enough in Japan undoubtedly to tempt our social philosophers to experiment ;— but the garotting going on in the heart of our own capital is scarcely better than the cutting and maiming by Samourai in the streets of Yeddo.

Notwithstanding these disheartening reflections, which are too apt to intrude upon all who seek to lift the veil and search into the true character and meaning of any civilisation yet attained, — the task of examining closely into the working of institutions, the social and national characteristics of the different families of man under varying conditions, and the determining influences of good and evil socially developed, — is one full of interest, if not of obvious utility. Let us proceed with our inquiry into the civilisation and social science of the Japanese, who, although they may not really have lived, as their history asserts, five hundred millions of years, are undoubtedly descendants of an ancient race which was possessed of many of the elements of civilisation largely developed, as far back as the Christian era, and has ever since occupied a more or less isolated position as a nation.

There is a little republic isolated by mountains on

every frontier lying between the Pyrenees of Arriège and
the Pyrenees of Catalonia, included neither in France nor
Spain, but intervening between the two countries, consisting chiefly of three valleys.  Its greatest length is under
thirty miles, and its greatest width under twenty, with a
population of about 8,000.    This little commonwealth,
we are told by a writer in the ' Edinburgh Review,' who
has recently ' disinterred this living relic ' of a past age,
was carved out by Charlemagne and his son Louis le
Débonnaire during their Moorish wars, and apparently
preserves the same frontiers and principles of government
which it at first assumed, now more than a thousand years
ago !   It is a peasant's commonwealth based upon aristocracy.   Long descended patricians who derive the grant
of their lands from Charlemagne shear their sheep with
their own hands.  But they are not the less proud of their
unbroken descent and patrician lineage, more ancient than
the Montmorencys and Rohans, though the nation has
been too motionless to rise above a peasant's civilisation.
A body of untutored rulers is here so brave that every
man's religion is the defence of his rights.   They are a
race of nobles who, during ten centuries, while all around
them has been movement and change, have steadily maintained their separate existence and immobility as a people
— and strange as it may seem, we are told ' the feudal
theory of nobility nowhere receives a more complete
acceptance than among the Andorrian landholders, with
whom luxury and education are preeminently wanting.
They still defend and govern the land which their fathers
conquered.'

Andorre is the Japan of Europe, and Japan is another
example of the power of isolation to produce stationary
types of civilisation and forms of government.   Here, as
in the valleys of Andorre, isolated by the ocean, as
Andorre is by its mountains, from all other nations except
China, until discovered in the sixteenth century, and then
only in momentary communication with the rest of the
world, is a petty nationality whose annals go far beyond

Charlemagne—with a proud and feudal aristocracy and an absolute government, but a torpid administration and a laborious people ; ' a land unequalled for the beauty of its scenery and the simplicity of its race, yet poor withal ; ' ' a phenomenon of social poverty and conservative tradition, a perpetual infancy of the arts in unchanging antithesis with the everlasting luxuriance of nature.'   It would be really difficult to give any more perfect or accurate description of Japan than this epitome of the characteristics of Andorre and its conservative race; except that being a larger country, with a population of millions instead of thousands, they have developed more material wealth. How the little republic has preserved its insular liberties intact, wedged in between two of the greatest Powers in Europe, amidst the general wreck of small kingdoms by ' the growth of empires and the violence of power,' is scarcely a greater marvel than the long-maintained conservatism and isolation of Japan.   But the hour seems approaching when even this Japanese stronghold of mediæval and feudal institutions must disappear before the ever-advancing tide of European invasion and civilisation.   It may well happen that the Andorrians will still preserve their antique freedom and feudal tenure, when the waves of revolution and change shall have swept over the Japanese soil, obliterating the very landmarks of their past history ; for Andorre is still fast locked in its mountain barriers, and has little to tempt the cupidity of the great.   It has nothing to tempt the restless energy either of missionaries or merchants, while Japan, less fortunately situated in this respect, is on the great highway of nations, the coveted of Russia, —so many believe—the most *absorbing*, if not the most aggressive of all the Powers ; and a perpetual temptation alike to merchant and to missionary, who each in different directions, finding the feudalism and spirit of isolation barriers in their path, will not cease to batter them in breach, or undermine them to their downfall.   Such seems to be the probable fate of Japan, and its consummation is

little more than a question of time. When all is accomplished, whether the civilising process will make
them as a people wiser, better, or happier, is a problem
of more doubtful solution.   One thing is quite certain, that the obstructive principle which tends to the
rejection of all Western innovations and proselytism as
abominations, is much too active and vigorous in the
Japanese mind to leave a hope that there will not be
violent and obstinate resistance; and this inevitably
leading to corresponding violence in the assault, there
must be a period of convulsion and disorder before the
change can be effected, and new foundations laid for
another social edifice.   Looking forward to this impending future, the actual state of a people and their
institutions, so long and successfully maintained in mediæval forms, and with a fully developed feudalism,
is worthy of careful study.   This feudalism has left
the nation, if not free in our estimate of freedom, yet
in enjoyment of many blessings which all the boasted
freedom and civilisation of Western States have failed to
secure for them in an equally long succession of centuries.
National prosperity, independence, freedom from war and
material progress in the arts of life—these are all among
the possessions of the Japanese as a people, and the inheritance of many generations.

How to arrive the most rapidly and certainly at some
just estimate of the degree of civilisation actually attained
in a strange country, and what the agency and machinery
employed, is a question of great interest.   It has been
suggested by Mr. Meadows in an essay on Civilisation
contained in his work on China, that the artificial means of
communication and the size and value of private dwellings
and public buildings, exclusive of fortifications or other edi-
fices for warlike purposes, will give a very ready criterion.
I cannot say I think so.   These constitute but a very small
portion of the outward and palpable signs even of a material civilisation, and entirely fail to give the necessary
insight into that which is intellectual and moral.   Judged

by these criteria, Japan may vie with ancient Rome, for, like
the Romans, the Japanese are great in roads. Their highway, the Tocaido, the imperial road throughout the kingdom, may challenge comparison with the finest in Europe.
Broad, level, carefully kept and well macadamised, with
magnificent avenues of timber to give shade from the
scorching heat of the sun, it is difficult to exaggerate their
merit. But if from roads we pass to means of artificial
communication in the larger sense, including post-offices,
mails, telegraphs, and means of rapid transit, they are immeasurably behind the least advanced of European nations.
Railroads and electric telegraphs, though known to the
Rulers by report and working models brought both by the
American and Prussian Missions, are wholly unthought of
in the country. There are no public carriages, or carriages
of any kind indeed, if we except the Mikado's carriage
drawn by buffaloes, or something quite as cumbrous borne
on men's shoulders, for ordinary means of travel.

Indeed the usual rate of all travelling in Japan is from
five to ten Re a day (fourteen to twenty-eight miles), and
while the first is the more usual distance performed on foot,
horseback, or in norimon, the last is rarely attempted
except under conditions of urgency. You cannot travel
farther or faster than men on foot and beasts of burden can
follow with your baggage. In my own journeys, though
well-mounted myself, I found five-and-twenty miles the
extreme limit, and that could not be done several days in
succession. As to postal communication, it is all conducted
by runners. Government couriers run between the ports at
stated periods, doing the distance between Yeddo and the
extreme north or south, Hakodadi or Nagasaki, in about
twenty-five days, the distance being 290 Re to Hakodadi
(say 650 miles), and 350 Re to Nagasaki (say 875 miles).
By express, paid at the rate of eighty itziboos or six pounds
sterling, letters can be conveyed in nine or ten days.
Thus, with some of the best roads in the world, they
are three centuries behind the rest of the civilised world
in all that concerns speed and means of communication.

And even this very primitive post has no reference to the wants of the people, but serves merely to keep up the communication between the Government and its officers. The merchants combine among themselves to send couriers express from one trading city to another, but so far, as I could learn, at no regular periods or in any permanent form. The Chinese even seem in advance of them here, for in most of the large cities in the North, there are regular posts established by the people or certain guilds of merchants for them.

There are no newspapers and no public press; occasionally penny sheets appear in Yeddo, and possibly other large cities, and circulate items of news, which the Government has no interest in suppressing. They have had in the old times a system of signals all the way from Nagasaki to Yeddo, by means of guns, to announce the arrival of any foreign ship, but since they have come by hundreds, the authorities have ceased to waste their powder.

As to the size and value of private or of public buildings, it would go hard with the Japanese if their civilisation, either mental or moral, were to be judged by such a test. They have no architecture. They live on a volcanic soil, the surface of which is affected with a tertian ague, thus denying the first conditions of the builder, a stable foundation, and imposing a law of construction fatal to all architectural pretensions or excellence. Houses for dwelling in seldom consist of more than one story, those of the wealthy never, I fancy, and those of the busy and commercial classes in large cities where land is valuable — more valuable than life in Japan — consist of a ground-floor and garret above.

These are all constructed of solid wooden frames strongly knit together, the walls being merely a thin layer of mud and laths to keep out the cold and heat; the whole surmounted in the better class by rather ponderous and overhanging roofs, as may be seen in many of the sketches scattered through these volumes. These, as may easily be understood, are not very easily shaken down;

nevertheless, once in about every seven years, according
to Japanese report, the inhabitants of Yeddo must lay
their account for seeing their wooden city reduced to
a heap of ruins by an earthquake, too violent, even, for
such constructions to resist, and completed by fire, which
inevitably follows.  We need not look for architecture,
then, here ; and nothing, accordingly, can be more mean
or miserable looking than the streets of Yeddo, one of
the largest cities in the world.  The Daimios' *Yaskis* are
merely a low line of barracks of the same construction,
rather higher in the roofs, and occasionally they venture
upon a modest attempt at a three-storied pagoda.  The
temples are more ambitious, and, moreover, afford safer
ground for architectural experiments or pretensions, as
people do not usually live under their roofs.  These
furnish the only specimens of Japanese architecture.  The
woodcut on the opposite page is from a photograph of
the belfry at the temple where we were lodged at Osaca,
and is a very fair specimen of all their temple and
gateway architecture.

It will be seen that no fair criterion of their civilisation or advance in the arts can be drawn from such
a source, the special conditions of the soil exercising
an absolute controlling power over all architectural developement.  In all the mechanical arts, the Japanese
have unquestionably achieved great excellence.  In their
porcelain, their bronzes, their silk fabrics, their lacquer,
and their metallurgy generally, including works of ex-
quisite art in design and execution, I have no hesitation
in saying they not only rival the best products of Europe,
but can produce in each of these departments works we
cannot imitate, or perhaps equal.  It is quite true that
Europe may also make a similar boast with justice. There
is much, especially in the province of art properly so
called, to which the Japanese cannot make the slightest
pretensions.  They cannot produce, by any effort, works
to be compared with the noble specimens of Repoussé
carving, from the chisel of a Vechte, a Morel Ladeuil, or

BELFRY IN COURTYARD OF TEMPLE

a Monti, which the Great International Exhibition showed ; yet the Japanese bronze castings are, some of them, scarce inferior in skilled workmanship and mixture of metals to anything we can produce of the same kind.   No Japanese can produce anything to be named

in the same day with a work from the pencil of a Landseer, a Roberts, or a Stanfield, a Lewis, or Rosa Bonheur, whether in oil or water colours ; indeed, they do not know the art of painting in oils at all, and are not great in landscape in any material.   Their knowledge of perspective is too limited, and aërial effects have scarcely yet entered into their conception.   But, in figures and animals, I have some studies in Indian ink, so graphic, so free in outline and true to nature, that our best artists might envy the unerring touch and facile pencil so plainly indicated.   In the rendering of animals, whatever the material employed, they seem to have studied not only the mere forms, but the habits and character of each with such accuracy and closeness of observation, that they gain a perfect mastery over their subject, and by a few lines, and a dash of the brush, produce a faultless imitation of nature.   This is especially true of the stork, the emblem of longevity, and nearly as much admired and revered by the Japanese, as ever was its kindred ibis in Egypt.   Hence, on porcelain, lacquer, in enamels, on ivory, in basso-relievos, in steel and iron, in bronzes, it is everywhere to be met, and with a marvellous perfection of workmanship and artistic power.   On the preceding page is a rough specimen cut out of a common picture-book, of which it formed the fly-leaf.   Whoever has seen a flight of these birds, must be struck with the fidelity of the sketch.

Here, again, is a wild goose in flight, than which nothing can be better.

I need say nothing of the lacquer ware.   The Japan-ese are in all probability the originators of the manu-facture, and have never been approached in Asia or in Europe.   Neither Soochow, Canton, nor Birmingham appear to possess either the material, or the skill neces-

sary ; and certainly have yet to show that they can even
make a near approach to some of the fine specimens of
old lacquer which I collected for the Exhibition, to
illustrate the progress of the Japanese in the mechanical
and higher industrial arts, and as evidences of their civilisation.

Perhaps in nothing are the Japanese to be more
admired, than for the wonderful genius they display in
arriving at the greatest possible results with the simplest
means, and the smallest possible expenditure of time and
labour or material.  The tools by which they produce
their finest works are the simplest, and often the rudest,
that can be conceived.  Wherever in the fields or the
workshops, nature supplies a force, the Japanese is sure to
lay it under contribution, and make it do his work with the
least expense to himself of time, money, and labour.  To
such a pitch of perfection is this carried, that it strikes
every observer as one of the moral characteristics of the
race, indicating no mean degree of intellectual capacity
and cultivation.

They have been familiar with the art of printing in
various colours by blocks of wood — a process similar to
our lately discovered art of lithochrome printing — from
an unknown date,—similar, at least, so far as the employment of several blocks in the same design for different colours.  They do not seem, however, to print
one colour over another to produce depth or richness, as
we do.  Mr. Leighton, an artist himself, who saw some of
these colour prints in the Japan Court at the Exhibition,
informs me he has discovered, upon close examination,
'that they have the power of reducing their prints by
some process, as doubtless of enlarging also, — a thing
patented by us some few years since, and used by Mr.
Leech in his enlarged pictures from "Punch."'  If this be
true, it is only one more instance in which by their own
unaided genius and ingenuity they have anticipated by
centuries some of the most recent inventions and discoveries of Europe.  Another improvement in colour

printing, only lately patented, also is evidently known to them — graduated shading.*

They meet the popular taste for pictures and bright colours at the cheapest possible rate.   There are countless works on drawing, filled with illustrations of the styles of their different masters, from which it would be easy to select any number of groups and figures worthy of Teniers, Van Ostades, Jan Steens, or any of that school of Dutch Painters—and much in the same style of broad farce— of humour and fidelity in the representation of the life of the people, too faithful in many instances, like their Dutch compeers, to be always very delicate or refined.   But on this subject I may as well say, *en passant*, and not to revert to it, that, although there is no doubt a wide-spread taste for gross and obscene productions (of which evidences will occasionally thrust themselves upon those who seek them least, proving how widely the demand exists for such things,—since the supply is so large and various in type), yet, upon the whole, they are not usually obtruded upon a casual observer, either in real life, or their books and toys — although they do exist in these last, to an extent that speaks ill both for their taste and system of juvenile education.   In the ordinary run of illustrated works and pictures, however, of which I made a large collection, the scissors of the censor are but rarely required, unless in very prudish hands.   Of course, where the customs of the country present quasi-nude figures everywhere to the eye, in the streets and houses, without any consciousness of in- delicacy attaching to such absence of costume, a painter of

---

* The following opinion of artistic characteristics, as exemplified in the specimens sent to the Great Exhibition, will be interesting as coming from an artist.   Mr. Leighton writes to me on this subject : —
 'The quaintly-picturesque seems to govern all in Japan — harmony of colour with extraordinary finish, avoiding symmetry and delighting in sharp angles — just the reverse of all other nations.   They have many things in common with the Chinese, but a far finer touch.   A great deal of this comes, I think, of their buildings being of wood, having a wooden architecture rather than an enduring one in stone ; — had they been masons, then would they have worked on a grander scale.   They seem fond of sensations — the sweet, the soft and pretty, is heightened by the grotesque, yet all is in harmony.'

popular manners will necessarily reproduce what he constantly sees, and in attitudes ill-suited to European notions.
But he does so without the slightest consciousness of
offending against any of the proprieties—and under such
circumstances we must take his works as we habitually
do those of Phidias, or the sculptors of more modern date,
more graceful it may be, but quite as scantily draped.
With this proviso, there is nothing to deter the most fas-
tidious student of art, and the manners and customs of
Orientals, from turning over the leaves freely.

Very many of these clever and graphic studies of Japanese
life have been already introduced as illustrations of manners
and customs— being so good and perfect in their kind
that no European pencil could improve upon them.    Their
enamels are quite equal to those of China, which at the
Great Exhibition of 1851 were for the first time seen in
England among some objects which I sent from thence,
and attracted great admiration.    Finally, their carvings
in ivory of groups of figures and animals, are often in the
best style of art ; and although by their cheapness, they
are evidently the fruit of a kind of skilled labour by no
means uncommon, they could only be produced in Europe
by some of our best artists, and at a proportionate cost.
Some twenty or thirty of the finest of these were also
sent to the Exhibition, but the large and not very discriminating demand for such things at the Consular Ports
has sadly deteriorated the quality of all those that come
now into the Japanese market.

I had intended giving a more detailed description of
their works of art in metal and in ivories, as illustrating
their life and traditions ; but having already far exceeded
the limits I originally proposed, I must pass them over
with a cursory notice.    I close, however, with the less
regret, feeling that no description could convey any perfect
idea of the kind or degree of excellence attained : and
that numerous specimens of the best were in the Exhibition.
Among other things there was sent a collection of some
three hundred medallions and intaglios in mixed metals in

iron and steel, silver, gold, and bronze to the Exhibition, many of which I should have no hesitation in placing side by side for comparison with the best works of the kind bequeathed to us by mediæval art, not excluding Benvenuto Cellini's chef-d'œuvres. This no doubt will read to many as the exaggerated praise of a biassed judgement, or the admiration of an indifferent connoisseur of art. The public will have been able to form its own judgement, so no harm will be done. Their power of blending and producing artistic effects out of mixed metals is, so far as I am aware, an art scarcely known in Europe. They were carefully examined by Mr. Hunt of the well-known firm of Hunt and Roskill, as one of the jurors at the Great International Exhibition, and in his report he makes the following statement, which, coming from so competent a judge, will be read with interest:—

' This collection is very remarkable. The smaller fancy objects, such as brooches and clasps, are admirably executed. In all the figures, the national character is represented with perfect truth and expression. These objects are principally in iron relieved by partial overlaying of gold and bronze. Great aptitude is evinced in these works.'

I may add that many of the specimens are elaborate and highly finished: and the legends attached to some, and the indications of character which may be traced in all, make them highly instructive as well as interesting. I can only venture upon a description of four or five which happen to be under my eye as specimens while I am writing. The first and largest represents *Mongaku shonin*, a priest of Buddha, supposed to be sitting under a waterfall, and praying that he may have much knowledge given him; while praying, two gods appear to answer his prayers. The face of the priest with gold teeth and rings to his mouth, is an elaborate work in iron; while the gods in the vision are also in gold, and wonderfully minute in their workmanship. The next is one of *Hotai oshir*, and represents a Chinese Buddhist priest of high rank, who having fallen asleep, his servant is endeavouring to awaken him by tickling his nose with a piece of twisted paper. Absurd and worthless as the subject is the faces of both are very perfect in expression. *Ubi sakino sambato* is a juggler, supposed to be balancing a weighted image upon his little finger. *Kairaishi* is a toy-merchant crying his wares, a practice said to be long since out of date, but I have often seen something very like it in the streets of Yeddo. These men used to walk about the streets singing, and trying to entice people to purchase their goods; but my Japanese expounder of these medals tells me the practice died out at Miako.

*Mukashi banashi bakamono tszasyra.* This represents the last act of a fable, which shows the Japanese have also their fairies, who know how to bestow good and evil gifts.

The following is the popular legend.

An old couple were living together, when one day the old man brought home a sparrow in a cage, but its twittering annoyed the wife. She determined to rid herself of the annoyance, but could find no reason for so doing. One day, however, while she was out, the sparrow picked all the stitches out of a new garment she had been sewing, which so enraged her, that she cut a piece of its tongue off and let it go. Her husband on his return inquired for the bird, and was very angry when he heard what his wife had done, and upbraided her with her cruelty to a bird which he loved as if it had been his daughter. So he went out in search of the bird. As he was walking on the hills, an apparition of a beautiful girl appeared to him; thanked him for his kindness to her while in his house, and offered him his choice of a present, asking him if he would prefer a heavy basket, or one of less weight. He, being an old man, preferred the lighter, so she gave him a basket to open when he got home. On opening it, he found it full of most beautiful clothes. His wife on seeing them, and hearing where they had come from, thought she would try her luck, so she went on to the hills in search of the sparrow. The beautiful girl appeared to her, and after upbraiding her with her unkindness, gave her also her choice. She chose a heavy basket, and took it home ; but to her disgust and surprise, on opening it, two goblins jumped out. This is the moment chosen by the artist ; the old woman is on her back prostrated with alarm, and her heels in the air, while the goblins rising out of the cage are faintly indicated by the graver, but full of ghoulish expression. This also is wrought in two metals, giving relief and colour to the figures.

A somewhat similar legend is attached to a very delicately chiselled medallion of the collection, where the good spirit inhabits the body of a favourite dog, the property of an aged couple who had no children. He takes the old man into a wood and shows him where a treasure lies buried. This coming to the ears of a vicious neighbour, he borrows the dog of his good-natured master, but though he is shown where to dig, he finds nothing but stones ; and he kills the dog in his rage. Grieved by this cruel act, and the loss of his canine friend, the old man demands where he was buried ; and cutting down the tree by which the body lay, he fashions a temple to his memory, and out of the trunk a mortar to beat his rice. No sooner does he employ this, than gold also comes. The evil neighbour again comes to borrow ; again fails in getting gold by the same process, and in his rage burns the mortar. The owner only humbly begs the ashes, and in a dream his dog appears and tells him to go with the ashes to a certain spot, and when a Daimio passes not to kneel, but if summoned, to say that he is a magician, with power to bring flowers on dead trees, or out of their season. Accordingly, taking his post, when the procession passes, and the terrible word is echoed along the road, *Shitanirio*! kneel down! he finds courage to keep his feet. The Daimio's attendants hearing the reason, determine to report it to their lord instead of inflicting summary punishment. The Daimio demands the proof of his power.  Whereupon throwing some of the ashes upon the tree over his head, it suddenly burst into bloom. This is the moment chosen by the artist, and the delight and amazement of the old man to see the golden flowers is admirably rendered.   The end of the story soon comes ; he is taken to the Daimio's house, who retains him and gives him presents. The vicious neighbour, still pursuing, asks for some ashes ; with inexhaustible good-nature this also is granted, and now comes his punishment.   Waiting the arrival of a Daimio's cortége, he makes the usual supple joints rigid, and on being approached, declares his power ; but on throwing the ashes, instead of covering the branch and producing flowers, they fly into the Daimio's eyes, who instantly draws his sword and hews the culprit down, while his attendants finish the work by cutting off his head, and so the evil-minded gets his deserts—in a way perfectly characteristic of the country and its rulers.

While studying this branch of the subject, and collecting materials for a judgement on the progress of the Japanese in the fine arts, amidst the hundred volumes accumulated about me, I came upon one work which, after a world of explanation — perfectly unintelligible, I found, at last, consisted of a series of illustrated charades or rebuses, such as Charivari delights in.  Many of the drawings, all coloured, are inimitable, both as drawings and illustrations of popular life and manners.  I confess utter incapacity in reference to the solution of the various ingenious enigmas they are meant to illustrate.   I never, in my life, could guess a conundrum or a rebus, in plain English or French, how much less in ' Japanese *hirakana*.' Yet, as specimens of art, and illustrations of the civilisation and every-day life of the people, I cannot resist introducing some of them ; and should anyone feel inclined to try their talent in deciphering, the written characters have been given in many cases also, by Mr. Pearson, with the most perfect skill and fidelity.

Here is a courtier in full costume who is evidently

in great anxiety to carry a tray to its destination,
with a speed which the interminable prolongations

SPECIMEN OF GROTESQUE

of his trousers must render unsafe, if not impossible.
The whole expression and action of the figure is admirable.  Then we have a Japanese, it may be your
servant, taking his ease and enjoying the luxury of being
well shampooed—and one he will by no means forego,

BARBER

though you should want him ever so much.  He engages
to serve you only on those well-understood conditions.
Or if he is not being shampooed, then he is being shaved
and having his hair dressed, with a stiff cue twisted and

JAPANESE PHYSICIAN.

laid over the crown of his head,—a daily operation also, or if it is not it ought to be, to make him look cleanly and decent, therefore you know the alternative if you make difficulties. Then comes a doctor, feeling the pulse of his patient. The barber and the surgeon were one, not so long ago even in England, as Holbein's painting of the barber-surgeons receiving their charter from bluff King Harry proves. But in Japan the physician enjoys a good social position, and holds his head as high as any other in Europe. Our Japanese friend has thus been to the shampooer, and the barber, and even the doctor, a very habitual round with them all; but he has not yet had his bath, a matter of still greater importance. A little conjugal scene awaits him when he returns to his domestic hearth. I do not pretend to know the cause of quarrel, but it is quite evident the lady has the best of the argument, and is not disposed to forego her advantage until she has obtained full satisfaction, and it seems precisely one of those cases in which no one else has any business to interfere, or chance of doing so with advan-

CLOTHES MERCHANT

tage. He appears to have got over his troubles; perhaps, after all, it ended in the *pace di marcolfa*, of which Prince Puckler Muskau used to write so mysteriously.

And now he is engaged in buying a new robe :* possibly his last may have suffered some damage the night before. If so, he is evidently prepared to console himself with a new one, and the merchant is eloquent on its merits. But there is an end to all things, and even this chapter must be brought to a close, although the portfolio is full, and the materials are inexhaustible. A very few more samples, and we will close up the books illustrating 'y^e manners and customs of y^e Japanese.'

The Japanese are celebrated archers, and, like the Tartars, regard the bow with predilection. Like our own Saxon and Norman ancestors, the sword, the spear, and the bow are their national weapons, and they are

MAKER OF BOWS

no mean adepts in the use of all three. Here is a maker of bows and arrows; and how well, in a few lines, his craft is told, while he himself is represented in the act of stringing one to try its strength. Here are some ladies at their toilet—quite as often performed with open windows, as in the privacy of an inner chamber—and it has its merit as regards fidelity and truth of detail also. The toilet-stand, with the polished metal mirror (that

* See preceding page.

SHAVING THE LADIES.

might have been dug out of Herculaneum or Pompeii), is faithfully rendered, as is the lady in the centre, painting her lips with the bright red of the hollyhock or the thistle—a dye extracted from the flower.   A group of beggars trudging along the road forms the subject of one

LADIES AT THEIR TOILET

of the happiest illustrations—already given in a former chapter.* The figures are barely sketched in, yet, so felicitous is the touch, that you see at once they are blind,

GOING UP HILL

and of the type vagabond.   And this scene on the road is scarcely inferior — wayfarers of the humbler clas

* See Vol. I. p. 112.

ascending and descending — the poor Coolie, with his
heavy burden, evidently feeling the hill unpleasantly
stiff.  Or still on the road, see this peasant in his coat of
rushes.  How much expression, again, is there in the

SNOW COAT

mere rough outline of these men towing.  You do not
see the boat, but you can have no doubt that it is close

MEN TOWING

behind, and heavily laden too.  And, to show that they
are not, as artists, servilely copying a stereotyped pattern
here is the same subject, but quite differently handled,
yet equally good.  I had proposed passing in review
some of the principal incidents of the life of a Japanese,
as these are painted by themselves; but it would carry
me too far for the limits of a chapter, if not for the

patience of my readers.   Out of the mass of illustrations
before me, I will only take at hazard half-a-dozen more.
We have seen how little conjugal differences may arise

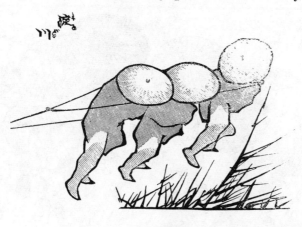

MEN TOWING

and be settled in Japan.   Here is a courtship behind the
screen; and emerging into the streets, we are caught in

JAPANESE WOOING

a shower of rain—a good 'evendown pour,' as we
sometimes see in Yeddo.   This is very well rendered,
with a good deal of humorous bye-play in the grouping.
But better still, as a specimen of perfect effect, with the
fewest possible touches, is the snow-storm.   I was just

shutting the book, when I came upon a whole series of
a celebrated professor, who teaches how to obtain the

CAUGHT IN THE RAIN

greatest effect in single lines and one colour ; and all his

A SNOW-STORM

specimens are certainly admirable, both in outline and
effect.   One, a dame and her child, preceded by a servant

with a lantern — very perfect in its way — has already.
been introduced to the reader.*

Another sample of the mistress and her servant is very
characteristic, and whoever has been in the country
would recognise the type. A little domestic scene, the
mother-in-law and the daughter, is also very graphic, and
tells a tale not new in England or other lands, though
it may be daughters-in-law are not so reverential under
censure from that quarter in all countries.†

THE MISTRESS AND HER SERVANT

How far they have profited by Dutch instruction in
the course of the last two centuries, it may be difficult to
determine accurately. That they have had, and communicate to each other, instruction, even in perspective, is
proved by a volume of drawing lessons, in perspective,
which I found in turning over a book-stall.

They not only have an eye for form and picturesque
grouping; and understand effects of light and shade, but
they evidently have a considerable amount of humour, and

* See. Vol. I. p. 264.                    † See next page.

are very fond of the grotesque.    If somewhat Rabelaic in
its grossness, it is not the less humour, and betokens a

MOTHER-IN-LAW AND DAUGHTER

keen sense of the ludicrous.    Here * is a very pleasing
specimen ; full of life and fun, and worthy of Hogarth for
its truth to nature, it needs no explanation.    It shows
plainly how children of large growth blow soap-bubbles
to amuse their progeny, and are not above enjoying the
sport.    When they yield themselves fairly up to the grotesque, they give loose rein to their imagination, and produce some of the most absurd and monstrous combinations
and distortions of humanity.    Sometimes they are simply
monstrous or laughable, at other times they are grim in their
significance.    One now before me is of a gentleman who by
some accident (not an uncommon one in Japan) has lost his
head, or at all events it has flown from  his shoulders, and

* See next page.

although the body expresses considerable discomfort, the
head evidently thinks it a capital joke.

BLOWING BUBBLES

Another grotesque from the same pencil shows an
uncommon tenuity about the epigastric region, but a happy
state of mind notwithstanding, and is very laughably rendered ; while for *vis-à-vis* he has a friend whose lower limbs
have shot upward so immeasurably that he cannot help
laughing himself on finding his head in the clouds. Then
follow a couple of amphibious-looking wayfarers with
wings on their backs, and carrying a packet between
them by means of a monstrous nose.   They are intended
to represent some kind of gnomes or spirits.  This pro-
longation of the nasal organ, sometimes not in very
decent shape, is a favourite exemplification of the grotesque with the Japanese.  It is very common in their
masks; and in the leaves which I am turning over, there is
a grand display of what noses may become, and to what
strange uses perverted.  On the following page will be
found a rebus, in which a lantern-maker is represented

at his work; and face, attitude, expression, and accessories, are all perfect in their way.

GNOMES

Let us close up the list with the artist himself at his
work.   Here is one of the guild painting flowers, and

LANTERN-MAKER

following him another painting with two brushes at
once, — a *tour de force* by no means uncommon, though

it seems quite as difficult and incomprehensible as the lady's performance, who, having no hands, used to paint with her toes, an example of which I saw, by the way, the last time I visited the picture gallery at Antwerp. Lastly, welcome to the enthusiastic genius, who, not contented with a brush in each hand, has a third in his mouth, and a fourth and fifth between the great and small toes of each foot. I do not think dexterity in art can go beyond this, and it forms a fitting finale, therefore, to our exhibition of the Japanese school of painting.

Having thus passed in review some of the leading traits of character, and endeavoured to trace the chief influences under which their national life has taken form and deve- lopement, if I were asked to give in a few words the conclusion to which I have been led as to the kind and degree of civilisation attained by the Japanese, without taking account of the various qualifications and reserva- tions already touched upon, I should say that theirs was a material civilisation of a high order, in which all the industrial arts were brought to as great perfection as could well be attainable without the aid of steam-power and ma- chinery — an almost unlimited command of cheap labour and material supplying apparently many counterbalancing advantages. Their intellectual and moral pretensions on the other hand, compared with what has been achieved in the more civilised nations of the West during the last three centuries, must be placed very low ; while their capacity for a higher and better civilisation than they have yet attained, should be ranked, I conceive, far before that of any other Eastern nation, not excepting the Chinese.

## CHAPTER XIV.

TEMPLES, RELIGION, AND AMUSEMENTS OF JAPANESE — STRANGE
COMBINATION OF THE TWO — DESCRIPTION OF ASAXA UNDER BOTH
ASPECTS — JUGGLERS — STORY-TELLERS — TOP SPINNERS—VARIOUS
GAMES—GAME OF THROWING THE BALL ON HORSEBACK—PIC-NICS
IN THE COUNTRY MUCH IN VOGUE AT SPRING FESTIVALS —
THEATRES — WRESTLERS — MATSURIS AND FEASTS — JAPANESE
CEMETERIES.

IN a former chapter I have referred generally to the
religion of the Japanese, so far as scanty information would permit, on a subject which, above all others,
requires a thorough knowledge of the people and their
language, to qualify anyone to speak with authority. Considering the religious doctrines and faith of a people,
as an important element of their civilisation, it was necessary to form some estimate of its character and influence,
however imperfect the data. But beyond the fact that
the Japanese with the written and ideographic language
of the Chinese, borrowed a philosophy and a religion,
and in both instances added it to their own, adopting
them more or less completely in their integrity, we really
do not know much. All that the Portuguese and Spanish
missionaries of the sixteenth century seem to have left
—and they were the only people in a position to know
and understand in what the different forms of religion
in vogue consisted — amounts to very little. Kœmpfer,
ever painstaking and indefatigable in his inquiries on all
subjects, has given a general view of the different sects,
and what they professed to believe in his day; and as
Japanese must doubtless have been his informants, we
may probably adopt his as a fair account, giving at least

some idea of the modification the two systems of Confucius and Buddha may have undergone in the Japanese mind. My own impression I have already stated to be, that religion in any form does not enter very largely into the life of the people ; and that the higher and the educated classes are all more or less sceptical and indifferent. The strange mode in which their religious ceremonies and temples are made to amalgamate with, and subserve their popular amusements, is one of the evidences on which my convictions rest. Plays are performed in their temple gardens, which also contain shooting-galleries, bazaars, tea-houses, flower-shows, menageries of wild beasts and exhibitors of models like those of Madame Tussaud in Baker Street. Such a medley can scarcely consist with any reverential feeling or serious religious convictions.

That the Japanese should nevertheless be very much addicted to pilgrimages with professedly religious objects may be taken, on the other hand, as an evidence that, among the lower orders at least, there is a religious sentiment of some vitality. There are pilgrimages to *Isje*, to the thirty-three chief *Quanquon* temples — pilgrimages to some of the most eminent Lin and Cami or Buddhist temples, celebrated for miracles wrought there and the *benefits conferred on pilgrims*, which, no doubt, is a powerful motive with the votaries, giving the hope of participating in their turn. A true and orthodox disciple of Sinto visits only those of his own gods, and Kœmpfer adds, the ' Temple Saif in Sicousin, where Teentin died, is one of the most esteemed.' On the other hand, both Buddhists and Sintoists seem to go to the Quanquon temples as a means to obtain happiness in this world, and bliss in that to come. In reference to the Sintoists there seems to be a strong analogy in the laws of purity and purifying observances enjoined by their creed with those of the Mosaic dispensation, while their priests give to the pilgrims an *ofarrai* in a small oblong box, which is an absolution and remission of their sins — whether preceded by a confession or not I cannot say — sometimes it is wrapped in white paper in 'order to remind the pilgrim to be pure and humble, these two virtues being the most pleasing to the gods.' The effects and virtues of the absolution last only for a year, otherwise it is obvious the priests' treasury would not be sufficiently frequently replenished, something being always given for this valuable document. And even for the benefit of those who cannot make the pilgrimage, large numbers of *ofarrai* are sent throughout the country, for disposal like the indulgences that excited Luther's indignation. An indulgence or absolution, and an almanac, are generally supplied together at the new year, and in Kœmpfer's time might be had for an itziboo, or eighteen pence. It must be confessed neither could be considered very dear.

Making vows in times of trouble or distress, building temples as tokens of gratitude, and gifts to the poor, are not uncommon in Japan. There are several religious orders, hermits, and holy men, who dedicate themselves to a life of prayer and solitude for the mortification of the flesh ; nor are there wanting counter-types of the mendicant friars of Europe. Many of these seem to deal in charms and incantations for the cure of distempers, discovery of criminals, &c. and curiously enough their principal charm is called in the Japanese ' *Sin.*' There are two sects of the blind also, founded by two great celebrities in Japanese history, one, the third son of a Mikado, who wept himself blind for the death of his mistress ; and the other by a defeated general in the civil wars, who tore his eyes out that he might not be provoked to take the life of a generous victor in Youtomo, the founder of a dynasty. Into these two sects, half-religious, half-secular, persons of all ranks enter. They are generally, but not exclusively, musicians, and earn their subsistence by playing on musical instruments.

Engrafted on the Sinto or original religion of the Japanese, (which had the one great merit, at least, of not being idolatrous,) are the two derived from China—*Confucianism*, Chinese in origin, and *Buddhism*, which found its way across Asia from India. We have far less means

of information as to the Japanese version than we possess
in regard to the Chinese. Some contend that they accept
the doctrine of futurity and the immortality of the soul,
with more or less clearness of conception, but for both
men and animals. They are also supposed to believe in a
place of happiness after death to which the good pass, and
some place of punishment for the bad—the first, a sort of
Mahommedan paradise with various grades or degrees of
beatitude. *Amida* is the sovereign commander of these
heavenly regions, and through his sole mediation men
obtain absolution of their sins, and their portion of happiness hereafter. Leading a virtuous life and keeping the
commandments of Siaka are said to be the only way to
become agreeable unto Amida, and worthy of eternal
happiness, and the commandments are five : —

1. Not to kill anything that hath life. 2. Not to steal.
3. Not to commit fornication. 4. Not to lie (there can be
no true Buddhism in Japan). 5. Not to drink intoxicating
liquors (especially unobserved).

As there is an elysium with various degrees of bliss, so
is there a place of torment, also varying in degrees of
punishment, but not eternal. These may be greatly diminished by the virtuous life of their friends and relatives,
their prayers, and above all their offerings to the great
and good Amida, who is able to obtain their release
finally, and send them into the world again as soon as
possible, consistent with divine justice, but to animate
such vile creatures as are nearly identified with their former
sinful inclinations ; and so by successive transmigrations
they at last are suffered again to enter human bodies to
run a second course of virtue or of vice ; and so on to a
second future life of bliss or punishment *ad infinitum*.

According to the Japanese, Buddhism appears to have
come over from China and Corea about the sixth century
of our era ; whereas Confucianism was adopted in the
first. It is mentioned by the Japanese writers that the
somewhat arid doctrines of Confucius made slow progress,
whereas Buddhism rapidly found votaries, and the most

effectual and persuasive arguments were those which spoke of the immortality of the soul and the promises of a future life.

One can readily believe this, and agree with Mr. Edkins, a learned missionary who has devoted much labour to the study of Buddhism and Confucianism and their joint influence on the Chinese mind — when he says that ' holding such cheerless views as the Confucians did of the destiny of man, it is not to be wondered at that the common people should desert their standard, and adopt a more congenial influence.'  Nor can we avoid being struck with the phraseology of retribution and a future state wherever Buddhism has taken root.  An omnipotent Creator — a Divine Incarnation — a man-God who came into the world to enlighten and to show the way to salvation, are among the doctrines of Buddha — a vast religious system counting its votaries over all the East by hundreds of millions.  It is remarked upon by the late Abbé Huc in his travels in Tartary and Thibet, ' as containing a great number of moral truths and dogmas which form the basis of Christianity.'  That they should be united in a system of idolatry is sad enough, and that both should so long continue inseparably blended is perhaps disheartening ; yet may not these ideas of immortality, redemption, and retribution, which pervade their language and make a part of the popular faith of the millions of Asia, be the germs of a purer faith,—which, stripped of its debasing idolatry, is destined to spring forth in God's good time, and bear a harvest such as the world has not yet seen? It is impossible not to feel how wonderfully such religious convictions as these great fundamental truths of Christianity, are calculated to prepare the way for Christian truth.  We may even see in this long vitality of a system of doctrines blended with grievous errors, how, in the dispensations of Providence, the evil of such long persistence may, in the end, be overruled for good in the conversion of the Asiatic race, numbering more than half the whole population of the world, in far less time.  This, too, by a far

more natural and easy process than were the untutored
and semi-barbarous races of the North of Europe.    The
transition from such thoughts to those which their temples
suggest, with their busy, laughing noisy crowds, their plays
and their rope-dancing, has something in it incongruous
to one brought up under Christian influences.    But I
have undertaken to describe Japan as it is, so far as
my own observation extends ; and therefore, after this
glance at their religious systems, the reader must follow
me to their places of worship, their temples and their
cemeteries, and not hold me responsible for whatever
he may find there distasteful or startling.    There is a
strong similarity in all ; any difference, indeed, chiefly
consisting in the greater or lesser magnitude of the
temples, and the extent of their grounds.    One of the
largest and most celebrated in Yeddo is the temple at
Asaxa, situated in one of the most populous quarters of
the city ; and in describing what is to be seen there, I shall
have discharged my duty as a faithful cicerone, and leave
little to be regretted in the omission of visits paid to many
others, which I shall suppress, as possessing neither novelty
nor interest after one like that of Asaxa has been gone
through.    It is also called the temple of Quanonas, the god
Quanwon of thirty-six arms and a hundred hands, who
must be very popular, to judge by the crowding of the thousand idlers, who seem to be never wanting in its vicinity ;
and who rush through from one extremity to the other, to
catch a sight of the foreigner, with an uproar as loud as
distant thunder.    A long avenue intervenes between the
outer and inner gateway, as at Tozenjee, and on each side
are stalls or booths forming a vast bazaar of a very mixed
character.    Toys for children occupy a large space ; a few
little stone models of shrines, idols, tombstones and temples
were the only things I could perceive having the remotest
connection with the ascribed sanctity of the edifice adjoining.    Trinkets for women—especially metal pins for their
hair, and combs, almost the only ornaments they appear to
indulge in ; and perhaps to make up for any restricted use

elsewhere, they sometimes carry a forest of these on their heads; pins with hollow glass heads, filled with bright-coloured liquids, also seemed to enjoy great favour. The infant windmill, stuffed tigers, and barking dogs, drums and fifes, and miniature swords, bows and arrows, dressed dolls, and masks, kites, and even hoops, seemed to make the staple of the toy booths; so that our common humanity asserts itself even in toys for Japanese children. Of course picture books and gaudy prints were not wanting; nowhere in Japan apparently, certainly not in Yeddo, is the supply of these deficient.

The whole avenue is crowded with women and children, idlers, buyers, and votaries— the last in great minority to all appearance, and not very easily distinguishable even with the help of such sketches as the native artist furnishes.

It was late in November when I paid my first visit in returning from Ogee and its tea-houses, which Mr. Oliphant so pleasantly described some years ago, in his ' Narrative of Lord Elgin's Mission.' The autumnal tints of brightest scarlet were still on the maple-trees, but the country was beginning to look somewhat bare and wintry. Indeed the day in question might have been a November day in England. The sky was overcast and threatened rain, if it should not 'sna' as the Scotchman suggested on the Highlands, as the only alternative, for the air was raw and cold enough. There was a great crowd, and it was both noisy and boisterous, but it did not particularly incommode us. Some officers attached to the temple, or sent there to meet us, exerted themselves to prevent our being pressed upon. I have often been there since, and once or twice with ladies, but have never been molested, and what seemed to me to be a fair or semi-festival, appears to continue all the year round. The numerous amusements provided within the gardens, went far to account for this, and no doubt the principal revenues of the temple come from this source. We made our way through the dense crowd, not without some effort, as we had dismounted from

our horses outside, being told by our yaconins that such
was the rule.   And this, by the way, was one of the many
examples of how unfailingly they seek to place a Foreign
Minister in a false position in the eyes of the people, and
subject him to indignity, whenever they think they can
count upon his ignorance of their customs.   I afterwards
found that all officers entitled by their rank *to ride*, proceed
mounted up to the inner gate ; and upon the next occasion,
I did the same with my mounted escort, and evidently
guessing that I knew what I was about, my Japanese guard
had the discretion to avoid any remonstrance.   But now
we are at the foot of a high flight of steps through the
second gate.   We have passed the stable, where two
sacred white horses are kept for the god's exclusive use,
and before us is the temple.   It is a large, massive-looking
building, with a ponderous and elaborately carved roof
and ornamental pillars, and heavy folding door of lacquer,
a great improvement on the usual tawdry daubing of red
and blue paint.

On entering the temple, the same stereotyped altar,
image, and trumpery decorations of artificial flowers,
chandeliers, &c., strike the eye as leading features in
all.   The same ' bell and book,' priests in their robes and
scapulars, acolytes in attendance, and choristers to stand
behind the officiating Bonze.   The same burning of incense, the same reiteration and mumbling of prayers
and rituals in an unknown tongue, unknown even to
the priest who gabbles them ; at other times consisting
of three words, incessantly reiterated for an hour without
ceasing, ' Amida ! Amida ! Amida !' the name of the
god.

Taking all into account — the altar, the images, the
shaven priests, monastic life, and vows of celibacy, the
ritual in a dead language unknown to the people, and a
thousand other particularities, I never entered one of these
Buddhist temples, without a mental conviction of identity,
and the reflection that either the Buddhists of a later day
have borrowed from the Roman Church, or the Roman

Church of an early date borrowed from them. Two systems and ceremonials of worship, presenting such marvellous identity in small particulars and in larger characteristics, could not possibly have been born of chance, and wholly independent of each other. Which is the original, and which is the copy, I will not stop to inquire. The fact of identity in all outward ceremonials is there, let the explanation be what it may. The one

A JAPANESE PRIEST IN HIS ROBES

may be of apostolic or heaven-inspired origin, and the other the devil's counterfeit, as I believe the Abbé Huc roundly asserts — I only note the coincidence as it strikes a traveller — indeed, as it struck the first missionaries who accompanied Francis Xavier—and leave the explanation to other and abler hands. Here is a study from nature of a Japanese priest in his robes; and on the following page will be found another of a monk. Is he not the very type and presentment of a ' friar of orders

grey,' such as we could have shown before Harry Tudor
made the race scarce? The uproar created by the rushing in and out of the populace following our footsteps,
with small reverence for the house of worship, only
seemed to add another feature of resemblance; for in
St. Peter's at Rome, I have seen dogs and children on
high holidays, mingling in a crowd, which passed in
and out, and with quite as little outward show of
reverence, either for the temple or the Deity. Here,

A JAPANESE FRIAR OF THE MEDIÆVAL TYPE

certainly, nothing could be less impressive or calculated
to inspire reverence, than the row of ill-favoured monks,
with their shaven crowns, hammering monotonously at a
sort of wooden gong, placed before them as they squatted
on their knees and heels. At the side which would correspond to one of the aisles, in a Gothic church, my attention
was drawn to a large and elaborate picture of numerous
figures, Japanese ladies, dressed, apparently, in the height
of fashion. 'That,' said my guide, 'is the portrait of all

the most celebrated courtesans, or public women, in
Yeddo, and is placed there in their honour annually.'
The Social Evil would appear to be a national institution
in Japan, therefore, which is not without its honours!

And talking of strange coincidences of customs and
costumes, and the reproduction of familiar types in these
distant islands, far removed from all temptation or opportunity to imitate—is not this figure of a porter the very
picture of a serving-man in England, when a Plantagenet
was king?

PORTER

Passing from the temple and its monster idol with
lesser satellites, we wandered through the grounds, evidently laid out for the express purpose of attracting and
amusing the idle Yeddites,—a sort of Surrey Gardens,
with a good show of flowers; at this season consisting of a
fine collection of China-asters and chrysanthemums, many
very beautiful in size and colour. Dwarf and tortured
trees are here in quaint and brightly-coloured flower-pots.
Then to the zoological department, neither very cleanly,
nor rich in animals. The archery ground for women and

children, all had their votaries; and though last, not
least, a gallery of figures the size of life, with real dresses,
illustrative of national manners and customs, which was
quite worthy of Madame Tussaud.

There are christenings and marriages both, or something that corresponds to these ceremonies, in Japan, but

THE WEDDING PARTY

either they take place by ' special license ' in the houses, or
I have never been fortunate enough to come upon either a
wedding or a christening party — though more than once
I have encountered a burial procession.   Here are two
designs by a native artist who painted them for me by
order, but he has chosen to represent the costume of
Kioto or Miaco, the great stronghold of temple worship,
— of priests and monks, rituals and ceremonies — a sort

of Rome or ecclesiastical city, where the Mikado reigns supreme — the only spot in all his empire, it would seem, which he can even call his own. About thirty days after birth they shave the child's head, and the wet nurse or mother then takes it out for the first time to go to the temple to make the baby's first offering to the deities, of

THE CHRISTENING

a few cash. These are dropped into a box with a slit in it, always to be found at the entrance of every temple.

As illustrative of the people, the waxworks could not be without interest, though on other grounds, as works showing considerable artistic power and fidelity to nature, these wood carvings, painted to represent living figures with real dresses, formed a very curious collection. And

the difference between these as works of art — if that be
not too ambitious a term to apply—and the two guardian
monstrosities or colossal demons which guard the entrance
of the temple, took us somewhat by surprise.

In the first gallery, for there were several, we were
introduced to a scene of life in the country, I presume.
Two young ladies were taming a wild horse, each holding
a rope attached to his head, while the pony was careering
in a most untameable spirit, with his heels in the air.   I
could not learn whether this was really a customary amusement of the young ladies of Japan, or whether it was an
illustration of some popular history or tradition.   Then
came a scene in a barber's shop, in which both the barber
and the individual operated upon were very faithfully rendered, with a little of the grotesque.   Beyond this was a
beggar, looking quite as burly as beggars usually do in
this country I think, although there are many species of
them which may be studied along the public road  to
Kanagawa and elsewhere.   There is the jocose beggar —
often a group or family of them, and they salute you with
a jest or a grin, and with outstretched palm, and invite
you to bestow a *tempo*, equivalent to an Irish beggar
asking 'Your honour to give him a sixpence.'   They are
evidently beggars by vocation, but seem by their whole
bearing to say to the passers-by, 'We are beggars and must
live, but there is no need to be miserable about it.'   Then
there is the unsightly, diseased, and generally lachrymose
beggar, who seeks to make the desired impression upon
you by exhibiting as much misery as possible, bodily and
mental,—and these are generally crouched on all-fours on
a mat by the roadside, in tatters, with uncut hair—their
face but a little raised from the ground—unless it be
necessary to expose some loathsome limb covered with
sores.   And lastly, there is the decent, grave, and respectable beggar, like the gaberlunzie of 'Old Mortality,' or the
yellow-robed mendicant of China, who has an imperial
license to beg, and these are generally single, and only men,
I think, dressed something like a Bonze, and stopping at

each shop with a little gong or a bell or whistle, to call attention. I do not know whether they carry their privilege as far here as in China, where it is often a trial of endurance and impudence, for whether by law—or custom, sometimes stronger than law,—no shopkeeper may *send* a beggar away unless he has first given him something. It may only be a single coin, the five hundredth part of a shilling, but it must be of some current value; and as there is no reason why the same mendicant may not pay an importunate visit every day, and by a deafening noise wear out the patience of the most apathetic housekeeper,—if he thinks he may succeed,—and they are a legion in Canton, at all events;—it is simply a trial, as I have said, of the powers of annoyance on the one side, and of passive resistance on the other; and they are sometimes so evenly matched, that victory for either is often very long in declaring itself.

Occasionally the charity of the crowd is excited by the mendicant monks, carrying a sort of death's head and colossal wooden sword before them,—what may be its moral or peculiar attraction, I never could learn,—or the beggar and vendor of toys combine, with the mystery of a concealed face, thus joining several trades and attractions.

But the beggars have already detained us too long. In the next apartment with its raised platform, is an old man reading — very cleverly imitated, both as to attitude and expression — divers trades follow; presently we come to an aquatic scene by the sea-shore, with rocks, and men, women, and children bathing. But I fear these models after all cannot be taken to be very faithful representations of the habits and customs of the present day, for here they are all partially, if not modestly, clothed. Beyond this grand marine view is the interior of one of the houses which furnish the celebrities already alluded to in the temple. Two of these said distinguished personages have completed their toilet, and a most elaborate one it is, — with sweeping skirts of brocade and silk, — while another is shown in a less finished state; her tire-woman is engaged behind in dressing the hair with a broad grin on her face, while a slave, on her hands and knees, is tendering a pipe to the belle, who, without moving, her head held fast by the tire-woman, stretches out her hand for the proffered solace.   She is half-nude, and has just been well powdered with white, which they evidently conceive adds much to a lady's attractions.   This at all events is a faithful picture, for just such a scene was going on at the open front of a house, the last time I walked up the broad street of Yokohama.   Leaving these ladies to their toilet, we come upon a group of very various character.   There is a traveller equipped for his journey, with his basket on his shoulder.   The courier with his sealed letter stretched out before him in a cleft bamboo, and a little tinkling bell to give notice of his approach, at the sound of which every one must make way, while he at a swift trot—with very little clothing to embarrass his movements—pursues his journey, neither turning to the right nor the left.   Then there was a grand group of a most impressive character— a band of lonins of ferocious aspect have suddenly pounced upon a solitary traveller, leading his horse laden with baggage ; but nothing daunted, he has valiantly drawn his sword, and such is the effect of his air of determination, that the lonins themselves seem all paralysed in various attitudes of terror.   I should be disposed to conclude this was more theatrical than true to nature.

The collection was however, as a whole, well worth a visit, and many of the figures were admirably true to life. They all seemed carved in wood and painted to represent life. The last, I remember, was an heroic group of warriors suddenly attacked by tigers, and the remarkably affable way in which they met their formidable-looking assailants at the sword-point, was calculated to give a very high idea of their valour and coolness under very trying cir- cumstances. Tight-rope dancing, and a circus, may some- times be seen here, and rope-dancing in their peculiar wooden sabots must be worth seeing, but neither have been in play when I happened to be there.

Leaving the temple and its shows, we must give a glance at what constitutes the chief amusements of the people. Somebody has remarked that national amusements are often a more delicate index to character, than serious pursuits or public policy. Certainly with many nations, and I think with the Japanese, both their amusements, and their manner of indulging in them, do afford a fair index of prevailing taste and character. Whatever may be their religion, it is certain they abound in festivals: I used to think these occurred with astonishing frequency in some Roman Catholic countries, but Japan far exceeds in processions and holidays any of these. It has been suggested we might be called a nation of cricketers and fox-hunters, and some French do think we are made up of jockeys and boxers. The same hasty generalisation would make the Japanese a nation of top-spinners, in which they certainly have achieved greater excellence than any other people. I went upon one occasion to the American Minister's, to see a professor of the art. *We* leave spinning of tops, and flying of kites, to children in Europe, while the last is especially affected by grey beards in China, and the former is followed as a profession in Japan,—and very clever and wonderful are the performances of the professors. There is a company of them generally, who come to your residence, as do the jugglers, with stage properties, and all the accessories. The jugglers, however, ought to perform in the open air, and in a courtyard, with the solid earth for their stage, for so exceedingly delicate are many of the manipulations of their gyrating prodigies, that the slight tremulousness or vibration of a matted floor, even with the steps of the performers, is enough to cause the failure of some of their most dexterous *tours de force*, and moreover they require height for others. We were unlucky in our choice of day, for it began to rain almost as the performance began, and the stage had to be transferred to the house, with all its disadvantages of bad light, and unsteady matted floor. The tops are of great variety, both in size and construction,—the largest or father of all the tops being more than a foot in diameter, and proportionately heavy— and while some are like this solid, others of the smaller ones contain in their cavities a whole progeny of little ones, which fly out on raising the top, and figure away like the parent; others again pull out into a ladder or spiral of successive tops; a third draws up into a lantern, and spins cheerily in that form. The most remarkable fact connected with some, seems to be the marvellous persistence of the gyratory motion once communicated. This I thought at first might perhaps be in consequence of the form, which is a horizontal section of a cylinder, instead of being conical, as are those of Europe, with a thin iron rod passing through, forming a handle, a spindle, and a peg, each answering equally well for any of the three. But I afterwards ascertained that it was a top within a top.

With this glance at the properties and material conditions, the play begins. There are two men performers, and a young boy, whose chief occupation is to make a great noise on the table with two small wooden spatulæ, and to chime in with a sharp cry to every phrase and turn of the hand of his senior. He succeeded in making a most distracting noise with both instruments — the wooden and the vocal. The young urchin devoted himself to that particular branch of his business with a serious earnestness, and a degree of energy worthy of all praise,— for certainly he followed a scriptural injunction, and what his hand found to do, he did with his might.

The two seniors alternated their performances, each playing successively first or second part, with hand and voice. The play opens with the first performer coming gravely forward, and kneeling on the mats, he prostrates himself before the company, and makes a long and loudly intonated exordium as to what he purposes and hopes — ' if he may dare to show his small attainments to the thrice honourable and noble company,'— *Gozalimas* being one of the terms in every sentence, *ali* or *ari* meaning simply ' it is' or ' will be ;' *Go* and *Za*—with the final *mas* being cumulative honorific terms.

Having got over his preamble, he began with a running commentary of explanations and ejaculations, responded to by his companions with short sharp cries — in which the urchin played his part *con amore*, and with startling effect.   At first I thought all this bye-play was to distract attention, as it unquestionably is with the jugglers ; but as there are really no tricks here, and it is merely an exhibition of the most marvellous dexterity and cleverness, in the use of eyes and fingers — it seems rather intended to excite and keep up attention, and help to fill up the pauses while the tops are winding, and until the critical turns arrive.

I cannot pretend to describe half the performances, which extended over nearly three hours.   One of the most frequent, as well as the most curious, was their mode of throwing even very large tops, as the New Zealanders throw the boomerang, so that while it appears to be going straight at the head of one of the spectators, it inevitably is brought back to the hand of the thrower, who catches it on his palm.   It is a marvel to me, especially with some of the heavier, that the iron peg does not bore a hole in their hands.   When thus caught, they take it by the spindle, apparently stop it, set it down, and it immediately recommences ; turn it upside down, and it goes on just as merrily on its iron spiked head — they will balance it on any kind of surface, round or flat — on the edge of a fan — along a thin cord — and even on the edge of the sharpest Japanese sword — and after several minutes of such perpetual gyration, with intervals of apparent arrest in being transferred from one object to the other, it is thrown carelessly down on the table, and still continues spinning gaily, as if quite unexhausted, and inexhaustible. Occasionally the displays were marred as often as two and three successive times by the untoward conditions in which they were compelled to work ;  and it was impossible not to admire alike the grave humility with which the performer would bow his head in the dust, craving indulgence for his bad performance, and the indomitable patience and good humour with which again and again he returned

to the charge until a success *was* achieved.    One of these
was the building up of a series of little square boxes —
first, a single perpendicular column, one thick, then two,
— then four diagonal, making a sort of minaret, or com-
posite tower—on the apex of which was placed a cup
full of water, and the art consists, when all is complete, in
dislocating the column at the base, and catching the falling
column with one of the small boxes before the water is
spilt from the cup.    After three successive attempts,
however, it was shaken down each time by the un-
steadiness of the flooring before the moment came, and
they were begged to pass on to something else ; but this
was the only failure they could be induced to accept.

One of the most delicate of the performances consisted
in making a top spin in the left hand, run up the arm,
round the edge of the robe at the back of the neck, and
down the other arm into the palm of the right hand,
still spinning.    Another, again, was to toss a spinning top
into the air and catch it on the hem of the sleeve, without letting it fall.    A third was to fling it high in the
air, and catch it on the bowl or the angle of a Japanese
pipe, pass it behind the back, flinging it to the front, and
there catching it again.    Finally, one of the larger and
heavier tops was given its gyratory motion by simply
rolling the peg in the bite of a cord, one end being
held in each hand, then flung some ten or twenty feet in
the air, and caught, as it fell, with the same cord, spinning always, and this six, eight, and ten times in succession.    The last grand display, which consisted in sending
a top spinning up a rope to the head of a mast, was
unavoidably postponed, the rain having drenched the
cord, and rendered it impossible ; but I have seen it
since performed in the streets.

Certainly, I never saw a more perfect display of
wonderful tact and dexterity, and there is evidently a
great amount of humour and *vis comica* in the Japanese
character, which tends to make all these exhibitions doubly
amusing.

The Japanese seem to have many games and for all ages : those for children, many of them at least, are analogous to the games in Europe. I have seen the hoop trundled along, kites are much in vogue, battledore and shuttlecock, walking in stilts, playing at ball, and even playing at monster snowballs, as is evident from the illustrations, all drawn from native sources.

PLAYING AT BALL

I should say the children in Japan have a merit the tendency of modern education is to deprive ours of at home — namely, they are natural children, are well amused with the pleasures proper to their age, and have no wish to be thought above them. They will run after the strolling player with his droll monkey at his back, and desire no higher happiness than such pleasures give.

As to the games in vogue for the amusement of children of larger growth, I cannot pretend to be sufficiently initiated to give any complete description. They have a great variety of games with forfeits, often played by cards, which require verses to be made or written. There is also a game of the 'Fox,' which consists in the attempt to seize a piece of cake or a sweetmeat through a loop;

THE MATERNAL LESSON

if they are caught in it they pay a forfeit, which, if men alone are engaged, is generally to drink a cup of saki, and when both sexes are engaged the forfeits are more varied, without, if report speaks truly, being more decorous.

They have also a game similar to the *Moro* in Italy. Their musicians and jugglers are much patronised, and acrobats with strolling bands of masks are to be met with in all festive seasons in the streets. Nor must we forget the story-teller, who generally has a gaping audience.

Still less must we omit the wrestlers, for wrestling is to the Japanese what the ring is to us, and something especially national. Every prince has a whole troop of them, and their pride is to have the biggest, heaviest, and fattest, so that they generally look as bloated, over-fed, and disgusting as prize oxen for the butcher at Christmas. This so utterly confounds all our ideas on training, that I am at a loss to understand how such masses of flesh and fat can put out any great strength. They strip, and then squatting opposite each other, look exceedingly like a couple of white-skinned bears or well-shaven baboons. The pit is covered with sawdust. There is a judge of the sport seated in front just outside a circle made by wisps of straw, victory being his who pushes his antagonist, if but a foot outside. They grapple very fiercely, but seldom seem to throw each other.

THE WRESTLERS

Of feasts and festivals, religious and secular, there really seems to be no end. Besides the great annual feast of the new year, kept pretty much as it is in China, there are *Matsuris* for every town and village, and every month of the year, I believe. Their picture books are full of illustrations. Then spring-time, when the peach-blossoms are out, is a time for universal rejoicing, feasting, and pic-nics in the country and in tea-gardens for ten miles round. And withal there is a due regard for economy, as is proved by the collector of empty present boxes constantly to be seen with a load of them at his back gathered from the recipients, who do not part with them for nothing.

The Japanese have undoubtedly a very rural taste, and seem to enjoy their games with the greatest zest, even where the saki is sparingly indulged in. Festivals are high days for the temples, and they seem to take it in rotation to hold a sort of fair. Formerly lotteries were held there, of which I have many illustrations, but they have for some time been prohibited as immoral on the same ground as gambling with cards or dice, to which, however, the Japanese are greatly addicted. Dice are made so minute as to be concealed in a small scent-bottle worn at the girdle, the cube being scarcely more than a tenth of an inch.

The officers have a game on horseback, which consists in taking up a ball with a sort of racket, and throwing it through a hole at the end of the list. The players are divided into two parties, distinguished by their colours, and the fun consists in knocking the ball out of their rival's racket as he is approaching at speed to the throwing point. They play with great spirit, and it must also be said, great good-humour, though they have such wretched horse-flesh and heathenish saddlery. A light snaffle only is loose in the mouth — and great leather saddle-flaps effectually prevent their wheeling their horses by the touch of the heel — even if Japanese ponies had any mouths; but as their riders generally hold on by the reins, one in each hand, the beasts, to resent such heavy usage, generally go with their heads in the air, and become at last proof against anything short of a Mexican bit.

Of their theatres, I have already given some description. With this glance at the popular games, festivals, and amusements, the reader must be content. For seeing many of these, my position as a Minister was unfavourable, as it precluded much personal observation, and it would serve little purpose to describe at second-hand what I had not myself witnessed.

JAPANESE GAME ON HORSEBACK

In describing their temples, I ought not to omit some notice of their cemeteries, by far the most remarkable and pleasant part of their religion, and the one which is most in harmony with our own feelings of the sanctity due to a place of rest for the dead. They are generally beautifully situated, planted with fine trees and admirably kept. The graves are for the most part simple tablets, sometimes recording the names and dates, at other times a single name only, as 'True-heart!' which marks the grave of some one at Tozengee. The cemetery attached to the Legation temple is one of the finest and most picturesque in Yeddo. In front of each grave is always a vase for flowers and another for water, and it was pleasant to see how constantly these were renewed. They reminded me of the 'Field of God'—the cemetery outside of Copenhagen, where each grave is made a little garden, the resort of the families of all whose loved ones have been consigned to their rest. Some of our extra-mural cemeteries, I am glad to think, are fast becoming equally worthy of admiration, that of Highgate more especially perhaps, aided by its picturesque situation on the side of a hill, and the beautiful view it commands of the valley of the Thames.

The temple of Tozengee, the grounds and cemetery, cover an immense area. It was formerly, I have understood, the palace of a small Daimio called *Ito-sciuri-daibu*, who made a present of it to the priests, having built a better one in a more suitable place in Yeddo. It is in consequence of this that he *alone* is allowed to go under the portico in his chair, while the Princes of *Xendai* and *Bisen* (two other patrons who give large supplies of rice and undertake all repairs, &c.), though much higher and powerful Daimios, are obliged to get out of their chairs at the gate where the steps are.

The Government gave us this temple after having received the consent of the former Daimio, though it is well known that the other two, who had but an indirect voice in the matter and were not consulted, disliked exceedingly the idea of our occupying it even temporarily.

One morning, after the attack on the Legation, the Prince of Xendai sent an officer with a retinue of a hundred men or more, to remove one of his ancestors' tablets to another temple. The common people believed he did this because he was displeased that the temple should be contaminated with our presence, and the 'unclean' food we use, by killing sheep and fowls. My informant, however, thought he had taken this very unusual step to show his displeasure that the Legation was not removed, and his hatred to foreigners, which is commonly spoken of as something generally known.

Certain it is, that the evening before the tablet was removed, our chief of the yaconins on service, came to inform me of what was about to take place, with a sort of vague intimation that it would be as well if our own guard were on foot. They came, as it happened, at a much earlier hour than was announced; — so that, as far as any preparation on our part was concerned, they might have had us at a disadvantage; but it was observed that all our Japanese guards were mustered, and stood to their arms, lining the palisade which surrounded our courtyard and the entrance.

# CHAPTER XV.

### WESTERN DIPLOMACY AND EASTERN POLICY.

THE borders of the Mediterranean, with Asia Minor and Syria as the farther limit, long constituted the East in common acceptation.  The 'Levant' (*le soleil Levant*), as the region thus defined was styled in the middle ages, nearly marked the extent of European traffic and intercourse.  Later, when the discoveries of Vasco da Gama opened a sea route to India; though China and Japan were added to the countries with which we maintained certain relations of commerce, India monopolised to itself all popular conceptions of 'the East.'  It is only within the present generation that we have been compelled to acknowledge an East, far beyond the Ganges.

The West and the East, in this more extended sense Europe and Asia, present a moral and political antithesis, and an antagonism, quite as real as the geographical bearings at opposite sides of the globe.  The general character of the relations which have existed since the beginning of history between the East and West, whether in the original circumscribed limits, or now along the whole seaboard of Asia, bears the unmistakable impress of antagonistic and apparently irreconcilable tendencies, pointing to certain conditions which would seem inseparable from any intercourse between the two races.

If this not only be true, but admit of demonstration, it obviously behoves all European Powers to keep in view a fact of such vital importance to the success of their policy.  For it must be very clear that no treaties of amity and commerce can either give good fruit or promise of permanence if entered into without reference to these conditions. As regards ourselves, vast commercial interests, a large revenue and territorial possessions, which constitute an empire of no ordinary magnitude, are all at stake. And just on the same scale of magnitude, are the adverse influences and elements of untoward character, which constitute the difficulty of reconciling such opposite conditions; and bringing either our relations and interests in harmony with Asiatic tendencies and character, or effecting some needful change in these. Out of such complex and antipathetic elements, it can never be easy to frame a treaty which shall be good and durable. To make a treaty is indeed only the first and the least of the difficulties, as all history and experience prove. The real touchstone of success lies in the practical working. Given a demonstrated superiority of force and military means at command, any treaty may be extorted from an Eastern potentate, however repugnant the stipulations, or impracticable the details. Indeed, the more obvious the impracticability of the stipulations, the more readily will an Eastern Government subscribe, because, in the anticipated impossibility of giving effect to the obnoxious conditions, they see their future safety. They gain by the nominal assent, what to them is everything in such circumstances,—Time, and few people know better how to turn it to account, when an obligation is to be evaded.

Foremost among the sources of difficulty and antagonism here alluded to, apart from certain differences in the moral constitution, temper, and tendencies of the two races, are; first, the fear of territorial aggrandisement; secondly, the instinct of a great danger from the infiltration of European ideas and influences of a wholly subversive and revolutionary tendency, as regards their customs, policy, and religion. Lastly, the repugnance of Asiatics to relinquish or bate one jot of their long-cherished pretensions to an unquestioned superiority over all of an alien race.

In reference to characteristic differences in the constitution and habits of thought of the Eastern mind, closely

linked as these are with those same lofty pretensions to
superiority, there seems an unconquerable tendency in the
European race to run headlong against the barrier, and
fling down the gauntlet in mere wantonness, for the sake
of provoking a conflict.  A conflict, too, be it observed, in
which the strongest passions, and the most rooted convictions—all that enters most thoroughly and deeply into the
very texture and fibre of the Asiatic mind—is roused to
antagonism in nations never remarkable for pliancy ; and
very easily stirred up to stubborn and dogged resistance.
Europeans enter within the borders of Asia for the most
part with a feeling of indifference or contempt for all that
constitutes the life and the pride of an Asiatic.  And
setting aside the manifest impolicy of such a course, there
is perhaps as much vain pretension on our side, and for-
getfulness of the true claims to consideration which properly belongs to Asia, from the part her race has played
in the history of the world, as any that can be justly
charged against them.  Europe owes much to Asia, the
great cradle of the human race, besides mere parentage
and descent.  The European family is but the cadet
branch, and has been enriched and ennobled by all
the elder branches have done and suffered, thought,
and accomplished.  Each generation, it has been truly
observed, receives the benefit of the cultivation of that
which preceded it, and not only that immediately preceding, but of all former ages and generations.  Civilisation,
like capitalised profits, descends through ages, and the
civilisation of to-day, represents the accumulated wealth
and capital of all preceding ages.  The elder branch has
therefore some title to gratitude, in the fact that from
its progenitors, we have ourselves derived much that is
precious in our own life and history ; which is what it is,
not by our own efforts and superior intelligence alone,
but in great degree, by all we have gathered from the
past —not the past of Europe only, but also of Asia. The
creeds, doctrines, and faith of the millions that have
peopled Asia in successive generations, not less than the

discoveries, inventions, and material products borrowed from their soil, have all contributed to make Europe, her history and her civilisation, what they now are ; for its children to boast of — as something higher and better than any of Asiatic growth.  There are elements of civilisation, and germs of spiritual growth essentially due to the mind, the character, and the temper of the people of Asia, and which, but for them, might be wanting now in us.

We do not owe more to Greece and Rome,—to the cultivation of reason, taste, and the sense of beauty in the one, and the genius of government, or the spirit of order and legal organisation in the other,—than to Asia for its persistent and silent protest against the materialistic and essentially practical, but mundane tendencies of all of European race.*   Asia has had in all times a tendency to spiritualism, often dream-like and mystic, yet ever with a teeming imagination directed to the unseen, the spiritual, and mysterious elements of another world. She has often sought her inspiration in things above, while we have been grovelling in earthly and material aims, in which the conquest of nature, for our own immediate ends, has been the *primum mobile* of our efforts.   Often, in times past, as the hordes of Asia surged across the vast steppes for conquest and aggrandisement to the ends of the earth, they failed ; but even in failure they gave to Europe the new blood required to invigorate and lift up the worn-out stock of an effete and depraved civilisation, the legacy of Roman and Byzantine misrule.   They have ever recoiled and been baffled in any permanent settlement, when these mighty waves of invasion have swept over Europe.  Babylonian and Persian hosts, Attila and his myriad hordes, Genghis Khan and Tamerlane, with their Mongols and Turcomans, all, one after the other, in successive waves have been swept back from the fields of Europe, and failed in every

---

* I am in some degree indebted for this train of thought to the Essay of the Rev. Dr. Temple ' on the Education of the World,' in which he dwells upon the influence of the Asiatic mind and character.

effort to hold its fertile lands in permanency as Asiatic
dependencies.  The Mongols long held on to Russia in the
north, and the Turks fixed more tenaciously still on the
Byzantine fragments of empire, half European, half Asiatic,
in the south.  But may not this perpetual check to all earthly
progress have taught her children to seek, if not their inspiration, at least their greatness, in REPOSE, and to fix their
thoughts on things above?  So, it has been suggested*,
these two concurrent influences, may have moulded the
Asiatic life into the form it has now long assumed.
Contempt for earthly progress and mushroom nationalities, and scorn of utilitarian pursuits, combining to make
their very mode of being and living—a silent protest
against the unrest which is one of the chief characteristics of European life.  Modern society seems to have
adopted only half of Goethe's motto, ' Ohne Hast, ohne
Rest.' They do not rest, indeed, but they will hasten and
press onward.  Asia has had its philosophy also, into
which many things entered, not dreamed of in ours.  And
if even the Hebrews, as has been surmised, did not learn
from their Babylonian conquerors the doctrine of the
immortality of the soul (not, certainly, taught in their
scriptures), there is no doubt they emerged from a
long slavery with far clearer ideas on the subject than
they took with them.  There is a mystic grandeur in the
conception of eternal truths and divine law, familiar to
the imaginative Asiatic, which the positive practical
spirit of all the more advanced nations of Europe seldom
appreciates in others at its true value.  If Asia finds the
best elements of its life in rest and contemplation, and its
highest happiness in a dreamy repose—enemy to all
change and progress — Europe no less certainly is absorbed in material aims, where reason, and a practical
and thoroughly mundane spirit prevails over all the
more spiritual and mysterious elements of human nature.
The greatest happiness of the greatest number, as the
highest good to be striven for on a well-calculated and

* See Essay ' on the Education of the World,' by the Rev. Dr. Temple.

enlightened regard for our own best interests, which has ere now been held to constitute the highest virtue, are conceptions of the mind of Europe, and could hardly have emanated from Asia. What wonder that the two races should feel a mutual repulsion, and that the Asiatic especially should shrink from all contact, as bringing into his existence discord and confusion, — forcing upon him the cares of this world, and a struggle for the right to live as he deems best, abhorrent to his nature, and all his habits of thought and being. Ours may be the best developed form of life, and the tendency of Asiatic life may be towards stagnation, rather than progress or a spiritualising movement upward and outward, away from the ever-debasing, if not essentially absorbing thoughts of *self*. But Asia, as the counterpoise in the world's activities to the fly-wheel of European progress, and a mute and solemn protest against the all-absorbing pursuits of a more thoroughly mundane and rationalising existence, may supply, in the dispensations of this lower world, the corrective needed to check and rebuke the exaggerations of a more exclusively practical and unimaginative spirit in nations which, compared with those of Asiatic stock, are yet in their infancy as to age and experience, whatever they may be in progress and attainments. Even in these they can put forward high pretensions. Not only may the system of ethics, embodied in the thoroughly popular works of Confucius and Mencius, who lived nearly 600 years B.C., vie with the contemporaneous productions of the Greek mind in its best days ; but there is a current of ideas among all classes of Chinese, a shrewdness and power of observation, as well as a fund of knowledge on all the more practical duties and rela-tions of life, which will bear comparison with the state of enlightenment of the masses in the best civilised country in Europe. Although it is a form of courtesy for them in putting forward an opinion, even to a foreigner, to sign themselves, 'Your younger brother,' or even 'Your stupid younger brother,' it may be reasonably doubted whether, in many cases, the subscription would not more properly belong to the European. This rapid glance at characteristic differences in manners, customs, and habits, and the very stamp of the civilisation which exists in the East, compared with the type of Western developement, may suffice to show how many and how strong are the antagonistic influences in full operation against any efforts to draw closer the bonds of union for mutual advantage. Some may be disposed to treat lightly these social antitheses, as in no serious degree interfering with the interchange of merchandise, or the pressure and influence of material interests, when these demand the drawing together of nations, and make it one of the conditions of their prosperity. But this is to contend that men's feelings, prejudices, and passions are inert, and only called into play as a ' clear and enlightened view of their own interests' shall prompt. Slight worldly experience is required for the rejection of such a theory as utterly erroneous. Not only do our habits, feelings, and prejudices blind us to our own interests, but they lead us perpetually to consult the one in preference to the other, and without any regard to the moral worth of what we object to, or despise. The man who voids his rheum upon your hearth or carpet, shouts slang or barbarous language in your ear, and jars all the fibres of your organisation, is a man that you will dislike and avoid, even though he has good bargains to sell; especially if there are other fields where you can invest your money without being subject to such discords. As with a man, so with a nation. Uncongenial habits and customs, and the want of a common language, are great impediments to free intercourse. Now, that such uncongeniality exists, and antipathetic tendencies too, cannot be doubted; and that these involve distaste and contempt, facts sufficiently establish. The Chinese and the Japanese, like other people, are very apt to condemn what they dislike or do not rightly understand; and we may rest assured that the foreigner who finds the necessity for ' walking his thousand steps every day,'* or pulling like a bargeman for exercise, or shouting hurrahs with stentorian lungs after dinner for enjoyment, will be regarded as a ' barbarian ' by the Chinese, and despised and disliked accordingly, even if he could establish a more unquestionable and invariable superiority in moral worth.

If so many grounds of dissidence or antagonism may be shown to exist between the trans-Gangetic East and the West, between the Japanese, Chinese, or Mongolian, and the European races — in manners and customs, religion and philosophy — in all their characteristics, social and ethical, we cannot be surprised to find, upon inquiry, other and equally strong points of divergence in the political economy and commercial policy of this Eastern, yet scarcely Oriental people, as this term is popularly understood. That there should be such differences very clearly defined, seems to follow almost as an inevitable necessity. The state of civilisation to which a nation has attained, its acquired tastes and wants,—and the material interests of the country, always more or less influenced by those, must go far to determine their system of political economy and commerce, and China and Japan, in these respects, form no exception. In any foreign relations established between these Empires and the Western States, whether political or commercial objects may have been the end chiefly in view, these elementary conditions, without doubt, play a very prominent part ; and it is essential to know how far the influence is favourable or adverse.

It would be a great mistake to conclude that because the economic and commercial principles of Chinese writers, (borrowed and adopted by the Japanese,) on these confessedly intricate subjects are different from those most prevalent in the West, they have made no progress in the science of political economy (if science it deserves to be

* The way in which the daily exercise of the foreigners (when confined to the space within the Factory Gardens) used to be described by the Cantonese. It was supposed by the natives, in order to explain a proceeding otherwise so irrational and unintelligible to them, that this was the mode by which the foreign trader computed and made up his accounts !

called even in our day), or were in bygone ages without
the knowledge and practice nécessary to give developement
to the resources of a country, and the commercial interchange of products on a colossal scale.   In Europe, and
even in England, there is no such unanimity of opinion
on the cardinal points, as to entitle us to lay down the law
*ex cathedrâ* or very dogmatically, either to the Chinese, or
any other nation.   It was a science with them very certainly
before modern nations existed, and has ever since been
cultivated, with more or less success.   We can scarcely
hope to make much impression upon either the Chinese
or the Japanese mind in this direction therefore, without
taking cognisance of the current opinions and received
principles of that science, as *they* understand it.   If a
Chinese political economist had come among us forty
years ago, and pointed out the fallacy involved in protective laws for corn, we fear he would not only have signally
failed in any advocacy of a principle of free trade, but in
obtaining a hearing ; unless he could show that he at least
understood where the stress of the question lay, and what
were the arguments in vogue on the opposite side.
I cannot here show by many extracts what their views
are ; but that they should form the special study of
those charged with the extension of our trade in these
countries, cannot be doubted.   We should then see, as
M. Huc remarks, that ' the Chinese are as advanced as
we are in the art of making formulas.'   There is one example from *Tsien-tche*, a celebrated writer of ancient
times, who maintained that a legal interest of thirty per
cent. was calculated to facilitate commerce!   He says—

' A well-organised society would be that in which every
one labouring according to his powers, his talents, and the
public necessities, all property would be divided in such
proportions as should secure its enjoyment to every one at
the same time.   The richest State would be that in which
a small amount of labour would furnish the productions
of nature and art in abundance, superior to the number
and the wants of the inhabitants.   Wealth has necessarily

a relation to wants. The empire was richer with a smaller amount of property under the first dynasties, because less labour produced more in proportion to the number of inhabitants. The superabundant produce of some localities may be made to become a help to others that are deficient, and it is for commerce to undertake their transport. The necessity of commerce in the empire is equal to the necessity of exchanges, and the utility of commerce to their utility — that is to say, the necessity is absolute, and the utility universal and continual.'

Again, as bearing upon existing opinions and foreign commercial relations : —

' If all the goods of the empire belonged to the State, and the State would undertake the distribution of them, it must necessarily undertake those exchanges which are effected by commerce, by carrying the superabundance of one place to another. Merchants, however, undertake to render this important service to society, at their own risk and peril. The proportions and the correspondence of the exchanges of productions is neither uniform, constant, nor convenient enough to provide for the varied and continual wants of society ; but money, as the sign and equivalent of a fixed and recognised value, supplies this want so much the more easily, as it lends itself with facility and promptitude to all the proportions, divisions, and correspondences of exchange. Money is the spring and the leaven of commerce, and commerce can only be flourishing inasmuch as the circulation of money facilitates, accelerates, and perpetuates the multitude of exchanges.' *

But if we pass from the antagonistic influences at work in the far East, from Cochin China to Japan, under merely social and economical, or commercial aspects (though these, it will be seen, are neither few nor insignificant ; and in their cumulative force, constitute a barrier offering serious obstacles to farther advance) and consider the class of influences, of a different order, in which the

---

* It is passing strange that in a country where such doctrines were taught centuries ago, there is not even yet a gold or silver currency.

religious and the political elements predominate, both being closely intermixed, we shall find still stronger causes of dissidence and hostility.   It would be to give a very imperfect, and altogether erroneous view of the trans-Gangetic East, and its empires in their foreign relations; as well as of those influences among the Chinese, and Japanese more especially perhaps, which at the present moment are most active in respect to foreigners; if among the various causes of indifference or contempt on the one hand, and active hostility on the other, the religious and missionary conditions were omitted.   These enter into the question of further progress or improvement in our relations, in a manner so *effective and significant* as to determine and control the foreign policy at the courts of Pekin and Yeddo alike, but the latter more especially, far more decisively than any other of the many conditions, discordant or antipathetic, to which I have hitherto referred. And this because both rulers and people probably see in this direction, an element of greater danger, and one which strikes a key-note of fear, rousing a corresponding feeling of hatred and anger.  Religious or political propagandism they suspect is always contemplated by Western Powers. Some are more suspected than others perhaps, but all are held tainted with this, to them, pestiferous mania for converting and proselytising the Eastern races, changing their customs, and making them other than they are.  This unpropitious influence of a religious element in the state policy, and the bias of the rulers of Eastern nations, appear to be equally inimical to their *conversion to Christianity*, and to improved *political and commercial relations,*—on which latter, the only avowed objects of European intercourse, all access to the countries depends.   This is so important a fact, that even were it less likely to be hotly contested, I feel called upon to support my opinion by such evidence as leaving little room for doubt, shall bring the reader another stage towards a knowledge of the whole truth. If I am not greatly mistaken, it will lead him to this further conclusion, that the remarkable and admitted want of success in the missionary labours of the present time, as of all past ages in Asia, may be traced to well-ascertained causes, some of which are contingent on the means adopted, and the course taken by the missionaries themselves ; while others again are of a more absolute character, not contingent upon the shifting, misdirected efforts, or otherwise, of any body of men, but upon natural causes. Among the obstacles to any satisfactory progress, or permanent effect which I deem entirely conditional and temporary (contingent upon the means brought to bear, and not inherent in the subject) I trace throughout, first, a want of unity and accord among the teachers of religion, and in the things taught. Next, a glaring contradiction, patent to the observation of those whom it is sought to convert, between the doctrines and the practical illustration they receive, both in the lives of foreigners in the whole seaboard of Asia from Rangoon to Yeddo, and in the policy of Governments professing Christianity. Among those of a more absolute character and due in some measure to natural causes, we must take into consideration the hostility of the native Government. This hostility plainly takes its origin from a double source ; the one to be traced to the means adopted by the evangelising agents, with the open or covert support of Foreign Governments ; but the other inherent and inseparable from all efforts in this direction, — because they are, and must be, pregnant with a danger which menaces destruction to all governments founded on pagan creeds and absolute despotism.

It is only the latter that I propose to discuss here, as the former would take both myself and the reader too far away from the immediate subject of inquiry. M. Huc was certainly quite right when he said the Chinese emperors were neither intolerant nor bigoted, and are, indeed, too entirely without any religion to care for creeds, save in so far as they interfere with temporal things, and among these, as chief and paramount over all other considerations — their political supremacy and absolute power.  This which is true of China is doubly so of Japan, where there has been a life and death struggle, a long and a bloody war of a mingled civil and religious character, in which Christianity, as Jesuits and Dominicans taught it, formed the war-cry on one side, and that the losing one.

A Japanese as well as a Chinese may please his fancy as to what religion he professes, provided, as M. Huc says of the latter, it is not one connected either with secret societies or political objects.  ' Unfortunately,' as he goes on to add, ' the Chinese Government *has placed Christianity in this category*, and it is very difficult to correct this error and introduce more just ideas.'  Not only difficult but quite impracticable I should say, taken from either a Chinese or a Japanese point of view, with their right divine to absolute and undisputed rule over their subjects.  Is it an error to assume that Romanism militates against such rule?  Let us listen to the Emperor Young-tching, who, in 1724, proscribed the Christian religion and condescended to state his views to three Jesuit fathers who petitioned against the decree for their expulsion.

' Certain Europeans\* in the province of Fokien have been endeavouring to defy our laws and trouble our people.  The great men of the province have applied to me, and I must repress this disorder.  It is the business of the Government with which I am charged, and I neither can nor ought to act now as I did when I was a private prince.'

' Gentlemen,' said Frederick the Great, about the same time, at the opposite side of the globe, ' *Mon metier c'est d'être Roi.*'  So Young-tching evidently understood his duty.  But he continues :—

' You say that your law is not a false law, and I believe it.  But what would you say if I were to send a troop of

---

\* Spanish Dominicans settled in the province of Fokien.  Some of the following illustrations and extracts, with slight differences, may be found in an article which appeared in the ' Edinburgh Review ' for April 1857, on ' British Relations with China.'

Bonzes and Lamas into your country to preach their law in it? How would you receive them?—You wish to make the Chinese Christians, and this is what your law demands, I know very well. *But what in that case would become of us?* THE SUBJECTS OF YOUR KINGS. *The Christians whom you make recognise no authority but you;* in times of trouble they would listen to no other voice. I know well enough that there is nothing to fear at present; but when your ships shall be coming by thousands and tens of thousands, then, indeed, we may have some disturbances.'

Can anyone say that these were not, upon the whole, very rational views for the speaker as the despotic head of a great Pagan empire to take? Or can we feel surprise if a wide-spread opinion extending from the emperors to the lowest Mandarin or official in both countries, exists,— that political elements of disturbance are thickly sown with the spread of Christianity, tending to unsettle the minds of the people and subvert the national creeds and the traditions of absolute submission to the ruling powers? Can we doubt that this *is the greatest barrier at present existing to any successful negotiations* with the governments of either country for political or commercial objects? Certainly it is so in Japan. Universal tolerance is, to them, equivalent to deposition or the resignation of their authority; nor is it difficult to see that this must be to them a *vital question.* Not only our Christian enterprises to spread the faith, but all contact with Europeans on the part of Eastern races, has led to only *one of two results,*— either the rooting out of the sect itself in self-defence by the natives, and the total isolation of the country by a violent convulsion, as Japan to this day and China for a long period; or the assertion of a political supremacy, and the subjugation of the people, introducing foreign masters everywhere, of which they have living examples, —the Spaniards in the Philippines, the Dutch in Java, the Portuguese at their own doors, and the English (according to Abbé Huc) everywhere!

What, in effect, is the natural and the necessary tendency of Christianity as the Gospels have delivered it to us, when brought to the knowledge of a pagan race living under an absolute despotism, which draws from heathen superstition some of its authority, and mingles the worship of the gods and idolatrous practices with the reverence paid to the sovereign? *Is it not of necessity antagonistic, entirely subversive of the whole scheme of Government,* which claims for the head of the State divine honours, and places the will of the Emperor on the footing of a decree from heaven? Does it not involve the introduction of a dominion of principle and affection in a kingdom where another rule exists with which it has no affinity— bringing in 'a new *primum mobile,*' as Bacon has said in describing another principle, ' that ravisheth all the spheres of Government,'—that is, in this instance, threatening to ravish from the heathen rulers *all control over their own people, by the adoption of principles subversive of the established polity and institutions?* Statesmen — not in China only, but in other countries — have ever been prone to protect and cherish the popular superstitions as a useful engine of government, and submit to a mummery in public which they inwardly despised. This—which forced the philosopher in ancient times into being *a political not less than a religious reformer,* and cost Socrates his life — entails, unavoidably, *the same condition on the missionary in these Eastern countries.* A spurious mixture of the theocratic and patriarchal elements form the bases of all government both in the Celestial and the Japanese Empires, under emperors who claim not only to be each the Patriarch and father of his people, but also Divine descent. These are all alike, and inseparably bound up with a more or less false and demoralising faith ; and as there is no hope of amending the Government without changing the faith, he who preaches the religion of Christ does also — however peaceable his words or intentions — of necessity *preach revolution* ; in other words, *the subversion of all existing institutions and powers in those countries.* So, it is clear the emperors and all who derive authority and rule from them, *must* regard all Christian emissaries, whether Romanist or Protestant, as agents of a revolutionary propaganda. I repeat, they will inevitably be considered disturbers of the peace, — as teaching a new religion, which, in its Protestant and least aggressive form, inspires a feeling of equality and independence, often makes resistance to the civil power a duty; and indubitably strikes at the root of the institutions and polity of the empire as they now exist. It is evident that all connected with such a mission cannot fail to be obnoxious to those in power, and to be viewed with rancorous hostility as a source of danger and confusion. And what is true of China applies equally to Japan, Cochin China, and, I believe, Siam, and Burmah, but with special intensity to Japan.

The religion — be it Christianity or any other — which introduces as inherent to it a principle of independence to all earthly power,— where the subject is taught he must obey God rather than man, if the behests of the latter should be contrary to his duty, even though that man should be Emperor and styled the Son of Heaven, — is in its nature insurrectionary, when applied to a kingdom and countries governed as these are. This applies to Christianity, apart from all sectarian difference of churches, and questions of sacerdocy or polity. But, it cannot be denied, the argument applies with tenfold force when we come to consider Romanism. The Protestant missionary is bound, indeed, to teach his convert that he must obey God rather than man, whatever be the cost in worldly interests, even to the sacrifice of his life; but the Romanist adds the pretension of deciding *ex cathedrâ*, for the Ruler's subject who is his convert, in what obedience to God consists, and this in all the changing circumstances and relations of daily life, whether as regards his neighbour, his country, or his *sovereign*. The priest becomes the virtual sovereign. While the Protestant raises a standard of resist-

ance to despotic or heathenish power, by teaching as a sacred
right the duty of resisting authority, whencesoever emanating, *if it demand obedience contrary to another law and a
higher*, embodied in the Scriptures, and written in the
heart; the Romanist exacts obedience ostensibly to the
same Law, and resistance to any other—but the Law
as interpreted by him, and which *he shall prescribe*, as
the representative of the Roman Church, holy and infallible. Who can be surprised, if in both cases the Rulers
see only, in the efforts of missionaries to convert their
subjects to this Christianity, the introduction of a revolutionary element, not only antagonistic and hostile to the
monarch's supreme rule, but necessarily and directly
subversive of his authority in exact proportion to their
success? Or can we wonder, in so far as the Emperors
of China and Japan are informed of the distinction
between the two Churches, that in the case of the Roman
Catholics they should see an *additional motive for hostility
and alarm* in the pretension of foreign priests to direct
all these elements of disturbance and resistance to their
power, and to over-ride all authority claiming to be independent of and superior to that of the Church, and not
under its control? True, the Roman Catholic missionary
will reply, ' only in things spiritual;' but have we yet in
Europe, in this nineteenth century, been able to draw
with any accuracy this line between things spiritual and
temporal? Does it not still remain to be traced, the exact
boundaries being debateable ground, often threatening a
renewal of wars and persecutions, conflicts between State
and Church, nation and nation ranged on opposite sides,
— the temporal power and civil government on the one
side, and the Pope with the pretensions of a spiritual supremacy for the Church of Rome on the other,—conflicts only
less bloody and desolating than those of preceding centuries, because the power of the Papal Church is weaker,
and that of the State is everywhere stronger? Perhaps
it might be truly added, because there is less of faith,
—yet are these conflicts not liable to be renewed with the

pitiless hostility of the worst times, if a new field could be found *where these conditions were reversed*?   It is not that there is less of intolerance or bigotry in the world than in former days, I fear; but a larger developement of interests inimical to their free display.   What are the scenes passing around us in Europe at the present day? Do we require the Procession of the Shirt at Treves, or the denial of medical aid to the dying man who has not come to terms with his confessor, or the imprisonment of Protestant families for adhering to their faith, to tell us that the spirit of the Inquisition and the ashes of the martyr's faggot are yet smouldering, and capable of being again fanned into a destructive fire?

'Shall I,' writes the Editor of the 'Record,' in a leader which appeared but a few years ago,—'Shall I, therefore, fall in with this abominable delusion?  Shall I foster that damnable doctrine,—that Socinianism and Calvinism are not every one of them mortal sins, like murder and adultery?—or hold out hopes to the Protestant that I will not meddle with his creed?'

An *imperium in imperio* therefore, subversive of his own rule, hostile to his supremacy, and with a gauntlet of defiance ever on the ground against all who claim liberty of conscience, to be enforced, whenever the secular power is theirs, with the arms of flesh — by war and persecution,—this is the prospect held out to the potentates and rulers of China and Japan by the introduction of 'Christianity' into their empires.  Is there any rational ground of hope that either they or any of their successors will ever tolerate, much less *welcome as a benefit*, the propagation of the faith, of whatever denomination the agents may be, Romanist or Protestant?   And in proportion as foreign Governments are identified with these efforts, is it not evident that in this same degree will the presence of their subjects in the country be considered an evil imposed upon them by major force—to be acquiesced in only so long as that condition shall exist?   While, as regards political relations and efforts at negotiation for the extension of trade and commerce, with the view of obtaining the removal of disabling restrictions and barriers to a freer intercourse, nothing can be more vain or futile,—more utterly opposed to the ruling principle of the foreign policy of Japan, and the spirit of its rulers.

I have not discussed this question, it will be observed, upon any other principle than that which should govern all rational inquiry into the policy of States, and the action of natural causes.   The writer in the 'Record,' no doubt, spoke out in all sincerity — the more so that he discarded all suggestions of discretion, and it cannot be supposed he spoke only his own individual convictions. What he said was no less true than logical.   Romanism is not only the most intolerant of creeds, as has been observed, ' but *intolerance is its essence,*—that pervading spirit without which it would *not be itself, or be true to its own nature.*   It looks upon heresy, of whatever form (that is, dissent), not as a dangerous and deplorable error out of which men are to be persuaded or forced, but as a sin to be put down ; as an insult to the Divine Majesty, which calls for punishment ; as a crime against the best interests of society, which it is the duty of the State to repress and prevent, as it most effectively can, with the secular power and the arm of flesh.   It is bound to look upon matters in this light. *It would be untrue to itself, and self-contradictory, if it did not.'*

Neither have I entered into this examination of the influence and prospects of missionaries and proselytising labours in the far East with any feeling of hostility, or from any indifference to the success of well-advised efforts to spread the light of the Gospel over Asia; but with a mature conviction that they are not to be advanced at present, if ever, by any direct action, or political interference on the part of Foreign Governments.   I am led to this conclusion by the knowledge that this is precisely one of those objects which is the most liable to injurious interference, from the diversity of the thing sought by ourselves and other Foreign States; and the most open to objection, from the existing conditions and necessities of the Chinese and Japanese nations, living under pagan, despotic, and Oriental governments.

In considering the antagonistic influences in full operation, more especially in Japan, it was necessary to show, honestly, how the question of religion told upon our present relations and future prosperity. We have seen, independent of all antipathies of race, difference of language and customs, that there is a Political Economy opposed in all its accredited and fundamental principles to the developement of Foreign commerce. Behind this obstacle, sufficiently formidable in itself, is a great gulf, into which the bodies of thousands of martyrs have been flung, — victims to the political aspect of Romanism more especially; but to all Christianity, as subversive of the temporal power. Finally, ranged beyond, and ready to do battle to the death, stands Feudalism in full strength and vigour—feudalism, armed *cap-à-pié*, with its nobles and their followers, as it existed in Europe many centuries back. These feudal classes, with more or less intelligence as to cause and effect, but a true instinct, see the destruction of their privileges, and the subversion of their power in the progress of Foreign relations and the full developement of commerce. They see that we bring not only goods for sale, the purchase of which they believe will impoverish the nation; but new religions, new ideas of social order, liberty, and political rights, new customs and habits, all subversive of those now existing, and hostile to them and their order. Finally, I think they also see the line of progress as this has been traced in the Past. They may even have gleaned enough through the Dutch of European history, to know how feudalism fell in Europe by the growth of trade, and the enrichment and enlightenment of a burgher class, who ultimately became strong enough to make terms and extort concessions from both sovereign and nobles; and sometimes, even to fling the sword into the scales and turn the balance, when the two were in conflict and victory hung in suspense.

In this farthest extremity of Eastern empire, Western civilisation is *aux prises* with Feudalism, strong in its traditions and nationality, and defiant in its semi-chivalric and militant character. There are thus three great and well-defined obstacles to any progress — a POLITICAL ECONOMY opposed to free trade, a RELIGIOUS INTOLERANCE founded on purely political considerations, and, lastly, a rampant FEUDALISM. How these three enemies to all progress are to be dealt with, and by what means they may best be encountered and overcome, is the question of questions — the one difficulty which lies at the root of all others.

The reader will now be in a position to understand that in any policy or course of action to be adopted, there are inherent difficulties, which no art or skill can eliminate. Taking this knowledge with us we may proceed a step farther and inquire, what then are the essential, irrevocable conditions of all Western diplomacy in the far East? In other words what are the necessities and exigencies which govern its action; and the limits within which we may reasonably look for success? These questions have a direct bearing on momentous interests both in the Western and Eastern world, and the questions they embrace constitute one of the great problems of the day, so far as the far East is concerned. Two wars in China costing millions of treasure, and no small loss of life, have tended to fix public attention upon our relations in the trans-Gangetic East, as matters of too serious a character to be overlooked or uncared for. It has been seen that the national exchequer as well as commercial prosperity are deeply concerned in the relations we maintain with these trans-Gangetic Eastern races ; and that taxation, revenue, and the annual budget, are all directly affected by our position, and the means we take for practically asserting the rights, which treaties only nominally bestow. Serious considerations these, which even an English public, proverbially careless of Indian or Eastern affairs, and absorbed in Home affairs political and domestic, is beginning to perceive, demand, by the very fact of their influence upon the subjects of their predilection, the best attention that can be given to them, and fuller and more authentic information than it has hitherto been possible to obtain. Though we may not be over-sanguine if we look at the future by the light of the past, for—

> So many worlds, so much to do,
> So little done, such things to be,

may still describe the feelings with which such far-distant relations are discussed ;—yet on Paley's principle of ' an enlightened regard to self-interest,' the least discursive intellects in bucolic and manufacturing communities are turning their thoughts occasionally eastward, with a sense of the importance of what is passing there, as regards the more personal and immediate interests of their own boroughs and homesteads. Once this idea penetrates the native soil and takes root, it will not fail to bear a fruitful crop of inquiring minds, and an interest that will not die out. What is passing in those outlying regions of the farther Asia, among the Siamese and Cochin-Chinese— in China and in Japan, will be eagerly studied, until the earth is girdled round with a visible and continuous chain —link within link of reciprocal interests. Not as now invisible to many, and apparently broken short off at Vienna or Naples — beginning again at Constantinople — cropping up sometimes at Teheran in a fitful way, and finally dropping into the limbo of shadows and uncertainties at Calcutta, after traversing the Indian peninsula. Merchants, indeed, know this vital truth of continuity and reciprocal influences—the heads of the guild at least, for each day's transactions impresses the fact upon their minds, and prints it in their ledgers in characters far too legible and significant to be overlooked or mistaken. A murrain, an insurrection, or a war in the steppes and fertile plains of Russia, make sad havoc in the markets of tallow and hemp, and divers other articles

entering largely into the consumption of whole populations little knowing and little caring what is happening
in the political or physical conditions of the earth, out of
their own parish.   A civil war in a world beyond the
Atlantic, a world which did not exist for Europe or for
Asia three hundred years ago, has flung half a million
of thriving workmen here and in France into deepest
distress, and paralysed a whole industry.   The progress
of a disorganising process from the combined influence
of our wars with the vast Empire of China, over-popula-
tion, and feebleness with corruption in the government—
threatens us with the loss of our chief supplies of tea
and silk, both coming perhaps under the category of
luxuries and artificial wants, which our ancestors have
done without, and we might again learn to dispense with,
but now become almost necessities by long habit.  How hard
would be the lesson if it had to be learnt—how much
capital and industrial labour would be flung out of profitable employment — and though last, not least, what
new tax would supply the deficiency of six millions in
the budget, which none of us feel very seriously in its
present form on tea.  A war or a revolution, even in
Japan, small in its extent, and all but lost in the far
distant horizon, with an existing trade of scarce a
million sterling with all the rest of the world, has its
importance in this wider view of continuous and reacting
wants and interests which makes ' the whole world kin,'
however little there may be of the ' touch of pity,' or true
philanthropy in the acknowledged relations.   The supply
of tea, as of silk, we at present draw from Japan is but
small, compared with the whole supply which reaches the
English market ; but yet both have qualities not found elsewhere, and supplying something new and valuable.  Nor is
this all : what Japan now is in a commercial point of view,
is no criterion of what Japan *might* be as a new market
both of consumption and supply, could our relations with
it be placed on a more satisfactory footing.  What Belgium
and Holland, Spain and Portugal, Sweden and Denmark,

are to us at present, I have no hesitation in saying Japan might very speedily become under better and a less hostile régime. Whether this be worth striving for, and what may be the risk or cost, are precisely the questions each day arising and now pressing for solution.

Western diplomacy in these eastern countries necessarily involves, as in other fields, the consideration of the policy and interests of other Western Powers in the same regions ; and it is too much to expect, whatever may be the identity of these in some respects, that there should be a common accord in all. Yet such common accord is the one thing above all others most essential to any large or complete success in the inevitable struggle ! Diversity of objects and views, however, there will always be. Even when the ulterior ends are the same, there will be divergence and difference of opinion as to the means to be employed. What may be the actual policy and interests of the various Western States maintaining relations with the countries extending along the whole seaboard of Asia, and northward to Japan, the farthest limit of the East,—is therefore a legitimate subject of inquiry to all, and must enter essentially into the question of what our own, under any given circumstances, should be. What British interests *are* at the present day, and what the sole object of our policy, needs no explanation. Both should be, if they are not, patent to the world. Commerce is with us, in Siam, China, and Japan all equally (for with Cochin-China we have no relations yet) the one sole object. If any political interest be connected with it, this can only be in direct reference to India, and in the necessity of guarding ourselves from a loss of prestige, by a tame submission to wrong persistently, and intentionally, inflicted—and the like necessity of preventing, either our territories or our commerce in these seas being endangered by the occupation on the part of Foreign Powers of adjoining provinces and seaboard, which either seem to have this for the object, or may otherwise become a manifest source of danger. Such, for instance, are, or may be, certain acquisitions made and supposed to be further contemplated by Russia, in connection with both China and Japan. The vast acquisitions of territory and line of sea-coast made by Russia during the last few years at the expense of China, without a pretext of war, gives to the former an entirely new position in relation to Europe and commerce in all the adjoining seas, including the great highway of nations between China and the American continent, across the Pacific. No longer shut up the greater part of the year in frozen harbours, far removed from any great lines of commercial traffic on the northern shores of Okhotsk and Kamtschatka, at the farthest extremities of her Asiatic dominions, Russia has now well-nigh attained the great object of her ambition, so long sought in vain in the West—on the coast of Norway, in the Black Sea, and towards the Bosphorus —namely, a free outlet for her fleets and her commerce in unfrozen seas. A wide field has thus been secured for her navy, military and commercial, where vast interests and ever-increasing trade are in full developement. Olga bay, already in their possession, has two harbours, an outer and an inner port, and the former remains unfrozen during the whole winter. But Victoria and Broughton bays lie still farther south, and the one is already included in their newly-acquired coast-line, while the second is marked for acquisition—as being ' still indeterminate.' This last brings them to the northern limits of Corea, with merely the Straits between them and Japan, while the China seas and the great Pacific are before them. These are immense strides, and have been all made in the short space of ten years, during a time of profound peace, as regards Russia and the Chinese Empire. China has been made to yield up provinces larger in area than France and Great Britain by a process of simple pressure, which the government of Pekin felt too weak even to make the attempt to resist—otherwise than by words and protests, of small avail, as they must have foreseen, to avert their discomfiture.

The result has undoubtedly been to give to Russia a

commanding position as regards the territories of China and Japan.  Still more, perhaps, in reference to the great commerce rapidly developing from the Gulf of Pecheli to the western coast of America, with California in its centre, — intervening groups of islands on the one side of the globe, and those still more important centres of trade —Australia, Borneo, Java, and the Philippines, with the Chinese and Indian trade between those two countries, on the other.  To a government which knows how to turn to profit the weakness of an ally whose territories lie in tempting contiguity, proximity alone becomes a source of danger.  To annex a territory with nearly three hundred leagues of sea-coast, without war or other expense than the pay of a few agents, preparing the way by their ' scientific explorations,' must be considered the triumph of a policy of annexation, and a diplomacy which sees clearly the object to be attained, while it is deterred by no fears of resistance.  It is less necessary to canvass the real or possible interests and aims of other Treaty Powers—scarcely yet developed, perhaps.  Holland, no doubt, like ourselves, has no other aim than the extension of her commerce.  The same might probably be predicated with truth of America, North or South.  As regards France, apart from missionary protectorates, or Prussia, and Portugal—is it not rather a matter of national dignity than of material interests which has made them Treaty Powers in Japan?

Great Britain, America, and Holland, so far as our material interests are concerned, might most easily and cordially assimilate in their policy and interests,— all Protestant States, little given to impose missionaries upon an Asiatic people, undesirous of territorial acquisitions, and willing upon the whole to be both patient and tolerant of difficulties.  But unfortunately there runs beneath these superficial and apparent elements of combination an under-current of incompatible bases and pretensions.  The Americans have hitherto sought a ' platform ' of their own, as having loftier and less ques-

tionable claims to the full trust and confidence of the
Japanese than any other Powers.   Self-designated as me-
diators, if not protectors, in any differences that may arise
between Japan and the more 'bellicose,' 'unreasonable'
or 'aggressive Powers of the West,' they stand aloof.
This is the more to be regretted, as no two of the great
Western Powers should by identity of interests and
absence of aggressive tendencies, whether as regards
territory, or religious and political propagandism, be
more perfectly united in their course of action, where
Japan is concerned.   Nor could the cordial union of the
two Powers ever be more beneficial to both, and to the
interests of civilisation generally.   The Dutch, too, have
their pretensions of a special claim to good-will, in
their long-enduring relations, and patience under every
form of Japanese oppression in times past.   As the friend
and ally, *par excellence*, Holland is the agent for the
introduction and supply of all European appliances, arms,
ships, engineers, professors, &c.   I do not know that other
Western Powers should see cause of complaint in this,
viewed as a matter of business and a kind of official
agency.   Any tendency to special or exclusive relations,
however, unavoidably militates against a general accord,
which is the common interest ; and in this instance
undoubtedly it imposes on the Dutch the necessity of
standing aside when any question arises against the
Japanese Government, demanding the vigorous assertion
of a treaty right, though that right be the privilege of
all.   These are so many dissolvents preventing any very
close affinity in action or policy.   Russia, with no trade
but a repute for desiring territorial acquisitions, and
France with a protectorate of Roman Catholic missionaries in the Eastern Hemisphere, bring other uncombinable
elements into the alembic ; and thus the Treaty Powers,
isolated each from the other by irreconcilable objects and
lines of action, leave Japanese Rulers a fair field for a
policy directed perseveringly against the progress of all,

whether commerce, territorial acquisition, or religious propagandism, be the main objects in view.

In reference to all the Treaty Powers, and their supposed aims or tendencies, if no aggression be contemplated with territorial acquisitions for the result,— they could probably do nothing more effectually tending to smooth the way for real progress, in the way of commerce and friendly relations, than by a convention among themselves, formally disclaiming all acquisition of Japanese territory, and mutually contracting to abstain from any enterprise with that object or result.

This would dispose at least of one great obstacle to progress—the fears of the Japanese of any attempt to despoil or to subjugate them. The next, or religious element of jealousy, could of course be dealt with somewhat similarly — not quite so effectively, perhaps, from the nature of the enemy they fear, and the intensity of their feelings on the subject. But if the Treaty Powers were disposed to enter into a convention of reciprocal obligation, to abstain from all coercive action or intervention in favour of proselytising efforts on the part of their respective subjects, there can be little doubt it would greatly tend to allay the fears which lie at the foundation of the most implacable hostility. And by so much it would smooth the way for more friendly and cordial relations—on the maintenance of which must depend progress by peaceable means. For, let it not be forgotten that, beyond the limits of Western Europe, as has been truly said, the results which we understand by progress and civilisation, are neither desired nor understood. Whatever *aims* at these under the stipulations of a treaty it may safely be affirmed, therefore, *can only be a cause of distrust and an element of disturbance.* If progress and civilisation follow, as doubtless they will, if not injudiciously put out of their place and natural order — follow as the necessary attendants of commerce when this is in the hands of a Christian people, then will they come gradually to be understood and *in the end desired*; and not civilisation only, but a true religion also may

find its place, and take an ever enlarging field within
its fold.

But so long as treaties with Western Powers are not the
spontaneous acts of the Rulers of an Asiatic people, but forced
upon them,—it matters little whether by what is called
moral pressure or rifled guns, the reality of force is there
—and the vice of their origin will follow them to the end.
They can never be maintained in their integrity, save by
a command of the same means as those to which they
owed their birth.  Politicians and philanthropists therefore
who are opposed on principle to resort to coercion under
any circumstances, either for the advance of Trade,
Civilisation, or Religion, should be no parties to treaties
entered into with Eastern nations by Western Powers.

The relations established, I repeat, are all compulsory in
the first instance; and so long continue after the visible
compelling power has disappeared.  But to expect to
be able continuously to compel, without resorting to
the means of compulsion, is a simple absurdity.  All that
can be hoped is, that with the aid of time, patience, and
an honest desire to avoid all open or unnecessary appeal
to force, the necessity for its application in any material
shape will gradually diminish, and finally disappear.

There are fundamental conditions of all intercourse
inherent in the nature of things, and whatever may
be the special circumstances modifying their action,
they will still prevail in their integrity.  If treaties
of amity and commerce are entered into, they must be
maintained, if not by good faith on the part of the Eastern,
then by fear, and respect for the means of compulsion at
command.  For it were better a thousand times for them
and for us — for all the nations of the West alike, to
abandon them altogether, than sit down tamely acquiescent
under the flagrant and continuous violation of treaties—or
beat the air with idle complaints, and protests equally vain.
Submission to a wrong in Eastern States acts invariably
as a provocation to farther injury, until outrages multiply
and become intolerable to the most patient or pusilla-

nimous; and then war in its worst shape follows as a necessity,—a war, which carries devastation in the midst of unoffending populations at great cost both to the assailants and the country attacked, and from which a Western Power can reap neither glory nor profit.

The extension and free developement of commerce, without costly armaments of war, being the avowed and sole object of our treaties, it would be very important if we could determine, with some degree of certainty, under what conditions and to what extent it may be possible to attain this end in the far East? To secure new markets without danger of collision or risk of interruption, is the dream of Manchester and the hope of our manufacturing interests generally. But, although commerce shuns the evils of a belligerent condition, there is no doubt that in practice it often provokes the contests which it deprecates in theory. It has been said, with more or less of truth, that the appeal to physical force lies in the background in all national affairs, just as there is no law which does not rest on some force to give it effect. And if these axioms find illustrations of their truth but too often in the West, it may safely be concluded our treaties in the East will not be examples of the converse, or prove exceptions in any sense. It is manifest, that where force is habitually resorted to in questions between different races and Powers, as it assuredly is over the whole of the East; and where force, therefore, becomes the final arbiter, a corresponding obligation is imposed upon those Western nations who enter into treaties with them, to make themselves respected. For, without an appeal to unvarying experience, it must be clear that ' a nation which shows it cannot easily be trifled with, is in a much better position, *cæteris paribus*, than one with which liberties may be taken without fear of punishment.'

' Mankind,' it has been said, ' is going through a great fusion. It is being made one, not by conquest, not by the spread of a creed, but by the interchange of commodities.' Tested by actual experience, I am afraid, however,

this conclusion holds good only in a very qualified sense.
It may be true that commerce and the material wants
which it supplies, are among the most effective agencies at
work in the present day for the civilisation of the world
and the fusion of races.   For if the most barbarous and
the least advanced in mental culture or refinement, have
but few wants or appetites, the demand for their satisfaction is imperious and vehement, in strict proportion to the
smallness of the number.   Wants, on the other hand,
multiply with culture, and with civilisation ; they grow
by what they feed upon ; and are thus the best friends to
commerce.   But these however numerous, and their name
is legion, are more or less artificial in their origin, and
can only be called necessities in a very *conventional* way.
A public lecturer, not long ago, began by gravely announc-
ing as a *fact*, that ' ornamental art was a necessity of man's
nature.'   It is hard to say, then, what may not be considered a necessity ; but it may safely be concluded
that such necessities as these bear no comparison, as to
cogency, with the primary wants of less civilised
races.   Tea and coffee, in time, become very like
necessities to a whole population ; but less than three
centuries ago, neither was known in Europe ; — and I
suspect they might again be dispensed with, after an effort
perhaps, without any material diminution of the sum
of human happiness.   Partly because, at the state of civilisation we have now reached, the ingenuity of man would
find many substitutes in the whole range of the vegetable
kingdom, abounding, as it does, in stimulants and narco-
tics (and such, with all deference to teatotallers, most
unquestionably are these two favourite beverages of the
valetudinarian and the virtuous) ; and secondly, because,
in default, there are still a thousand other sources of
enjoyment and consolation to fall back upon.   But the
semi-civilised Oriental and Malay races have no such
resources.   Neither mind nor body has been so developed
as to enable them to find pleasure and occupation in an
infinite variety of ways.   As I have already said, the

only wants of which they are conscious are few, and imperious in proportion. For the supply of these Commerce is made welcome, opposed though it be by religious or political creeds of antagonistic tendencies, which would otherwise prohibit all interchange of thought *or* merchandise. Thus, and so far, it is true, as the writer I quoted in the beginning implies, commerce in our day is a great promoter of fusion and civilisation.

In past ages, nations were only brought in contact, and any fusion effected by Conquest. Then came the influence of Religious creeds, which often perfected what the sword of conquest began, but could not complete,— the fusion of different races. And last in the order of time, is Commerce. The tendency of the present day is nevertheless, I conceive, to attribute more to this agency of commerce, than often properly belongs to it. Like the Armstrong gun, it is very potent and far reaching, but there is much it does not, and *cannot* effect. It does little more, in truth, than open the way, predisposing men's minds to friendly intercourse and the interchange both of ideas and products ; and if on one side there be great superiority of mind and civilisation, progress in the higher order of ideas *may* be both rapid and great.

It has been very truly observed, however, in speaking of such progress, that one of the chief difficulties in the way arises from the want of pliability and flexibility, ' the deficient facility of accommodation to new circumstances, which belongs to a low state of intelligence and education.' What the king wrote to Lord Baltimore in the early days of colonisation in America, is especially applicable to the efforts we are making to spread our commerce and civilisation in Japan :—' New plantations have commonly rugged and laborious beginnings.' And in connection with the whole of this part of the subject, I cannot help quoting here one or two passages from M. de Tocqueville's Correspondence, which have a singularly just application to the influence and position of foreigners at the present day in Japan, though it is a country which was scarcely dreamed of, when the talented writer penned the letter in which it occurs to Mr. Reeve. He is speak-, ing, however, of European settlers in the East, when he observes—

'J'ai toujours remarqué que partout où on introduisait, non des chefs européens, mais une population européenne au sein des populations imparfaitement civilisées du reste du monde, la supériorité réelle et prétendue de la première sur les secondes se faisait sentir d'une façon si blessante pour les intérêts individuels et si mortifiante pour l'amour propre des indigènes, qu'il en résultait plus de colère que d'aucune oppression politique. Si cela est vrai pour presque toutes les races européennes, à combien plus forte raison cela est-il vrai de la race anglaise, la plus habile à exploiter à son profit les avantages de chaque pays, la moins liante, la plus disposée à se tenir à part, et (on peut le dire parceque ce défaut s'unit intimement à de grandes qualités) la plus altière de toutes les races européennes.'

He then goes on to say, as between Europeans and the Eastern races, that 'La civilisation et la race mettaient une si grande différence, que l'un s'apercevait à chaque instant que, non seulement il n'était pas l'égal, mais qu'il n'était pas *le semblable* de l'autre.'

And, finally, still referring to the same subject, in a letter to Lord Hatherton, he remarks, with admirable justness and power of discrimination:—'Une race inférieure par sa constitution ou son éducation peut bien supporter le gouvernement d'une race supérieure. Elle ne ressent que les bons effets de cette supériorité, et si le gouvernement est habile, elle peut le préférer à celui même de ses princes; mais le voisinage d'un particulier plus civilisé, plus riche, plus influent, plus habile que lui, ne peut manquer d'être un objet de haine et d'envie à l'indigène d'une race inférieure. Le gouvernement étranger ne blesse que les sentiments nationaux qui sont faibles. Le colon étranger blesse ou semble blesser de mille manières les intérêts particuliers qui sont chers à tous les

hommes.   On croit toujours qu'il abuse de sa supériorité,
de ses lumières, de sa fortune et de son crédit pour faire
de bonnes affaires et s'enrichir aux dépens de ses voisins,
et de toutes ces petites haines particulières la haine
nationale s'accroît infiniment.'

Such are a few of the difficulties opposing that progress of the higher order of ideas which the sanguine
and the theoretical would fain hope to see realised in the
intercourse now maintained between the Western and
Eastern peoples ; — but the history and the experience of
the past, it must be confessed, are very far from bearing
out such hopes.

The Japanese borrowed from China its ideographic language, and with it the Confucian philosophy,— a great deal
of the literature, and finally the Buddhist religion.   They
entered into commerce, each supplying to the other products in request.   And yet, despite all these pledges and
guarantees for peace, the history of both countries shows a
chronic state of war and antagonism, which can only be
compared to that existing so many centuries between
France and England.   Genghis Khan fitted out a great
armada for the conquest of Japan.   The Japanese,
aided by their iron-bound coast and stormy seas, repulsed it, and retorted by a century of aggressive
descents on the Chinese coast, and attempts to conquer Corea.   Thus it often happens, that a higher
order of civilisation, and commerce itself, are met
and checked in their progress by a hostile phalanx
of prejudices, interests, traditions, customs, and very
often religious creeds ; — and these supported by much
of the intelligence and all the strength and power of the
ruling classes.   They feel with a true instinct, that commerce never comes singly, but brings new elements of
thought in its train, and forms a wedge which will force
asunder the most compact structure, if not resisted at
the very beginning, and cast out.   And that which
begins by a conflict of ideas, ends almost invariably, and
it would seem inevitably, either by a war of conquest, or,

by civil convulsion and bloodshed among the natives. Such has been the history of all our relations with the East. We begin in perfect good faith by seeking only the interchange of commodities; and flatter ourselves that civilisation and the blessings of a true religion will follow, peaceably and naturally in the track of commerce. But here theory and practice, hope and experience, are woefully at issue. And for once it would be well, perhaps, to allow experience to have its weight;—for hope only deludes while the other enlightens and warns.

In the moral as in the physical, it would seem as if a process of disintegration formed the necessary preliminary condition to any new combination or radical change of form. The new product, whatever it may be, is only the result of much effervescence and decomposition, during which some dangerous elements are set free; while others, which served to give stability and body, evaporate and disappear. Powerful solvents come into operation, and the most destructive agencies are evolved in full activity. Thus all revolutions, social and political, generally are inaugurated; and commerce proceeding from the West to the East, is an agent of revolutionary character, however little the merchant may wish to make it so, or however much governments desire to prevent it. The cold blast by which iron ore is fused at a white heat, to a liquid mass of purified metal to be cast into a new form for the use and benefit of man, is not more fierce or irresistible in its action, than the processes by which two different civilisations and races are commingled and fused into a new phase of national life and developement. And the interests of the trader are powerless to prevent the disturbing and destroying processes by which alone the end is attained. The merchant may prostrate himself before the Eastern Juggernaut, in the vain hope of propitiating, or he may shriek and gesticulate his anger and despair; but the wheels of social and political change still roll on their course unheeding, and either crush or cast aside whatever lies in their way. The movement which commerce originates, all the commerce and the merchants in the world are unable to stop, until it has run its destined course. I have little faith in the milder and more gradual processes, sometimes vaunted as all-efficient to avert these evils. I see no examples in past history of the mingling of two different forms of civilisation — a higher and a lower — by the simple interchange of ideas and commerce. While, on the contrary, I see every-where, and in all ages, collision and conflict following, wherever the commercial wedge has effected an entrance, out of the range of European or kindred nationalities and institutions. Whether this is to be traced to some ever prevailing vice or weakness in the superior race seeking only its own ends, and not always very holy ones, — or qualities inherent in the body to be experimented upon, may be a question, and one admitting of much discussion. But so far as practical results are concerned, I fear it matters very little whatever conclusion might be come to. Still commerce will push its way over continents and seas, crying peace ; while war and confusion will as certain follow, when Eastern races are thus brought in sudden contact with new elements of thought, action, and government which they are unable to appreciate and unprepared to accept.*

Considerations such as these unavoidably present them-selves when the present state and future prospects of an Eastern people so long secluded and isolated as the Japa-nese have been are being discussed. Among the chief difficulties which beset the paths of commerce in these Eastern regions, there is yet one more that must not be passed over ; for although of less magnitude and impor-tance than those already examined, it still forms a very preg-nant source of danger, and adds no inconsiderable tributary

---

* The commencement of social and revolutionary changes, which the last mails from Japan announce, form a significant commentary on the above lines, which were written more than a year ago, while I was yet in the country.

stream, flowing into and deepening all the main channels of those waters of strife which obstruct our progress. The difficulty I allude to originates in the 'rowdy' and disreputable element which universally finds entrance with treaties and commerce, in Japan—as everywhere else in the Eastern seas when the former have opened new markets. The absence of any system of efficient control over all foreigners alike, whatever their nationality, if found in the country and bringing Europeans generally into disrepute by disorderly or dishonest conduct, is an ever-fruitful source of mischief. Such specimens of our civilisation there always are — ill-conditioned and unscrupulous adventurers claiming the benefits only to be secured by the maintenance of treaties, while they violate all the provisions. Sometimes there are subjects of Powers which have no treaties whatever with Japan, while in others a right of residence exists, but there is either no Consul to take cognisance of their acts, or none willing and with adequate means to deal efficiently with the cases which arise. To stipulate for a right of admission into a country like Japan, where the Sovereign has been stripped of his territorial jurisdiction by a clause of exterritoriality, and then leave him exposed to the outrages and disorders which lawless Europeans may at their pleasure commit, or without giving ample security against such license and gross abuse of treaty rights, can only be regarded by the Japanese in one of two lights. Either as an indication of indifference on the part of the Treaty Powers collectively, to whatever evil or humiliation we may bring upon them provided we attained our own end; or as an admission of incompetence to deal with an evil, which I have no hesitation in saying is both serious and discreditable. Were it only the spectacle daily given at the open ports, of drunken sailors reeling about and often committing actsof violence, as such men will when they are drunk, we should have much to regret. And this is no the least of our difficulties, for the sailors of men-of-war of the different nations, I am sorry to say, are no exception, and furnish their full contingent. Yet men cannot, especially after a long voyage, be kept for weeks in port close prisoners in their ships. So that the difficulties are neither few nor easily to be met. In China I have known three or four ruffians of a Western race, armed with revolvers and bowie knives, put a whole district under a levy of black mail by the terror they inspired; aided by an impudent assumption of authority to collect taxes!

There is no doubt that here, as in so many other cases, the omission to do what is right ourselves, is to sign a blank commission to others to do what is wrong; and in the present instance, the Treaty Powers find it lays a stumbling-block on the threshold of all negotiations, and until it is removed the ablest negotiators will work in vain. It lies, in truth, full in the pathway of all successful efforts for obtaining practically enlarged facilities for intercourse, and any access into the interior. Nor, while these abuses exist, can Foreign Powers pretend to deserve that there should be any such increased facilities. Good faith on our part in giving effect to treaty stipulations, with all the obligations they impose, is and ought to be the first condition of any effort urged upon the Japanese to perform theirs. A very solemn obligation has been accepted by every Treaty Power claiming for its subjects the privilege of exterritoriality,—to provide, at whatever cost or trouble, *adequate* means for performing the duty thus assumed of preserving the peace, repressing all lawless violence and illegalities, and rigorously punishing the offenders. How lamentably and persistently this has been disregarded in many instances in the Chinese and Japanese Seas by Western Powers is, unfortunately, too notorious to require farther evidence. But how fatal the neglect has been to the wrong and prejudice of the Chinese more especially, or how seriously the best interests of civilisation and commerce have been compromised in consequence, I feel it must be difficult to give any adequate idea to those who have not lived in the country and had opportunities of marking the effects. Fortunately, we can only be re-proached with wrongs of a less grievous kind in Japan. But little credit is due to foreigners for this result— since it is partly owing to our more restricted inter-course, and partly also to the fact, that there is an armed class quite capable of avenging on the spot any wrong or violence done them; and only too ready to find even a bad pretext for shedding the blood of a foreigner, and casting him out of the country dead or alive.

If Western nations are to maintain any relations of amity then with this people, there would seem a great necessity for some common basis of action. But as I have elsewhere observed, in this lies the main difficulty. Yet there are many grounds of mutual accord; and even where ultimate divergence may be more or less unavoidable, the causes are still in the germ, as it were, and many years will be required for their developement. In the interval there is a common interest in the progress of a civilising intercourse, which might serve as a bond of union; and some of those rivalries or antagonisms which loom in the future, may possibly melt and disappear with time and the march of improvement in all international relations. If the Japanese could be strong enough to assert and main-tain independence, and its rulers become sufficiently en-lightened to enter frankly into the family of civilised nations, acknowledging all the obligations which are held to be binding among these, the dark and lowering clouds now covering the horizon might be dispersed without a storm.*  It is the obvious interest of all Western

---

* Since this chapter was written, I have read a contribution to the 'North China Herald,' from a writer in whose knowledge of the Japanese language and long residence in the country, there is a certain guarantee for correctness of information. As this letter contains much interesting speculation on the present state of political affairs in Japan, and some details on matters of fact well worthy of consideration, I have given it a place in the Appendix (see Appendix G.), without, however, adopting the conclu-sions of the writer.

Powers having no other object than the extension of trade and civilisation, to promote such an issue out of existing dangers and difficulties. In this direction, indeed, lies our best hope of a peaceful and a general beneficial solution.

Existing relations are based on a fiction of exterritoriality, which assumes that the laws and executive power of Foreign Governments are in full force on the soil of Japan, as regards all foreigners, and effectually supply the place of the laws of the country, making adequate provision for the preservation of the peace and the repression of crime. But the right of exemption from the law of Japan is alone a reality, the other condition of the exterritoriality clause is too much a fiction.

A Government that undertakes what it does not perform, and which is either unwilling or unable to protect foreigners from insult or massacre, when these come to reside within its territories, on the faith of treaties, as we have recently seen at Jeddah, in the Red Sea, in Morocco, and in Japan, must bear the consequences of its own bad faith or imbecility. Because to hold such Governments free from responsibility upon any principle of Christian forbearance or political expediency, is to take away the best check on crime ; if not the only security for life and property in such countries. In other words, it is to render residence impossible, all developement of trade a delusion, and amicable relations or civilising intercourse alike impracticable. But, on the other hand, if it be impossible with Eastern races, still in their infancy as regards any knowledge of international rights, or the reciprocal obligations of treaties, to entrust the lives and property of foreigners to the Territorial Sovereign and the administration of justice prevalent in the country without some safeguard, such as the fiction of exterritoriality has invented, it specially behoves each treaty power to provide adequate means of its own on the spot, to do justice and maintain order.   There is a French proverb about the wisdom of not running after two hares at once, strongly inculcating the folly of attempting to compass two objects perfectly incompatible.   For conciliation to have its proper fruit, we must be just then in performing our part of the contract; and that forbearance may not provoke aggression, we must show determination to insist upon good faith towards the foreigner in return.   With due regard to both these conditions, will any amount of tact and forbearance bring Eastern rulers and the subjects they govern, to observe the stipulations of treaties forced upon them by Western Powers?

If we could really hope that anything approaching a perfect fulfillment of such conditions were possible, and not on the part of one Western Power, but of all equally, then indeed there would be solid ground to rest upon.   It is the want of combination of the two in just proportions, and the equal adoption by all the Foreign Powers of these principles, which constitute the main difficulty of dealing with Eastern races in the present day.   Every divergence in word or action among the Treaty Powers of the West, where the objects and interests are all ostensibly and professedly the same, is an element of weakness to them and of strength to the Eastern rulers.   Naturally distrustful of all western nations, and attaching little faith to mere words or the phraseology of treaties, they seek to read in the policy and action of each, a truer indication of real objects.   It no less naturally follows, attributing, as they do, a far greater degree of *solidarité* in the European family than really belongs to it, that they seize upon a dissidence as an Old Bailey lawyer pounces upon a discrepancy or a contradiction among the witnesses for the accused, and proceed to condemn without hesitation on the faith of it.   No doubt any principle of firmness and resistance to wrong, carries with it a contingency of war.   But, on the other hand, unlimited concession and submission is even more dangerous, and directly tends to war by encouraging in an Eastern race intolerable and increasing aggressions.  And although we may talk of retiring altogether, and abandoning treaty rights as not worth the cost of fighting for them,—or relinquishing trade and commercial privileges, because it is against our principles to adopt coercive means for their protection — when has a Western Power ever receded from Eastern ground on such pleas?  When has trade ever receded before the danger of collision, and the necessity of strife or war to cover its operations?  We sometimes hear, it is true, of such principles being put forward in the name of trading communities, and sometimes in higher places; but where is the Chamber of Commerce, at Manchester or elsewhere, that will endorse the policy—with the probability of its being really carried into effect by the Government in power?  On the contrary, did not the 'Times,' apropos to the last act of butchery in Japan, where a party of defenceless residents were cut down on the high road,—with its usual power of discrimination as to the tides and currents of national feeling, much more nearly approach the truth when it said, ' Some people turn away with impatience and disgust when they hear that another act of violence has been committed in Japan; others thoughtlessly cry out that we should keep away from places where there are factions, or robber princes, or individual ruffians, who render our presence insecure? All this is the impatience of ignorance or the cry of cowardice.  It is not thus we act in our own country, nor is it by giving up every enterprise directly it developes a danger that we have made England the great banyan tree of commerce and civilisation spreading over all the world. Little difficulties with uncivilised nations bound to us by treaty obligations will ever be as much a matter of course as lawsuits at Westminster, or police cases at Bow-street. This outrage must not pass unpunished.  If it be necessary

for the peace of this country to break down the power of
these robber chiefs, it must be done.'

The proposal to abandon a field of enterprise — a new
market for our trade, would no doubt be branded by the
mass of the nation as ' the impatience of ignorance, or the
cry of cowardice.' It is truly not thus we act, or ever have
acted, in this country. Only when the ' Times' speaks of
' little difficulties with uncivilised states bound to us by
treaty obligations,' in a lofty way, treating them as
matters of course, as much as ' lawsuits at Westminster,
or police cases at Bow-street,' it behoves us not to be
led away by such pleasant rhetoric. These ' little' difficulties arising perpetually with 130 millions of Asiatics
in India, 300 millions in China, or even a small 30
millions in Japan, make gigantic items in our national
budget; and constitute, in fact, some of the gravest
problems for the Statesman. The cost of wars, and
the growth of commerce — the first a heavy source of
taxation, and the second a main source of the wealth and
power of Great Britain — are all involved in these ' little
difficulties ' and the questions they suggest. It is many
years now since Mr. Gladstone, with the high authority
which attaches to his name, declared that we were
' more dependent than any other great people upon
external trade for the employment of our population.'
And the truth of the axiom only becomes greater and
more manifest each succeeding year. Trade is to our
national life what air is to the physical—a vital element
—a necessity, not a luxury—a thing we cannot dispense
with if we would, and must even fight for, if it is not
otherwise to be secured in the abundant measure our
ever-expanding lungs require. We cannot help trade
being paradoxical. It wants peace and security for its
developement—it cannot long last without such conditions of growth and well-being. But precisely because
this is a necessity of its existence, it imposes upon the
nation which profits by the wealth and power it brings
in its train, the onerous obligation of defending it from

all enemies. We must thus often fight first, and find the means, by taxation afterwards, of paying the costs of a war.

It is not that I am advocating a belligerent policy in the abstract, or desire to see hostile measures adopted in Japan to meet existing difficulties. The decision of a policy rests with other and higher powers, and, probably, no one of the staunchest advocates for peace and conciliation as our only weapons, would more deeply lament than I should do, the necessity, if such should arise, of a resort to arms in our dealings with the Japanese. I am merely concerned in pointing out the necessities and exigencies which must inevitably govern the action of Western diplomacy, whatever be the effort to control them or the desire to adopt a different course. The trade present or prospective in Japan may not be worth all it will cost to keep the ports open under treaties — and perhaps I might be the first to rejoice if it were determined to give it up. But my personal views, be they what they may, to the expediency of this or any other policy, have really nothing whatever to do with the question as I am now discussing it. I am endeavouring to ascertain and clearly state the *principles* on which we ought to act if we are to be either consistent or successful in pursuit of a plain end, about which there is and need be no disguise, that end being with us mainly, if not exclusively, trade and facilities for reasonable expansion and developement. The application of those principles and the choice of means to the end, I leave to the discretion and conscience of each individual. The principles, in so far as they are logical deductions from true premisses, will remain, whatever views may be entertained or policy adopted as to their application. It may be an indisputable truth, that ' war cannot be carried on with rose water,' and I believe it to be equally true that treaties are not to be maintained with Eastern rulers on whom they have been imposed against their will — by diplomacy, or protocols, unless these are known to be backed by something more irresistible.   But I do not feel any more responsible for this, than the author of the first truism could be held answerable for the necessary conditions of war.   On the contrary, to all who do not like war, it is clear, he who publicly announces in advance its true and inevitable conditions should be held the best friend of peace, since if anything would deter nations—only nothing ever does— from rushing into wars, it would be the full knowledge and clear perception of their cost.   I am only concerned here, therefore, with the problem as I find it.   Our commerce feeds a vital want—we seek trade, therefore, everywhere, although it is not without its risks and expenses.   We seek new and ever-expanding markets, to meet our ever-increasing wants and powers of production, and these seem to lie principally in the far East, and there we naturally, if not inevitably, go.*   Our first step is to obtain access by treaties to the markets they present.   The Native Powers being little disposed to enter into negotiations, we bring to bear the only effective means — pressure, and gain the document, which purports to give all the rights and facilities for trade required.   But one step more remains, and the end is ours.   The treaty has to be reduced to practice and made a working reality.   Unluckily, this is the principal, nothing having been farther from the intention of *one* of the contracting parties than such a result.   We are forcibly reminded of the courtier's dilemma in the play of 'Cinderella.'   In despair at the difficulty of finding a fit for the dainty but vacant slipper, he tries it first on one foot and then the other of the beauties, until at last, finding one smaller than the rest, he exclaims with joy, 'It is all in — except the heel!'

---

* I say these *seem* to lie principally in the East, but it may admit of question whether under existing antagonisms of race and differences of habits and wants — our most hopeful field for increased consumption really lies eastward.   The whole of our import trade with Eastern countries, even including India, is far inferior in amount to that which exists with one or two countries of the West, having a kindred civilisation and similar wants, real or artificial.   The United States for instance, which in one year took over 20,000,000*l.* of our manufactures.   Our colonies, again, are far more certain markets than China or Japan can ever be in the present generation.

A hard case ; for no shoehorn of smoothest ivory, or flattering words of the most refined courtier, will evidently get this recalcitrant heel into the slipper.

That is just the difficulty to be solved by diplomacy in the East—'the true point of difficulty,' as the Bonze replied to the Abbé Huc, who had expounded the cause of the want 'of faith and funds in China.' 'Your marvellous intelligence has seized the true point of difficulty.' But, until the heel *is* in, and some means, persuasive or forcible, shall have been found to accomplish that end, all the treaties and protocols in the world are little better than waste paper, or the title-deeds to an estate in Chancery—possession of which is the subject of litigation.

If, now, having considered what are the chief difficulties in the way of commerce, and any fusion of races or amalgamation of rival civilisations, we attempt to sum up the whole argument as furnishing principles of action — rather than a specific policy to be shaped out in their application,—I think that, with a clear conception of what are ' the essential conditions of all Western Diplomacy in the far East,' no less than ' the necessities and exigencies which govern its action,' the reader will have little difficulty in himself defining ' the limits within which we may reasonably look for success, and the conditions essential to any.'

There must, we have seen, be means of coercion in the background, and to this must be added the known *will and power* to resort to them—if all other means fail to secure the honest fulfilment of the stipulations of Treaties. This implies a possible contingency of collision and war, but if there be firmness and discretion in the employment of such means of diplomacy, there is the best chance, which circumstances admit, of avoiding the actual resort to force, or any overt acts of compulsion.

With such a policy firmly and consistently carried out, much of forbearance and patience may find profitable exercise. Too much precipitation, or wnat of judgement and temper, are just as much to be deprecated as timidity or vacillation and inconsistency. The one means war, and the other such a rapid deterioration and accumulation of wrong as must inevitably lead to one of two results: the destruction of all trade and treaty rights, or a crushing and more destructive war than otherwise might have been required to vindicate and maintain them.

Within the limits of a policy thus conducted, seeking only peace and the establishment of a mutually advantageous commerce as the end; and desiring of all things the avoidance of coercive means in the grosser forms of menace and war, success in some cases may be possible, though it can hardly be either absolute or complete. The traditions of a race cannot be eradicated, neither can national customs, habits, and modes of thought or action be wholly changed in one generation. Such a sweeping transmutation has never yet been seen in the history of the world, least of all can it be looked for in Oriental races over the face of Asia, which present the type of immobility and fixity in striking contrast to the spirit of progress and unrest which marks the descendants of Japhet, and more especially the modern offspring of Europe and its civilisation.

We must be prepared, therefore, whatever course may be followed, for many and persistent grounds of complaint on both sides—not wholly unfounded as regards either. If the Oriental is slow to yield and reluctant to change, the European is no less apt to be rash and aggressive in his spirit of innovation, especially where his interests are at stake. All that we might claim will not be attained— all that we owe to Eastern Governments and people will hardly be rendered; but, in the midst of these and many other drawbacks to perfectly friendly relations, there seems a possibility of a practical solution which may be accepted as satisfactory by both parties—as satisfactory, that is, as either party can hope, by any immediate action, to secure. Trade will be established and develope itself—prosperity and intelligence will grow under its influence, by a more gradual process, it is true, than the more sanguine could desire in the West, and somewhat quicker than Rulers in the East could wish, but that is unavoidable. The essential seems to be, that changes mutually beneficial, and preparing the way for a fusion of ideas and interests, *shall* ultimately take place. And those who come after us will probably see more clearly than we can now, that, tardy and halting as may have been the steps, no quicker or better line could have been advantageously followed with such antagonistic elements to contend against.

## CHAPTER XVI.

ARRANGEMENTS FOR THE DEPARTURE OF THE JAPANESE MISSION
TO THE COURTS OF THE SEVERAL TREATY POWERS IN EUROPE—
EMBARKATION ON BOARD H.M.S. 'ODIN'—CLOSE OF 1861—TRADE
OF THE YEAR AND COMMERCIAL PROSPECTS FOR THE INCOMING
YEAR OF 1862.

TOWARDS the close of 1861, it became necessary to make final arrangements for the departure of the Japanese Mission nominated by the Tycoon to represent him at the Courts of the several Sovereigns in Europe, with whom he had entered into treaty. H.M.S. 'Odin,' a fine frigate under the command of Commodore Lord John Hay, had been specially fitted up for the reception of the Japanese Ministers and their suite. The first difficulty was to reduce the number of these within any reasonable limits. When a Mission was sent to the United States the year preceding, they had been allowed to take any number they chose, and consequently, some eighty-four in all, I believe, had been accommodated on board the frigate conveying them to the American coast. Such a number, however, would not only have entailed great inconvenience during the passage, but have been still more objectionable in the long journeys to be made across the whole breadth of Europe, in passing from one country to another. It would have caused great superfluous expense to the respective Governments, and been a source of endless trouble and embarrassment to the several Courts where they were accredited. We had undertaken to convey them at our own charge to England ; the French Government agreeing in like manner to find transport for them back—but the travelling to Berlin,

St. Petersburg, the Hague, and Lisbon, would have to be arranged after their arrival in Europe. The precedent of the mission to America rendered my task additionally difficult and delicate, from the danger of appearing to wish to curtail the establishment they might have been led to think necessary to maintain their dignity, but which really had nothing to do with it. This I endeavoured to prove by enumerating to them the ordinary suite of Ministers and Ambassadors from the greatest Powers in Europe; while on the other hand, I described to them the incessant anxiety and trouble a number of helpless subordinates and servants would constantly occasion to the Ministers themselves, and those whose business it would be to make their residence at the different courts agreeable. Upon the whole, they were not unreasonable, and seemed fully persuaded in the end that I had both their proper dignity and their comfort equally at heart. Accordingly after the long hours required to possess them fully with the necessary information, some of the more useless of the subordinates were eliminated to the number of one half, and finally reduced to thirty-five in all,—an Envoy Extraordinary and Plenipotentiary, two Ministers Plenipotentiary, accompanied by thirty-two subordinate officers and servants — secretaries, ometskys, doctors, accountants, cooks, and barbers! But when this was effected we were only at the beginning of our troubles. As the period of their departure approached, the necessity for precise information as to the quantity of baggage, and of provisions fitted for a Japanese palate, became more urgent, while the difficulty of obtaining it only seemed to increase, as each day brought them nearer the date fixed for their embarkation. Then there was the question of sleeping appliances. A whole suite of cabins had been arranged for them by Lord John Hay with sliding panels, papered with Japanese patterns, and as innocent of furniture as their own reception rooms. Our advice to them was, to sleep either on a matted floor, as was their custom, or in cots, that could be removed by day, without lumbering their cabins.  But they finally decided on having bunks put up.  Nothing could have been more liberal or considerate than the arrangements as to space, &c., made for their comfort by the Commodore.  The whole of the main deck had been given up to their use.  The Ministers and superior officers were provided for abaft the main-mast, and the subordinates and servants forward.  To each set of cabins there were two or three bath-rooms, with moveable heating apparatus, on the Italian plan of a double tube and central heater.  A pantry also, and place for the storage of all their crockery and stores for daily consumption were attached to each class of cabins; for I should say they began by sending on board fifty crockery teapots, an immense supply of soy in five hundred champagne bottles; then a service of five porcelain cups for every individual, with saucers innumerable to answer for plates.  There were also some fifty *Hebachis*, or vessels for burning charcoal and warming the rooms, corresponding with the Spanish *Brazeiro*.  But I heard something about these being all stowed down below in utterly inaccessible places — a needful precaution if the Commodore ever intended to convey them as far as Suez, or arrive there himself, without a conflagration ;—which, by the bye, he did not succeed in doing, though from no fault of the passengers.  Notwithstanding every Japanese, at some time of his life, I suppose, is burnt out of house and home, and certainly lives in constant peril of such a catastrophe, there is no race in the world, perhaps, unless it be the Chinese, more reckless, or utterly devoid of common care and prudence in regard to fire, than they are.  On the fore part of the deck, immediately abaft the windlass, was a moveable kitchen, a galley upon wheels, so that when it was necessary to weigh anchor, it could be shifted ; and into this had been fitted their own cooking apparatus.  The Ministers were very anxious to go on board and see their future home, and, as ill luck would have it, the day chosen was rather boisterous ; the natural consequence of which was that the third Minister gave evident signs of being very miserable, and my old friend Matsudaira, the second Minister, the next time I saw him, was urgent in his entreaties to know if the Western people, who went so much in great ships on the seas, had no medicine or specific against sea-sickness? They were nevertheless much pleased with the imposing size of the ship, and its perfect order, as well as the liberal space and other arrangements made for their accommodation.

Some twenty days, I think, were consumed in launching this ' Great Eastern ' Mission. Many were lost in finding out with what amount of stowage for baggage they could be contented. Then it was necessary to get some of the subordinate members of their suite and servants on board, to remain and accustom themselves to the ship, that they might not be quite useless the first week ; which they proposed to accomplish by the notable scheme of sending on board substitutes ! Really there is a naïveté in some of the propositions of the Japanese, that quite takes one by surprise. To what extent the system of vicarious punishment goes I cannot say with any certainty, but a British merchant one day threatening a Japanese dealer, to whom he had made large sales, that he would complain to the authorities if he was not paid, intimating that imprisonment might follow ; 'Oh!' exclaimed his Japanese debtor, 'you do n't suppose *I* should go to prison—my substitute would go!' Though after all I do not know why we should be so much surprised at this, since not many days ago, precisely the same thing happened in London ; and a convicted offender, sentenced to a fortnight's imprisonment, managed between the police court and the gaol to arrange a substitute.

However, as regarded the motion and geography of a ship, it was quite clear the system of substitutes would not work at all, whatever it might do in trade, and the relations between debtor and creditor ; and so in the end I succeeded in getting some of the real personages caught, and caged on board.

Then the baggage could not be got ready in time, and at the last moment sundry bags of rice were sent on board, contrary to all instructions, in loose sacking, and under conditions which would insure its being all spoilt and useless in a few days.   I began to think they were determined after all to spend their new year in Japan (which did not begin until January 29), and were deliberately planning all these difficulties.   However, on the 20th, having ridden up to Yeddo the day previous, I went to present Lord John Hay and his officers on taking leave, and to my agreeable surprise, and still more, I am sure, to the surprise of the Commodore, the Mission was announced to be ready to embark the next day!   Indeed so much did it take us both by surprise, that I found to my dismay there were various and important matters which must be instantly settled with the Ministers, before the embarkation *could* take place.   They had sent me only at the eleventh hour a copy of credentials, in which they had given no title or rank to their several Ministers ; and had merely recommended each by their names to the good offices of the Queen.   It appeared they had but one name for an Envoy or Ambassador to a foreign court, *Sisetzu*.   Naturally they had no titles in their language to correspond with Envoy Extraordinary, Minister Plenipotentiary, &c., and were slow to understand that unless they adopted these in the letters of credence, or something that could be understood as equivalents, it would be impossible, in the system of European etiquette, to assign them any especial rank ; or to regulate the salutes and other honours to which they would be entitled.   In the end they yielded, convinced of the necessity ; and Takeno Votschie Shemod-Zeno Kami was named Envoy Extraordinary and Minister Plenipotentiary ; Matsudaira Iwamino Kami and Kiogok Notono Kami second and third Ministers Plenipotentiary.   But the amended credentials had to be sent after them, as it was impossible to prepare them in time.   Then there was the question of salutes ; for although they had previously agreed with me to accept frankly, on a principle of perfect

reciprocity, the European system, they had, or pretended
to have, conceived some doubts, from an intervening discussion with the French authorities, as to what they were
undertaking in regard to salutes to the National Flags.
It was too late to enter upon a new discussion, so the
matter was arranged by dividing the subject into two — one
the system of salutes for diplomatic authorities, and the
other for the national flag.  The first they formally accepted, and the second was deferred for farther discussion.
At last even these multifarious difficulties were brought to
a close.  Some trifling presents of arms and silk were
offered to the officers, in token of the Government's gratitude for—'favours yet to come;'—the lively Frenchman's
definition of the only real gratitude to be found in this
world,—and which Lord John Hay was very much disposed to decline.  But as I felt that would at least be a two
hours' work, and we had already been engaged three, I
protested in self-defence, that all the silk in the room was
not worth an hour's discussion, and so with a reluctant
consent they were assigned to their several proprietors,
to be sent on board.

The next day they were to be embarked between one
and two o'clock ; and Mr. Macdonald of the Legation was
sent on board to receive them as their future equerry.
But two o'clock, three o'clock, four o'clock passed and no
salute was heard.  I began to think there was a failure,
when just before dusk set in unmistakeably, the guns of
the 'Odin' boomed across the Bay, and announced that they
were on board!  I now felt perfectly satisfied ; being
very sure they would never get out of the Commodore's
grip while the ' Odin ' was in Japanese waters ; even for an
hour.  Indeed, so anxious was he to secure them and be
off, that, as I afterwards learned, he had performed
Joshua's feat, and put back the sun nearly half an hour
to enable him to give them their salute ; but everybody
knows the sun's progress on the dial on board a man-of-
war is subject to the fiat of the commander ; it may be
noon, or sunset, or eight o'clock, to the rest of the world,

but it cannot be so on board until the word has gone forth — ' make it so ! '

And thus the Japanese Mission took its departure. The next morning, January 23, at the first dawn of day, the ' Odin's ' steam was up, and she was steering down the Bay. Opposite Yokohama the Commodore made a halt of a couple of hours to pick up an unfortunate Interpreter, Ota; who had been designated as needful, and had only received notice of this voyage to the Antipodes during the night; and Ota was as effectually impressed into the service of the Mission, as though a pressgang had been employed. They *can* move sharply and decisively in Japan, when they themselves have made up their minds as to the necessity. A few proofs are as good evidence as a thousand.

The Mission away, I had now little farther to do before taking my own departure on leave, long and anxiously looked forward to, except to wind up some pending affairs, and gather in the trade and other reports for the year just ended. The despatches with my final instructions, it is true, had not yet appeared; but each succeeding day might bring them — they were already long overdue.

The year 1861 had closed, and as the trade reports came in shortly after, I cannot do better here than give a brief summary of their contents, showing the state of foreign commerce at this period, just two years and a half from the opening of the ports, with a few remarks on its prospects. Trade had been nearly limited to the two southern ports, Kanagawa and Nagasaki—the first by far the most important. As to Hakodadi in the north, nothing deserving the name of trade had been found possible, and at this time not a single British merchant or agent was left on the spot, nor of residents of any other nation, who could really be placed in the category of merchants.

Kanagawa enjoys the lion's share of the infant trade, and despite all the multifarious impediments, small and great, which the artificial system and natural obstructiveness of Japanese officials create, it appeared at the end of

1861, after a thirty months' trial, to be thriving fairly. In round numbers it gave employment to about one hundred vessels in the year and was worth a million sterling, of which more than half was carried in British vessels, and considerably more, probably, on British account, as two of the largest American ships among those loaded were despatched to London.

The import trade increased in 1861 some thirty per cent., from 197,023*l*. to 307,981*l*. ; but there was a corresponding decrease in the exports, for in 1860 they were estimated at 823,812*l*., and in 1861 only at 558,948*l*., taking both at a low rate of 4*s*. 2*d*. for the exchange of the dollar, to which, however, from ten to twenty per cent. might fairly be added as the current value of this coin at the port.

The export trade, which began with bulky articles — edibles chiefly for the Chinese market — employed more shipping in 1860, but it settled down in the last year to a more valuable trade if less bulky in its staples. The chief exports being these last years tea and silk, both of which realised well, but more especially the former, taken up eagerly to supply deficiencies in the supply of China green teas. Rags for paper furnished cargo for three ships, and, at first, were said to have realised a large profit. Unfortunately the reverse proved to be the correct version. Had it been otherwise, the vexed problem of a supply of rags might have been considered settled, so far as an unlimited quantity was concerned, for all China and Japan produce rags in abundance, and consume none in the manufacture of their paper or anything else. The only question was, whether they could be made to cover the extra cost of freight; and that unfortunately seemed to be settled in the negative.

Among the imports the only novelty was an attempt to supply raw cotton and cotton yarns to the Japanese, and after a little attempt to shut both out as 'unenumerated articles' by a prohibitive duty of twenty per cent., I succeeded as regarded the yarns in removing the obstacle,

and getting them received at five per cent.  Since which
they have held their place among the imports to the
extent of some 2,500 piculs of 133 lbs. valued at 15,291*l.*
Among the curiosities of imports, I find duly entered two
tigers !— upon which I fancy a larger profit was realised
than on any other article in the tables.  Worth about *$*100
in the Straits, they sold here to Japanese for purposes of
exhibition for three or four thousand.  And in this, as in
other things, the appetite appeared to grow by indulgence,
for the tigers led to an order for a brace of elephants.
But even here, as in all other novelties, there was an impediment in the first instance to be got over on the part of
the Japanese authorities, and the following story was in
circulation: — Whether they objected because tigers were
not in 'the tariff,' or on some other equally valid
ground, certain it is they did object, and, as the im-
porter was a Dutch subject, it became a matter of
discussion with the Dutch Consul, who solved the difficulty with great readiness.  When the Japanese Custom
House and the Consul seemed to have come to a dead-
lock, the question arose, what was to be done with the
article?  The Custom House would not pass it, the ship
could not take it back—what was to be done with the
beautiful beast?  'Oh, very well,' said the Consul, seeing
it was time to make a last stroke for his countryman's
merchandise ; 'since you say it is impossible to allow it
to be entered and sold, there is nothing left but for the
merchant to lose his money and let the beast out.'  'Let it
loose !' exclaimed the officials, in various tones of horror
and dismay, 'why, it will eat us all up !'  'Really, I do n't
know ; perhaps he is not very hungry ;—but, in any case,
I cannot compel the merchant to keep him.'  It is superfluous to add, that all interdict on his sale was soon removed, and, instead of making a meal of the Japanese,
he served as a feast to the eyes of thousands in the
different cities, at so many cash per head.  The moral of
which seems to be, that it is the nature of the Japanese

officials to object; but it does not answer to be too soon
discouraged, when new imports have to be introduced
into Japan!

I am surprised glass is not more rapidly adopted by
the Japanese. Perhaps one reason is, that the paper,
after all, besides being less costly, does really keep out
both heat and cold better than a thin sheet of glass. In
the Tycoon's new palace, I am told, however, there has
been a tolerably free use of glass for screens and windows.
They have attained no small skill in manufacturing glass
for themselves, in great variety of forms, though I am
not aware whether they have attempted window glass;
but lamp chimneys, ground-glass shades, bottles cut and
moulded, these they can manufacture at about English
prices, and scarcely, if at all, inferior in material or
workmanship.

At the end of this third year that the ports had been
opened, the foreign community consisted, at Kanagawa,
of—

| | |
|---|---:|
| British . . . . . . | 55 |
| American . . . . | 38 |
| Dutch . . . . . | 20 |
| French . . . . . | 11 |
| Portuguese . . . . | 2 |
| Total . . . . | 126 |

At Nagasaki the number was considerably less, thirty-
nine if I remember right, but the proportion of Dutch
was, I believe, larger.

The trade at Nagasaki, I have said, was much inferior
to that of Kanagawa in value—rather a strong argument
against the idea broached by a Dutch partisan of the
Japanese policy for not enlarging the boundaries of
foreign intercourse beyond Nagasaki, as offering all the
facilities that could be required for trade, without any of
the disadvantages attending its extension, and the residence of foreigners at other ports. The total value of

imports in the year 1861 amounted, according to the returns made up on the spot, to $669,261, and of exports, $1,000,317, or say, 140,000*l.* and 203,000*l.* in round numbers, against 308,000*l.* and 559,000*l.* at Kanagawa,—giving, of imports, a total of 448,000*l.*, and of exports, 762,000*l.*, or a little over twelve hundred thousand pounds sterling for the whole trade of Japan with Foreign countries.

This is not a very large result for the trade taken collectively, but when it is remembered in what a state of isolation the Japanese have lived, and how entirely the country has been from the most remote times *self-sufficing*, there is nothing discouraging in the result. Indeed, could the policy of the Government be modified, and be made less restrictive and hostile to the extension of trade, there is not the slightest doubt that the country possesses resources, hitherto undeveloped, which would supply an export trade of ten times the amount, and afford a market for a large, if not an equivalent, increase in the imports. In tea and silk alone there is every reason to believe they could produce in two or three years, and afford to part with, an enormous surplus. I fear we are yet distant, however, from the period when any great or fundamental change in the policy of the rulers of Japan can be anticipated with confidence; and in the meantime whatever trade is developed will be only, with constant efforts, both on the part of foreign merchants and their authorities on the spot;—and despite of a system of obstruction, expressly designed to prevent all rapid extension, and only too well adapted to the end in view. We have undoubtedly the largest interest at stake in this trade ; yet in proportion to the whole import and export trade of Great Britain, nothing Japan is likely either to take or to give can be considered otherwise than trifling. One, or a half per cent., on the whole of our export trade, is much too small a proportion to induce us lightly to incur unnecessary risks in preserving, or to

resort to any very costly or serious efforts to extend it.
More than the half of what trade there is has fallen into
our hands; we cannot complain, therefore, of our share,
whatever may be the value of the whole, and I fear we
must be content with this, as the only result attainable
for the present.   Not all the merchants, with all the
Consuls and Ministers combined, can make any essential
change in the system and action of the Japanese authorities, high and low.   This can only come with time,— or
political and social revolutions.

I rode down from Yeddo to Yokohama after having despatched the Mission to Europe, and some other business
with the Ministers of Foreign Affairs, and on my way had
to pass one of the execution-grounds, lying just off the
Tocaido, by the edge of the bay, a short distance from the
capital.   As I came up, three gory heads fresh severed
from their trunks looked grimly down upon me from their
unenviable elevation on a little platform at the top of a pole.
Were these the heads of any of the assassins who penetrated into the Legation on July 5 ?   One struck me as
singularly like the only man I closely scanned as he lay
wounded on his back the following morning.   The
face, and even the expression of the villainous-looking
ruffian as he lay bound and a prisoner, eyeing me
with a sullen look of baffled vengeance, were suddenly
recalled to my mind.   And, what is more remarkable,
the same idea of resemblance struck one of my attachés without our exchanging a word.   The Ministers had
informed me secretly that either two or three of these men
were to have been executed that morning in their prison,
the man I allude to among the number.   But I alone knew
this.   If they were the heads of my would-be assassins,
however, the Government did not dare to state it on the
placards beneath, for these, I ascertained, described them
as highway robbers, who had entered a temple, and stolen
property.   As I pursued my way, I could not help musing
on the strange state of uncertainty in which we were left
as to the actual position of the Government in this country,

and its relations with its subjects and great feudatory princes ; and how thorny the path of those, who in the midst of such imperfectly understood conditions, had the task of establishing commercial relations, and maintaining a good understanding with both rulers and people.  The wind blew cold and keen, right down from the snowy peak of Fusiyama, and the range of mountains below equally clad with a mantle of white, as we crossed the bleak causeway leading over the salt lagunes by which Yokohama is cut off from the main road.  How admirably the situation had been chosen for isolation and espionage, for a system of control and surveillance, such as only Japanese could, I think, carry out to the same perfection !  Not a soul can enter the settlement of foreigners at Yokohama without being noted, scrutinised, and *passed* by officials stationed at different points along this raised causeway.  Not a bale of goods can enter or leave without licence, and undergoing such inspection and taxation as may seem good to the Japanese so employed. How can trade take any healthy developement under such a system, and in such a locality?  The foreign merchant, it is true, had preferred it to the opposite side of the bay, where such utter isolation and minute surveillance would have been more difficult, if not impossible.  Granted that the facilities for loading and unloading ships may have been greater on the Yokohama side, was it not possible to pay too dear for these advantages?  The die was cast, however, and under an army of lynx-eyed Japanese officials — hemmed in on all sides, the very merchants of native race ticketed and labelled before they can obtain permission to enter its water-girt limits (and under what conditions as to traffic who can say?)—the trade must henceforth be carried on, so long as the policy of the rulers remains unchanged.  If Yokohama is not another Decima, it is at least a very excellent imitation, and answers nearly all the purposes except that of keeping the foreigner a close prisoner, and even that seemed about this time to have entered into their conception as a possible consummation and worth at least an attempt. On the occasion of the marriage of the young Tycoon with a sister of the Mikado, the Government sent an earnest request to the Foreign Representatives to prevent their countrymen going on to the main road between Kanagawa and the town beyond for two days, as it would be filled with the retinue of the princess returning to Miaco. But the third day they intimated the same impediment existed, and both the French Minister and I demurred to this continued exigence. Although they paid us the compliment to ask our assent, it appeared they took their own measures to make the prohibition imperative by closing the gates which bar all ingress or egress across the raised causeway already referred to, leading to the high road. The whole foreign community, therefore, were by this means made close prisoners, so far as any exit on that side was concerned. Outraged by this high-handed proceeding in violation of express treaty stipulations, it was determined by my colleague and myself, that a communication should be forthwith sent to the Governor by each of us, expressing our surprise at the course taken, and giving him notice that if the gates were not instantly thrown open, and all impediment to the egress of our countrymen withdrawn, a party of armed men from the British and French ships-of-war should be landed, to raze the gates to the ground. Before an officer from the Legation could reach the spot, an express from the Governor had arrived, and the gates were thrown wide open. It was explained to have been a mistake on the part of the subordinate officials at the port! Of course it was a mistake, when it was no longer prudent to persevere. It so happened, however, that the officer I sent heard one of the officials at the post say to his comrade, ' Why don't you say we had orders from the Custom-house ? ' When I spoke to the Ministers on the subject, pointing out that no stipulations of the Treaties had been more expressly and distinctly framed than those which interdicted all attempts to enclose or shut in foreigners by gates or walls, they replied instantly, 'When you speak to us on this subject we have nothing to say. It was totally contrary to Treaty, and a most unpardonable and stupid mistake of the inferior officers, and we are very scrry it ever happened.' It is difficult to pursue a complaint in the face of such an admission, and I could only say that I was satisfied, and felt assured it would never happen again. But who that has lived in Japan can doubt, if this first attempt had passed without notice, or less decided protest, that it would have formed a precedent inaugurating a system of locking every European up, within the boundaries of the settlement?

On the other hand, and in the face of such determined resistance and dangerous encroachments on the liberties of foreigners, and their privileges under Treaty, the local press beginning in Japan and extending in widening circles to Shanghai and Hongkong, teemed with abuse and aspersions directed more particularly against myself, for ' appeasing and conciliating the Japanese by a course of pusillanimous concessions, to which there was no limit ; ' apropos to a short set of regulations, issued under the Queen's order in Council, for Japan, and under the reiterated instructions of Her Majesty's Secretary of State for Foreign Affairs, for ' the peace, order, and good government of British subjects within the dominions of the Tycoon.' How essential some rules were, making it a punishable offence to commit certain acts of dangerous tendency, and calculated to provoke collisions with the Japanese, fatal to the peace or security of the foreign communities, must be obvious where British subjects of very promiscuous character might take up their residence,—from the simple fact that no violation of Japanese laws could, *per se*, constitute a punishable offence, without such regulations prohibiting it were in force. And after all, the prohibitive clauses amounted only to five, pointing to the most likely causes of danger, as shown by past experience. These were, furious riding ; — firing loaded arms in the settlement ; — taking the

wrong side of the road, which is often filled with large
retinues and processions composed of Daimios and their
followers, only too prone to come in collision with
foreigners, if they could find a plausible ground of quarrel
(as has since been most fatally exemplified) ;—sleeping in
distant localities, where no adequate protection could be
afforded, or knowledge of their habitat and conduct could
exist ;—and lastly, shooting game, strictly prohibited
to all natives within ten Re of the Tycoon's residence.
These abominable 'restrictions on the liberty of the
subject, really repugnant to the feelings of Englishmen,'
which could have no other object than to 'oppress
and lower them in the eyes of the natives,' nor better
motive than 'to appease and conciliate the Japanese Government' by 'pusillanimous and unworthy
concessions,' seemed to me at the time, I confess, so
innocent and reasonable, that, with less experience of
the spirit in which all official action is judged in these
localities, and handled in the local newspapers, I think I
should have been taken by surprise on learning the storm
of vilification and abuse, of which they and their author
had become the object. But against abuse which we
feel is undeserved, and an evil we know to be inevitable, the most sensitive become hardened by time. It
was rather amusing, at this moment, to fall in with a
memorial by the 'Citizens of the United States resident
at Yokohama,' which by chance came under my notice in
one of the San Francisco newspapers, dated some time in
the past year. It was a memorial to the President of the
United States praying for the removal of their Resident
Minister (whom 'they did not recognise as their Representative except nominally'), and the Consul of his nomi-
nation. I do not care to give circulation to all the grievances they set forth against their own functionaries, but
I could not help smiling, as I threw down the paper, at
the similarity of result with the dissimilarity of provocation. To believe the American memorialists, neither
their Minister nor Consul had done anything 'either

directly or indirectly ' to serve or help them or uphold their treaty rights. Some of my countrymen, had they been memorialising the Queen, would evidently have based their grievances in a pernicious activity thwarting them, controlling their liberty as free-born Britons, and interfering with their right to construe treaties and pursue trade, or any other object as seemed best to themselves.

# CHAPTER XVII.

THE year 1862, the third subsequent to the opening of the ports under treaty, instead of an assassination and a menace of general massacre, with which each of the preceding years had begun, opened more propitiously, as I have related, with preparations for the departure of a Diplomatic Mission from the Tycoon, to the Courts of all the Sovereigns in Europe with whom he had entered into treaties — Great Britain, France, Holland, Russia, Prussia, and Portugal, six in all.

The Mission despatched, I only waited for my instructions in answer to the Tycoon's proposal respecting the delay in opening more ports, to take my own departure on sick leave, and follow as quickly as possible, in order to overtake the Japanese Envoys before they should leave England. The necessary arrangements in anticipation of their arrival before me would, I knew, be made, to secure the good employment of their time in the examination of all the elements of our wealth and power — our manufactories, arsenals, and mines; but it was very desirable that they should not suffer any long detention.

Waiting for the mail, and anxiously counting the days and weeks before it could well be expected, taking into

account the various causes of delay, and chances of a break-
down in the chain of many links which connects Japan
with Europe, the 14th of February arrived, and no
mail.   We had begun to seek consolation in the reflection
that, at least, our new year was so far unstained with
blood, when, on the evening of that day, a message was
received by the French Minister and myself, both temporarily resident at Yokohama, from the Governor of the
place, to inform us that two Governors of Foreign Affairs
had arrived express from Yeddo, intrusted with a communication of importance from the Gorogio.   Evil news,
we knew, they must bring; what was it?   Monsieur de
Bellecourt happened to have been dining with me, so
that we were together at the moment when the message
came, and vainly speculated upon what it might be.
Was it to warn us of another gathering of lonins, and a
plot to attack the settlement? or had anything disastrous
happened either to our American colleague in the capital,
or any of the members of the Tycoon's Cabinet?

We were not far from the truth.   About ten o'clock at
night the Governors arrived, and made their communication, which was to inform us that a band of eight men had
that morning attacked Ando Tsusimano Kami, the second
of the Foreign Ministers, and the one supposed to be most
favourable to the maintenance of Foreign relations.   It appears they had taken their measures pretty much as they did
when the Regent was attacked and killed ; only, if possible,
looking to the smaller number engaged, they had shown a
more reckless and desperate courage, determining to kill,
and willing to be killed, in the accomplishment of their
object.   The Minister was in his norimon and proceeding
to the palace in the midst of an armed retinue befitting his
rank as a Daimio and a member of the Cabinet.   The distance between his official residence and the palace is very
short, and he had but to cross an open space or glacis to
gain the bridge leading over the broad deep moat which
surrounds the Tycoon's castle. Short, however, as was the
distance, and exposed to view, these desperadoes were

nothing daunted; for, as the train approached the bridge, a shot was fired, wounding one of the officers by the side of the norimon. Ando Tsusimano, it appears, instantly divined that he was to be attacked, and throwing himself out of the norimon, drew his sword to defend himself. It was well he lost no time, for already his people were being cut down by the desperate band of assassins. The next instant he received a sabre-cut across the face, and a spear thrust in the side that had well nigh proved fatal. As in the previous case of the Regent, the life-and-death struggle was brief as it was bloody. In a few seconds seven of the assailants lay stretched, wounded or dead, on the ground, and one only (the eighth) escaped. Among the wounded, however, were some who lived long enough to have confessions extracted from them as to their motives and associates. The Ministers told me one of the wounded had confessed that, among the assailants, were some of those who had attacked the British Legation in July, and that it was partly from the same motives, and partly to avenge the execution of three of their confederates. Was this the fact? If so, it would be a sufficient answer to all those who amused themselves and their readers in the local press of China by pretending to find a personal motive for the attack on the British Legation, founded upon some dislike to the individual Minister. But if the policy it was my duty to carry out was the cause of hostility, then it is clear that the Japanese Minister of Foreign Affairs must have been thought to approve, and was held equally obnoxious and amenable to the wild justice of these summary judges and executioners.

We were long in a state of painful doubt whether the unfortunate Minister had not, as in the Gotiro's case, been slain on the spot. The declarations of the officials could be taken as no certain evidence; that at least we knew by what had passed when the Regent's head was on its way to Miaco. Popular rumour now, as then, rather favoured the report of his death, and neither I nor my colleagues could regard such a possibility without pain

and regret. We could only consider the attack upon
him as another blow aimed at ourselves, and a Foreign
policy based on the obligation of treaties. And, despite
my frequent struggles for the better maintenance of treaty
rights, entailing of necessity much official interchange of
conflicting opinions and discussion of rival interests, my
relations personally with Ando Tsusimano Kami had always
been of a friendly and courteous character. Moreover,
I had the same conviction as his assailants, that he was, of
all the Ministers we had discussed affairs with, the one
*best disposed* to take a fair and a reasonable view of the
exigencies inseparable from the treaties entered into ; and
the most willing, so far as his position would admit, to
place the relations of Japan with Foreign Powers, if not on
a perfectly satisfactory footing, at least on a friendly basis.
The former, perhaps, he knew better than anyone else, was
for the present not possible. ' When sorrows come, they
come not single spies,' Shakespeare has said, and in no
country does this rule seem to hold good more truly than in
Japan. It was midnight before the conference was over,
and scarcely had the Governors taken their departure, and
M. de Bellecourt wished me good night, when there was
an alarm of fire in the European settlement. It lasted
several hours, and a large block of houses was destroyed.
The danger of its spreading over the whole settlement
was at one time very great, and that which made the
event more serious was the fact of some men, dressed like
the Japanese police, having been discovered by Lieut.
Aplin, at the commencement, actively engaged in spreading
the fire to an adjoining house.

This troubled night over, the arrival of my despatches
again occupied my thoughts. It was late in February before
they reached me. Captain Craigie in H.M.S. 'Ringdove'
brought the mail, with orders to wait a week to bring
me away, if I at once undertook to be on board within
that time. As it was obviously impossible for me to do
this with the necessity of first returning to Yeddo and
there carrying through to some definite result difficult

negotiations with the Government of the Tycoon, I had no alternative but to let the 'Ringdove' spread her wings without me, and return to Shanghai in the twenty-four hours peremptorily prescribed by the Admiral. The same mail brought orders to the only remaining ship of war, the 'Charybdis,' to proceed to Vancouver's Island ; and thus again, and at the least auspicious moment, the station was destined to be left for weeks and even months without a British ship of war. After waiting in vain for some time for Ando Tsusimano's recovery, and partly in the hope also that, before I proceeded to Yeddo, a vessel of some kind would have been despatched by the Admiral on the return of the 'Ringdove' without me, in conformity with the instructions from home not to leave the station without a ship of war ;— I finally had no alternative but to proceed to Yeddo, and I accordingly rode up on March 4, with my escort. I had no guard for the Legation of course, but Captain Faucon, with his usual courtesy, was good enough, at the suggestion of my excellent colleague the French Minister, to send a small guard of his men—blue-jackets from H.I.M.'s transport ship the 'Dordogne'—to supply the place, as far as he might, of a guard of marines from one of our own ships. Fortunately, it seemed not to have entered into the plans of those from whom so many murderous attacks had come, to make any attempt at this time to remove me out of their path before I might make any further arrangements with the Tycoon's Government. The next attack was reserved for my successor and H.M.'s Chargé d'Affaires some months later, and when he least anticipated any danger. But considering that, less than a month before, they had fallen, sword in hand, upon one of the Ministers of Foreign Affairs for his supposed leaning to Foreigners, the position of H.M.'s Minister at Yeddo could hardly be considered a very secure one.

Ando Tsusimano, though badly wounded, survived, and my negotiations with his colleagues of the Council detained me in Yeddo nearly three weeks. I saw Ando Tsusimano

no more, however, to my regret.   It was reported he was
not sufficiently recovered to see me when my last interview with the Minister took place ; and shortly after my
departure, his retirement from the Cabinet was officially
announced, on the ground of promotion to *Tarnalid-
soomay Kakf* — whatever that office or grade may be —
his translation being accompanied by a change in the
characters forming his signature.   Thus not only his
destination, but his name was changed.   It is difficult
to understand how there could be *promotion* from the
Cabinet Council of the Tycoon.   Was this a change in
the interest of Ando Tsusimano to secure his life from
further attempts, which nothing could avert if he remained
Minister ?  or was it a concession to the hostile party, which
had declared their implacability and determination to
sever the link of connection between him and the Foreign
Representatives ?   An honourable dismissal, with a desire
to preserve his life, seemed the most probable explanation ;
the Government of the Tycoon yielding to a pressure
they were unable to resist.

As to my negotiations, H.M.'s Government* had instructed me to make no concessions without equivalents,
and to demand, in the first place, indemnity for Messrs.
Oliphant and Morrison, the punishment of any of the
assailants arrested, and finally, a defensible site for the
Legation. As I found them wholly unprepared to concede
any equivalents in return for the deferred opening of the
ports, I declined entering into any engagements respecting them, and contented myself with obtaining the satisfaction I had been instructed to demand in reference
to the attack.   This done, I referred them to H.M.'s
Government for any answer as to the ports ; telling the
President of the Council that it would be for the Tycoon's
Government to enter into negotiation by their own Representatives when they should arrive in London, and that I
would charge myself with the safe delivery of any fresh

* See Parliamentary Papers.

instructions they might desire to send. Or, should they prefer it, I even offered to take charge of a confidential officer of their own, who, in addition to any written instructions, might convey verbally a fuller statement of their views and policy. I mentioned Moriyama, present at the time as interpreter, knowing him to be more conversant with all that had passed, whether in interviews or correspondence, with Foreign Representatives since Commodore Perry's first arrival; — and at the same time more intelligent, and, as I inferred, more trusted, than probably any other officer whom they could at once select and despatch. At first, this took them by surprise, and Koodgi, the President of the Council, in thanking me, observed they could scarcely spare one so constantly in requisition as Moriyama, and so useful to them; but the Council would nevertheless take my proposition into serious consideration. I confess to being somewhat surprised the next day, when Moriyama presented himself at the Legation, and with a face which did not betoken any serious misgiving or feeling of regret at the lot which had fallen to him, he told me that the Gorogio determined on accepting my offer, and that he was to accompany me as the bearer of confidential instructions to their Mission in Europe. I could not but be sensible of such a mark of trust and confidence as regarded myself, on the part of the Cabinet. That they should commit to my keeping one of their own officers, who probably knew more of their secret counsels and policy than almost any other in the Tycoon's service, far away from spies, and without any safeguard or impediment to the most unreserved intercourse day by day during a voyage of two months, was indeed an innovation on all the established principles of Japanese policy and government. It either betokened intense anxiety in them to secure the main object — the deferred opening of the ports (and, seeing they failed with me, it might seem their last chance and well worth some risk of indiscretion in their agent), or a degree of trust in his fidelity, as well as confidence in

me that I would not take undue advantage of my opportunity, or abuse their trust—for which I was scarcely prepared. I think it probable that all three motives existed
and may have influenced their decision. I may as well add,
while on the subject, that Moriyama, and the second officer
who went in the capacity of his attendant, but spoke no
word of any European language, were in perfect readiness
in five days ; and from the hour of our departure until I
handed them over to the Mission in London, I never
had a moment's cause to regret having taken charge of
them. They not only were most careful to give me no
unnecessary trouble, and to conform scrupulously to the
rules and regulations they found established in the
steamers, but made friends for themselves everywhere by
their unobtrusive manners and gentle bearing. Moriyama
with several Dutch passengers felt quite at home, speaking
their language fluently ; and even with the English, he
spoke and understood quite enough to obtain and give
information. Nor do I think the Japanese Government
will ever see cause to regret the trust they placed either
in their own servant or Her Majesty's Representative on
this occasion.

The time had come for my departure, which indeed
had been only too long delayed, if the Japanese
Mission had to be overtaken before they left London.
But although I was ready, no ship had come to take
me across to China. It was now the 20th of March ;
the 'Charybdis,' the last British ship in the Japanese
waters, had been gone just a month; and the 'Ringdove,'
going straight back to the Admiral at Shanghai, had left the
week before the 'Charybdis'— still there was no sign of a
British pendant. In this dilemma, my Dutch colleague
M. de Wit, and Captain Buijs, commanding H.N.M.'s ship
the 'Admiral van Hoopman,' kindly came to my rescue,
and were good enough to offer me and my protégés also a
passage to Nagasaki, where, if no British ship of war had
arrived, I might possibly find a merchant ship proceeding
to Shanghai, and so make my way. We embarked on

March 23, but baffling winds, too strong to allow the auxiliary steam-power to make any headway, kept us eleven days at sea—so long indeed as to make it scarcely possible that I should save the mail leaving Shanghai on the 7th. My illfortune seemed, however, to have exhausted itself, and I found a gunboat in harbour on her way up to Yeddo, detained by the sickness of the commander, who had an attack of small-pox. As he was in quarters on shore, I found no difficulty in obtaining the vessel to run across with me, and in fifty-six hours I was steaming up the Hwangpo. Even then I had the narrowest escape of missing the mail, and being detained a whole fortnight; for the regular mail steamer had passed us at the mouth of the river without being recognised. Fortunately a second steamer was on the berth, having been detained twenty-four hours by the Admiral for his despatches, by which I was enabled to proceed on my way.

Amidst all the reserve and self-possession, natural and acquired, of the Japanese, the surprise of Moriyama and his friend at all they saw, mingled with intelligent observation, could not be concealed on our journey homewards. As we came to each colony—first Hong Kong, then Singapore, Penang, Point de Galle, Aden and Malta, in succession— I pointed out that these were so many links in a chain of colonies with which we girdled the globe. When we came to Malta, I took them to see Sir Gaspard le Marchant, the Governor, and he was good enough to send an officer over the fortifications with them. On their return, I asked them what they thought of the place. They had evidently been impressed with its strength, and on my casually remarking that it was but a small island, and of no importance as a colony, Moriyama rejoined, with more emphasis than was usual to him, ‘Ah! a small place to you, *but to us*’—leaving his phrase unfinished.

On my arrival in England, the Japanese Envoys were very eager to give instant effect to the instructions Moriyama had brought them. It is only necessary here to remark that the delay of five years in opening the new ports, and the city of Yeddo, — the object of so much effort and anxiety on the part of the Japanese Government, was conceded conditionally, that certain specific grievances should be removed, and greater security to life, as well as increased facilities for commerce at the ports actually open, *should be effectively enjoyed.* There was, indeed, but one of two alternatives. We must either grant the delay which the Japanese Government declared to be essential for their own security, no less than ours,— and thus give them the means of making head against hostile factions and internal difficulties, trusting that in the interval they would keep faith, and employ the time in preparing the way, as they promised, for the fulfilment of all the stipulations of the Treaty; — or refuse, and be prepared to enforce execution at the period fixed by Treaty. That is at the end of the year — and this, whatever might be the circumstances of the country, or our own convenience. By adopting the first, making the concession *distinctly conditional* on a tangible and manifest improvement in certain specifically enumerated directions, one of two things must follow. Either we and all Foreigners must gain such advantages in security and facilities for trade, as would be far more valuable than any extension of points of contact with perpetual danger, obstructions to trade, and threatening of civil war ;—or failing these, we retained the right of withdrawing the concession, and insisting upon the due fulfilment of all the stipulations, at the time and in the way that might be deemed most expedient and suitable to ourselves. There seemed by such an arrangement much to gain, and little to lose. Of course, it was quite possible the Japanese Government, under the dictation of the hostile Daimios, might act in bad faith, and, instead of clearing obstacles and preparing the way for a better order of things, turn the time to a totally different account. But assuming this, in what worse position should we be, having the right distinctly re-

served, on failure of engagement, to cancel the concession at any time, and take action precisely as if it had
never been made? Whereas, on the other hand, we
should have the advantage of demonstrating to the world
that we had been willing to trust them, and of satisfying
ourselves at the same time that, having granted largely and
without diminution what they asked as essential to their
progress and stability,— nothing more could be hoped from
effort in that direction. If called upon to assert our rights,
it would only be when driven to it, by this second and
continued failure on their part to keep faith. We should
have nothing to reproach ourselves with, for we should
have done all the Japanese Government had themselves
asked as needful to their stability and success. Under such
circumstances, not only the whole country would probably
be with any Government that might take measures for
exacting a better observance of treaties; but the other
Treaty Powers might be disposed, upon this evidence, to
join Great Britain in a more perfect accord than could
well be hoped for, prior to any such effort and experience
of its futility.

On the other side, there was reason to believe that,
had Her Majesty's Government resolved to insist upon
the opening of the ports at the time fixed by Treaty,
and peremptorily refused to listen to the representations
of the Tycoon's Government, we might have had to
undertake the task of enforcing the condition alone,
or nearly so. The United States of America had already
consented to the postponement, when their Resident
Minister negotiated an indemnity of $10,000 for the
murder of Mr. Heuskin, their Secretary of Legation, as
a provision for a widowed mother — at least, so I was
informed by the Japanese Ministers; and I have no
reason to doubt that assurances to that effect had been
given. Russia had no commerce,— seeks none in Japan,
keeps no Diplomatic Agent at Yeddo, and probably has
no wish or care for more ports to be opened. Holland,
bound by peculiar antecedents and old relations with

Japan, would not have been very likely to take a decidedly hostile course. There remained, then, France, with whom alone any probability of accord or alliance for such objects could have been contemplated, and even there the material interests at stake were small, and, as has been already pointed out, certain elements of dissidence in ulterior objects and lines of action are not wanting to weaken any united action, with whatever good faith both parties may enter upon such a course. Taking all these considerations into account, there could be little question that the best and wisest course was to give the Government of the Tycoon the benefit of any doubt as to their ability and willingness to repress all hostile action and keep better faith ; — before proceeding to extremities involving expense or chances of war. It may indeed be alleged that the Treaty Powers had only to be resolute, and insist upon the opening of the ports to succeed, and strike discouragement into the hearts of all now raising pretexts for delay and non-fulfilment. But nothing is easier than to make such assertions, and one condition of such a course could not be overlooked—namely, that it neither admitted of retreat nor delay. Either the ports *must* have been opened in that case at the day fixed, whatever the risk, real or supposed, to the existing order of things in Japan—or action prompt and decisive must have been taken to enforce execution. No one could be certain, no Foreign Representative assuredly, that a determined front (even in the supposition of a common accord, to all appearance unattainable) would or could secure the desired end without internal convulsion and a resort to menace or coercion from without. And which was the Government or Foreign Power willing to accept the alternative ? *

* While this sheet is going through the press a China paper has reached me containing an oracular leader on Japanese affairs — by a writer who it is to be presumed has never seen Japan,—in which we are confidently told, 'It was a mistaken policy to assent to a postponement of the opening of Miako (Osaca it should be—but that is a trifle) to foreign commerce. The Western Powers have been fairly outmanœuvred by the Japanese diplo-

The wisest course was, no doubt, taken by the Foreign Powers, with more or less of concert and identity of action. If, in point of time, the United States had taken precedence, the circumstances were such as, no doubt, favoured a double arrangement at one and the same time, very much in accordance with the general course of American policy in the far East. The Resident Minister had to obtain indemnity for his murdered Secretary, after a year had passed over, without any action taken ;— and the Japanese Government had a concession on their side to ask. By being the first to concede the postponement, two objects would be gained. The Americans would act independent of other Treaty Powers in a sense favourable to the wishes and prejudices of the Japanese Government ; and the more hesitation other Powers might show in following a similar course,—the more would the Japanese be likely to appreciate the initiative in the American Government. And on the other hand, if ultimately the remaining Powers, any or all of them, should refuse,—the ' most favoured nation clause ' secured the United States from any possible prejudice ; while their previous action would save them by anticipation, from the cost and damage of participation in any coercive measures.

If I were asked whether I felt sanguine that the concession ultimately made by Her Majesty's Government and other Treaty Powers would ever realise the hopes professedly entertained by the Japanese Ministers ; or secure to foreigners the advantages promised, I should be very much disposed to answer in a trans-Atlantic fashion by another question : Who is ever sanguine of results contingent on Asiatic good faith ? Or who that has ever passed years in constant intercourse with Asiatics, rulers or subjects, feels any implicit trust either in the most solemn engagements they may enter into, or the reliability of their judgement, even when most honest — as to the

matists.' What a pity it is that none of these very clever and able commentators on public affairs can ever have an opportunity of trying their hand in settling the destinies of nations, — always provided that it could be at their own risk and peril, and not at the expense of others.

probable result of political measures and the action of chiefs and armed retainers in a given order of circumstances?

So the Mission ended its course in Europe — visiting all the Courts of the Sovereigns with whom they had treaties, failing in all subordinate objects, but succeeding in the one and great end of their diplomacy — a conceded delay in opening the Ports.　For notwithstanding this, which was conditional in our case, and I believe, that of France, was indefinite as to limit of time in the case of Holland, &c., yet such variations in the terms in nothing affected the identity of result.　Although this was a main object of the Mission to Europe, the Envoys had other instructions and hopes—as to objects which European Governments would consider either secondary or utterly frivolous.　And I confess when I saw what these were, and how eagerly and pertinaciously they sought to engage Her Majesty's Secretary of State for Foreign Affairs in their consideration, after the primary end was gained, I could not help feeling how doubtful must be the result of any concession Foreign Powers might make.　The list of their grievances and the restrictions they wanted to be imposed on foreigners were so thoroughly expressive of the very spirit of reaction and a retrograde policy of isolation ;—that although they did not actually propose among the number, the restriction of foreign trade to Nagasaki with an enlarged Decima, (as it had been reported they contemplated,) it was difficult to believe that such a desire did not lie at the bottom of their hearts.　Nothing probably but a conviction of the utter hopelessness of such a proposition had prevented the Government of the Tycoon from including this too among the exigencies of their political position!　There were nine of these demands, of which it may be truly said, that with the exception of the Currency, which stands first, and another of mere custom-house detail, there is not one that a reasonable government desiring to carry out the stipulations of existing treaties in good faith could well have proposed.　Most of them had been frequently discussed in Yeddo between the Ministers of Foreign Affairs and myself, as with the other Foreign Representatives; and therefore they were perfectly aware in giving instructions to press them on the Governments in Europe, that they were going counter to the opinion of the Ministers accredited to the Tycoon from the different Courts.

The following is the list :—

1. Currency.—Proposed alterations — on which there is much yet to be said.

2. Prohibition of the *export* of *manufactured* copper.—Copper in bar having virtually been prohibited by the Japanese Government refusing to sell to foreigners, or to permit their subjects to do so.

3. Prohibition to Japanese to leave Japan by foreign vessels.— This at the very time that they were sending a numerous mission to Europe, and fitting out European-built vessels to trade with China and other foreign countries.

4. Prohibition to men of war to practise ball-firing in harbour. —They had already been told of the willingness of the Representatives to enter into any arrangements analogous to those prevailing in like circumstances in Europe, but they wished to insist the ships should always go out to sea, out of gunshot of the coast, on a plea of danger to their subjects, though no case of injury had ever occurred.

5. Foreign cavalry escort not to be kept in Japan.— In the face of their own notorious inability to protect the life of a Foreign Minister in their streets or high roads.

6. No exemption from duty of the private effects of foreign officials resident in Japan.— Some question of abuse had arisen as regarded stores, imported under this head, but really for sale; and as to the privileges of merchant-consuls, in which, no doubt, there might be something requiring alteration.

7. Prohibition to bury the dead anywhere but at the consular ports.— A question had arisen on the death of an officer on board one of Her Majesty's ships in the inland sea, who was buried in an uninhabited spot. They had even induced Admiral Hope when at Yeddo to consent to its disinterment and removal to Nagasaki; and not on any religious, but a purely political ground — the absence of any right to land elsewhere than the open ports.

8. Claim to exercise the right of examining Japanese servants before passing into foreign employment.— In other words, the right to prevent any Japanese serving foreigners without a permissive license, in the teeth of an express stipulation to the

contrary in all the treaties.   This violation of a very important treaty-right, has always been persevered in, under plea of a protective measure, but there is no doubt, with a view to perfect a system of control and surveillance utterly incompatible with any sense of liberty or freedom of action.   One consequence is, that none but the lowest class of coolies can be obtained for the household work of foreigners, and with no better guarantee, as experience has proved, for their honesty, soberness, or absence of treacherous intent, than if they were picked up promiscuously by foreigners themselves in the highways.

9. Limitation of the foreign settlements or quarters at all the consular ports.— In a word, isolation and means of effective surveillance, as effective as ever established at Decima.   This is what they have persistently aimed at from the first hour, and they have as invariably met with a determined opposition on my own part, and that of some, if not all, of the other Representatives at Yeddo.

This is not an encouraging list to contemplate.   There is too clearly one unvarying tendency towards the isolation of the foreigner, and the seclusion of the nation from all intercourse, save with the salaried officials of the Government, and a few of the lowest classes.   There is but one stereotyped idea in their brains as to foreigners.   We are a cross between barbarians and wild beasts, ferocious and dangerous if let loose, only safe and tractable when securely caged, watched, and in the hands of responsible keepers.   Their one idea of a port for foreign trade, if such must be, and a foreign settlement, is Decima ; and so far as in them lies, they strive that no other shall exist.   They have laboured incessantly and indefatigably to convert every other port into a facsimile on that much-admired model, and *per fas et nefas* to cage up and imprison in Yeddo the Foreign Representatives, as the most dangerous of all the wild beasts, so long as their presence *must* be tolerated under any conditions.   He who least likes the régime, or is most difficult to confine within the prescribed limits, will always be the first marked out to be removed, as Japanese Samourai best know how.

The currency comes under a very different category, and as upon the satisfactory settlement of the questions which have arisen, must greatly depend all our future commercial, if not our political, relations with the country, the whole subject has received the most careful consideration. The monetary system of the Japanese, conducted on restrictive principles, and adapted only to their own use when they had no foreign trade or treaties, had been shaken to the centre by the American Treaty of 1858, negotiated by Mr. Harris, and subsequently copied by all the other nego- tiators. On matters of trade and currency, the Japanese could not apparently be so fairly charged with ignorance of European practice, as of having simply, in their intercourse with the Dutch, sought information to suit their own wants. They had—far in advance of their neighbours the Chinese —both a gold and silver currency from the year 708, the first money coined, Kœmpfer tells us, being under the reign of a female Mikado, *Teutsy*, the daughter of the preceding Emperor or Mikado, to whom she succeeded by hereditary right. And this although gold was not discovered in Japan until half a century later, and was previously imported from China. On the first renewal of foreign relations by Commodore Perry's negotiations, their coins were found on assay, in London, to be well fabricated, and to possess much greater uniformity than is usually to be found in other Eastern countries.

I do not think therefore that when the first discussions took place between the Americans on the currency, that the charges of ignorance and perversity freely brought against them in Mr. Hildreth's account of the negotiations were altogether deserved.* Indeed the conclusion to which any well-informed mind would naturally come, upon careful consideration of the facts and statements on both sides, would be that the Japanese had the best of the argument; and showed a tolerably correct appreciation of the real question at issue, which was one of vital impor- tance to them in their future relations with Europe. It had been well, perhaps, for them and for us, if the resolution

* 'Japan as it Was and Is,' by Richard Hildreth, author of the 'History of the United States,' &c., 1856.

they came to on this occasion had been firmly adhered to, when four years later Mr. Harris was negotiating a new treaty.

The question was no other than this, upon what principle of exchange should American coins be received in payment for goods and supplies?    As regarded their relative value with Japanese coins, and the condition of their currency at that particular period, one fact appears to have been known to both parties, namely, that silver coins were over-valued in relation both to the gold and copper money.    When an endeavour was made therefore by the Representative of the United States to obtain a recognition of the Mexican dollar as of equal nominal value with the silver coin of Japan, the Japanese Commissioners insisted that the Foreign coin was but bullion to them, while the American Finance Commissioners — nominated by Commodore Perry from among his pursers to discuss the question — contended the effect of this would be to put their silver dollar, so far as payments in Japan were concerned, on a level with the silver itziboo, which weighed only one-third as much.    But if the relative value of their silver and gold coins was (as we know it to have been) in that proportion, the Japanese were perfectly justified in objecting to the dollar being circulated with equivalent weights of itziboos. No inquiry appears to have been made regarding the relation which the silver coins of Japan bore to their gold and copper, yet this was essential to any equitable arrangement, and lay at the root of the whole matter in question.

By careful assay at the British Mint, it was subsequently found that silver coins in the currency of Japan, bore the relation of hardly five to one with the gold, and were over-valued therefore to the extent of two-thirds above the average proportion (viz. fifteen and a half to one), which silver bullion bears to gold in the general market of the world.

So again in reference to the copper, the silver itziboo,

not quite one-third the weight of a dollar, was worth in Japan 1,500 good copper cash, whereas in China the Mexican dollar, containing three times as much silver, had long ceased to be worth more than 1,200, and often was rated at less.

Here then clearly it is established, that the silver money of Japan consisted, as the Government alleged, of token coins greatly overrated in reference to their contents of precious metal ; and representing in exchanges a wholly dispro-portionate value in the two extremes of gold and copper coins. In round numbers, the silver coin was overrated in the proportion of two-thirds, both as regarded the gold and copper currency.

Probably what greatly tended to obscure this view and confuse the question with the American Commissioners, was some fallacy confounding value and prices, a very common source of perplexity in discussions on currency. There is no possibility of denying the greatly overrated value of the silver itziboo, in reference to both gold and copper coin. But there is still this other perplexing fact, no doubt present to the minds of the Americans, as it has been forced upon the attention of all the Diplomatic Agents since resident at Yeddo under later treaties, that although the dollar's weight in *itziboos* would purchase, or be exchangeable for, three times the quantity of copper cash, or of gold, that it could procure in China, such increased amount of cash or gold *would not purchase more goods or unskilled labour* in the markets of Japan, than *a third* of the number of cash or quantity of gold would command in China. How was this to be accounted for ? On this aspect it seemed no less clear that the silver token or coin did *not* represent more value than properly belonged to it, *in refer-ence to its purchase power in the markets of labour and com-mon articles of consumption,* the best of all tests of value, if not the most unvarying throughout the world. Thus a coolie for common labour could be hired by the day in China for 150 to 200 cash, say from $\frac{1}{6}$th to $\frac{1}{8}$th of a dollar. The same labour could only be obtained in Japan for exactly three times the amount of cash, for 450 cash to 600, say $\frac{1}{3}$rd of an itziboo—or from $\frac{1}{6}$th to $\frac{1}{8}$th of a dollar. Or in other words, in each country, taking the price of the lowest labour, one dollar in China, or 1,200 cash, would buy the services of from six to eight men per diem, and in Japan the same labour could be only got for some 4,800 cash, or for three itziboos, equal in weight to one dollar. So of things in general; and accordingly when the Japanese carried their point with Commodore Perry, and had it not only ruled, that the rate of exchange, but the prices of every supply should be fixed by themselves, they made the fleet of the negotiator pay $28 a ton for native coal, though the range of prices at Nagasaki has been for several years since the last treaties from $6 to $8 per ton, and we may be sure they are not sold at a loss.

There is something in this that may well have perplexed the American negotiators, as it has proved a cause of embarrassment to all who have had to enter on this discussion. One thing alone seems perfectly clear. If the silver itziboo, under such circumstances, without other and corresponding changes, is to be taken in exchange for dollars as a token worth two-thirds more than the weight, or intrinsic value of the precious metal it contains ; Japan will be by far the dearest country in the world,—so exceptionally dear as to put all foreign merchants out of its markets, unless they can barter their goods for equivalent values in Japanese produce. At least this would seem to be the natural and legitimate result, unless it can be safely concluded that the Japanese rulers, with their peculiar and only imperfectly comprehended system of Government, and mysterious power over the transactions of every subject in the realm, may have hitherto brought this to bear in some manner unknown to us, to compensate for what they regarded as a robbery ; and to counteract the forced circulation of the dollar against the itziboo, weight for weight, by affixing to *all labour and goods supplied to foreigners* a purely factitious price. I believe they possess such a power. I know that they have cognisance of every merchant who gains access to a foreigner ; that they examine, tax, and I *believe* fix the prices of every article sold, the officials reserving such portion as may seem to them good or fitting in view of the price obtained. Perhaps, even in such a view, the best remedy would be found in abandoning on our side anything false or not justly tenable in the monetary clause of existing treaties — article X in our own.

One error begets another—one false step is the parent of many. If Foreign Powers in the Treaties of 1858, have been mistaken in imposing upon the Japanese an engagement for the exchange and circulation of foreign coins, which is anomalous as regards international principles of intercourse between European Powers, and in its essence erroneous and vicious ; the sooner it is departed from the better, even at some risk of monetary derangement and great embarrassment to commerce in those regions. As it now exists, it cannot continue. Nor, indeed, is it desirable in view of our own interests that it should ; for I believe the two greatest and most generally pervading causes of hostility are to be traced to the feudal element and the monetary perturbation reacting especially upon the military retainers and official classes, and giving them an additional and special motive of hostility. They believe the whole nation has suffered wrong and injury by Mr. Harris's original clause in the American Treaty, stipulating that American coin (and therefore in the sequel all foreign coins, more especially the Mexican dollar) should pass current for the corresponding weight in Japanese coin of the same description.

I am not aware what motives may have led Mr. Harris to propose, and it is still less easy to conceive what possible inducement the Japanese could have had for yielding consent, to a proposition which they had four years before resolutely and consistently refused to accede to, when proposed by Commodore Perry. No inquiry appears to have been made as to the effects of the well-known relation which the silver coins of Japan bore to their gold and copper coins, on nominal prices. The neglect to ascertain this point, and to provide for it, has no doubt been productive of much evil. It has tended more than any one circumstance since foreign relations began to vitiate the position of foreigners, and hold them up to popular odium as despoilers and impoverishers of the land—a character only too well justified in appearance by the rise of prices and depreciated value of their silver. Necessary consequences, in some degree, of a sudden developement of trade in a country long isolated, and a currency only adjusted, like their supplies, to their own wants; but undoubtedly the pressure and perturbation must have been greatly increased by this radical vice in the first arrangements.

Whether the Japanese negotiators were clear-sighted enough or sufficiently well-informed, to duly estimate and foresee the exact influence and degree of perturbation such an engagement as the clause in question involved, may be questioned. Seeing, however, that four years before the whole subject had been maturely considered and discussed; and that the Japanese Commissioners had said, that 'the Mexican dollar was but bullion to them,' and thus 'hit with precision the point at issue,' as has been well observed by an impartial authority in financial matters in this country, I cannot but conclude that they did not enter into the engagement blindfolded, or fall into a trap, as by some has been supposed. I am still farther confirmed in this conclusion by the fact that when the first correspondence on this subject took place after the opening of the ports between the Japanese Government and the Foreign Representatives, the Ministers of Foreign Affairs wrote to me in the following terms:—'As we mentioned in our former letter, it is merely stipulated in the Treaty that coins of the same weight and the same sort shall be exchanged, and not that no new coins should be issued without a previous notification. Therefore, we supposed that no objection would be raised to our issuing a new coin. *And for that very reason we did not allude to it when the Treaty was concluded.'*

It must be abundantly evident, therefore, that whatever be the true history of the negotiation which took place with Mr. Harris; or the motives by which the American negotiator was induced to impose so unprecedented or anomalous an engagement, and the Japanese to accede to it — the latter signed under a mental reservation to alter their silver currency in the way they subsequently attempted by reducing it as much as they deemed it overrated, that is two-thirds — issuing a coinage of *half itziboos*, two of which should contain the same weight of silver as *three* of the then current *itziboos.* That Mr. Harris had not contemplated this as one of the contracting parties is to be inferred by his joining the other Foreign Representatives in resisting the change, at all events until farther discussion and a reference to our respective Governments should give time to clear the question of all doubt and obscurity.

In point of fact, although there was a certain craftiness in the silent mode in which they prepared a totally new coinage on the opening of the ports—acting, as they thought, within the letter of the Treaty, and in the exercise of their sovereign right to regulate their own currency as they themselves might deem best — there was great clumsiness also. For while they had this clear and indefeasible ground to stand upon, they vitiated all right in the matter by making a coin too palpably designed only for foreign trade and dealings with foreigners, while they left the coin current when the treaties were signed still in circulation as silver tokens for the natives. With their unlimited power in the country, it was quite clear they could thus maintain a special and restrictive currency for foreign trade only, and compel the Japanese dealers to bring back to the Mint the new and weighty silver coins to exchange for the silver tokens.

This involved a clear infraction of Treaty, since coins

issued for a restrictive purpose could not properly be classed with Japanese coins ; British and all other merchants would have had the right to avail themselves of the coins in general use.   This was the ground taken by H.M.'s Representative and his colleagues in remonstrating against the proceeding, and the matter has been in abeyance ever since.

At the end of the first year, during which, according to Treaty, they were bound to exchange dollars for itziboos, weight for weight, in order, as the Article expressly states, that the Japanese might become familiarised with the value of foreign coins, it became necessary to consider whether any, and what steps could be taken by the Foreign Representatives, to secure the ends apparently contemplated by the contracting parties to the Treaties, in regard to the free exchange at par of foreign coins with those of Japan.   The Treaties stipulate that, ' All foreign coin shall be current in Japan, and shall pass for its corresponding weight in Japanese coin of the same description ; ' and further, that ' British (foreign) and Japanese subjects may freely use Foreign or Japanese coin in making payments to each other.'

The equity of this singular engagement the Representatives of Foreign Powers were not called upon to discuss — that was a question for their respective governments. But the practicability of interposing in any way calculated to ensure its execution according to the terms of the Treaty, was necessarily a subject for their consideration.

As H.M.'s Consul subsequently stated to a public meeting of the merchants at Yokohama.*   While there was ' no dispute about the obligation of this government (the Japanese) to do all that is in its power to give effect to this clause, there is a question, and a difficult one, as to how far it is in the power of this or any other government to force a foreign coinage into general circulation, and at a fixed rate or valuation.   The Japanese Government

* See Minutes of a Public Meeting.   Appendix B.

says it cannot ; and even in the case of a single coin, the dollar, that it has already, as a government, done all it can do, and failed ; that it has issued an edict throughout the empire making all foreign coins legal tenders, weight for weight ; that it has even attempted, with the concurrence of the Foreign Representatives, to secure the circulation of the dollar (at something less than weight for weight, in view of the facility of exchange), and stamped a certain number with a government stamp of three itziboos, but still they only find circulation at the ports, and that varying at a depreciated rate of two, or two and a half itziboos, while in the interior there is reason to believe they have no currency.

' Is there any remedy for this ?

' That is the question for consideration.  Because it is to be remembered, that no treaty can be invoked to effect an impossibility.  Many may believe that the Japanese Government are not acting with good faith in the matter, but are themselves the chief impediments to the free circulation of the dollar at its full value, and that in any case they have the power, if they had the will, to secure their currency both at the open ports and elsewhere.  But it must be remembered, on the other hand, that the difficulty not to say impossibility, of forcing a foreign coinage on a people is of universal experience — however despotic or absolute the government.  In China, where they have no coinage to displace, where a coinage of any kind is a desideratum, and where dollars of Spain and of American States, all of the same (or nearly the same) intrinsic value, have for the last twenty years been in circulation at five ports on the coast, — with the government of the country passive in the matter, having no obvious interest one way or the other,— this free circulation throughout the country is as far as ever from being attained.  Even in the case of those districts where our large dealings in tea and silk have, so to say, forced foreign specie into circulation, the result was not the general circulation of all dollars bearing a pretty equal value, but an unmeaning preference for the only one of those that was obsolete and could not be reproduced, the Carolus dollar ;—to which obsolete coin an entirely fictitious value was attached by the Chinese, continually increasing until they were at last used up, and not to be had at all, to the depreciation of all other dollars, some thirty or forty per cent. The circulation of a western coinage in an eastern country must then be admitted to present great difficulties, and some that may be quite insurmountable, even where there is no active influence of a government to prevent its currency, or no want of good faith to help. On the other hand, although it is to some extent an evil to the foreign merchant not to be able to circulate the coinage of his own country and buy produce with it, weight for weight against native coins, the committee have rightly shown it is not so great an evil as has been often represented ; nor is it altogether unmixed with good. If it tends to restrict the export trade of Japanese produce, it certainly no less serves to increase or develope a trade in imports. And, again, whether the dollar be nominally rated by the Japanese at two and a half itziboos or at two, it does not follow that more dollars must be paid for a chest of tea or a bale of silk than if they were rated at three or more, because it is to be assumed, that the foreign merchant will only give as many dollars as he calculates it is worth, to leave him a fair profit ; and if they were to circulate at their weight value of 311 or 312 per $100, competition would still keep up the price of Japanese produce to the same margin of profit.

' Lastly, no large trade could be conducted by means of this coinage only, any more than it could by shillings and sixpences. Such at least are some of the considerations which it appears desirable should be carefully weighed, and kept in view, before any proposals are made, by means of more or less determined effort and action upon the Japanese Government, to alter what actually exists, and which perhaps may only be altered by risking some greater or unforeseen derangement in monetary and commercial relations. These suggestions are thrown out in view also of a considerable diversity of opinion among the community here, which is at all times an additional reason for caution, and for mature deliberation in any steps recommended. It may be true, that the government does in effect prohibit the circulation of the dollar in the interior, and will only give two and a half itziboos in exchange when Japanese take their dollar to the mints (or that there are extortions and bribes which bring it down to that), but we shall never be in a position to prove it; and Her Majesty's Envoy, I know, believes it a very profitless, and not a very dignified or politic course, to persist in assertions reflecting on the character of the government which he cannot support by proof, and they meet by a flat denial.

'It seems probable that they have the means of purchasing the produce, or otherwise working the silver mines in Japan, so as to obtain the bullion at a less rate than two and a half itziboos for a dollar weight. Of course, by so much less as they can thus obtain it, the exchange of dollars is a dead loss of revenue. If this be the fact, it is vain to hope the Japanese Government will frankly and honestly subject themselves to this loss, whatever treaty stipulations may require to the contrary.'

This public statement was made under my instructions some months after the close of the first year, when it was clearly ascertained that the average exchange of dollars against itziboos, at the different ports, was never more than some two itziboos and a third, instead of a fraction over three, which would have been the rate if they had been exchanged according to the terms of the Treaties, weight for weight.

The Foreign Representatives had therefore, as the Consul reported, to consider how far it was in the power of the Japanese or any other government, to force a foreign coinage into general circulation, and at a fixed rate or valuation? The Japanese Government affirmed that they had done their utmost and failed;—and to invoke the terms of a treaty to effect an impossibility was obviously absurd, as well as unjustifiable and mischievous.

Again, there was a want of unanimity among the leading foreign merchants themselves, as to the wisdom or expediency of any attempt to intervene in a forcible manner to regulate the exchange, beyond what had been done in the first instance by edicts declaring the equivalent value of coins, and stamping the Mexican dollars with a mint mark of three itziboos.

Under these circumstances, it was resolved by my colleagues and myself to take no further action until something could be definitively determined by our respective governments, as to the proper course to be adopted.

But another difficulty arose as regarded the Legations in Yeddo, *where no dollars would pass current at any rate.* The members of the several establishments, with a fixed stipend paid in dollars, and no business transactions as the merchants had at the ports, whereby exchanges might be effected in the course of their trade, were suddenly exposed to the danger of being left without any means of purchasing the necessaries of life ; or at best incurring all the risk and expense of sending their dollars to the port of Yokohama, and there employing a commercial agent to negotiate the exchange for itziboos, as a distinct monetary operation, at whatever rate might under such disadvantageous conditions be imposed either by foreign or Japanese merchants. I did not think this a position in which public servants ought to be placed. They were already exposed, in a way and to an extent unknown to merchants engaged in trade at the ports, to every species of extortion and robbery, from the Government officials in charge of the Legations in the capital, the tradesmen, and their own servants. The latter, be it remembered, imposed upon them by these same officials, and all in collusion together for the purpose of carrying out a system of wholesale plunder. If, in addition to these drains upon very limited salaries, there was to be a further and unlimited tax levied under

the name of exchange, and subject to no control, a
residence in their isolated position at the capital might at
any time be rendered simply impossible. They not only
might, at the will of parties at the ports, be deprived of
the fair use of their salaries, but would, in effect, be
always at the mercy of others, to the destruction of their
independence. Moved by these considerations therefore,
I determined to state the circumstances to the Japanese
Government, and propose that, until something should
be definitely settled by reference of the whole question
of currency to the Treaty Powers, they should exchange
from the mint monthly, the amount of dollars absolutely
required for the disbursements of the Legations in salaries,
wages, and other contingencies payable out of the public
chest, — allowing four per cent. for the cost of coinage,
as the estimated expense to the mint. This was readily
acceded to as a temporary measure, and extended to
the consular establishments at the ports, where so far
as Her Majesty's servants were concerned, all were
equally precluded from entering into trade, or profiting
by any of the facilities and advantages which those engaged in trade possessed. My colleagues put forward
similar claims, extending the terms to their Consuls who
*were* engaged in trade. The Japanese Government saw
fit to accede to this also, although such an arrangement
obviously rested upon a different principle, but with
this I had nothing to do. I had claimed for the
members of the Consular establishments because they
were not allowed to trade — had fixed salaries and must
live upon them — and I carefully estimated for each Consulate as for the Legation, the average disbursements for
salaries, wages, and contingencies, paid out of the Legation
and Consular chests on public account. In so far as
wages, rent, and other contingencies were concerned, the
public, of course, benefited equally by the arrangement.

I have been induced to enter more fully into the
details than I should have otherwise deemed necessary
for the general reader, because I find occasion has been

taken since my departure from Japan, to make them the subject of a series of scurrilous attacks in the local papers. It was impossible to show that the merchants were damaged or made poorer, because the Legations and Consulates were enabled to obtain itziboos direct from the mint for their daily expenses, at a somewhat more favourable rate than traders could effect an exchange in the market for *their* household expenses.    And, as regarded trade, it is admitted the operations were untouched.    Even the writers seem to have felt ashamed to appear to contest an advantage which, whatever it might be, cost them nothing, as merchants ; and consequently were driven to the necessity of considering the difference of exchange as a premium paid by the Japanese Government to buy over the Foreign Representatives, and induce them to connive at an infraction of the Treaty, to the prejudice of trade, which they could and would otherwise have prevented !

The plain answer to all this vituperation, lies in the fact that none of the merchants themselves could suggest any means by which Japanese could be forced to take foreign coins at a foreigner's valuation, or any fixed rate. Such a thing had never been done or attempted, so far as I know, in any country in the world, before Mr. Harris introduced the singular clause in the American Treaty. Merchants were not entitled by Treaty to have their dollars exchanged at the mint,— in any quantity, large or small,—after the expiration of the first year.    What they *were* entitled to (according to the exact terms of the Treaty), namely, that their coins should pass current, weight for weight, with Japanese coins of the same metal, was declared by the Japanese Government to be out of their power to secure.    I believe that great as their power is over the lives and property of their subjects, this might well be impossible.    It was clearly out of my power, or that of my colleagues, in the face of such a declaration,— and equally beyond our province,—to adopt any measures of coercion.    What had the merchants to complain of then, or what could a bribe avail one way or the other, to alter the conditions of the currency? But the calumnious object of such detractions of a Minister, three years of whose life was passed under a continual menace of assassination in defending their interests, is manifested by their carefully keeping out of view the fact that all my colleagues, not Her Majesty's Minister alone, entered into the provisional arrangements objected to, and were consequently to be held equally responsible and open to any charge of venal motives. If it be meant by the suppression of all reference to these, that they had no voice in the matter, and were entirely led or overruled by me, I am constrained to repudiate a compliment to my influence at the expense of the integrity and independence of the Representatives of every other Treaty Power in Yeddo. Though apart from this, I should accept without hesitation the whole responsibility of this, or any other act of my administration, however endorsed by the common consent of my colleagues. I have not usually shrunk from responsibility when it properly devolved upon me, and I feel less inclined than ever to do so in this instance. As for the grasping after pecuniary advantages implied in all these imputations, the calumny is pointless against a public servant, who, after more than twenty years of arduous service, chiefly in the East, returns poorer than when he first entered.

But to resume the consideration of the general question of the currency, thus temporarily in abeyance: it was evident that it could not so remain indefinitely, or for an unlimited time, and it was natural that the Japanese Government should seek a final solution in negotiations with the respective Treaty Powers in Europe, on the occasion of sending a mission to them. Accordingly it was brought prominently forward by the Envoys, and they received an assurance, that although no immediate decision could be taken in a matter of such importance, it should receive the careful consideration it demanded; and upon reference to the department to which questions of finance and currency more specially appertained, instructions should be sent to Her Majesty's Representative at Yeddo. And the whole subject has since then been most carefully considered and examined in all its bearings by those most competent to give information, and assist in arriving at a right conclusion.

A financier in Europe and a diplomatic agent in Japan would naturally approach the subject from two very opposite points, but if both were simply desirous of arriving at the truth, they could hardly fail in the end to come to very similar conclusions. The financier would naturally take his starting-point from broad principles of international law as governing the relations of States in matters of currency as in everything else; and taking with him also certain equally fixed principles of political economy regulating matters of trade and currency. The diplomatic agent, without rejecting these, would quite as naturally be inclined to look at the arrangements actually entered into or proposed, with a direct reference to local conditions calculated to influence in some special manner the practical result. It would be next to impossible for him not to take into account the very peculiar character of the system of Government: its mysterious and far-reaching power not only over prices and currency, but the produce of the mines of gold and silver and the minutest transactions of daily life in its subjects. With the knowledge of such power existing, it would be equally impossible not to take into account as of preponderating weight, the question of good or bad faith in the Government employing it.

Starting from such opposite premisses, it could be no matter of surprise if the financier should unreservedly condemn the original clause in the Treaties,—whatever might be the history of past transactions, and however questionable the acts which might have been practised in Japan with the object of evading or remedying the consequences of the Treaty ;— as strange and anomalous, in violation of every principle of international law, and utterly unjustifiable both politically and financially considered.

Both would, however, see in this question of currency, a matter which ultimately affects, not only the interests of trade, but at the same time the social and political condition of the Japanese, and in each of these directions would inevitably react upon our future relations with the country and its Government.

So sudden and violent a rending of the monetary arrangements of a country produced by the interference of foreigners, is without precedent in modern times. Depreciation of currency in other countries, however rapid, has generally been foreshadowed and sufficiently gradual to admit of a progressive readjustment of prices, and to a certain extent of contracts. But in the case of Japan the value of the current money was at once reduced to one third of its former rate, by external pressure, and for the advantage of foreign merchants.

It is beyond all doubt under these circumstances that the inconvenience occasioned by the consequent derangement of money prices and of contracts expressed in money must have been immense. In one respect, moreover, the disturbance of wages had no less manifestly a political bearing, which may, or rather which must, seriously affect our future relations with the Japanese. The Daimios have in their service large bodies of retainers who in addition to their food and clothing receive a very small allowance paid in itziboos. This, barely sufficient before to enable them to dress themselves and support their families, by the depreciation of the currency became altogether inadequate. The discontent and irritation caused in the mind of this class is intense, as we have had evidence written in blood. The Daimios, whose pecuniary interests have probably been little benefited by foreign trade, owing to the profits of the sale of all produce being intercepted by the Tycoon's officials at the consular ports ; and who are alarmed and

exasperated by the danger these foreign relations bring to
their feudal privileges and rights, and the institutions of the
country generally, have obviously no motive if they had
the means of allaying this discontent by increasing the
money-wages of their retainers.  On the contrary, there
is very little doubt they have profited by the circumstances
to incense their followers more against foreigners.  Under
these circumstances, the Japanese Government appear impressed with the necessity of taking measures for the
purpose of allaying this general discontent.  This is their
avowed object in the change which they now propose in
their currency, and such a change, if suggested with that
motive and for that object, is as much in our interest as
theirs.  They propose to withdraw the present silver
coinage and substitute for it pieces to be denominated half-
itziboos, two to the dollar in weight.  It is contended
financially that the natural effect of this arrangement
would be that two half-itziboos would be equal in weight
to three itziboos of the present coinage, and the two
coins would represent the itziboo in the denomination of
account.  The purchasing power of the itziboo would
thus be raised to an equality with that of the dollar,
unless other causes operated to prevent the recognition
of the dollar as a tender of payment on an equality,
weight for weight, with Japanese coins.  If 1,500 iron
cash continued to represent the nominal value of one
itziboo, the purchasing power of the cash would be raised
equally with the value of the itziboo.  Consequently, the
nominal value of the dollar expressed in the term ' cash,'
would be reduced two-thirds ; but its real value in relation to cash would remain unchanged, as the purchasing
power of 1,500 cash would be the same as that now
possessed by 4,500 cash representing the value of three
itziboos.

If this be correct, the objection hitherto offered, that
the dollar would be exchangeable for no more than one-
third .of the quantity of cash for which it is now exchanged, and that its *purchasing power* would thus be

reduced by the change to the extent of sixty or seventy per cent., falls to the ground. It would in that case appear to be founded on a confusion between the real value of coins derived from intrinsic contents of precious metal, and the nominal value of token coins representing parts of the standard money.

It is not, however, perfectly clear to me that the purchasing power of the dollar will suffer no diminution. I confess to a belief that it *will* suffer, though to what extent it may be difficult to say, from the power the Japanese Government possesses to control and modify the course of exchange. But whether the reasoning on this point be correct or not, it does not seem that there is any ground on which Her Majesty's Government can claim a right to object to the present proposition of the Japanese Government, on the plea of its involving an infraction of Article X. in the Treaty. The Tycoon must be held at liberty to regulate the designation and weight of the coins current in his dominions as he pleases. All that can fairly be contended for is, that the manner in which it is brought forward, and the serious considerations affecting our international arrangements with Japan which the currency question has raised, would point to the policy of cooperation with the Government of the Tycoon, in their attempt to remedy the evils which originated in foreign interference; while the clause admitted into the Treaty gives us a claim to be heard.

Such a settlement of the currency question in Japan should be undertaken in the view only of what is just to the Japanese, and if with a frank acknowledgment of error in the past, it would not, I venture to believe from what I know of Japanese Ministers, detract from our merit in their eyes. I quite agree with the financial authorities, that the real claims of foreign merchants in Japan, and their commercial interests cannot be affected, certainly neither wrongfully nor injuriously, by a proper regulation of the currency of a country with which they trade. If foreign money is wanted for the settlement of their transactions, it will find its way; but the attempt to force foreign coin upon the Japanese by compact in a treaty, can hardly be regarded otherwise than as showing a disregard of the laws of political economy, no less than of the principles which govern international relations between civilised nations.   Japan is rich in minerals, and to require them to take silver, of which they have already a supera-bundance, in exchange for other produce, such as tea and silk, which our merchants require, cannot be regarded otherwise than as a one-sided operation, which violates the principles of commerce.   The proper use of the precious metals in international transactions, it may safely be affirmed as beyond dispute, is to adjust the balance of exchanges.   This fundamental principle, it may not less safely be asserted, can never be disregarded without incon-venience; while in the case of Japan, it is to be feared the attempt to contravene it could only lead in the end to very serious results, the reverse of those which were anticipated from the Treaty.   It seems an unavoidable conclusion that the dollars sent to Japan will remain in that circum-scribed territory as there is no vent for them.   The Japanese will not require them for the purchase of com-modities from other nations.   The inevitable consequence, therefore, must be a glut of silver in Japan, and a rise in prices until they reach a point at which it will be no longer profitable for the British merchant or any other foreigner to transmit dollars for the purchase of Japanese produce, and thus all trade would be brought to an end quite as certainly as it could be under any equitable adjustment of their currency, were even the worst fears of those who would deprecate such a course realised to the fullest extent.   But there would be this difference, that in the latter case we should ourselves be the authors of the mischief by persisting in a wrong course — one equally open to condemnation on the best ascertained principles of political economy and international law—while in the former, Foreign Powers would have nothing to reproach themselves with, and could no more be held responsible for the result, than for the changes of the seasons, or the operation of any other of the immutable laws by which the relations of supply and demand are regulated all over the world, whatever may be the efforts of man to change their course. This is the more worthy of attention, perhaps, as opening a view of the subject in which the immediate interests of our merchants connected with the country may be opposed to the permanent objects of commerce; and Treaties of amity and commerce, if they have not nobler ends should at least have wider aims than the temporary enrichment of a few individuals, even if these may have an interest in promoting the introduction of British manufactures into a new market. Such were the conclusions which seemed naturally to follow a searching investigation into all the various phases of this long-debated question of the Japanese currency. And as material interests must be affected by any action that may ultimately be taken by the Japanese Government, not only the investments and trade of the merchants actually in the country at the time, but the future prospects of all foreign trade with Japan, it will no doubt be satisfactory to many to know what the real points at issue have been. And farther, to know in what direction it is considered in this country we may most safely look for a readjustment upon equitable principles, of the monetary system of Japan, entirely broken up by a forcible interference from without, — and at this moment in a transition state which it is impossible to perpetuate. Impossible, I say, even if it were not otherwise demonstrably unsound, and calculated to create the most serious prejudice to the true interests of foreign commerce, no less than to the country with which we seek to maintain relations mutually and reciprocally beneficial.

This year of 1862 in respect to the progress of events and the foreign relations of Japan, we have seen, has been, up to the period of the negotiations in Europe, chiefly marked by two events — the departure of the Japanese Mission and the attempt on the life of the Japanese Minister of Foreign Affairs. This last had one special feature worthy of note. For the first time in these onslaughts a fire-arm was used by the assailants. Already before my departure I had information of a manufactory for revolvers; the political significance of which is greater than may seem; for assuredly the life of a foreigner and our whole position will be very much less secure if revolvers get into the hands of those who are hostile. Hitherto the superiority enjoyed by the foreigner in the exclusive possession of these, has been a great element of security.

The first six months of the year had passed, however, with only a suspicious fire in the foreign settlement at Yokohama, in addition to these leading events; and on the same day as the attempt on the life of Ando Tsusimano. One circumstance indeed occurred well deserving of a passing notice, if merely as demonstrating the persistent intolerance of the authorities in matters of religion. The Abbé Girard, a French missionary of the Romish faith, had built a chapel at Yokohama, to which no objection had been made; but as soon as it was finished and Japanese were found to go, attracted chiefly by curiosity, they pounced upon thirty of them, and M. de Bellecourt had the greatest difficulty in saving their lives.

Lieut.-Col. Neale, the new Secretary of Legation, did not arrive from China until after my departure, with instructions to take charge in my absence as Chargé d'Affaires. He resolved to take up his residence in the Temple of Tozengee again, while the new Legation was being completed. So recently arrived from Pekin, he may have thought the people and circumstances were alike; but if so, he was destined to be very quickly and painfully undeceived. The anniversary, according to the Japanese calendar, of the last attack on the Legation had come round. One of the Governors of Foreign Affairs paid him a visit of congratulation in the afternoon, and all had gone to rest in the building save the two or three solitary sentries (blue-jackets, and marines of H.M.S. 'Reynard,') posted at intervals round the house, when suddenly Lieut.-Col. Neale, who was still awake, heard the sentry outside his door challenge. Although the parole was correctly given, something suspicious or unsatisfactory apparently, made the sentry advance towards the party approaching, when suddenly a cry of mortal anguish broke the stillness of the night, and the sound of blows reached him as he lay. To leap out of bed and make his way across his own apartments to the guard-room was not the work of many moments. All were suddenly roused and sprang to their arms, to feel how desperate was their position if any attacking force had to be resisted. At the same moment the sentry staggered among them, covered with wounds and frightfully gashed. To gather together in one place, the largest room in the house, and stand prepared to resist from whatever quarter assailants might come, was indeed all that could be done, in their ignorance as to the nature or extent of the danger, the numbers to be met, or the direction from whence attack might be expected. After a pause, a corporal of marines was missed who it appeared had been going his rounds, when the alarm was first given, and Lieut. Aplin with some of his men went in search of him. He was found lying dead across the door which gave entrance from the outside to Colonel Neale's rooms, and by which, during my residence there, the retreat of the sentries at that side had to be effected. He had received numerous sword and spear wounds, and had fired one barrel of his revolver, but so sudden and murderous must have been the assault that he was probably at the first blow disabled. The Japanese Government wished it to be believed there was but one assailant, but it is astonishing in that case how quickly the one succeeded in overpowering two men both armed,— and inflicting some thirty or forty wounds.

The night must have passed drearily enough for that band of foreigners, taken at sore disadvantage, and caught in something very like a trap, so entirely open on all sides to attack, and so incapable of defence from within.  From the dying sentry, a sailor of the 'Reynard,' some few particulars were gleaned before he breathed his last.  The night was very dark, he had as usual a Japanese sentry by him, who it is to be presumed had his dim paper lantern by his side, when he perceived something approaching across a rustic bridge immediately opposite, which gave passage over a large pond.  On challenging, he received back the word for the night, ' Tama,' but not liking the appearance of the object in the dark, he stepped down from the platform, and advanced towards it, when a man suddenly sprung to his feet from the end of the bridge, where he had been on all-fours, and thrust at him with one of their fifteen feet lances.  The next instant, with a sweep of a sword the hand that held the musket was nearly severed from the wrist, and thus rendered defenceless he received a succession of sabre cuts before the corporal of marines appeared on the scene.  The latter approached from the verandah at the end of the lawn, some twenty paces off, and advancing to the rescue, the assassin or assassins, (for whether there was more than one does not seem to have been ascertained,) left the sentry, and rushed upon the corporal, who, after firing a single shot, was hewn down in the same ferocious manner, having apparently maintained some sort of running fight until he reached the steps leading to Colonel Neale's bed-room, where he was found lying quite dead.  One of the murderers had evidently taken refuge under the verandah, for the next morning a pool of blood was found, and spots all along the verandah showed his track across another small bridge, directly past a Japanese guard-house.

There seems to be no doubt that this man was a retainer of the very Daimio who furnished the Japanese guard or a portion of it—for more than one Daimio was charged with the defence of the Legation.  The man in question, however, appears to have been a retainer, some said a confidential officer, of Matsdaira Tembanus Kami ; and wounded by the shot from the corporal's revolver, he made his way unmolested, or rather aided by his comrades, back to his own house, where he killed himself, after confessing (or boasting) that he had attacked, and killed some foreigners. The Japanese sentry admitted that he ran away—to call assistance! Then as ever, disarming vigilance by a show of protection and support, which was wholly illusory. Whether he was in collusion or not, or how many of the man's comrades were in complicity with the more active instruments, we shall never know with any certainty. But a very significant incident marked the following day. Lieut.-Col. Neale demanded to see the body of the murderer, and after some demur, the request was acceded to—accompanied, however, by an intimation, the sinister and menacing purport of which admitted of no mistake, that the body would be brought, to be laid in the temple, and surrounded by a large body of his comrades, the retainers of Matsdaira. It was afterwards reported that they had determined to massacre every foreigner if a desecrating finger was laid upon their comrade! Of course the Chargé d'Affaires declined the visit, but no satisfaction could be obtained for the atrocious character of the proceeding.

As there was a speciality in the circumstances of the attack on Ando Tsusimano, distinguishing it from all previous attempts of the same nature—the first use of fire-arms—so was there in this a similar and discouraging difference, in the special fact, that whereas in the first attack on the Legation by an armed band, the Japanese guard, though it allowed itself to be surprised, and tardily came to our rescue, yet at least fought in our defence, and struck manfully at the assailants, who moreover were, so far as we knew, lawless and nameless men. But here it was the Japanese guard itself, from whose ranks the murderer came; and if only one, it is impossible to doubt that he had many accomplices and well-wishers. It was precisely because I felt no confidence in the fidelity of the Japanese guards by which we were surrounded, of whom we *could* know nothing, and in the selection of whom we had no voice; that I had come to the conclusion if life was to

be protected at all, it must be by a guard of Europeans —
both in the house and in the streets.    Many small
incidents—some as light as feathers, but like feathers
indicating prevailing currents — had satisfied my mind
that the men about us could never be trusted, and might
at any moment, as had now actually happened, supply the
instruments of attack or murder.    For this reason I had, so
long as I remained at Yeddo, always doubled the sentry
near the door by which a retreat was to be effected, and
further secured them a light by which they could observe
the approach of anyone.    I felt nothing short of such
precautions could protect life, either that of the sentries or
our own.

The year was not to close without another frightful
tragedy, but this time it was on the high road between
Yeddo and Kanagawa.    The victims were British residents at Yokohama, and invested with no official character
to render them specially obnoxious or more exposed to
hostility.    And this time too, as if it was decreed that each
successive deed of blood in the year's series should be
marked by a more sinister character, this was distinguished
from all preceding by the worst feature that has yet
been observed.    Residents had before been set upon in
and near the port, and butchered in the streets, but all,
with one exception, had been under cover of the darkness,
and by unknown assailants.    In this case, and for the first
time, a whole party, among whom was a lady, were set
upon, not by unknown or lawless outcasts, but by the
liveried retinue of one of the proudest nobles in the land,
and at the order of his secretary.    Under his own eye
the party was attacked, and one of them, after being des-
perately wounded, was slain outright by a farther order as
he lay on the ground.    So at least it is confidently reported.
Two of his male companions, dangerously wounded, together with the lady, only escaped with their lives by
riding through the band of armed ruffians.

Let us hope this will close the series for the year, though
none may safely venture to predict that it will, or what a

day or a month may bring forth in such a country under
existing circumstances.   Life in Japan is in the present
day, under a feudal and military system, no more secure
than it was in the Anglo-Saxon era in our own land,
with which lawless and ferocious period in our history,
the present social state of Japan has, as I have shown,
many points of close resemblance.   There is and can be
no security to life under such conditions.   Yet as I wrote
now two years ago to the Japanese Ministers : —

'It is for the Government to answer, for they are responsible by the Law of Nations.   In the eyes of all the world
they are responsible for the maintenance of order, and
that respect for the laws which protect life and property ;
if they fail in this, they cease to preserve the essential character of a Government, and lose their best title to the
respect of Foreign Powers, who can only treat with those
who govern *de facto*, and not merely in name.   This is,
indeed, the very condition of their permanence as a Government, and they cannot forget it without imminent peril.
The Government of Japan is menaced, therefore, in its own
existence, in such a state of misrule ; and, in their own
interest, I must urge the actual situation upon their most
serious attention.' *

Nor can I better close this chapter and the boo
devoted to an exposition of the true nature of our relations
with Japan, than by the following extract from the same
despatch addressed to the Japanese Minister of Foreign
Affairs to be laid before the Council immediately after Mr.
Heuskin's murder, in which, in concert with my four
colleagues, I sought to rouse them to a true sense of the
impending danger to them, as a Government, and to their
subjects :—' My long-continued personal relations with one
of your Excellencies, and their uniformly friendly character,
lead me to hope that, sharing in the regret I feel for these
untoward impediments to a good understanding, you will
see the necessity for similar decided action with your col-

* See Correspondence respecting Affairs in Japan, March and April 1861,
presented to both Houses of Parliament by command of Her Majesty, 1861.

leagues in the Government, that this standing reproach may be removed. The faction of violent and unscrupulous advocates for a system of terrorism and assassination whom I must suppose to be the real authors of such troubles, must be controlled, whatever may be the rank or number of those concerned, or nothing but grievous consequences, from which Japan will be the first and greatest sufferer, can follow, in spite of the sacrifices and efforts I am now making to prevent such a catastrophe. The Government, in a word, must show that it has both the will and the ability to impose respect on all the disaffected or violent spirits who would seek, for their own ends, to disturb the good relations hitherto existing between the Treaty Powers and Japan, and which on the part of Great Britain, the Government of Her Majesty is most anxious to maintain for the mutual advantage of both countries. They must no longer be permitted to take life with assured impunity, and follow out a system of intimidation in the vain hope of driving foreigners out of the country by murder and terrorism. Europe, united, would resist the attempt, render its success impossible, and punish the authors of such an outrage on the laws and rights of nations. Could they even temporarily effect their object, and murder every foreigner, Japan would be the most grievous sufferer. Were such a flagitious policy ever to be carried out, the whole country would fall under the ban of civilised nations, and be dealt with as a common enemy. I trust, for the interests of humanity, such deplorable contingencies may be rendered impossible, and that both the Government and people of Japan will be convinced that their best policy is faithfully to fulfil their engagements, and to maintain friendly relations with a Power which has at its disposal ample means for obtaining, in case of need, full redress for injuries done to its subjects.'

I had already at a much earlier date been compelled to write in a similar strain a despatch, and with a single paragraph, I may sum up the whole of this dismal chapter of violence, treachery, and murder:—

'It is the desire of my Government and the interest of Great Britain to be at peace with all nations, and cultivate only the best relations; but it is not permitted to any nation, with large interests at stake and national honour to defend, to shrink from the due maintenance of its treaty rights; and least of all can Great Britain allow them to be trampled under foot here or elsewhere.'*

As to what may be the best policy for this country, or for other Treaty Powers, under such conditions, I will not here express any opinion. The whole question is surrounded by difficulties of the most serious kind. That there should be an accordance of views among all the Treaty Powers, and some unity of action, were it possible—would appear to be a first important result to be aimed at, as a preliminary condition in the success of any course ultimately adopted. Not that each one is not strong and powerful enough to exact retribution for itself, if that be deemed the one thing needful. But having entered into relations with a people presenting this strange anomaly that, while their material civilisation is not far behind our own, and the mass of the nation is well-ordered and peaceable, with as much of culture and intelligence as any nation in Europe: they are governed by a feudal and military class, for a parallel to which we must go back to the ferocious and turbulent periods of our own history,— to a period when Anglo-Saxon, Dane, and Norman had fought over the whole land, and divided the kingdom among the respective chiefs and followers, and no sovereign that ever held the sceptre of the whole or a part could maintain order, or insure peace among his bold and savage feudatories. How to deal with two such opposite social states and conditions of existence in the same nation, is a problem which has never before been presented to any Government for solution, and one which may well prove perplexing to the best statesmen of Europe. The feudal element is the true obstacle for the moment to all

* Correspondence from Her Majesty's Envoy, &c., in Japan, presented to both Houses of Parliament by command of Her Majesty, 1860.

progress towards a pacific and satisfactory solution. How is it to be dealt with? That is the first question which seems to present itself, in any review of possible alternatives or conditions of settlement. The dual sovereignty of Mikado and Tycoon follows close upon it, and equally requires to be grappled with before any satisfactory conclusion can be arrived at by one, or all the Treaty Powers combined. No doubt various answers might be suggested more or less satisfactorily dealing with the real questions at issue. They would be out of place, however, here. I have merely endeavoured in the history of our past relations, which this narrative may in some degree, I hope, supply, to indicate where the real difficulties seem to lie, and what the nature and extent of the obstacles to all progress towards a better state of affairs, in which security to life, and reasonable facilities for a legitimate commerce are the chief ends. How such difficulties and obstacles may best be dealt with, remains, of course, for each Treaty Power to decide as it may see fit. I can only hope to have contributed some materials in the way of information on the actual state of the country, and our present relations, which may assist in the formation of a right judgement. As to both these, and the policy best calculated to bring about the desired end in the interests of commerce and civilisation, it is hardly possible to speak in any decisive terms at this moment above all others. A great change is being effected in the fundamental relations of suzerain and subject. The whole Feudal power is profoundly moved, and their organisation, political and social, is crumbling under the shock of a sudden contact with Europe. Whether all this can take place, and a new social and political basis be attained, without an interval of disorder, violence, and bloodshed, must be very doubtful. The danger is undoubtedly great. The changes indicated by the departure of the Daimios and their families from the capital are of the most sweeping and fundamental character. It is, in a word, a revolution, effected either by compromise and compact between the governing classes and the Tycoon; or it is the preparation for an appeal to arms, in which latter case foreigners are likely to be the first objects of attack, as their presence has undoubtedly been the immediate cause of such fermentation. If, on the other hand, any compromise has been entered into, on a basis of mutual concession between the Tycoon and the leading Feudatory Princes, the object of which is to remove to a distance from Yeddo the Daimios and their armed retainers, better days may be in store for Western nations and Japanese alike, than could reasonably have been hoped for, after such a troubled and inauspicious beginning. A very short time must show which of these two phases of national life the Japanese are now entering upon; and equally tell the foreigner what his prospects are in Nipon — whether he is to be allowed to dwell in peace, or must stand prepared to resist desperate and continuous efforts for his expulsion from the Japanese territories.

# APPENDIX.

——◦◦⦂◕⦂◦◦——

## A

THERE has been a question raised as to the elasticity of the trade in China — in other words, the tendency of that and other Eastern countries to take a continually increasing quantity of our manufactured goods. Mr. Lay, the able Superintendent and Chief Commissioner of the custom-houses, under the Chinese Government, put forward a statement in answer to some observations of Mr. Cobden, in the House of Commons, from which the statistics in the note referred to are taken as of undoubted authority. But when the *opium* and *treasure*, forming by far the greater portion of the whole import trade, are subtracted, I do not think the statistics by any means prove the converse of Mr. Cobden's assertion that the trade was *not* elastic. The imports, apart from opium and bullion, for instance, keep no pace with, and bear no sort of proportion to the rapid and steady increase in our demands for their staples, tea and silk. And nothing short of this could, I think, be accepted as a satisfactory increase, in regard to the question of elasticity and expansive tendency.

The following is the ratio of increase in two or three of the principal articles at Shanghae — by far the most important of the Consular Ports —·

### IMPORTS.

|                        | 1854—1855       | 1858—1859         |
| ---------------------- | --------------- | ----------------- |
| Dyed and fancy cottons | 90,000 pieces   | 540,000 pieces    |
| Long cloths            | 520,000 ,,      | 1,400,000 ,,      |
| Drills                 | 120,000 ,,      | 560,000 ,,        |

It is true, they have quadrupled in three years, but yet the whole quantity is comparatively small, and this at the end of twenty years trade under treaties, with access, more or less real, to some four hundred millions of customers. Compared with the sum total of the exports of our staple manufactures, and the quantity taken with progressive increase either by European nations or our colonies;—it will be seen that, so far as we can judge from the past, there is no ground for extravagant hopes of large, or any rapidly progressive increase. The truth is, that between their capacity for consumption in woollen or cotton fabrics, and their disposition to take these from the foreign market, there is a wide disparity—and a void, which no ingenuity of the foreign producer or merchant can have any present hope of bridging over.

# B

*Minutes of a Meeting of British Residents at Yokohama, on February 19, 1861, convened by Her Majesty's Acting Consul, for the purpose of taking into consideration a Report and the proceedings of a preliminary Meeting on the subject of existing grievances and obstructions at this port.—Capt. F. HOWARD VYSE, H.B.M. Consul, in the Chair.*

THE Chairman having explained the object of the meeting in the terms of the Circular of the 14th inst. convening it, said he would be glad to receive any proposition, or hear any explanation bearing on the subjects for discussion.

Mr. Edward Clarke begged the chairman to read the report of the preliminary meeting referred to, as he (Mr. Clarke) was yet ignorant of what was embodied in that report.

The report being read,

Mr. Clarke said:

Mr. Chairman,—I rise to claim the privilege of addressing this meeting on behalf of myself and also those parties present who may not have had an opportunity afforded them of reading the reply sent in to Her Majesty's Consul, by those merchants of Yokohama who received invitations to attend the private meeting held at Mr. Keswick's parlour, on the 7th inst., and I beg to take this occasion of heartily thanking you, Sir, for the kindness and consideration which you have shown to this meeting by reading the contents of that document, with which I am now made acquainted for the first time, barring what I have learned by hearsay: and I must now claim the indulgence and patience of you, Sir, and also of this meeting, if, in my attempt to criticise portions of a document with which I can only be very imperfectly acquainted, I may unintentionally commit some errors, arising chiefly therefrom, and partly also to the short space of time during which I have been resident in Japan.

Without wasting the valuable time of this meeting on minor topics of grievances which others are, or have been, so much better able to deal with, I will now venture to approach at once what I consider to be of the pith and marrow of that which concerns this meeting; I allude, Mr. Chairman, to the *Currency Question,* and however simple it may appear in the abstract, to

hear that a resolution was carried by a majority, at the preliminary meeting held on the 7th inst., to the effect 'that the
Mexican dollar be allowed to find its own level,' &c., &c., still, I
humbly think, that it will be trenching too much on the good sense
and patience of this meeting to suppose for one moment that the
Mexican or any other dollar or coin whatsoever could ever find
its own level, so long as the Japanese Government, for obvious
reasons, is determined that it never shall. It is, nevertheless,
quite true that Article X. of Lord Elgin's Treaty apparently
tends somewhat in support of that resolution; but if, Mr. Chairman, we give to this article the careful consideration and
interpretation which it deserves, we shall find that it is subject
to the same rules which guide the Queen's judges, in giving
interpretation to clauses in Acts of Parliament, which, however
well framed at the time of being enacted, are sometimes found
in practice to be almost inoperative: in these cases the judge is
permitted to take upon himself the responsibility of interpreting
the meaning of the Act, and the motives of the law makers for
framing the clause. Following out this principle in its integrity,
I will, Mr. Chairman, with your permission, endeavour to elu-
cidate to this meeting what I take to be the meaning and
intention of Article X. of the Treaty with Japan, or rather such
portions of that Article as appear to me to bear practically on
the aforesaid resolution.

In the third paragraph of Article X. it reads thus:

'As *some* time will *elapse* before the Japanese will become
*acquainted* with the *value* of foreign coin, the Japanese
Government will, for the period of one year after the opening
of each port, furnish British subjects with Japanese coin, in exchange for theirs, equal weights being given, and *no discount
taken for recoinage.*'

I am of opinion, Mr. Chairman, that nothing can be clearer
than the intention and meaning of the third paragraph of Article
X., and I think also that it is quite competent to this meeting
to interpret it in a *large sense*. It was self-evident to the
framers of the treaty (and the foresight displayed does them
infinite credit), that *some* time must elapse before foreign coin
could become current in this country; but, as it was desirable
to fix a definite period, twelve months was the short space
accorded for the exchange of weight for weight coins, and doubtless the framers (for the major part at least) thought such
a period ample; but, unfortunately, the contrary is the fact,
twelve months has *not* been enough—and such being the case,
I humbly think, Mr. Chairman, that *we have a right* to fall back
on the *meaning* and *intention* of Article X. of the Treaty, and
in accordance with this I beg, Mr. Chairman, to put the following
resolution to this meeting:

'That, in the opinion of this meeting, it is desirable, that Her Majesty's Envoy and Minister Plenipotentiary be humbly requested to take such steps as he may see fit and desirable to obtain from the Japanese Government a fresh grant of time for the exchange of Japanese for foreign coins, less the deduction of such a per centage as will be found to remunerate the Japanese Mint, but which in the opinion of this meeting should not exceed a maximum royalty of four per cent.'

Mr. W. Keswick begged, that before pronouncing on the currency question, the meeting would well consider whether the exchange system would, in the end, be to the advantage of foreign trade. He (Mr. Keswick) was of opinion it would not; and certainly thought it wiser, with a view to the future, to abide by the treaty, and to endeavour to make the foreign coinage take up a position and find its way here as elsewhere. Where a large trade had to be conducted, the expense of coinage and the delays that would attend in every stage of such a system in Japan, and the evident impolicy of such a step in its future consequences, all spoke strongly in favour of abiding by the treaty stipulation on this head.

Mr. Clarke again rose and made the following rejoinder:

At the risk of repetition, he must beg to remind Mr. Keswick, that he was but very imperfectly acquainted (for reasons already stated to the meeting) with what was termed the chief point at issue; but in reverting to that portion of the Currency Question which tended in the direction of making a legal tender of the Mexican or any other dollar, in what he believed to be an independent State, populated by a people of high spirit, and who moreover possess a coinage *superior* in some important respects to that of the States of Central Europe (*more particularly those composing the Zollverein*), to wit, the admirable bronze coin of one tempo, which he then held in his hand, and he must beg to record it as his deliberate conviction, that the French might with *equal* justice insist on the five franc piece being made a legal tender in England.

Mr. Clarke's motion, seconded by Mr. Elmstone, was then put to the meeting—For the motion 10, against it 24; resolution carried by 14.

No other motion being put, the Consul then addressed the meeting, stating that he was very glad to meet so large a body of the British residents at this port, not only to hear what observations they might wish to make on the several matters to be taken into consideration, but on his own part to give them such information as might be in his power, to assist them in coming to a right conclusion. In furtherance of this object, there were some data in respect to the steps which had hitherto been taken by the British authorities that he would avail himself of the present occasion to put them in possession of, the better to enable them to deal in a practical manner with the question to be discussed. To prevent doubt or misapprehension as to the details, he had committed them to paper, and before proceeding to read them, he would further say, that he not only was glad to have this opportunity of meeting them for the purpose of taking into consideration many questions directly affecting their interests, because the full and fair discussion with a free interchange of opinions was, he thought, one of the best modes of arriving at the truth; but he hoped the proceedings of that day might go far to remove many misconceptions, and prepare the way for a better understanding in future, in all that concerned their mutual relations and the position of residents in the country. The following statement was then read by the Consul:—

'I ought in the first place to inform you, that the letter of the committee nominated at a preliminary meeting, and which was addressed to me on the 15th instant, enclosing the minute of the proceedings, was duly laid before Her Majesty's Envoy Extraordinary, and I am directed to inform you, that he read the whole with great interest, and observed with satisfaction the excellent spirit in which you had set about the consideration of the grave matters brought under your notice. I am further to assure you of his earnest desire to contribute by every means in his power to the improvement of your position generally, and the removal of any grievances that can be shown upon full information of all the local conditions to admit of practical remedy.

'He has instructed me accordingly to afford you every information as to the steps which have hitherto been taken with the Japanese Government and authorities towards the improvement of trade, the security of life and property, the custom-house system at this port, and the occupation of land for building purposes; and, to enable me to do so more effectually, I have had access to all the sources of information the Legation affords. I think you will see, in what I shall now lay before you, abundant evidence of watchful regard for every legitimate interest, and that no efforts have been spared by Her Majesty's Envoy in communication with the Government at Yeddo to advance these interests, and avert the dangers which have menaced both you and them. It will probably best promote the objects of the meeting if, in the data I now wish·to lay before you, I follow the order observed in the dispatch of Her Majesty's Envoy Extraordinary, and subsequently in the proceedings of the preliminary meeting and the letter of the committee.

'*The Currency.*—The treaty stipulates, that "all foreign coin shall be current in Japan, and shall pass for its corresponding weight in Japanese coin of the same description." That has not hitherto been the case; and while there is no dispute about the obligation of the government of this country to do all that is in its power to give effect to this clause, there is a question, and a difficult one, as to how far it is in the power of this or any other government to force a foreign coinage into general circulation, and at a fixed rate or valuation. The Japanese Government says it cannot; and even in the case of a single coin, the dollar, that it has already, as a government, done all it can do, and failed; that it has issued an edict throughout the empire making all foreign coins legal tenders, weight for weight; that it has even attempted, with the concurrence of the foreign representatives, to secure the circulation of the dollar (at something less than weight for weight, in view of the facility of exchange), and stamped a certain number with a government stamp of three itziboos, but still they only find circulation at the ports, and that varying at a depreciated rate of two, or two and a half itziboos, while in the interior there is reason to believe they have no currency.

' Is there any remedy for this?

' That is the question for consideration. Because it is to be remembered, that no treaty can be invoked to effect an impossibility. Many may believe that the Japanese Government are not acting with good faith in the matter, but are themselves the chief impediments to the free circulation of the dollar at its full value, and that in any case they have the power, if they had the will, to secure their currency both at the open ports and elsewhere. But it must be remembered, on the other hand, that the difficulty, not to say impossibility, of forcing a foreign coinage on a people is of universal experience—however despotic or absolute the government. In China, where they have no coinage to displace, where a coinage of any kind is a great desideratum, and where dollars of Spain and of American States, all of the same (or nearly the same) intrinsic value, have for the last twenty years been in circulation at five ports on the coast, with the government of the country passive in the matter, having no obvious interest one way or the other, this free circulation throughout the country is as far as ever from being attained. Even in the case of those districts where our large dealings in tea and silk have, so to say, forced foreign specie into circulation, the result was not the general circulation of dollars bearing all a pretty equal value, but an unmeaning preference for the only one of those that was obsolete and could not be reproduced, the Carolus dollar, to which obsolete coin an entirely fictitious value was attached by the Chinese, continually increasing until they were at last used up, and not to be had at all, to the depreciation of all other dollars, some thirty or forty per cent. The circulation of a western coinage in an

eastern country must then be admitted to present great difficulties, and some that may be quite insurmountable, even where
there is no active influence of a government to prevent its currency, or even no want of good faith to help.   On the other hand,
although it is to some extent an evil to the foreign merchant not
to be able to circulate the coinage of his own country and buy
produce with it, weight for weight against native coins, the
committee have rightly shown it is not so great an evil as has
been often represented ; nor is it altogether unmixed with good.
If it tends to restrict the export trade of Japanese produce,
it certainly no less serves to increase and develope a trade in
imports.   And, again, whether the dollar be nominally rated by
the Japanese at two and a half itziboos or at two, it does not
follow that more dollars must be paid for a chest of tea or a
bale of silk than if they were rated at three or more, because
it is to be assumed, that the foreign merchant will only give as
many dollars as he calculates it is worth, to leave him a fair
profit ; and if they were to circulate at their weight value of 311
or 312 per $100, competition would still keep up the price of
Japanese produce to the same margin of profit.

' Lastly, no large trade could be conducted by means of this
coinage only, any more than it could by shillings and sixpences.
Such at least are some of the considerations which it appears
desirable should be carefully weighed, and kept in view, before
any proposals are made, by means of more or less determined
effort and action upon the Japanese Government, to alter what
actually exists, and which perhaps may only be altered by
risking some greater or unforeseen derangement in monetary and
commercial relations.   These suggestions are thrown out in view
also of a considerable diversity of opinion among the community here, which is at all times an additional reason for caution,
and for mature deliberation in any steps recommended.   It
may be true, that the government does in effect prohibit the
circulation of the dollar in the interior, and will only give two
and a half itziboos in exchange when Japanese take their dollar
to the mints (or that there are extortions or bribes which bring
it down to that), but we shall never be in a position to prove it;
and Her Majesty's Envoy, I know, believes it a very profitless,
and not a very dignified or politic course, to persist in assertions
reflecting on the character of the government which he cannot
support by proof, and they meet by a flat denial.

' It seems probable that they have the means of purchasing the
produce, or otherwise working the silver mines in Japan, so as
to obtain the bullion at a less rate than two and a half itziboos
for a dollar weight.   Of course, by so much less as they can thus
obtain it, the exchange of dollars is a dead loss of revenue.   If
this be the fact, it is vain to hope the Japanese Government will

frankly and honestly subject themselves to this loss, whatever treaty stipulations may require to the contrary.

' The second subject for consideration has relation to the various impediments traceable more or less distinctly to Japanese officials, in the way of trade; and restrictions not in accordance with the treaty, or the free sales and purchase of goods.

' The non-observance or enforcement of contracts, the committee place at the head of these, and no doubt it is a serious grievance. Within the last month, it is true, greater efforts have been made by the Japanese authorities here to fulfil this obligation than in all the antecedent period; yet this, I fear, is rather to be traced to circumstances connected with the present political situation, than any settled determination to give effect to contracts.

' But in reference to a practical remedy being found, I confess I am not sanguine. In China, I am told, after twenty years of effort and experience, little progress has been made in this direction, though precisely the same grievance exists; so much so, that a mode of transacting business has grown up which, except in the case of Chinese of well-established character, rarely leaves it in the power of the native dealer to inflict loss upon the foreign merchant. In exceptional cases where this has not been done, an appeal to the native authorities, in nine cases out of ten, leads but to one of two results: if the Chinese dealer is a man of means and only dishonest, he is squeezed as long as he has anything squeezable, for the benefit of the mandarins and their subordinates; if poor, he may get a bambooing or imprisonment; but in neither case does the creditor get anything for his pains.

' Something may be done by persistent representations and remonstrances, but I fear it will be long before either my best exertions on the spot or those of Her Majesty's Envoy at Yeddo will remove all cause of complaint under this head. It is true, the governor, upon more than one occasion, has proposed to take off the head of the defaulter by way of a caution to others, and possibly it might be effective, but I confess to some scruples in accepting such composition for the payment of debt, and some doubt whether it would be as satisfactory to the plaintiff as even a small dividend.

' The official interference with the sale of Japanese produce is, I conceive, a much more serious evil. I wish I could honestly tell you I thought it easier of remedy. I have not the slightest doubt in my own mind, that the grievance exists to the full extent stated; but the evidence is unproducible, and were it otherwise in any one or two cases, the only result would be a more secret and astute mode of going to work for the same end. The spirit of official meddling and restriction seems a part of the very constitution of Japan. The government and whole class of officials seem incapable of abstaining, or even understanding how the country could be governed without it. The ruling classes believe the country is being ruined, as it is, by too large and unrestricted foreign trade. The ministers tell Her Majesty's Envoy this nearly every time he sees them. They have long been urgent, on the alleged ground of public opinion and general discontent from the enhanced price of everything (attributed exclusively to foreign trade), for the deferring of the opening of any other ports. And they urge it on the double ground, of a necessity for the country, and to prevent a revolution or sanguinary outbreak, which would be fatal to foreigners themselves, and possibly put an end to all relations. The last menace of general massacre was referred to by them as a proof of the truth of their statements on this head. Whether the restrictive and retrograde policy is founded on Japanese views of political economy, combined with the hostility, on other purely political grounds, of a large party among the ruling classes, or the result of a hostile public opinion and general discontent with a view to prevent a catastrophe, is open to question. Whether, in fact, the repeated menace of attack and series of assassinations have a political origin, and are to be taken as part of a policy which has been carried out either by the government of the country or in spite of it by those who wish to create political troubles, is matter for grave consideration, and a question on which even the foreign representatives are not unanimous. But as respects the hope of inducing the Japanese authorities, under such circumstances, to abstain from meddling, with a view to promote and not restrain the free developement of trade, I confess I see little of promise in the future. When pressed on this subject, they have even hinted, by no means obscurely, to one of the foreign representatives at Yeddo, that there were more evils than breaking a treaty, if it should be found really ruinous to a country in its operation; and upon another occasion, they proposed openly to seek the consent of all the Treaty Powers to a limitation to be fixed for all articles of export for a term of years, especially oil, silk, tea, and vegetable wax. I am authorised to mention these facts of deep interest to you all, and in order to show you clearly how great the difficulties to be encountered in any efforts to secure the full and honest execution of treaties, in respect to trade, with a government that can deliberately contemplate the rupture of all relations with foreign powers, as a lesser evil than a rigorous execution of treaties, which they regard as impolitic and imperious, and have indicated plainly enough that if they are driven to choose between a civil and a foreign war, they should not hesitate to accept the latter in preference.

' The want of system in the custom-house and inadequate
wharfage accommodation are, of all the obstacles to trade, those
which may best admit of gradual and certain improvement, and
I am quite ready to endeavour to give effect to your suggestions;
and the same I should say in reference to the interference with
labour and cargo-boats, respecting which all you propose is I
think perfectly reasonable.

' We come now to the occupation of land, in which the committee speak of " unaccountable " and, what has appeared to many,
"vexatious" delays, in obtaining building sites.  Yet nothing
admits of more easy explanation.  I need hardly remind you,
that when the port was first opened it was a question between
the Japanese authorities and the foreign representatives which
side of the bay offered the most eligible site for the permanent
objects of trade.  The British and American ministers both saw
cogent reasons for preferring Kanagawa, in a permanent point
of view; while the majority of the merchants, arriving by ones
and twos, seemed to find greater advantage in view of immediate
facilities, on the Yokohama side, where the Japanese desired
to fix them, and had gone to great expense with that object.
Both may have been right from these separate points of view:
the ministers looking to national and permanent interests, the
merchants to what was individual and temporary.  That is a
question which need not be discussed now, and it is not in fact
before the meeting; but as there has been no little misconcep-
tion (I do not wish to use any harder word) as to the real facts
and the action of Her Majesty's authorities, it may not perhaps
be without advantage to all if I offer a few words in explanation
in respect to the past, as tending to clear the way to a good
understanding for the future.

' We will not discuss who was right or wrong, or whether anything better could have been done at first than to leave the
question to be decided by events, the progress of the settlement
being left to itself, in a great degree.  It is no very grave reproach
to those who have only temporary interests at stake, to charge
them with preferring these to any future permanent advantages,
so neither is it a very legitimate subject of reproach to consul
or ministers, who by office are the representatives of interests
that are national and permanent, if they should keep these
constantly in view as the more important, whatever may be the
pressure of that which is individual and fleeting, and follow the
line of duty thus indicated without fear, or seeking after
popularity.  Of course, the two classes of interests cannot always
be very perfectly reconciled to each other, and this will lead to
a conflict of interests and opinions.  But in such a contingency
you have at least the satisfaction of knowing that neither the
consul nor minister can have any personal interests to consult —

they neither trade, nor deal in land. And it is going very far
a-field for adverse motives to attribute to either petty feelings
of spite and illwill, because British subjects may have thought
their own views the best, and acted upon them to the best of
their power, in a matter so nearly concerning their interests. I
will not tell you, therefore, no such feeling has ever existed,
because I will neither pay you nor myself the bad compliment
of assuming that you ever believed it possible, or that this could
be a rational mode of explaining the difficulties you experienced
in getting land. In truth, the impediment and sources of delay
lay so completely on the surface, that but for the assertion in
the letter, that they were considered unaccountable, I should fear
to take up time by telling you what all must know, and could
apply for yourselves to the solution of the supposed mystery.
However, to make further misapprehension impossible, I will
remind you that as the Japanese authorities desired nothing
better than that the merchants should settle themselves at
Yokohama rather than at Kanagawa, the former needed no aid
from minister or consuls to get all the land available for their
purposes into their hands; and things were allowed accordingly
to take their own course, without official intervention or obstacle
on my part, while an ample site was being secured on the opposite side of the bay at Kanagawa, as a measure of precaution, if
nothing more, to meet future contingencies. But in this interval,
the few who had first arrived had got into their hands all the
land available, and a cry arose, that there was no more room,
and as fresh merchants arrived no more building sites could be
obtained. This might perhaps have been foreseen when the
Japanese offered the site; but as it did not particularly affect
those who first arrived and were enabled to secure what they
themselves wanted or desired, it had not prevented a settlement
being formed, where no provision existed for increase or
expansion. The question then arose, what was to become of
merchants arriving each successive month with equal claims as
their predecessors to building sites, space, and accommodation
to follow their vocation? Some of those already in possession
may have had more than was really required for their legitimate
wants, and it was certainly true that they held their land without
any legal or valid title; but to resume possession of the land, and
re-distribute, in a more impartial way, the whole area, already
built over, was an undertaking open to many objections, besides
its difficulty and the trouble it would entail, however consistent
with legality, and even with strict justice. What then was to be
done for the houseless and landless? The merchants were themselves powerless to obtain more than the Japanese authorities
had already assigned for the whole foreign settlements. It was
under these circumstances that Her Majesty's Envoy came to

their aid, and insisted, since the Japanese Government had made Yokohama the site, that the limits should be adequately extended and more land be given. It can hardly be supposed, by those who have the least experience of Japanese officials and local conditions, that this could be effected without effort or expenditure of time. Even when a large additional tract was conceded in principle, it was still necessary that it should be cleared, by buying out and removing a considerable village population; and the merchants who most desired land evinced no readiness to advance the necessary funds. Yet this was obviously the first step towards obtaining possession. Not only the land then had to be obtained by the unaided efforts of Her Majesty's Envoy, but the funds, and they were finally obtained from the Japanese Government by him, as an advance on the security of the land. The ground too was, after this, cleared and surveyed. The process of clearance was a slow one, with infinite difficulty effected, and it proved a source both of delay and difficulty, which can be deemed unaccountable by those only who never considered the circumstances. And yet this same process of eviction and clearing land in occupation is notoriously difficult, and often a very slow operation in many countries more civilised than Japan, especially when people are forcibly dispossessed for the benefit of others, and those of an alien race. Even then, unless the whole tract, as in the old site, was in the first instance to pass into the large grasp of a few, not unwilling to invest their funds in land as a stock in trade, more or less to the prejudice of all who might be less amply provided with funds, and certainly to the damage of all who might come after, it was obviously necessary some principle of allotment and distribution should be agreed upon, and certain conditions of tenure, in order that every one might possess a clear legal title to his property. But to any such arrangement, however useful or obviously necessary, there were necessarily many parties, all of whom must be consulted, as they had each a voice in the matter: the foreign consuls and local Japanese authorities here, the ministers, both foreign and Japanese at Yeddo. Is there any one here who thinks agreement on such matters, involving both principle and detail, is so simple and easy a matter that no differences of opinion could arise—no impediments or causes of delay and difficulty? I trust to have sufficiently explained then, why those who desired land, after the old location had been all absorbed and appropriated by the first comers, could not immediately get their wants supplied. So far from the delays already experienced being "unaccountable," I cannot help thinking, as I look back on all that has been gone through, that the most unaccountable of all things would have been the absence of delays and serious difficulty. It is at all events in my power to assure you, that no exertion has ever been wanting, either on the part of Her Majesty's Envoy or myself, for their removal ; and I am happy to be able also to inform you that the last of the difficulties (as I hope and so far as I know) has now been removed.

' The conditions of tenure have been settled, as you will find them embodied in the printed Land Regulations, and form of lease or Certificate of Title on the table, subject only to the final confirmation of the Japanese and Foreign Ministers, in which I do not anticipate any difficulty, as they have already been submitted in draft and approved. It is in the nature of a leasehold tenure; transferable, without fine or charge of rent, in perpetuity — the next best thing to a freehold, and equivalent in all but the rent. You will perceive only one scale of rental has been referred to, nevertheless it seems desirable here, as at Nagasaki, that a difference should be made between front, middle, and back lots. The rental for land demanded by the Japanese authorities does not appear unreasonable, and they assure my colleagues and myself that it is estimated on the actual value in the locality to Japanese. It is 10,875 mommé for one tsoboo, a tsoboo being six feet square, which is little more than a tempo according to the present rate of exchange. In round numbers that would give for a square area of 100 tsoboo, that is 600 square feet, a rent charge of 108¾ tempos, a little more than six itziboos, and as there are 4,840 square yards to an acre, unless I have made any mistake in the calculation, they offer you building ground at the rate of 144 itziboos, or, say at the present rate of exchange, about $57 per acre.* But as the front lots are undoubtedly more valuable than the middle or back lots, it would probably be fairer — as the government demands for the whole area, as laid down on the plan before you, a sum equivalent to the rate specified — to fix different rentals for the different lots according to situation. Nothing, however, has been finally determined on this point yet, and I am quite ready to hear any opinions on the subject. The total amount paid for clearing the ground has been $10,211.66, of which $3,398.66 was raised by the sale of choice in lots, and the remainder has been advanced by the government to be repaid without interest, as the remaining lots are taken up. I hope shortly now to see the streets according to the plan laid down, and all the lots acquired fenced in, when nothing stands in the way of the proprietors turning them to account, and building such accommodation as they require.

' Finally, as to the security to life and property, which is the first and most essential condition to any developement of trade. I appreciate the reserve the committee have manifested in dealing

---

* Note by the Chairman.— There was an error here, it was found later that the rate stated was per mensem and not per annum, thus multiplying the rate by 12 for the year, or say $684 per acre.

with a subject which, if it has its special dangers and difficulties, has also its paramount interest; and if I am constrained in some degree to follow their example, I am sure you will believe it is from no indifference, either to your security or your natural desire for information. The steps recently taken by Her Majesty's Envoy, in concert with the representatives of France, Prussia, and Holland, while it must satisfy you that he regards in the most serious light whatever menaces your security, is also a sufficient indication that he thought some considerable danger existed, or at all events, that there was that in your position, and of foreigners generally in Japan, which rendered it an imperative duty in him to take some decisive step. Whether this may prove successful and attain the objects he and his colleagues have in view, as fully or as promptly as I would feign hope, it is impossible in the present state of impending negotiations to say with any certainty. In the meantime, his temporary removal here among you is itself a security and a pledge of safety, for it lessens the danger of any attack, by increasing the responsibility of the government, and gives it therefore additional motives to prevent it. And when he leaves us, either to return to Yeddo or to proceed elsewhere, you may rest assured the security of your position here will equally occupy his attention. It was not his own personal security he came here to ensure, but the improvement of yours and our position generally in Japan; and, whatever steps he may feel called upon to take, I am authorised to assure you all, that they will be taken with due deliberation, having in view the equal necessity of averting by every means in his power any interruption to trade, or disaster to yourselves. I would only say in conclusion, that I am sure you will readily see the necessity of contributing to this end by avoiding, to the utmost, all causes of quarrel or collision with the Japanese, either officials or others, and by abstaining from all unnecessary exposure in going about the settlement after dark; with such precautions I trust this alarm of dangers menacing foreigners generally will, like many preceding, pass over without more serious consequences, and that it may be with permanent advantage to our future relations.'

After some desultory conversation on the subject of a church, no one having any farther observations to make on the subject announced for discussion, the Consul concluded by suggesting the desirability of forming a committee to give effect to the wishes of the community regarding the erection of a church.

It was then proposed by Mr. S. Maine that Messrs. Ross, Clarke, Marshall, and Bell, with the Consul as chairman, should form the committee.

Mr. Bush seconded the motion.

Mr. Boyle thought the affairs of state should be finished before those of church be introduced.   He therefore proposed that the other topics touched on in the merchants' letter be discussed before this meeting.   This motion finding no seconder fell to the ground.

Mr. Marshall proposed, and Mr. Boyle seconded, a vote of most cordial thanks to the Consul for the manner in which he had conducted the meeting, for the admirable statement he had made, and for the valuable information given upon all that concerned them.

The meeting was then dissolved.


(Signed)          F. HOWARD VYSE,

H. B. M.'s Acting Consul for Kanagawa.

(True Copy)  F. BLEKMAN.

# C

EXTRACT FROM MR. MEDHURST'S COMMUNICATION.

During my recent visit to Japan, I have been much struck by the general and familiar use made by the Japanese of the Chinese written language in its own proper construction, and I avail myself of your suggestion to submit the following few remarks on the subject, in the hope that they may prove useful to you in directing the studies of the young gentlemen of your suite, who are now trying to acquire the Japanese language.

Until I came here I was always under the impression that the Japanese written language merely had its basis in the Chinese character, and that although the Chinese symbols did appear in Japanese books and writings with their own proper meaning attached, yet it was rather an exception than a rule, and even then they were isolated here and there, and never combined so as to be readable by a Chinese in the idiomatic construction peculiar to his own country. This impression I believe to be general amongst all persons who have ever given any thought to the subject. The brief opportunity, however, which I have now had of observing the people and their customs, has led me to conclude that the case is materially different; and that not only the Japanese can read Chinese to a much greater extent than has been supposed, but that Chinese can understand a considerable portion of what they see written in Japan, and from their knowledge possess peculiar facilities for acquiring its hieroglyphic and syllabic languages, as well as for learning its vernacular. I doubt not, moreover, that with larger opportunities for observation I might discover even more grounds for believing this to be the case.

That a Japanese can understand Chinese to a considerable extent I have repeatedly tested by writing short sentences for people of various classes, and the following instances will show that a person conversant with Chinese has only to walk through a Japanese town and look about him to be at once convinced how largely and intelligibly the Chinese character and construction are used. The tea and saki shops, which are so numerous,

are all scribbled over with the words, 御茶 'Royal Tea;'
御酒 'Royal Wine;' 御休所 'Royal Resting Place.'
Fruit shops show invariably the sign 御菓 'Royal Fruit,'
and often 水菓子, the very term used in China for 'Fresh
Fruit.' The fruit themselves are labelled with prices exactly as
in China, the character 文 being used to represent the copper
coin.  Jinseng and drugs are distinguished, as in China, by a
more flaming or elaborate sign than usual, and are represented
by the same characters likewise.  Advertisements by quacks of
life pills, and a hundred other medicines, might be Chinese but
for the walls and posts on which they are exhibited.  The
notice seen everywhere in China answering to our 'Commit no
nuisance,' I have met with here, worded in the same peculiar phraseology which the Celestials have adopted.  Public
bathing places have two doors side by side with the notices
男浴 'men's baths,' and 女浴 'women's baths,' which are,
however, not separated farther in, as in China, by a corresponding discrimination in a more tangible shape.  On roadway
gates, over entrances to enclosures which are public or Imperial
property, and over particular bridges, may be observed the
車留 and 下馬, which in China hint the necessity of
dismounting from chair or horse whilst treading sacred ground.
On one bridge in the highway leading to Yeddo, I noticed the
warning 御用之外車留 'unless on Imperial service
dismount,' in which sentence the construction is strictly and
purely Chinese.  I even observed one day in the main street of
Yeddo a plank stuck up by the workmen in front of a portion
of road under repair, with a notice in Chinese to pass by on the
other side.  These instances will suffice to prove the familiar
use of the Chinese written language in common life.  In books,
maps, pictures, and printed publications of all kinds the use of
Chinese is quite as decided and remarkable.  Chinese prefaces
are common in the books I have seen, and the titles or headings,
not only of the books, but of any illustrations they contain, are
invariably in Chinese.  The outer covers of maps seem always
to be superscribed in Chinese, and every town in the kingdom
appears to have a distinct Chinese name applied; it would seem
as in China, in reference to the site or some other association
connected with it, the Japanese sound of the character having
in some cases the same meaning as the characters themselves

possess. Yeddo is written 江戸, 'River's Door;' Yokohama, 横濱, 'Cross Shore;' the highway between the two towns, 東海道, 'East Sea Road;' Fusiyama, 富士山, 'Rich Scholar Peak;' and so on.

Pictures the Japanese seem peculiarly partial to, and they are to be met with of every description and rate of value; and I think I may say with truth that by far the larger proportion I have seen had Chinese titles attached, and answered perfectly to the description given. The few envelopes of official letters from the Japanese authorities which I saw in the Legation office were all superscribed with the minister's title in Chinese, and his name in Japanese, the identical characters being used for the former which are employed for the corresponding title in China, with the single exception of the translation 全權 for 'Plenipotentiary,' a term introduced by Morrison, and since discarded by Mr. Wade for another more correctly Chinese.

The facts above detailed, I think, warrant me in the opinion that a person conversant with the Chinese language possesses vast advantages for the observation of the people, habits, and language of Japan; and it follows as a consequence that a student wishing to acquire the language, will, if previously grounded in Chinese knowledge, master the difficulty with more ease than the man who attacks it without that aid. The former has only to apply the knowledge already gained, in much the same way that a Japanese would do who is grounding himself in his own language; for Japanese boys, I am told, have first to learn the Chinese symbols in which their phonetic letters are founded, and in doing so not only accustom themselves to the sight of more or less of the rest of the Chinese collection, but acquire the habit of writing them with such rapidity and facility that they eventually learn to excel even the Chinese in their ability to reduce the characters from the square into the cursive style. The student, on the other hand, who commences, ignorant both of Chinese and Japanese, has before him not only the labour of mastering the many and arbitrary modes of writing Japanese, but he has to learn whatever Chinese characters he finds employed, whether with their meanings or as mere sounds. Nor is this all, for such characters will be met with in all stages of reduction into the cursive style of writing; and I defy any man to fix in his memory the Chinese character in this shape, without first learning its component parts and accustoming his eye to the entire character whilst yet in its square form.

In a word, I am of opinion that a young student who has had, say two years' grounding in Chinese under a competent master and teachers, will master Japanese in far less time than another who starts without such introductory knowledge; and if I am right, it becomes a matter of serious consideration whether some steps should not be taken to save Her Majesty's Government and the students they send here the expense, time, and labour, now to a certain degree wasted, in endeavouring to acquire a knowledge of this difficult language.

That it is necessary to have competent interpreters of our own, both for the written and spoken languages of Japan, is a desideratum which I know you appreciate as highly as any person can do, and the sooner that it is secured, the better for our commercial and political interests here. I never in all my experience of interpretation witnessed such a slow, trying, and laborious process of communication as that to which you were obliged to have recourse in the interview with the Ministers, at which you kindly permitted me to be present a few days ago, when you had first to state what you had to say in English to the Dutch interpreter, he in Dutch in his turn to the Japanese go-between, and he afterwards in Japanese to his principal. Every sentence must have lost materially in force, perspicuity, and point, and abundant opportunity was given, I observed, for that tricky evasion of the true question at issue in which the Japanese so well rival their near neighbours the Chinese.

**D**

# LIST OF DAIMIOS AND THEIR REVENUES, &c.

LIST OF DAIMIOS HOLDING OFFICES IN THE TYCOON'S GOVERNMENT.

| | Offices, Titles, and Councils of the Tycoon's Government | Daimios holding these Offices | Territorial Revenues in Kokous of Rice | Value of Revenues (at 13s. 10d. per Kokou) | Fortresses belonging to these Daimios | In the Province of | Remarks |
|---|---|---|---|---|---|---|---|
| 1 | The 'Gotairo,' or Regent of the Empire (in event of minority or illness of Tycoon). Said to be hereditary in the family of Ikamo no Kami | This high office, instituted for the event of the minority or sickness of the Tycoon, is always filled by a Daimio of the 1st Class, elected by the Councils of State and the majority of the Daimios | . | £ . | . | . | Vacant since the murder of the Gotairo in March 1860. The Prince Ikamo no Kami, possessor of 350,000 kokous of revenue (224,000l.), had occupied this post for seven years |
| 2 | The First Council of State, 'Gorogio' (5 members), Daimios of the 3rd Class | 1. Koussé Yamato no Kami† | 68,000 | 43,520 | Seki Yado | Simosa | Ministers for Foreign Affairs. Entered the Council in 1860 |
| | | 2. Ando Tsousima no Kami† | 50,000 | 32,000 | . | . | Ditto 1860 |
| | | 3. Matsdaira Bouzan no Kami | 50,000 | 32,000 | Mourakami | Etsigo | Ditto 1853 |
| | | 4. Naito Ki no Kami | 60,000 | 38,400 | . | . | Ditto 1860 |
| | | 5. Honda Mino no Kami | 50,000 | 32,000 | Noumatzou | Sourouga | |
| 3 | The Tycoon's Aide-de-camp, Grand Messenger of State. Daimio of the 3rd Class ('Osoba Goionine') | Midzouno Dewa no Kami | | | | Sourouga | In charge since 1859 |

† Both changed recently. The second after an attempt to assassinate him in February 1862, on his way to the Palace.

LIST OF DAIMIOS HOLDING OFFICES IN THE TYCOON'S GOVERNMENT (*continued*).

| | Offices, Titles, and Councils of the Tycoon's Government | Daimios holding these Offices | Territorial Revenues in Kokous of Rice | Value of Revenues (at 13s. 11d. per Kokou) | Fortresses belonging to these Daimios | In the Province of | Remarks |
|---|---|---|---|---|---|---|---|
| 4 | Second Council of State ('On-wakadouchiori'), 7 members, Daimios of 3rd and 4th Classes | 1. Hori Idzumo no Kami | 10,000 | £ 6,400 | . | . | Entered the Council in 1850 |
| | | 2. Midzoumo Idzoumi no Kami | 50,000 | 32,000 | . | . | Ditto 1860 |
| | | 3. Enda Takouma no Kami | 12,000 | 7,680 | . | . | Ditto 1838 |
| | | 4. Soua Inaba no Kami | 30,000 | 19,200 | Taka Sima | Sinano | Ditto 1860 |
| | | 5. Sakai Oukiono-souke | 10,000 | 6,400 | . | . | |
| | | 6. | | | | | |
| | | 7. | | | | | |
| 5 | Council of the Mikado, at the Court of the Tycoon (24 members), Daimios of the 3rd and 4th Classes, of whom ten have fortresses | Kouchiki Omi no Kami | 32,000 | 20,480 | Foukoutchi Yama | Tamba | |
| | | Matsdaira Hoki no Kami | 70,000 | 44,800 | Myatsou | Tango | |
| | | Inoie Kawatsi no Kami | 60,000 | 38,400 | Nama Matsou | Totomi | |
| | | Awoyama Daizen-noske | 78,000 | 49,920 | Ghef | Mino | |
| | | Matsdaira Souronga no Kami | 35,000 | 22,400 | Iwatsi | Igo | |
| | | Matsdaira Idzou no Kami | 70,000 | 44,800 | Ioshida | Mikawa | |
| | | Nishnô Oki no Kami | 35,000 | 22,400 | Jokoska | Tango | |
| | | Makino Kawatchi no Kami | 35,000 | 22,400 | Tanabé | Tango | |
| | | Midzouno Sakounsiogen (ou Daiken Montsen) | 50,000 | 22,400 | Jamagata | Dewa | |
| | | Ota Bitjou no Kami | 50,000 | 32,000 | Kakegawa | Totomi | |
| 6 | The Tycoon's Representative at the Court of the Mikado (at Kioto Onzoushidai) | Sakai Wakasa no Kami (Daimio of 1st Class) | 100,000 | 64,000 | Obama | Wakasa | |
| 7 | 16 Aides-de-camp in ordinary to the Tycoon ('Osobashiou') | Possessing from | 2,000 to 5,000 | 1,280 to 3,200 | | | |
| 8 | 24 Daimios, Ambassadors of the Tycoon at the Courts of Daimios ('Gokokishiou') | Possessing from | 1,000 to 3,000 | 640 to 1,920 | | | |

LIST OF DAIMIOS HOLDING OFFICES IN THE TYCOON'S GOVERNMENT (*continued*).

| | Offices, Titles, and Councils of the Tycoon's Government | Daimios holding these Offices | Territorial Revenues in Kokous of Rice | Value of Revenues (at 13s. 10d. per Kokou) | Fortresses belonging to these Daimios | In the Province of | Remarks |
|---|---|---|---|---|---|---|---|
| 9 | 4 Daimios, Ambassadors of the 2nd Class ('Gokôkishiou Sonai Siki') | Ghino Wakasa no Kami · | 1,532 | £ 980l. 10s. | | | |
| | | Hataké Yama Membou Noské · | 5,000 | 3,200 | | | |
| | | (2 vacancies) | | | | | |
| 10 | 26 Daimios entrusted with the defence of the Tycoon, and obliged to furnish special military contingents. Daimios of the 2nd and 3rd Classes ('Onzoumeshiou') | Tsoutjia Ouemeno Sono · | 95,000 | 60,800 | Soutioura · | Fitats | |
| | | Mabe Simosa no Kami · | 50,000 | 32,000 | | | |
| | | Akimoto Tsousima no Kami | 60,000 | 38,400 | | | |
| | | Itakoura Sao no Kami · | 50,000 | 32,000 | Matsyama · | Bitjou | |
| | | Toda Yasnoské · | 77,000 | 49,280 | | | |
| | | Matsdaira Kiosaboro | 82,000 | 52,480 | | | |
| | | Makino Bizen no Kami · | 35,000 | 22,400 | | | |
| | | Doi Noto no Kami · | 40,000 | 25,600 | O-no · | Tomoti | |
| | | Awoyama Simodzouké no Kami | 60,000 | 38,400 | | | |
| | | Nagai Ghida no Kami | 36,000 | 23,040 | | | |
| | | Naito Souronga no Kami · | 23,000 | 14,720 | Takato · | Sinano | |
| | | Nagai Fizen no Kami | 32,000 | 20,480 | | | |
| | | Itakoura Naizen no Sono · | 30,000 | 19,200 | | | |
| | | Itakoura Kazoué no Kami | 30,000 | 19,200 | | | |
| | | Kourouda Izen no Kami · | 30,000 | 19,200 | | | |
| | | Matsdaira Seenoské · | 30,000 | 19,200 | | | |
| | | Okoubo Sado no Kami · | 30,000 | 19,200 | | | |
| | | Oka Ghioga no Kami | 23,000 | 14,720 | | | |
| | | Honda Hoki no Kami · | 40,000 | 25,600 | | | |
| | | Matsdaira Oribe no Sono · | 20,000 | 12,800 | | | |
| | | Ishikawa Wakaza no Kami | 20,000 | 12,800 | | | |
| | | Abé Inaba no Kami · | 16,000 | 10,240 | | | |
| | | Mioura Din-noské · | 23,000 | 14,720 | | | |
| | | Naito Kiniziro · | 15,000 | 9,600 | | | |
| | | Mabe Awa no Kami · | | | | | |
| | | Doi Oljitji no Kami · | | | | | |

LIST OF DAIMIOS HOLDING OFFICES IN THE TYCOON'S GOVERNMENT (*continued*).

| | Offices, Titles, and Councils of the Tycoon's Government | Daimios holding these Offices | Territorial Revenues in Kokous of Rice | Value of Revenues (at 13s. 10d. per Kokou) | Fortresses belonging to these Daimios | In the Province of | Remarks |
|---|---|---|---|---|---|---|---|
| 11 | 27 Daimios holding different military commands under the Tycoon's orders ('Onzoumé-nami') | Possessing revenues to the amount of | 20,000 | £ 12,800 | | | |
| 12 | 4 Daimios, Superintending Governors of Justice, and Comptrollers of Temples and Monasteries ('On-Disha-Bongnios') | Matsdaira Hoki no Kami. Matsdaira Idzon no Kami. Midzouno Sakonsiogen Awoyama Daisen Noske | 70,000 70,000 50,000 78,000 | 44,800 44,800 32,000 49,920 | | | |
| 13 | 8 Daimios, Superintendents of Passports at Hacone and Arai ('Onroussoui Tosijorishiou') | Having revenues from | 2,000 to 7,000 | 1,280 to 4,480 | | | |
| 14 | 12 Daimios, commanding Imperial Fortresses ('Ogoban Shiou') | Having revenues from | 3,000 to 10,000 | 1,920 to 6,400 | | | |
| 15 | 20 Daimios, Lords of the Bedchamber ('Goshiou Goban') | Having revenues from | 300 pios to 7,000 kokous | 4,480 | | | |
| 16 | Grand Ometskés, Councillors of State ('Dai Omitski'), 5 Daimios | Having revenues from | 400 pios to 3,000 kokous | 1,920 | | | |

GOVERNMENT OFFICERS, NOT DAIMIOS, BUT BELONGING TO THE 'HATTAMOTTO,' OR VASSALS DIRECTLY DEPENDENT ON THE TYCOON.

| | Posts and Offices of the Tycoon's Government | Salary in Kokous of Rice | Value of in English money (at 13s. 10d. per Kokou) |
|---|---|---|---|
| 17 | 2 Governors of the city of Yeddo ('Matchi-Bounios') | 3,000 | £1,920 |
| 18 | 4 Governors of Finance ('Gokanjo-Bounios') | 1,500 | 960 |
| 19 | 1 Governor of Public Works, Roads, and Rivers ('Osa-Koudji-Bounios') | 1,500 | 960 |
| 20 | 2 Governors of Public Buildings and Fortresses ('Ongo-Foushion-Bougnios') | 1,500 | 960 |
| 21 | 2 Governors of the Navy ('On-Gounkang-Bougnios') | 200 pios | 38l. 8s. (about) |
| 22 | 3 Governors superintending the registering of the Daimios' Banners ('Onghata-Bougnios') | From 4,000 to 9,000 | 2,560 5,760 |
| 23 | 4 Commanders-in-chief of the Imperial Guard ('Hacounine Goumi') | 5,000 | 3,200 |
| 24 | 3 Generals of Archers ('O youmi kata') | 500 | 320 |
| 25 | 5 Generals of troops armed with lances ('O yari kata') | 1,800 | 1,152 |
| 26 | 2 Generals of Musketeers ('O teppo kata') | 9,000 | 5,760 |
| 27 | 10 Generals of troops armed with swords ('On-sakki Tenkata') | 500 | £320 |
| 28 | 24 Generals of the 2nd corps of Musketeers ('Onsakki teppo gata') | 1,200 | 778 |
| 29 | 5 Generals of Artillery ('On moutji tsoutsou grasira') | 1,500 | 960 |
| 30 | 3 Governors of Military Stores and Ammunition ('O teppo tama ksouri Bounio') | 400 | 256 |
| 31 | 1 Officer for preventing the discharge of fire-arms within a radius of 10 Re of Yeddo ('Dsiou ri yo hon teppo hong aratami') | 3,000 | 1,920 |
| 32 | 1 Governor-Inspector of the Schools of Musketry, established in 1860 ('Koboushio Bounio') | 5,000 | 3,200 |
| 33 | From 15 to 20 Governors of Foreign Affairs and of the open ports* ('Gaikokon-Bougnio') | From 1,000 to 2,000 | 640 1,280 |

* From this class are chosen the Tycoon's Ambassadors and Envoys to Foreign Powers.

STATEMENT OF THE FEUDAL PRINCES OF THE JAPANESE EMPIRE, ARRANGED ACCORDING TO THEIR REVENUES.

[The Daimios to whose names an asterisk is prefixed (twenty-four) are all more or less independent.]

I.—DAIMIOS HAVING LAND REVENUES OF FROM 1,200,000 TO 200,000 KOKOUS (769,728*l.* TO 128,000*l.*), AND POSSESSING FORTRESSES.

| Daimios, with their Names and Titles in full, taken from the Japanese 'Official Almanack' | Their Revenues in Kokous of Rice | Value of, in English money £ | Fortresses, Strongholds, and Castles in their possession | Situated in the Provinces of | Remarks |
|---|---|---|---|---|---|
| *The Prince of Kanga, Maida Kaga no Kami | 1,202,700 | 769,728 | Kanasawa, Daisodgi, Koumatsou | Kaga and Noto . | Bearing the title of 'Tsounagon,' a high dignity conferred by the Mikado, and answering to the title of 'First Officer of the Court of Kioto.' Purely honorific |
| *The Prince of Satsouma, Matsdaïra Satsouma no Kami | 760,800 | 486,912 | Kagosima, Sadowara . | Satsouma and Fouïgo | Known also by the name of 'Siouri no Taïon,' but less generally |
| The Prince of Owari, Tokungawa Owari dono | 629,500 | 402,880 | Nagosa, Inu Yama . | Owari . | Of the three families from whom the Tycoon is elected, called 'Gosankay,' or 'Brothers of the Tycoon' |
| *The Prince of Moutsen or Xendaï, Matsdaïra Moutsen no Kami, or Xendaï | 626,000 | 400,640 | Siraisi, Xendaï, Taïra . | Moutsen, or Oshiou Xendaï | |

DAIMIOS HAVING LAND REVENUES OF FROM 1,200,000 TO 200,000 KOKOUS (769,728l. TO 128,000l.), AND POSSESSING FORTRESSES (continued).

| Daimios, with their Names and Titles in full, taken from the Japanese 'Official Almanack' | Their Revenues in Kokous of Rice | Value of, in English money | Fortresses, Strongholds, and Castles in their possession | Situated in the Provinces of | Remarks |
|---|---|---|---|---|---|
| The Prince of Ksiou, Tokungawa Kidono, or Ksiou | 555,000 | 355,200 | Wakayama, Tanabe, Singo | Ki, or Ksiou | Also one of the three families from whom the Tycoon† is elected |
| *The Prince of Etzu, Hosokawa Etzu no Kami | 540,000 | 345,600 | Koumamoto, Jatsosiro, Oudo | Chigo or Figo | |
| *The Prince of Mino, Matsdaïra Mino no Kami | 520,000 | 332,800 | Foukôoka | Tzikoudzen | |
| *The Prince of Aki, Matsdaïra Aki no Kami | 436,000 | 279,040 | Ghirosima | Aki | |
| *The Prince of Daïsen, Matsdaïra Daïsen no Taion | 369,000 | 236,160 | Yewakuni, Tokuyama, Hagi-Chiofou | Nagato and Soulio | |
| *The Prince of Fizen, Matsdaïra Fizen no Kami | 357,000 | 228,400 | Saga | Fizen | One of the three families whose members can be chosen Tycoon |
| The Prince of Mito, Tokungawa Mito Dono | 350,000 | 224,000 | Mito | Filats | |
| Prince Ikamono, Ikamono Kami | 350,000 | 224,000 | Ghikomé | Oömi | The regency of the Empire was hereditary in this family‡ |
| The Prince of Igo, Matsdaïra Igo no Kami | 330,000 | 211,200 | Wakamatsou | Oshiou, or Moutsen Xendaï | |
| *The Prince of Itsumi, Todo Itsumi no Kami | 323,950 | 207,320 | Wérno | Iga | |

† The present Tycoon is the son of the reigning Prince of Kiusu; he ranks but as Fourth High Officer in the Imperial hierarchy.

‡ The last Regent or 'Gotaïro' of the family of Ikammono was assassinated in March 1860 by the officers of Prince Mito. The Regent has left no children. The family is reported to be extinct. No new Regent has been appointed.

DAIMIOS HAVING LAND REVENUES OF FROM 1,200,000 TO 200,000 KOKOUS (769,728l. TO 128,000l.), AND POSSESSING FORTRESSES (continued).

| Daimios, with their Names and Titles in full, taken from the Japanese 'Official Almanaok' | Their Revenues in Kokous of Rice | Value of, in English money | Fortresses, Strongholds, and Castles in their possession | Situated in the Provinces of | Remarks |
|---|---|---|---|---|---|
| | | £ | | | |
| *The Prince of Etsisen, Matsdaïra Etsisen no Kami | 320,000 | 204,800 | Toukôsi . . . | Etsitsen | |
| *The Prince of Koura, Matsdaïra Koura no Kami | 310,000 | 198,400 | Okayama . . . | Bidzen | |
| *The Prince of Awa, Matsdaïra Awa no Kami | 250,000 | 160,000 | Sôomoto, Tokusima . . | Awa and Awadzi (Island of) | |
| *The Prince of Tosa, Matsdaïra Tosa no Kami | 242,000 | 154,880 | Takatchi . . . | Tosa | |
| Prince Okoubo Raga, Okoubo Raga no Kami | 213,000 | 136,320 | Odawara . . . | Sagami | |
| *The Prince of Ghemba, Arima Ghemba no Kami | 210,000 | 134,400 | Koormé . . . | Tsikongo | |
| *The Prince of Okio, Sataké Okio no Taiou . | 205,000 | 131,200 | Akita . . | Dewa | |
| *The Prince of Nambou, Nambou Sinano no Kami | 200,000 | 128,000 | Morioka, Hatchinoké . | Oshiou, or Moudzen Xendaï | |

II.—DAIMIOS HAVING LAND REVENUES OF FROM 180,000 TO 100,000 KOKOUS (115,200l. TO 64,000l.) AND FORTRESSES.

| Daimios, with their Names and Titles taken from the 'Official Almanack' | | Their Revenues in Kokous of Rice | In English Money | Fortresses in their Possession | In the Province of |
|---|---|---|---|---|---|
| *The Prince of | Matsdaira Dewa no Kami | 180,000 | £ 115,200 | Madzi | Idzumo |
| The Prince of | Matsdaira Kai no Kami | 150,000 | 96,000 | Koriyama | Yamato |
| The Prince of | Matsdaira Okino Kami | 150,000 | 96,000 | Ousóo, Takou, Matsyama | Igo or Iho |
| | Okasawa Sakio no taïou | 150,000 | 96,000 | Kokourà | Boudzen |
| | Okoudaira Daisen no taïou | 150,000 | 96,000 | Nakatzou | Boudzen |
| | Sakai Sayemon no dzio | 150,000 | 96,000 | Shouaï | Dewa |
| * | Wiezongui Danio no Daihitzou | 150,000 | 96,000 | Igouesawa | Dewa |
| | Sakakibari Sikibou no taïou | 150,000 | 96,000 | Takata | Etsigo |
| The Prince of Ooto, Sakai Ooto no Kami | | 150,000 | 96,000 | Ghimedgi | Harima |
| * Tachibana Sakou Siogen | | 120,000 | 76,800 | Yanagawa | Chikongo |
| The Prince of Awa, Kourousima Awa no Kami | | 102,500 | 65,600 | Takeda | Boungo |
| The Prince of Simosa, Matsdaira Simosa no Kami | | 100,000 | 64,000 | Oshi | Mousachi |
| Toda Ouemenou no Zió | | 100,000 | 64,000 | Ogaki | Mino |
| The Prince of Sinano, Sanada Sinano no Kami | | 100,000 | 64,000 | Matsiro | Sinano |
| The Prince of Igo, Abe Igo no Kami | | 100,000 | 64,000 | Sirakawa | Oshiou |
| *The Prince of Etjou, Tsougaro Etjou no Kami | | 100,000 | 64,000 | Ghiéromasé | Oshiou |
| The Prince of Wakasa, Sakai Wakasa no Kami | | 100,000 | 64,000 | Obama | Wakasa |
| Maaïda Keenoské | | 100,000 | 64,000 | Togawa | Etjou |
| *The Prince of Inaba, Matsdaira Inaba no Kami | | 100,000 | 64,000 | Sikano Totori, Yonoka | Inaba, Houki |
| The Prince of Mikawa, Matsdaira Mikawa no Kami | | 100,000 | 64,000 | Tsouyama | Mimasakka |
| The Prince of Isen, Abé Isen no Kami | | 100,000 | 64,000 | Tokouyama | Bingo |
| The Prince of Matsmaï, Matsmaï Sima no Kami | | 100,000 † | 64,000 | Matsumaï | Island of Yesso |
| The Prince of Totomi, Daté Totomi no Kami | | 100,000 | 64,000 | Owadzima | Igo |

† Derives a considerable revenue from the fisheries and products of the chase, in the Island of Yesso, given to him as an appanage.

III.—DAIMIOS POSSESSING LAND REVENUES OF FROM 100,000 TO 60,000 KOKOUS (64,000l. TO 38,400l.) AND FORTRESSES.

| Daimios, with their names and Titles, taken from the 'Official Almanack.' | Their Revenues in Kokous of Rice | In English Money £ | Their Castles and Fortresses | In the Province of | Remarks |
|---|---|---|---|---|---|
| *The Prince of Tsousima, Tsousima no Kami | 100,000 | 64,000 | Foutchou | Tsousima (Island of) | One of the Commanders of the Tycoon's Guard |
| The Prince of Ouémene, Tsouzya Ouénémi no Kami, or Sono | 95,000 | 60,800 | Soutioura | Fitats | |
| Matsdaïra Okionoské | 82,000 | 52,480 | Taka Sakié | Kodzouké | |
| Makino Ghiobouno Sono | 80,000 | 51,200 | Kasawa | Fitats | |
| Matsdaïra Hiobonou taïou | 80,000 | 51,200 | Akaza | Arima | |
| The Prince of Owi, Doi Owi no Kami | 80,000 | 51,200 | Touroukawa | Simosa | |
| Onoyama Daïsen Noské | 78,000 | 49,920 | Ghef | Mino | Member of the Council of the Mikado at the Tycoon's Court, and Governor of Courts of Justice, and Temples, and the Priests |
| The Prince of Yamasiro, Toda Yamasiro no Kami | 78,000 | 49,920 | Outzounomia | Simodzouké | |
| Nakagawa Siouri no Taïou | 70,400 | 45,040 | Oka | Boungo | |
| The Prince of Itsou, Matsdaïra Itsou no Kami | 70,000 | 44,800 | Joshida | Mikawa | |
| The Prince of Bouzen, Makino Bouzen no Kami | 70,000 | 44,800 | Nagaonaka | Etsigo | |
| Matsdaïra Yas no djo | 70,000 | 44,800 | Simabara | Fizen | |
| The Prince of Noto, Naïto Noto no Kami | 70,000 | 44,800 | Nobonôka | Chiouga | |
| The Prince of Hoki, Matsdaïra Hoki no Kami | 70,000 | 44,800 | Myatsou | Tango | Member of the Council of the Mikado at the Court of the Tycoon, and Governor of Courts of Justice, and Temples, and Priests |
| Koussé Yamato no Kami | 68,000 | 43,520 | Séki-yado | Simosa | Principal Minister of Foreign Affairs, member of the Gorogio since April 1860 |
| The Prince of Iki, Matsdaïra Iki no Kami | 61,000 | 39,040 | Firando | Firando (Island of) | |
| The Prince of Itsoumi, Matsdaïra Isoumi no Kami | 60,000 | 38,400 | Nishiou | Mikawa | |
| The Prince of Tonomo, Ishikawa Tonomo no Kami | 60,000 | 38,430 | Kami-yamo | Isse or Idze | |
| The Prince of Kawatchi, Inoié Kawatsi no Kami | 60,000 | 38,400 | Hama-matsou | Totomi | Member of the Council of the Mikado at the Court of the Tycoon |
| The Prince of Ghiobou, Honda Ghiobou no taïou | 60,000 | 38,400 | Djen-shô | Oômi | |
| The Prince of Tamba, Matsdaïra Tamba no Kami | 60,000 | 38,400 | Matsmoto | Sinano | |
| The Prince of Tajima, Akimoto Tajima no Kami | 60,000 | 38,400 | Fatsi-Bajasi | Kodzouké | |
| Soma Daïsen Noské | 60,000 | 38,400 | Nakamoura | Oshiou | |

IV.—DAIMIOS POSSESSING LAND REVENUES OF FROM 60,000 TO 50,000 KOKOUS (38,400*l.* TO 32,000*l.*) AND FORTRESSES.

| Daimios, with their Names and Titles, taken from the 'Official Almanack' | Their Revenues in Kokous of Rice | In English Money | Fortresses in their Possession | In the Province of |
|---|---|---|---|---|
| The Prince of Soôto, Matsdaïra Soôto no Kami . | 60,000 | 38,400 | Tanagoura | Oshiou |
| The Prince of Kasousa, Tosaoua Kasousa Noské | 60,000 | 38,400 | Sin . | Dewa |
| The Prince of Ki, Naïto Ki no Kami† | 60,000 | 38,400 | Mourakami | Etsigo |
| The Prince of Simosa, Owayama Simosa no Kami | 60,000 | 38,400 | Sinoyama | Tamba |
| Matsdaïra Oukou Schiogen | 60,000 | 38,400 | Hamada . | Iwami |
| The Prince of Satou, Oga Souara Satou no Kami | 60,000 | 38,400 | Karaouô | Fizen |
| The Prince of Naïzen, Okabé Naïzen no Kami | 59,000 | 37,760 | Kishou Ouada | Idzoumi |
| The Prince of Bitzu, Yenaba Bitzu no Kami | 56,000 | 35,840 | Oz en Kiné | Boungo |
| The Prince of Souri, Hoa Szuri no Taïou | 51,000 | 32,640 | Ebi | Chiouga |
| The Prince of Dewa, Mitsouo Dewa no Kami‡ | 50,000 | 32,000 | Noumatzou | Sourouga |
| The Prince of Iga, Matsdaïra Iga no Kami | 50,000 | 32,000 | Whouéda | Sinano |
| The Prince of Totomi, Makino Totomi no Kami | 50,000 | 32,000 | Koumoso | Sinano |
| The Prince of Sou, Hakoura Sou no Kami§ | 50,000 | 32,000 | Anaka | Kodzouké |
| The Prince of Awa, Akita Awa no Kami | 50,000 | 32,000 | Miharo | Oshiou |
| The Prince of Daïken, Midzouo Daïken Motzo, or Sakonsiogen | 50,000 | 32,000 | Yama-gata | Dewa |
| The Prince of Chinga, Arima Chinga no Kami | 50,000 | 32,000 | Marôka . | Etzizen |
| The Prince of Fizen, Misogoudtzi Fizen no Kami | 50,000 | 32,000 | Sibata . | Etsigo |
| The Prince of Ki, Matsdaïra Ki no Kami | 50,000 | 32,000 | Kamiyama | Tamba |
| The Prince of Awatsi, Wakisaka Awatsi no Kami | 50,000 | 32,000 | Tazouno | Harima |
| The Prince of Soo, Hakoura Soo no Kami | 50,000 | 32,000 | Matsyama | Bitzou |
| The Prince of Nagato, Kisgotori Nagata no Kami | 50,000 | 32,000 | Marougame | Sanoki |
| The Prince of Kaï, Kourouda Kaï no Kami | 50,000 | 32,000 | Akidzouki | Chikouzen |
| Honda nakats kasa no taïou | 50,000 | 32,000 | Okasaki | Mikawa |
| The Prince of Bitzu, Ota Bitzu no Kami ‖ | 50,000 | 32,000 | Kakégawa | Totomi |

† Member of the 'Gorogio' since 1853.
§ A Commander of the Tycoon's Guard.

‡ Messenger of State ; Chief Aide-de-camp to the Tycoon since March 1859.
‖ Member of the Council of the Mikado at the Court of the Tycoon.

V.—Daimios possessing Land Revenues of from 46,000 to 25,000 Kokous (29,440*l.* to 16,000*l.*) and Fortresses.

| Daimios, with their Names and Titles, taken from the 'Official Almanack' | Their Revenues in Kokous of Rice | In English Money | Fortresses in their Possession | In the Province of |
|---|---|---|---|---|
| | | £ | | |
| The Prince of Totomi, Nagaï Totomi no Kami | 46,000 | 29,440 | Kotching | Setsou |
| Matsdaïra Totomi no Kami | 40,000 | 25,600 | Amagasaki | Sourouga |
| The Prince of Bouzen, Honda Bouzen no Kami † | 40,000 | 25,600 | Tanaka | Etsisen |
| The Prince of Uoto, Doi Uoto no Kami † | 40,000 | 25,600 | Oue | Totomi |
| The Prince of Oki, Nishono Oki no Kami § | 35,000 | 22,400 | Totooka | Totomi |
| The Prince of Kawatchi, Makino Kawatchi no Kami § | 35,000 | 22,400 | Tanabé | Tango |
| The Prince of Souragano, Matsdaïra Souragano Kami § | 35,000 | 22,400 | Iwadzi | Igo |
| The Prince of Higo, Nagaï Higo no Kami | 32,000 | 20,480 | Kano | Mino |
| The Prince of Omi, Kontchidi Omi no Kami § | 32,000 | 20,480 | Foukondgi Yama | Tamba |
| The Prince of Setsou, Inagaki Setsou no Kami | 30,000 | 19,200 | Toba | Xima |
| Matsdaïra Setsou no Kami | 30,000 | 19,200 | Takatzou | Mino |
| The Prince of Noto, Matsdaïra Noto no Kami | 30,000 | 19,200 | Iouamoura | Mino |
| The Prince of Sona, Sona Juaba no Kami | 30,000 | 19,200 | Takasima | Sinano |
| The Prince of Tosi, Tosi Tambano Kami | 30,000 | 19,200 | Mibou | |
| The Prince of Okonbo, Okonbo Sado no Kami ‖ | 30,000 | 19,200 | Krani Yama | Simodzouké |
| The Prince of Itakoura, Itakoura Uaïgeu no Sono ‖ | 30,000 | 19,200 | Toukousima | Oshiou |
| The Prince of Nakaskasa, Matsdaïra Nakaskasa no Sono | 30,000 | 19,200 | Kami Yama | Dewa |
| The Prince of Hori, Hori Tambano Kami | 30,000 | 19,200 | Mouramatsou | Etsigo |
| The Prince of Saki, Matsdaïra Sakio no Taiou | 30,000 | 19,200 | Saidzio | Igo |
| The Prince of Akidzouki, Akidzouki Sado no Kami | 27,000 | 17,810 | Saifou | Chouiga |
| Omoura Tanga no Kami | 25,000 | 16,000 | Omoura | Fizen |
| Kinosita Yamato no Kami | 25,000 | 16,000 | Shidé | Boungo |
| Matsdaïra Sayemon no djô | 25,000 | 16,000 | Foumayé | Boungo |

† Member of the Council of the Mikado at the Court of the Tycoon.
§ Members of the Council of the Mikado at the Court of the Tycoon.

‡ A Commander of the Tycoon's Guard.
‖ Commanders of the Tycoon's Guard.

## VI.—DAIMIOS POSSESSING LAND REVENUES OF FROM 25,000 TO 10,000 KOKOUS (16,000l. TO 6,400l.) AND FORTRESSES.

| Daimios, with their Names and Titles, taken from the 'Official Almanack' | Their Revenues in Kokous of Rice | In English Money | Fortresses in their Possession | In the Province of |
|---|---|---|---|---|
| The Prince of Oumoura, Oumoura Dewa no Kami | 25,000 | £ 16,800 | Takatori | Yamato |
| The Prince of Nickawa, Mioura Bingo no Kami | 23,000 | 14,720 | Katzou-Yama | Mimasakka |
| The Prince of Naïto, Naïto Sourouga no Kami† | 23,000 | 14,720 | Takato | Sinano |
| The Prince of Ooka, Ooka Sizen no Kami | 22,000 | | Ionaski | Morashi |
| The Prince of Mionaké, Mionaké Tosan no Kami | 20,000 | 12,800 | Taouara | Mikawa |
| The Prince of Moari, Moari Awa no Kami | 20,000 | 12,800 | Saéki | Boungo |
| The Prince of Mori, Mori Etsou no Kami | 20,000 | 12,800 | Akô | Harima |
| The Prince of Zengokou, Zengokou Sanoki no Kami | 20,000 | 12,800 | Desi | Tadsima |
| The Prince of Ghoinga, Matsdaïra Ghoïnga no Kami | 20,000 | 12,800 | Itowogawa | Etsigo |
| The Prince of Rokougio, Rokougio Shiogo no Kami | 20,000 | 12,800 | Hounguio | Dewa |
| The Prince of Sakaï, Sakaï Sima no Kami | 20,000 | 12,800 | Mayabashi | Kodzouké |
| The Prince of Honda, Honda Bongo no Kami | 20,000 | 12,800 | Hie Yama | Sinano |
| The Prince of Omi, Ichikaoua Omi no Kami | 20,000 | 12,800 | Simodate | Fitats |
| The Prince of Tamba, Naïto Tamba no Kami | 20,000 | 12,800 | Kolomo | Mikawa |
| The Prince of Kawatsi, Madyama Kawatsi no Kami | 20,000 | 12,800 | Nagasima | Idzé |
| The Prince of Shinga, Midzouno Shinga no Kami | 18,000 | 11,520 | Youki | Simosa |
| The Prince of Hiogo, Hori Hiogo no Kami | 17,000 | 10,880 | Jeda | Sinano |
| The Prince of Samouki, Matsdaïra Samouki no Kami | 12,000 | 7,680 | Takamatzo | Sanouki |
| The Prince of Shieda, Otawara Shieda no Kami | 11,000 | 7,040 | Otaoura | Simozouké |
| The Prince of Bittjou, Hota Bittjou no Kami | 11,000 | 7,040 | Sakoura | Simosa |
| The Prince of Etjou, Matsdaïra Etjou no Kami | 11,000 | 7,040 | Konano | Idzé |
| The Prince of Sakio, Noiona Sakio no Taiou | 10,000 | 6,400 | Nihon-Matz | Oshiou |
| Hitotsou Yanaghé Niobonoské | 10,000 | 6,400 | Komadzou | Igo |
| Godjima Saijemmo no Djo | 12,000 | 7,680 | Fukaï (Island of) | Fizen |
| The Prince of Kawatchi, Matsdaïra Kawatchi no Kami | 22,000 | 14,080 | Kidziki | Boungo |
| Shto Sayemmo no Dsio | 22,000 | 14,080 | Fkoui | Fizen |
| The Prince of Simano, Sagara Simano Kami | 22,000 | 14,080 | Nagasa | Igo |
| The Prince of Oki, Kame Oki no Kami | 30,000 | 19,200 | Tsouano | Iwami |

† A Commander of the Tycoon's Guard.

# E

## NOTES ON THE AGRICULTURE, TREES, AND FLORA OF JAPAN.
### By Mr. JOHN G. VEITCH.

### *Agriculture of the district of Yokohama and Kanagawa.*

AGRICULTURE forms the chief occupation of the lower classes. Land is brought to a very high state of cultivation, arising in a great measure, firstly, from the country having to provide for an annually increasing population; and, secondly, from the fact that all rents are paid in produce. The revenue of the princes, and other proprietors, is derived almost solely from their landed estates. The greatest landowners are the princes and the crown. Some of the former are possessed of immense estates, their annual incomes being sufficiently large to give them great power in the country, and often to menace the ruling powers.

It is somewhat difficult to arrive at the relative position of landlord and tenant. It is however known that all payments are made in *rice*. The Japanese measure is termed *Koku*, weighing about 100 lbs. English. A landed proprietor calculates his income by Kokus; his retainers and attendants are again paid in rice, and thus but very little money passes. Each estate is surveyed once or twice a year, when an approximate value is placed on the crop, and at the time of harvest each tenant pays six parts in ten (this is as near as can be ascertained) of whatever the valuation was. The crown tenants, it is said, do not pay so much as those of other proprietors.*

The land in this neighbourhood is exceedingly fertile, a friable loam extending to a very considerable depth, and easily worked. There is a great amount of waste land, which might be cleared at a very slight expense, and cultivated if necessary; but, on the other hand, there is not a spot of ground which, having been once under cultivation, is not taken the best advantage of.

* There is reason to believe the proportions vary under different proprietors or in different provinces.

Cropping and the rotation of crops are thoroughly understood by the Japanese. Rice forms the chief food of the entire population. The great number of rivulets and streams of water, which are found alike in all parts, renders the growth of rice everywhere practicable. There are several varieties of rice; some adapted for growing on irrigated lands, and others on higher and drier situations. There are entire valleys of immense extent planted with rice in this country. No hedges or fences of any kind are necessary. All domestic animals are stall fed, and there being no necessity for protection against wild animals, does away with the obligation of dividing and fencing lands, which is so common in England.

There is one particularly striking feature in every Japanese farm; viz. the cleanliness and order everywhere prevalent. Each man seems to take a pride in keeping his land in perfect order and clear of everything in the shape of weeds. The use of manures is well understood and appreciated. Human manure is the commonest and that most generally in use. It is given in a liquid state, during the younger stages of the growing crops. Horse manure and seaweed are both used, but the latter only suits a certain few crops.

## THE CHIEF CROPS OF THE DISTRICT.

RICE.— It is grown as in China. The fields are ploughed and irrigated. The seed is first sown in small nurseries, and transplanted in April, in small tufts of eight to ten plants, in rows about eight inches apart. The plants at this time are about six inches high. The harvest commences in October.

WHEAT.— This is extensively grown in some parts. It is sown in November and December, and harvested in May and June. Generally sown in drills.

BARLEY.— Grown in the same way as wheat. It is used principally for feeding cattle.

MILLET.— There are five kinds grown in this district. They are sown in drills in March or April, and harvested in September and October. Millet forms a common article of food. It is generally made into cakes.

COTTON.— This a crop of some importance. It is sown in March or April, attains a height of twelve to eighteen inches, and is harvested in September and October.

BEANS.—There are numerous varieties: some in the way of the English field-bean, and others similar to French beans. They are largely grown for several purposes. As food they are eaten in a green state, and also when ripe. Some kinds are ground down into powder, and made into cakes. Cattle are fed on some kinds; and from others, soy and different condiments are made.

BUCKWHEAT. INDIAN CORN.

RAPE.— Grown for its seed, from which large quantities of oil are made.

PEAS.— Several kinds grown for food, and eaten both in a green and dry state.

HEMP. TOBACCO.

The labour of the district is almost entirely manual. A plough is sometimes met with, but, generally speaking, the land is prepared with implements used by hand. Women and children take an active part in field labour throughout the year. The agricultural implements in Japan are very few. A plough drawn by bullocks or horses is sometimes used for preparing paddy fields, but they are not at all general. Mattocks and hoes are the common implements, with which almost everything is done. Flails, similar to those in England, and used in the same manner, are employed for threshing. Winnowing machines, upon the same principle as those in England, are in common use. A smaller article is also used for cleaning grain. It resembles two fans, joined by a piece of bamboo at the handles. The grain is allowed to fall from a height during which the fans are worked, and the dust blown away. To separate the rice from the exterior husk, the Japanese use a large wooden mortar, and pound the grain by hand. They have also a machine, upon the same principle, worked by water, or by means of a man's foot. It consists of a number of pestles, which rise and fall into wooden mortars containing the grain.

The domestic animals of Japan are very few. The inhabitants never eating animal food has been the cause of their not paying due attention to the breeding of animals. Horses of a small breed are plentiful. They are used exclusively (with the exception of riding-horses for the high officers of the land) for purposes of draught. There are no carts in this district. Everything is transported from and into the interior by horses and bullocks. Oxen and cows are used for purposes of draught *only*. They are never killed, nor is any use made of milk. Sheep and pigs have both been introduced by foreign nations, at various times, but have never become distributed throughout the country. Neither of these animals are known by the Japanese living at some distance in the interior.

## THE VEGETABLES OF THE DISTRICT.

The collection of vegetables is considerable, and great attention is paid to their growth, in consequence of their forming so large a portion of the daily food.

They are generally grown in small corners of land about the farms, and particularly near the dwelling-houses. There is no great peculiarity in the manner in which they are grown. Liquid manure is much used to bring them to a large size. From this cause, to a great extent, is to be attributed the great want of flavour in all Japanese vegetables.

Annexed is a list of the principal kinds of vegetables grown in the district.

Beans, peas, potatoes, turnips, carrots, lettuce, beet, arums (commonly grown for the sake of their roots — the commonest in cultivation is *Arum esculentum*), yams (*Dioscorea Batatas*), tomatoes, ginger (the young roots are boiled before being eaten), the egg plant (*Solanum esculentum*), gourds, chilies, cucumbers, mushroom, horseradish, lilies (the roots of various kinds are eaten), spinach, leeks, radishes, the young shoots of bamboo just as they appear above the ground, garlic, capsicums, endive, fennel.

## THE FRUIT TREES OF THE DISTRICT.

The fruits of Japan are, generally speaking, not good. The want of flavour is the great fault. No attention is paid to improving the various kinds of fruit trees, and consequently the same sorts continue without alteration from year to year. Both the climate and soil are very favourable to their growth, and, with proper attention to the subject, the fruit of Japan ought to equal any in the world.

The following is a list of the principal kinds met with in the district :

Apple, pear, plum, peach, grapes (one of the best fruits in Japan), chesnut, persimmon, pomegranate, figs, oranges, lemons, citrons, strawberries (growing wild, and very insipid), melons (several species).

## THE FLORA OF THE DISTRICT.

The flora of this district is very remarkable, principally (as indeed is that of the whole of Japan) for the great abundance of evergreens. Four-fifths of the plants growing wild in this neighbourhood belong to this class, so that even during the winter months the country has a clothed and cheerful aspect. Coniferous plants play a conspicuous part. There is a great variety, most of which are peculiar to Japan.

The assortment of showy flowering plants is not so great as might be imagined, but for this the abundance and variety of foliage fully compensates. The land throughout the district is undulating — one continued succession of hill and valley. The former is for the most part uncultivated, and contains some of the most interesting botanical specimens in this quarter of the globe.

The Japanese are great amateur gardeners. Every cottage of any size has its garden attached to it. Plants are brought from all parts of the country, and high prices often paid for rare specimens. The annexed list contains an enumeration of the principal genera and species found wild in the neighbourhood of Kanagawa :

Abies. One species.
Acer. Three or four species.
Alnus. Two species.
Amaranthus. Many varieties.
Aralia japonica.
Ardisia crenulata.
Aucuba japonica.
Azalea. Many varieties.
Balsamina hortensis.
Bambusa. Five species.
Bambusa foliis variegatis.
Benthamia japonica.
Berberis japonica.
Camellia japonica. Very common.
Camellia Sasanqua.
Celosia cristata.
Celosia pyramidalis.
Cephalotaxus Fortuni.
Cerasus flore pleno.
Chamærops excelsa.
Clematis. Two species.
Convolvulus. Several varieties.
Cornus officinalis.
Cryptomeria japonica.
Cryptomeria species nova.
Cupressus. Many varieties.
Daphne.
Deutzia. Two species.
Dianthus. Many varieties.
Diervilla versicolor.
Elæagnus.
Eriobotrya japonica.
Euonymus japonica.
Filices. There are fifty species in the vicinity of Yokohama.
Forsythia suspensa.
Gardenia florida.
Hedera Helix.
Hibiscus. Two species, very common.
Hydrangea. Several species.
Hypericum. Two species.
Illicium. Three species.
Indigofera.
Iris. Several varieties.

Jasminum.
Juniperus. Three or four species.
Kerria japonica.
Laurus.
Ligularia gigantea.
Ligustrum japonicum.
Lilium. Many varieties.
Lychnis. Two species.
Magnolia. Two species.
Morus papyrifera.
Nandina domestica.
Nelumbium speciosum.
Nerium Oleander.
Nymphæa. Two species.
Olea. Three species.
Orchis. Three or four species.
Oxalis.
Paullownia imperialis.
Pæonia. Many varieties.
Pinus. Five or six distinct species.
Primula. Two or three species.
Prunus flore pleno.
Quercus. Several species, both ever-green and deciduous.
Retinospora. Many species.
Rhus vernix.
Ruscus sempervirens.
Rosa. Two species.
Sciadopitys verticillata.
Skimmia japonica.
Spiræa. Two species.
Stauntonia.
Taxus.
Ternstroemia japonica.
Thujopsis dolabrata.
Thuja. Two or three species.
Tradescantia.
Ulmus. Two or three species.
Viburnum. Two species.
Vinca.
Vitis.
Weigela. Two species.
Wistaria sinensis and others.

## THE PRINCIPAL TIMBER TREES GROWING IN THE VICINITY OF YEDDO AND KANAGAWA.

| Japanese Names | General Remarks; also the Botanical Names as far as they are procurable |
|---|---|
| 1. Eng-o, *s.* | A good wood in common use for building purposes. |
| 2. Mo-ku, *s.* | A very fine timber, hard and of close grain, used for saddles and turning purposes. |
| 3. Mo-mi, *s.* | *Abies firma.* A common pine in the district, growing to a height of 120 feet; the wood is good but 15 feet. In common use for building and other purposes. |
| 4. To-yo-matsu, *s.* | *Pinus parviflora.* One of the common pines of the country, used in building. |
| 5. It-su-ga, *s.* | *Abies Tsuga.* A wood much valued by the Japanese. It is a white strong wood, used for house building. |
| 6. Su-gi, or Sun-gi | *Cryptomeria japonica.* Commonly called the cedar of Japan. It is common throughout the entire empire. The wood is light and soft, but being very cheap, it is one of the most generally used timbers. |
| 7. Ki-a-ki, *s.* | *Planera acuminata.* The Japanese elm. This is probably the finest timber in Japan. Planks 4 to 5 feet in width are often seen. The wood is *hard, very strong*, and of a dark brown colour. The grain is beautiful, but rather coarse. It polishes well, and is used for the facings of houses, doors, furniture, cabinets, lacquer-ware, &c. |
| 8. Kay-a | *Cephalotaxus drupacea.* Used principally for ship building. |
| 9. A-cang-a-shi, *s.* | *Quercûs species.* One of the oaks of Japan, but not the common oak of the country. The timber is very good and highly valued. It is very hard, and of immense strength. Used for ships, their rudders, sculls, &c. &c. |
| 10. Shi-rong-a-shi, *s.* | *Quercûs species.* A close-grained heavy wood, very similar to No. 9, and used for the same purposes. |
| 11. Sa-wa-ra, *s.* | *Retinispora pisifera.* A common tree in this part of Japan, but does not attain a *great size.* Used for making tubs, barrels, baths, &c. &c. |
| 12. Icho | *Salisburia adiantifolia.* This tree grows to a great size, and assumes a very fine habit. The wood polishes well, and is used for light boxes, cabinets, tables, &c. &c. |
| 13. Ku-a | A coarse-grained light wood. Used chiefly for small polished articles. |
| 14. Sa-wa-ku-ri, *s.* | *Thuja species.* Not extensively used. The wood is soft and light. |
| 15. Ku-ro-bi | A very nice light wood. It is dark-coloured and light. Used for facing walls, ceilings, &c. &c., in houses. |

| Japanese Names | General Remarks ; also the Botanical Names as far as they are procurable |
|---|---|

16. Kir-ri . . . *Paulownia imperialis.* A very light wood. Used for the bottoms of Japanese shoes, &c. &c.

17. Hi-no-ki, *s.* . . *Retinispora obtusa.* One of the finest and most beautiful timber trees of Japan. The wood is much valued; temples and chapels are generally built of it. It stands well in water and under ground. Ships are built of it. Used for house building, and especially for flooring. The wood is light, white, and fine.

18. Asu-na-ro, *s.* . *Thujopsis dolabrata.* One of the most beautiful trees in Japan. The wood is coarse and light. It is used for building.

19. A-ung-kir-ri . *Paulownia species.* A variety of No. 16. The wood is very similar, and used for the same purposes.

20. Cash-y, *s.* . . *Quercus species.* The oak of Japan. There are many varieties, both evergreen and deciduous. The trees attain a great size. The timber is very fine, and probably equal to any oak in the world. It is used for all purposes where great strength is required. The handles of Japanese swords are chiefly made of cash-y.

21. Ging-di-su-gi, *s.* . *Thuja species.* A light wood. Used for house work.

22. Mee, *s.* . . . A fine wood, very heavy and hard. It polishes beautifully, and is one of the woods selected for making the finest boxes, cabinets, &c. &c.

23. Hi-ba . . . *Retinispora species.* Nearly allied to No. 17. Used chiefly for building.

24. Mo-mo, *s.* . . A heavy, strong wood. It polishes well, and is used for boxes, cabinets, &c.

25. Kat-su-ra, *s.* . A beautiful wood; it has quite a silky appearance when planed, and is of a very fine grain, dark brown colour, and medium weight. It is considered by the Japanese as one of their best woods for fine neat work, and is highly prized.

26. Ho . . . A light white wood. All the sword sheaths in Japan are made of it.

27. Shi-ra-bi . A light white wood, used for building.

28. Ya-ma-na-ra-shi . Used for shoes, sword handles, &c. &c.

29. Ka-ki . . . *Diospyros Kaki.* Not very extensively used. The wood is hard, but somewhat brittle, and will not stand exposure to weather.

30. Mats-u, *s.* . . *Pinus densiflora and Massoniana.* The common pines of the country. The trees attain a great size. The timber is large and fine in quality. These trees are valued by the Japanese, who plant them to form avenues, and on all prominent positions. *Mats-u answers to the deal of* Europe. Rosin is also made from them.

31. Kats-u-no-ki . An unimportant timber tree. Used for chop-sticks, and similar small articles.

32. Na-ra . . . Used for small boxes.

33. Ku-rong-no-ki . The wood is almost black, very like ebony. It is very scarce in Japan, and used for the finest lacquer cups, &c. &c.

| Japanese Names | General Remarks ; also the Botanical Names as far as they are procurable |
|---|---|
| 34. Sing-y . . . | In common use for building and rough work. |
| 35. Ya-na-ny . . | Common wood of little value. |
| 36. Momids-y . . | *Acer species*. The Japanese maple. There is a great variety of maples in Japan. The wood is not much used in this country. The trees are chiefly planted for ornaments. |

The above is a list of the principal timber trees. Taken as a whole, I think the timber of Japan will equal that of any other country. It is very plentiful and cheap. Most of these trees would probably thrive well in England.

Those marked thus (*s*) are found only in Japan and the neighbouring islands.

---

## ADDITIONAL NOTES ON THE TREES AND FLORA OF JAPAN.

### THE CONIFEROUS PLANTS.

THERE is probably no country in the world, of the same area, which produces so great a variety of conifers, as the group of islands composing the Empire of Japan. From Nagasaki in the south to Hakodadi in the north conifers are everywhere abundant, and in great variety ; and as foreigners have hitherto been enabled to explore but an exceedingly small portion of these islands, it is more than probable that the numerous mountainridges of the interior produce a great number of entirely new and, as yet, undiscovered species.

The Japanese are great admirers of evergreens, and great trouble is taken to cultivate them to the best possible pitch. The greater portion of the timber used for building, and for all ordinary purposes, is that of coniferous trees. The annual demand is exceedingly great throughout all parts of the empire, and it is said that land-owners are compelled to plant a certain number of *forest* trees *yearly,* in order that the stock in the country may not be diminished. Conifers are also employed very largely for ornamental purposes. Clipped hedges of the Cryptomeria, Retinosporas, Biotas, &c., are very general ; and scarcely a garden can be met with that does not contain specimens of coniferæ, many of which are cut and trained into the most grotesque forms.

The main roads which intersect this country are very generally planted on either side with rows of *conifers*. Pinus densiflora and Massoniana, Cryptomeria japonica, and Thujopsis dolabrata, are probably the kinds generally employed for this purpose. These trees are seldom or ever cut down, and consequently they attain a great size, and form specimens of the greatest beauty.

Altogether conifers constitute the most useful and the most generally employed trees in Japan. As most of the kinds which have been discovered by travellers have now been introduced to European gardens, and there being every prospect that most of them will prove of sufficient hardiness to withstand the most severe of our winters, it is confidently hoped that ere long many of the beautiful species indigenous to this country may be distributed throughout our pleasure grounds, and flourish as luxuriantly as they do in Japan.

Annexed is a list of the principal conifers, and other plants, which have been described as coming from the Japanese islands :

| Japanese Names | Botanical Names and General Remarks |
|---|---|
| | *Abies Alcoquiana.* A noble tree, discovered in 1860, during Mr. Alcock's trip to Mount Fusiyama, and named in honour of that gentleman. It grows at from 6,000 to 7,000 feet elevation on Fusiyama, where it attains a height of 90 to 100 feet. |
| Saga-momi . | *Abies bifida.* A variety peculiar from the ends of the leaves being divided into two sharp points. Only seen cultivated in gardens in Yeddo and Kanagama. |
| Momi . . | *Abies firma.* A common tree in the mountainous districts, growing at an elevation of 3,000 to 4,000 feet. It attains a height of 80 to 100 feet. |
| Itsuga . . | *Abies Tsuga.* Found growing on Mount Fusiyama, at an elevation of 6,500 feet. It attains a height of 80 to 100 feet, and is much valued as a timber tree. |
| Jesso matsu . | *Abies jezoensis.* A tree growing some 60 feet in height on the island of Jesso. |
| Fusi matsu . | *Abies leptolepis.* Found at an elevation of 8,000 to 8,500 feet on Mount Fusiyama. It is remarkable as being the tree which grows at the greatest elevation on this mountain. Its greatest height is 40 feet; but on ascending the mountain dwindles down to a bush of 3 feet. |
| | *Abies microsperma.* A species hitherto found only in the vicinity of *Hakodadi*, where it was seen attaining a height of 20 to 30 feet. |
| Tora-momi . | *Abies polita.* A large tree growing on the mountains in the north of Niphon. Attains a height of 80 to 100 feet. |
| | *Abies Veitchii.* A species found at an elevation of 6,000 to 7,000 feet on Mount Fusiyama, where it grows over 100 feet *in height.* |
| Siwa . . | *Biota orientalis.* A bush of 18 to 20 feet. Commonly found near Yeddo. |
| Ito-sugi . | *Biota pendula.* A growing bush found on the mountains of Hakone. It is largely planted in gardens for ornamental purposes. |

| Japanese Names | Botanical Names and General Remarks |
|---|---|

Isa-bo-hiba  .  *Biota japonica.*  A low bush, cultivated in gardens.
*Cephalotaxus drupacea.*  A tree growing to a height of 35 to 40 feet, on the mountains in the south of Japan.

Inu-kaya .  .  *Cephalotaxus pedunculata.*  A tree growing 20 to 25 feet in height.
*Cephalotaxus umbraculifera.*

Sugi  .  .  *Cryptomeria japonica.*  The cedar of Japan.  Perhaps the commonest conifer in the empire.  It grows exceedingly straight, attaining a height of 80 to 100 feet. It is found in all parts, from Nagasaki to Hakodadi. There are numerous varieties of this cultivated in gardens.

Liu-kiu momi .  *Cunninghamia sinensis.*  A very graceful tree with drooping branches, growing to a height of 20 to 25 feet.
*Juniperus japonica.*  A dwarf shrub, found in most parts of Japan.
*Juniperus rigida.*  A handsome tree, attaining a height of 20 to 30 feet, found on the Hakone ridge of mountains, and at Atame.  There are several other species of junipers not yet described by botanists.
*Nageia cuspidata.*  A small-growing tree, said to be found in a wild state in the island of Jesso.  It is cultivated in the gardens near Yeddo.

Nagi  .  .  *Nageia japonica.*  A tree growing from 30 to 40 feet in height.  It is found on the mountains of the interior, and is cultivated in the Yeddo gardens.

Aka matsu  .  *Pinus densiflora.*  One of the commonest pines of the country, the timber of which is in very common use. It attains a height of 40 to 50 feet, and is found throughout the whole empire.  Both rosin and ink are prepared from this and the following species.

Wo-matsu  .  *Pinus Massoniana.*  A pine very similar to the latter, but attaining a greater size.  It is very commonly planted to form *avenues,* and is the favourite species for dwarfing and training horizontally.

Wiomi matsu .  *Pinus ———.*  A tree largely cultivated in gardens, but not found in a wild state in the localities to which foreigners have had access.

Go-yo-matsu .  *Pinus parviflora.*  A species growing on the Hakone mountains, and much cultivated in *gardens.*  It grows from 30 to 40 feet in height.  There are several other species and varieties of pines as yet undescribed.  One of the most remarkable of these is the *Shi-ro-y matsu* of the Japanese, the foliage of which is variegated.

Maki  .  .  *Podocarpus Maki.*  A small growing tree, planted in gardens for ornamental purposes.
*Podocarpus japonica.*  A tree found in Japan by Dr. Siebold, and planted for ornament in gardens.

Fou maki .  .  *Podocarpus macrophylla.*  A tree growing from 20 to 30 feet in height.

Hinoki  .  .  *Retinispora obtusa.*  This is one of the finest conifers in Japan.  It is much valued, both for its timber and for ornamental purposes.  The Japanese call it 'The Tree of the Sun.'  It grows commonly on most of the mountain ridges of the island of Niphon, from 50 to 60 feet in height.

| Japanese Names | Botanical Names and General Remarks |
|---|---|

**Sa-wa-ra .** . *Retinispora pisifera.* A tree growing from 20 to 30 feet in height. It is very graceful and ornamental, but does not attain a sufficient size to be very valuable as a timber tree.

**Sinobu hiba** . *Retinispora squarrosa.* A small growing tree with glaucous foliage, largely planted for ornament in gardens. There are several species of Retinospora still undescribed.

**Koya maki** . *Sciadopitys verticillata.* The umbrella pine. This remarkable tree, which derives its name from having its leaves in whorls at the end of the shoots, is the only species yet discovered. It is a dense pyramidal tree, found abundantly on the *Koya mountains,* in the province of *Kiudin,* and on other mountain ridges. Its greatest height is probably from 70 to 80 feet; and being clothed with branches to the foot, forms one of the handsomest trees in Japan. This and its numerous varieties, one of which has variegated foliage, are largely planted in the gardens of the Japanese.

*Taxus tardiva.* A small shrub with dark green foliage, found on the mountains of Japan, and in the gardens of Yeddo.

**Ara-ra-gii** . *Taxus cuspidata.* A dense growing shrub with dark green foliage. It is found at the foot of Mount Fusiyama, on the Hakone mountains, and on the island of Yesso. It grows from 15 to 20 feet in height.

**Asu-naro .** . *Thujopsis dolabrata.* One of the most beautiful evergreen trees in Japan. It is found on the Hakone mountains, and on other ridges in the north of Niphon. It is also found near Hakodadi, in Yesso. It forms a most elegant and graceful tree, from 30 to 40 feet in height, with dark green drooping branches. It is largely cultivated by the Japanese in their gardens, and highly prized. There are several varieties, one of which has beautifully variegated foliage, and another with foliage smaller and of a light green colour.

**Kaya** . . *Torreya nucifera.* A tree growing from 25 to 30 feet in height. Its foliage is of a dark green colour, and the nuts are carefully gathered by the Japanese, the kernels of which are eaten. It is found common in the midland and southern provinces of Japan.

*Veitchia japonica.* An entirely new genus, of which this is the only known species. Nothing is yet known
. about the habit of this tree.

**So-cho** . . *Fraxinus excelsior. The ash of Japan.* A good useful timber, coarse grained, heavy, and strong. It is not in very general use in *this district.* Employed chiefly for oars, bows and arrows, &c. &c.

**O-row-schy** . *Rhus vernicifera. The Japanese varnish tree.* A tree 15 to 20 feet in height, grown exclusively for the sake of its sap, from which the celebrated lacquer is obtained, and its seed, from which oil and wax are pressed. The lacquer is taken from the tree during the early spring months. A ring is cut with a sharp knife round the trunk of the tree, from which the varnish exudes, and is received in vessels placed for the purpose. It is white, and of the consistence of cream, when first coming from the tree, but turns black on exposure to the air. The seed of this tree, like that of its near ally (*Rhus succedanea*), from which the vegetable wax is made, contains a large quantity of oily substance. From the seed itself oil is pressed, whilst the husk produces the substance from which the bulk of the Japanese candles are made.

Ka-so　. 　. 　*Broussonetia papyrifera. The paper tree of Japan.* This shrub is grown exclusively for its bark, which forms the chief material used for paper-making. The shoots are cut annually in December or January, after the leaves have fallen, having grown some four or five feet in length. They are then immersed in water for several days, after which the bark is taken off. The inner and whiter bark is separated from the outer, and the former selected for making the better qualities of paper. The bark is then beaten into a pulp and afterwards well washed and cleaned. This done it is allowed to accumulate in a vessel, and is ready for being converted into paper. In making the paper, a portion of the pulp is taken up in a tray with a very low (almost imperceptible) projection round the edge. Sufficient pulp is thus retained to make the paper the desired thickness, and the remainder runs off. The paper being made by hand, these trays are small, which accounts for the Japanese paper being always made in small sheets. It is dried in the sun after this latter process, and becomes fit for use. There are three plants grown in this district for paper-making, viz. *Broussonetia papyrifera, Buddlea species,* and *Hibiscus* species. The bark of the two former, and the *root* of the latter is employed. The Broussonetia is, however, by far the commonest, only comparatively small quantities of the two latter being mixed with it.

## NOTES ON JAPANESE PLANTS

INTRODUCED TO ENGLAND BY MR. JOHN G. VEITCH, AND NOW IN CULTIVATION
IN THE ESTABLISHMENTS OF MESSRS. VEITCH AND SON.

THE following additional notes have been supplied me while the work is going through the press; and, as affording the latest information in reference to the plants now in the country, they will doubtless be acceptable to all interested in ornamental gardening: —

Many of these plants will unquestionably be most valuable additions to our gardens, their hardiness adding much to their value.

Amongst deciduous trees *Planera acuminata*, the Japanese elm, will occupy a prominent place, not only as an ornamental tree but from the value of its fine timber which the Japanese use for their best work. The Maples also will prove very handsome trees from their rich autumnal tints. (See vol. i. p. 298.)

Conifers are abundant, and amongst those at present most admired, perhaps because most known, the graceful *Thujopsis dolabrata*, numerous elegant species of *Retinispora*, both green and variegated, the singular and distinct Umbrella Pine, *Sciadopitys verticillata*, the *Abies Alcoquiana* rendered peculiarly interesting by the seeds having been plucked on our pilgrimage to Mount Fusi'yama with other beautiful species of *Abies, Picea, Pinus*, &c.

Our collections of hardy shrubs are enriched by the addition of many fine things, including the evergreen female *Aucuba japonica*, producing copious branches of red berries in the autumn. It is from this original species that our well known *variegated Aucuba* originates, and now we have several *variegated* additions.

There are also many fine species of *Ligustrum, Euonymus, Elæagnus*, &c., both green and variegated as well as the beautiful Holly-like *Osmanthus aquifolius*, a charming little shrub, of which there are several varieties. Nor must the various *Bamboos* be omitted, which, from their very distinct and peculiar habit, are calculated to form most useful objects for ornamental planting, especially near water.

Of *Ferns* also a great number have been received, and are now under cultivation.

Annexed will be found a list of the principal Japanese plants now in cultivation in this country, many of which have been already referred to in previous portions of this Appendix. In addition to these there are many others, the character of which is not yet sufficiently developed to allow of their correct determination.

Abies Alcoquiana.
„  firma. A very fine and distinct species.
„  microsperma.
„  polita.
Acer (*maple*). Several species, with great variety of foliage.
Aucuba japonica vera. Many beautiful varieties.
Ardisia. Many beautifully variegated kinds.
Bambusa. Several very fine and quite new kinds, one of which is variegated.
Biota (Thuja) falcata.
Buxus sempervirens. Two distinct varieties.
Berberis species nova.
Camellia japonica foliis variegatis; Camellia Sasanqua variegata. Two nicely variegated forms of this beautiful genus.
Catesbæa spinosa variegata.
Cryptomeria species nova. A very distinct and beautiful plant.
Daphne. Several varieties.
Elæagnus japonicus variegatus. A beautifully variegated plant.
Euonymus ovatus aureo variegatus.
„  radicans variegatus.
Eurya latifolia variegata.
Farfugium species nova.
Ficus species nova.
Hypericum. Several new forms.
Hemerocallis species foliis variegatis.
Ilex Fortuni (?).
Illicium. Several new kinds.
Iris. Many new sorts.
Juniperus rigida.
Ligustrum japonicum aureo-variegatum. A beautiful variegated plant.
Lilium auratum. One of the most remarkable and beautiful plants introduced from Japan.
Magnolia. Several species.
Melastoma. New species, very beautiful
Osmanthus ilicifolius; Osmanthus ilicifolius variegatus. Two beautifully variegated plants, with holly-like foliage.

Paulovnia species nova.
Planera acuminata. The Japanese elm, a fine timber tree.
Planera acuminata. Two distinct varieties.
Pinus densiflora.
„  Koraiensis.
„  parviflora.
„  Several other new species.
Photinia (?) ovata. Splendid evergreen shrub.
Podocarpus. Many new kinds, several of which are variegated.
Primula. Two distinct and very fine species have already flowered.
Quercus. Many new ones, both deciduous and evergreen.
Retinispora obtusa. The Japanese Tree of the Sun.
„  lycopodioides.
„  pisifera.
„  squarrosa.
„  Several beautifully variegated forms of the foregoing species.
Rhapis flabelliformis.
„  „  foliis variegatis.
Rhynchospermum jasminoides variegatum.
Rhus succedanea. The vegetable wax tree of Japan.
Rhus vernicifera. The lacquer tree of Japan.
Rhododendron. Two distinct species.
Sanseviera carnea variegata.
Sedum carneum variegatum.
Serissa fœtida variegata.
Sciadopitys verticillata. The umbrella pine.
Taxus. Two distinct species.
„  pygmæa. A most singularly dwarf and beautiful species.
Thujopsis dolabrata; Thujopsis dolabrata variegata; Thujopsis lætevirens. This genus is peculiar to Japan, and is one of the most beautiful known.
Viburnum. Several new species.
Weigela. A very beautiful new kind.

FILICES (*Ferns*) &c.

Adiantum.   Two species.
Cheilanthes mysurensis.
Cyrtomium falcatum.
Gymnogramma japonica.
Lastræa opaca.
   „   Several distinct kinds.
Microlepia strigosa.
Niphobolus Lingua corymbiferus.
   „   hastatus.

Onychium japonicum.
Polystichum setosum.
   „   Two other distinct species.
Pteris.   Several distinct kinds.
Selaginella.   Many new varieties.
Woodsia polystichoides.
   „   „   Veitchii.
Woodwardia japonica.
   „   orientalis.

The following lists of seeds and plants sent from the Legation to the Royal Gardens at Kew may also be interesting:—

## LIST OF SEEDS SENT TO SIR W. HOOKER IN 1860.

1. Pinus species.  Hakodadi.
2.   „   parviflora (cones).
3.   „   „   (seeds).
4. Cunninghamia sinensis.
5. Cephalotaxus species.  Yeddo.
6. Salisburia adiantifolia.
7. Retinispora obtusa.
8.   „   pisifera.
9. Paulovnia species.  Yeddo.
10. Chamærops excelsa.
11. Acer species.  Yeddo.
12. Ilex species (?).  Evergreen shrub.  8 to 10 feet.
13. Rhus vernix.
14. Abies species.
15. Biennial.  Unknown.
16. Nandina domestica, fructu rubro.
17. Paulovnia species (?).
18. Euonymus species (?).
19. Ilex latifolia.
20. Ilex species.  (Smooth leaved.)
21. Nandina domestica, fructu luteo.
22. Lilium species.

## CONTENTS OF CASES FOR THE ROYAL GARDENS, KEW.

### CASE No. 1.

1. Abies species, from Mount Fusiyama.
2. Thujopsis dolabrata variegata.
3. Zanthoxylon species (?)
4. Abies species (larch), from Mount Fusiyama.
5. Magnolia species, from Mount Fusiyama.
6. Pernettya species, from Mount Fusiyama.
7. Canna species (?).
8. A tree (unknown) from which the Japanese are said to make varnish.
9. Azalea species.
10. Osmanthus species.
11.   „   „   variegatus.
12. Rubus species, from Mount Fusiyama.
13. Gardenia radicans variegata.
14. Carex species variegata.
15. Thuja species.

CASE No. 2.

2. Thujopis dolabrata variegata.
8. A tree (unknown) from which varnish is said to be made.
9. Azalea species.
15. Thuja species.
16. Thujopsis dolabrata.
17. Retinispora obtusa.
18. Melastoma species (?).

19. An orchid (unknown).
20. Creeper with variegated foliage.
21. Chrysanthemum. A handsome and novel variety.
22. Shrub (unknown).
23. Platanus species.
24. Acer species.
25.　　,,　　　,,

Quantities of Seedling Pines, Oaks, Maples, &c., &c., planted in both cases.

# F

## TITLES IN JAPAN.

[*From the 'Japan Herald.'*]

THE subject of the titles of officers in Japan is to the uninitiated a maze of obscurity. It is a labyrinth in the mazes of which one is immediately lost without a guide, but through which it is easy to steer when the clue has been obtained. Not one of the many Japanese officers (whether their titles be hereditary or not) is so often misnamed, by those even who know his position and his proper titles, as he who holds the position of what foreigners style Temporal Emperor. The titles of officers generally is too large a one to take up at present, but it may not be amiss to discuss, or to throw out a few hints for the discussion of, what is the proper title of the Temporal Emperor.

In our last number, we, in noticing another subject, expressed an opinion, in a passing way, that there was little or nothing of spirituality in the ideas that the Japanese have of the Mikado beyond what is contained in the doctrine of the divine right of kings. The title of almost any one of the rulers in Christendom contains some expression to denote more or less plainly that the person of his or her majesty is most sacred, and that he rules by the grace of God. That Easterns should call the highest individual in their respective empires by the title of the Son of Heaven, or that these should so style themselves, is not a matter of surprise. But in Japan it is supposed by foreigners that there is something in the official titles of the one and of the other to constitute them co-equals in rank, to one of whom is given the execution of the laws, to the other the dispensation of honours only as from a sacred fountain.

If, however, it be granted that there is anything which would denote an idea of spirituality in the office of Mikado, there is nothing we shall find in the titles of the other to denote any idea of imperial or kingly power whatever.

The name by which this officer is commonly known is 'the Tycoon of Japan.' In all the Treaties made between the respective Governments of England, France, America, Holland

and Portugal, and Japan, he is styled 'his Majesty the Tycoon of Japan,' and in the Japanese text of the Treaties he is also styled Tycoon.    There is, however, no such word as Tycoon in the language of Japan.    There was no such title given in Japan to any officer before the arrival of Commodore Perry in Japan. Whence has it arisen that an officer is, in such an important document as a Treaty, given a name which is not known in the country with which the Treaty is made ?

The two words Tycoon or Taikun are Chinese, the first signifying 'great,' the second is translated in Williams's dictionary, 'a chief, head of society, a prince, sovereign or ruler honourable, exalted; to rule, to fulfil the duties of a sovereign, &c.;' the two words therefore imply that the bearer of the title is the 'great sovereign or ruler of Japan.'    The word emperor in Medhurst's vocabulary is translated Sohera Mikado, and another word is given for the Spiritual Emperor, no word being given for Tycoon.    But this is only an old word for Emperor, and ought to be Smera Mikoto.

We may then inquire whether (if this high-sounding name be a foreign importation), it is born out to the full extent or to any extent by the titles by which he is known in Japan.

And in the first place, we may state what we have learnt on the spot as to the origin of the name Tycoon in the Treaties. When Commodore Perry arrived in the Bay of Yedo, the Government was naturally anxious to find out exactly what he wanted, what his powers were, and how far he was likely to go in pushing his wishes.    The expedition was heralded with such a flourish of trumpets so loud and so long, as to reach the shores of Japan long before the Commodore himself.

The Government, no doubt, consulted long and anxiously about the diplomatist whom they should send down to carry on a negotiation: they seem, not with their usual skill and wisdom, to have deputed a man who was more notable for his knowledge of the Chinese language than for worldly wisdom or practical shrewdness.    This was Hyashi Daigaku-no Kami.    Not the Prince of Daigaku, as the American official report styles him, but the head of the Chinese college, or professor of Chinese in the college of Miako, and at the time teacher of Chinese to the Tycoon.    He happened to be a pedant.    He was devoted to the study of Chinese literature.    During the conferences which took place at Yokohama, the question of the proper title of the Emperor, as he was then called, came up, and, so far as we recollect, the question was put if the 'Tycoon' was the proper title to embody in the text of the Treaty.    The answer given by Hyashi implied that it was the proper title by which to designate the person intended in the text of the Treaty.    Poor Hyashi, in consequence of his diplomacy on this occasion, fell into disgrace and poverty, died some years ago despised by his countrymen and neglected by his friends, and an object of aversion to the Government by whom he had been accredited. With such an authority, and with interpreters who were acquainted with Chinese only, it was natural that the style should be adopted.

At what period, the name was first adopted by foreigners we have no means at hand of discovering.

Kœmpfer calls him the secular Emperor, secular Monarch, a Crown General; but we cannot find that he alludes to any such title as Tycoon. The old Jesuit fathers called him the Kubosama, the Xogune, Daifusama at different times, according to the exact title he received from the Emperor at the time they wrote.

He is never spoken of in public documents by the title of Tycoon. So far as we can learn, nearly all his titles are given to him by the Mikado, and he goes through the several grades of rank in succession. Such being the case, we may conclude that Tycoon is not a title to which he has any right, and the more especially that it seems to convey an idea of superiority and of sovereign rule which is not included in, or to be inferred from, any of the titles conferred on him by the Mikado. The very giving of such a title and the assumption of it, is likely to create a feeling of jealousy when none would have existed, had his own honours been strictly adhered to.

So far as we can learn, the son and heir or the 'Temporal Emperor,' whether his father be alive or not, goes, till he is fifteen years of age, by the name of 'Take-cheoo,' two Chinese words meaning a bamboo shoot green for ten thousand years. If his father is dead and he has succeeded him, this title is changed when he is about eight or nine years of age. He assumes the *toga virilis* at an earlier age than is usual—i.e., at fifteen — has his head shaved and assumes the name by which he is afterwards known, such as Iyeyas, Iyaymitzno Iyaytzna.

But if he have succeeded to the vacant seat even at an early age, there are two titles which are inherent in the position. The first Junna Shongakoo drio een no Bettowo, which means that he is the head or principal of the two colleges of Junna and Shongakoo. These were formerly in Miako, but are now in Yedo. This title always is assumed by the person who holds the next — viz: 'Genjee no-choja.' Genjee is the family which opposed the Heji, and after a lengthened civil war overcame them. Genjee is the Chinese sound of the characters of the word Minnamoto. Sometimes the title is given with the latter instead of the former word — Minnamoto-no Choja; Choja means the head of a large house or family. The title signifies ' the head of the Minnamoto family.'

These two titles appertain to the individual, whoever he may be, who is the real or supposed lineal descendant of Iyeyas and other lines upon which this line has been engrafted. So soon as this officer assumes the *toga virilis,* and shaves his head as a man, the Mikado gives him titles and honours. Those which we have just noticed may be called family and literary honours. Those which he receives from the Emperor are civil and military, and of rank or position. Of each of these there are several with differences. Three years ago, shortly after his elevation, the present Tycoon was Dainangoong (Ta-nah-yen in Chinese); since then we believe, and shortly before his marriage with the Emperor's sister, he was advanced to either Nai-dai-jin or Oodaijin—i.e. to be either middle or right great Minister. He was not advanced to this without some opposition from officers of high rank at Miako. He receives from the Emperor generally at a very early period after his elevation the title of Daisiogoong (in Chinese Ta-tsiang-kiun), the great commander of the army. This is a title given in China to the commander-in-chief of the Tatar troops only. This is the highest military rank in Japan, and has been generally hereditary; it carries with it no actual military duties; but, as the Japanese consider themselves a nation of soldiers, the holder is in fact the head of the executive.

To this title is sometimes, but not always, added Se-i or Savee (in Chinese Ching-i) the chastiser or subjugator of barbarians, as we translate the word ' I,' the use of which is prohibited by the last treaty with China. This title was originally given with reference to the Ainos in the north of Japan and Yezo, but this has lately been applied to foreigners in communications from the Mikado to the Tycoon in which he asks him — ' I have given you the title of Se-i, why do you not fulfil the expectations I had of you in conferring the title ? ' Se-i f'oo is one of the names of the Tycoon's castle in Yedo.

In addition to these titles he has one denoting by a number the rank he holds. All officers of the rank of Daimios and upwards are thus denoted; and, if this number be high, it is placed first. If a high office be held, the number of his rank comes after. Iyeyas was No 1 of the 2nd degree while he was alive, and after death was elevated to No 1 of the first degree. But such high rank is very rarely given ; No. 2 of the second degree being the highest rank ordinarily given during life. These are the whole of the titles that are inherent in or given to the holder of the Tycoon's chair.

The titles of Iyeyas were as follows :

Jiu itchi (No 1 of the second degree).

Oodaijiu (right great Minister).

Se-i dai Shiogoong.

Junna Shongaku drio een no Bettowo.

Genjee no Choja.

Minnamoto no Iyeyas.

Besides these the Mikado gives frequently, but not always, the title of Kubosama. This was first given to old Ashikanga, when he had retired from the office of Dai Shiogoong. Kubo is the title given to a retired or abdicated Emperor when his son has succeeded him. Sama means originally 'the same as.' The Emperor who wished to confer as high an honour as he could upon the ambitious old man, gave him one implying that he was 'the same as my father when he has abdicated.'

It is a name by which the Tycoon is frequently spoken of even when, as at present, he has no right to it. It has not as yet been conferred upon the present young man. The name Daifusama, by which the Jesuits designated Iyeyas, is a sort of corruption of Nai dai jin, being Nai or Dai fhos sama, meaning, according to the subsequent conversion of Sama, Lord of the Inner Office.

Occasionally other official titles are added, but as these are of lower rank and would require an explanation of the whole list of titles, our space does not permit of our entering on so extensive a subject.

From the above we see that the title of Tycoon is by no means a correct one. The title by which he is most commonly spoken of appears to be Dai Shiogoong or Kubosama. But as neither of these came so easily to a foreigner's lips as Tycoon, he, in all probability, will continue to be called by that title to which he has no right, but which, having been introduced into a high State document, has some authority for its use.

# E

A FEW REMARKS ON AN OPEN LETTER TO THE REPRESEN-
TATIVES OF THE WESTERN NATIONS AT YEDDO.'

## To the Editor of the ' North China Herald.'

SIR,— The merit of this letter may be variously appreciated :
its assertions have been a matter of discussion. But whatever
may be the *objections proposed*, the judgement of the Japanese
has made a victorious reply to them.

Among the Japanese, either friends or enemies to the
Government at Yeddo, all those who have been able to become
acquainted with the contents of ' An Open Letter' were aston-
ished at the precision and exactitude with which their most
inward constitution was explained, and at the interesting details
upon the organisation of the various powers in Japan. The
only fault the Japanese could find with it, was that the letter
did contain so much correct information concerning their laws
and government.

If then I venture now to make a few remarks on the letter,
it is less to criticise it than to complete and correct certain
facts, which the judicious author of the letter could hardly have
known in all their particulars. I must even confess, that notwithstanding my long studies on the same matter, I had at first
arrived at the conclusions so boldly deduced by the writer of
that letter.

A summary of the actual constitution of Japan may be thus
rendered : —

Whenever a law, or a measure of general interest for the
Empire — that is a law which does not concern only the dominions of the Taikong, but also the estates of the Daimios — is
to be decreed or adopted, the Taikong, (the chief of the executive Power — the Lieutenant of the Micado) proposes by
himself or by the *Go-ro-tjo*, the law which is submitted for the
approval or the criticism of the Daimios; who examine the said

law either in a general meeting at Yeddo, or by their deputies. If the new measure which is to be adopted, is of minor importance, the Government at Yeddo consults the Daimios by deputies sent to them for that purpose. If the law is adopted by the majority, it is immediately presented to the Micado for his sanction. Should the majority of the Daimios disagree with the Court at Yeddo, the Taikong may pass them over unheeded, and submit the law to the examination of the Micado — who simply approves the law or consults the Daimios.

The opening of Japan to foreigners by the treaties, was not only one of these general great measures with which the interests of all were highly concerned, but it caused a radical revolution in the Empire. It required then, to be voted and sanctioned by all the requisite forms, in agreement with the constitution.

In fact, the Daimios were consulted in drawing up the treaty of Commodore Perry. The question was laid before them in these terms: 'Does it please your Lordships to conclude a treaty of such and such tenour, as an experiment, and for 6 or 8 years only?' The Daimios examined and discussed the matter with care and deliberation. Some of them consulted the various classes of people of their estates — Yakoonins, bonzes, physicians, &c. &c., and most of them brought back to Yeddo an affirmative answer. Still the decision of the majority was opposed by a strong minority, in proportion as 2 to 3.

When the year 1858 arrived, with all its momentous events in China, Japan was requested, or summoned to bind itself by definite engagements to the Western nations. The Government of the Taikong either could not, or would not, take the advice of the Daimios; who by this time would have proved almost unanimously favourable to the new treaties. The four years elapsed since the first treaty with the United States, had been actively and usefully employed in discussing the opening of Japan to foreign trade. Several pamphlets — of which their lucid argumentations have more than once excited our sincere admiration — circulated freely among all the classes of the people.

It is impossible to read these pamphlets — all written by servants of Daimios — and not be convinced that not only the Daimios were not hostile to the new policy, but were rather ahead of the Government at Yeddo; which, with all its sleepy inertia, could hardly join in unison with the general opinion. It is therefore to be regretted exceedingly, that the Taikong's Government neglected a very essential formality. The Daimios were long since on their guard against the encroaching policy of Yeddo endeavouring to centralise all the powers — long since, they were wearied with what we might call the plague of the Landholders, viz. the journeys to and ruinous residence at

Yeddo. These wealthy and powerful nobles were stung to the quick by this new blow aimed at their constitutional rights, and many of them turned to be the irreconcilable enemies of the treaties. Many learned Japanese explained this neglect of the Government by the fear which Yeddo entertained towards the rather too liberal policy of the Daimios ; that is, the Government of the Taikong was willing to open Japan, but with endless restrictions, and the firm mind to monopolise the new trade to its own profit. On the contrary, the Daimios wished to open Japan in such a way as to enable every estate to profit by the treaties. A learned Japanese of the province of Nagato — who was treacherously put to death by the agents of Yeddo — in a very remarkable address to the Micado, urged the Emperor to compel Yeddo to open Japan in the most liberal way, that the whole Empire might be benefited by the new course of policy. The quarrels between the two families of *Kishoo* and *Mito* for the succession of the late Taikong augmented the number of the malcontents against the Government of Yeddo, which has always been exposed to the secret hostility of the Daimios. The Landholders are indignant at the new charges laid on them, on account of a commerce of which they derive no profit. But let us come to the main point, viz. has the Micado been consulted, and has he sanctioned the treaties? To these questions we answer in the affirmative, although we have at first warmly defended the negative. A few words will explain our former error. The Government at Yeddo, affecting to see in the new treaties nothing but a continuation of the first convention made with America, and for which the consent of the Daimios and the sanction of the Micado had been duly obtained, could not remain consistent with itself and openly consult the sovereign. The Micado sanctioned the treaties really and fully; but owing to the irregularity in which the Taikong stood towards the Daimios, he could not promulgate his sanction with the ordinary solemnity. The Daimios therefore feigned to be ignorant of this sanction, and contrived, in addresses more or less ambiguous, to prove to the Micado the nullity of the treaties. The Micado, strictly watched by the Taikong, and entirely ruled by his influence, answered the Daimios by a series of acts equivalent to a sanction. He continued to receive the envoys of the Taikong, and to send him various solemn messages of great import; finally he wedded him to his sister, and by so many acts, gave a new sanction to the treaties.

Most of the Daimios, without being less bitter against Yeddo, accepted at last the *statu quo*. Many of their servants tried at various times to raise an insurrection. Their boldest attempt was made this year at Miako ; but, not being supported by the Micado, their camp dissolved of itself.

It is not my intention in these few lines to follow step by step our interesting writer. I am by no means willing to contradict him on the number of the Daimios; the relative importance of the eighteen great ones, &c. &c. The 'Open Letter' leads the reader to a practical conclusion, and to this too I am anxious to arrive.

Without wasting time in discussing, whether the explicit consent of the Daimios was required or not, whether the sanction of the Micado ought to be published with a certain degree of pomp, I will simply say that the conclusion of the 'Open Letter,' viz. 'To have the treaties recognised by the real Government of the Empire or to abandon them as worthless,'—is in the first place *useless*, and secondly *practically impossible*. It is useless; for whatever may have been the want of forms in the conclusion of the treaties, they have, as already stated, received a double sanction from the Micado, and been finally accepted by most of the Daimios.

Undoubtedly the weakness of the Government at Yeddo, that kind of antipathy, a mixture of hatred and contempt, in which we are held by the great number of the two-sworded men, may lead us to form wrong conclusions. The weakness and the unpopularity of the Government at Yeddo is to be attributed to many causes which I will not now discuss.

The kind of hostile antipathy which we meet from the privileged class cannot but surprise those unacquainted with the character of a two-sworded Japanese. The Government at Yeddo in opening Japan reserved to itself, in petto, the right to overrule with an absolute authority the new relations. The energy and dignity of our Representatives have singularly disappointed their pretensions: all those who are attached to the Government, whose national pride has not forgotten the homages rendered to the great Nippon by *Desheema*, are scandalised to see the foreigners make the treaties a serious thing, and acquire in Japan an influence more or less fatal to their privileges. A Japanese official cannot understand how a merchant dares to appeal to *what is right*, as the sole arbitrator between himself and the *Yacoonin*. He cannot bear that a *despised akindo* (merchant), should be more enlightened than himself, and should prove it daily to him.

I said, the conclusion of the 'Open Letter' was practically impossible. The Miaco would certainly not receive the European envoys, but would send them back to Yeddo, where the Taikong is the official deputy to treat on such a matter.

Moreover, such a measure would be most dangerous. The Daimios would move heaven and earth, and intrigue in every manner, to influence the Micado, to ruin the detested Government in condemning its policy towards foreigners. The Daimios

would necessarily be against us, because they are the enemies
of a Government whose cause is fatally connected with our interests.

Such are the reflections which the reading of the 'Open
Letter' has suggested to me, and which I submit to your appreciation with all possible respect.

E. E. M. * * * *

# INDEX.

# INDEX.

THE END.